GHOST RANCH

Trinity and Billy Raglan cross the deserted ranch — a dry, dead land of lost dreams and broken spirits. So why does the wealthy Boss Clark want to buy it? The land supports few cattle — and they are being herded away by the former owner, Polly Travers. Meanwhile, Boss Clark, Polly's greedy son Cole, and the killer and escaped convict Calvin Dancer fight a deadly war for ownership . . . whilst Trinity fights the seemingly futile fight and digs the graves for the dead.

C. J. SOMMERS

GHOST RANCH

Complete and Unabridged

LINFORD
Leicester

First published in Great Britain in 2011 by
Robert Hale Limited
London

First Linford Edition
published 2013
by arrangement with
Robert Hale Limited
London

British Library CIP Data

Sommers, C. J.
    Ghost ranch.- -(Linford western library)
    1. Western stories.
    2. Large type books.
    I. Title II. Series
    823.9'2–dc23

    ISBN 978–1–4448–1421–7

Published by
F. A. Thorpe (Publishing)
Anstey, Leicestershire

Set by Words & Graphics Ltd.
Anstey, Leicestershire
Printed and bound in Great Britain by
T. J. International Ltd., Padstow, Cornwall

This book is printed on acid-free paper

2-21-13   Uiverscraft $21.06

1

They spotted the first casualty lying in the dirt road leading to the Bar-D Ranch which was still about ten miles distant across rugged, red country.

'Who in hell do you s'pose would do that?' Billy Raglan muttered, swinging down from his gray to take a closer look.

'There aren't many rules in war,' Trinity answered. He sat his piebald horse, hands crossed on the pommel, while his older companion crouched over the victim of violence, his hat tilted back.

'Damned shame, damned waste,' Raglan muttered, looking up at his tall companion.

'Most death is,' Trinity said philosophically, popping out his canteen cork to take a drink of tepid water. The sun was riding high in the pale sky. 'But

1

there isn't much we can do about it. Not when we've hired out to do what we're doing.'

Raglan was still concerned and confused. 'They just cut her throat, Trinity! Left her lying in the sun. Hell, a Comanche wouldn't do that.'

'No.' Trinity was tired of the conversation. The day was sweltering. Mirages danced before his eyes across the long flats all the way to the far-distant red hills that seemed to ripple in the heat haze.

'Damn!' Raglan said once again before he roughly kicked the bloated body of the white and red heifer that someone had left along their road.

'Think she had calves?' Raglan asked, swinging into the saddle, tugging down his hat to shield his eyes against the sun-glare.

'Too young by the look of her,' Trinity guessed, 'Besides, we don't have the time to search around for them if she did. Supposing we found calves? What would we do with them?'

'I don't know,' Raglan said, sniffing. 'You're right, I know. It's just the waste . . . Sometimes I hate our line of work, Trinity.'

Which was that of hired guns, to put it as bluntly as possible.

As Trinity sat his pony, watching the long land, the dry wind drifted over him and outside of the constant scent of sage and lightly drifting sand, there was no sound or smell across the prairie, no evidence of anything you'd expect to see and hear around a working ranch: cattle bawling, men shouting to one another, woodsmoke hanging in the air.

'Kind of eerie, isn't it?' Billy Raglan commented.

'What's that?' Trinity asked, as if he hadn't noticed it himself.

'Even out on the open range . . . all we seen so far is one dead cow. Who are we supposed to be fighting, anyway? And what does Boss Clark even want with this dead country? He's already got about a million acres.'

'Ten thousand,' Trinity corrected. And even that was not considered a lot in west Texas where an acre of land could barely support two or three steers.

'All right, ten thousand!' Raglan said as they started their horses forward again. 'This here spread,' he commented, waving a dismissive hand, 'won't add much of use to his holdings.'

'There's water here,' Trinity replied.

'Yeah.' Billy snorted dismissively. 'I know — Shamishaw Creek. I've heard it described as the 'Shamishaw Trickle'. Tell me, Trinity, do you see any green grass anywhere around us?'

'I suppose it's a seasonal creek,' Trinity said as they crossed a dry arroyo, dotted with dry willow brush and stands of flat-paddled nopal cactus. 'Besides,' he continued as they achieved the flat once more, 'It's not our business to figure out why Jefferson Clark wanted the land. The fact is that he bought it and now these people won't move off it.'

Billy sniffed and wiped his cuff across his nose. 'It sure looks to me like they moved.'

'Taking the cattle and still owing Boss Clark the title for the land,' Trinity reminded his saddle mate.

'I can't figure how a canny man like Boss Clark could have let that happen,' Billy said. 'I'd hate to deal with him myself — or play poker with him!' Billy chuckled.

'It was a woman who sold the property to him,' Trinity said, as if that explained a lot.

'Oh,' Billy said, understanding. 'They do have their ways.'

In silence they rode across the land which was barren, dry, clumped here and there with greasewood and stands of mesquite, nopal and always sage. Once they passed a blackened cottonwood tree; it was the only sign of healthy vegetation they had seen, and now it stood barren and black as wrought iron against the pale sky.

'Those hills,' Billy said nodding

toward the distant sawtooth range on the horizon ' — that's up in New Mexico, isn't it?'

'I don't know,' Trinity responded. 'We're near to the line. That's for sure.'

'I'd like to see that territory,' Billy said with some wistfulness.

'What for? The land's not going to look any different from what it does on this side of the line.'

'I don't know,' Billy Raglan answered. 'Just to say I've been there, I guess.'

Trinity reined in sharply. Billy looked a question at him. Then Trinity shook his head.

'It's nothing — I thought I heard some cattle lowing over to the west. I must be starting to imagine things.'

'Well, keep on looking sharp,' Billy advised. 'If we run across anyone who knows who we are, they might just go to sniping at us.' He fell silent as the horses plodded on toward where the Bar-D ranch house was supposed to be situated. 'A woman foxed old Boss Clark, did she?' Billy asked with a chuckle.

'I wouldn't know — that seems to be what the old man thinks.'

'Well, a man can get silly around them, even the shrewdest of us.'

Trinity smiled. 'Is that what happened to you, back in Topcka? I know you were carrying a lot of gold when we rode in and didn't have the money to pay for stabling your horse when we rode out again.'

'Oh, that!' Billy answered. 'It wasn't anything like this. You mean Gloria?'

'I don't think I ever knew her name — you two were always off alone somewhere.'

'Well,' Billy insisted, 'she wasn't one of those gold-diggers or cheats. We just didn't get along.'

'Why was that?' Trinity asked, trying to keep the irony out of his tone.

'My God, Trinity, didn't you ever hear her talk! She had that squeaky mouse voice, like fingernails on a slateboard. Maybe it was a little amusing at first, but a weary man wants to hear a soothing voice to

7

comfort him in the evening. When I was a schoolboy . . . did you ever go so school, Trinity?'

'There was none where I grew up.'

'Well,' Billy said, 'we had a little red schoolhouse. Dad made me go there when I was not needed at home. I guess I did not so much get any schooling, but used school as a place to act up, and learn about girls,'

'What did you learn?' Trinity asked.

'I'll tell you another time,' Billy said with a flip of his hand. 'Anyway, when I was in school there was a smug little girl with pigtails seated behind me named Marcia . . . Marcia something, and she dragged her fingernails across her slateboard. It put my teeth on edge, that sound, and I told her so. So she continued to do it forever after, every day. It about drove me crazy.

'So you see, when I met Gloria back in Topeka, I thought I had struck gold. But she had this voice . . . ' Billy made a fist and shook it, 'I tell you, I couldn't take it.'

'So that was the reason you gave up on her?'

'Sure — what were you guessing?'

'I don't try to guess about women,' Trinity said. Then he dropped the subject as they crested a hillrise topped with golden-dry wild oats and came upon the Bar-D ranch house. 'Check your loads, Billy,' he advised. 'We might be about to raise some hell.'

They saw no one, heard no animals or voices as they trailed down the long dry-grass slope toward the log ranch house, but they rode cautiously, wary of a trap. Trinity described a circle in the air with his finger and motioned toward the rear of the house. Billy Raglan nodded and started that way, rifle across his saddlebow.

The place was as silent as the fine blowing dust. By the time Trinity swung down at the hitch rail in front of the small ranch house and tied his piebald, Billy had finished circling the place.

'There's no one around,' Billy said, tipping back his hat from his sweating brow, 'And it makes no sense.'

'No, it doesn't.' There were only two ways to look at it: either the former owners of the Bar-D had decided just to give it up and ride off, leaving the place to Boss Clark, or they were hiding out somewhere, determined to fight Clark off. Either way, they were going about this wrong. Boss Clark had paid good money for the Bar-D and the owner had failed to deliver the property deed to the county courthouse as agreed upon. It was starting to look as if the woman who owned the Bar-D had indeed bested Jefferson Clark — or was trying to. Trinity knew his employer well enough to know that he would not accept the slight. He would fight for what he believed to be his.

Which was why Billy and Trinity were here on this hot, dry day. To do a little fact-finding and warn off anyone still occupying the land that they had no choice — they had to leave.

'Who the hell pulls out and slaughters his own cattle along the way?' Billy grumbled to the sky as he swung down from his horse. He was still thinking about the dead heifer they had come across.

'Maybe they did get attacked by Indians,' Trinity suggested. 'That would explain why no one's on the ranch.'

'No it wouldn't,' Billy said with some heat. He was thirsty and trail-beat. 'They'd stay right here behind these log walls and fight. Besides,' he added, 'why would an Indian kill a perfectly useable cow and leave it to bleach in the sun?'

'A warning?' Trinity suggested for the sake of conversation.

'No, sir! Wasn't no Comanches involved in this,' Billy said positively. 'Can we get out of this sun now, Trinity? I reached my limit about an hour back.'

'All right,' Trinity said, slicking his Colt revolver from his holster. 'Do you want to go in first, or you want me to do it?'

Billy Raglan seemed for the moment to have forgotten that they had no way

11

of knowing if the house, abandoned as it appeared, was empty. 'You go,' he muttered, drawing his own pistol.

Trinity approached the door, holding his revolver high. He looked at Billy, tapped three times on the door, then nudged it open with his boot toe. Finally he administered a healthy kick, entered, and crouched beside the open door. He and Billy fanned out through the musty-smelling house, searching for inhabitants. Trinity already knew there was no one there. An empty house always feels that way — empty. Absent is all warmth of human bodies, scents of cooking, echoes of long-ago laughter. You can tell when a house is empty even from the outside.

Nevertheless, this was no time for taking chances.

They met back at the living room with its low-beamed ceiling and open-mouthed native stone fireplace. Billy shook his head. 'No one living or dead.'

'I wonder what we're supposed to do in a situation like this?' Trinity said, seating himself on a broad chair covered with natural leather.

'Do? We rest up and ride back and tell Boss Clark that he can move his cattle and men on anytime he likes; the place has been deserted.'

'There's the matter of legal claim to the land, Billy,' Trinity said. 'Say Boss Clark mounts a cattle drive and comes out here with thirty or so drovers and some sheriff demands to see the deed to this property, which he happens to know belongs to Mrs . . . what was her name? Polly Travers?'

'If you say so,' Billy said, glumly, taking Trinity's point.

'That's a lot of expense and time. Boss Clark won't like finding he still has no clear title to the land.'

'What do you suggest we do?' Billy asked wearily.

'I only see one way — we find Mrs Polly Travers and settle this.'

'I saw a well out back, Trinity. I have to have some water. Maybe you could see if there's something left around here

13

to eat. I knew we were packing too light.' But then, a thunderstorm had settled in as they were crossing Heeler's Canyon, forcing them to shelter up for the day and the following night, and a lot of their provisions had been tapped while they waited for the rain to stop.

Billy Raglan walked out of the house, squinting against the glare of the white sun, and trudged around to the back of the house where he had seen the well on his earlier circuit of the ranch grounds. On his way he nearly stepped on a spotted brown hen. A small light flickered on in Billy's skull — dinner! Or so he thought, but as he lunged to his right, the chicken darted to his left. When he moved left, the hen ran right. It stood still for a moment then, feathers ruffled, craning its neck. Billy tried approaching stealthily, his hand stretched out as if offering food. The chicken watched his approach with cocked head and bright eyes, and just when Billy thought he could catch its neck, the chicken fluttered away, clucking with alarm.

It was too hot for this game. Billy went to the well, drew a bucket of water and poured it over his head and shoulders. Then he drank deeply.

Trinity was at the rough plank table in the kitchen when Billy returned. There were two plates set. 'Found something?' Billy asked curiously.

'These.' Trinity had found a tin of sardines hidden away in the furthest corner of a high cupboard. The tab meant to be used to open the tin was broken off, but prodding and prying with his sheath knife, Trinity had finally managed to peel back the top of the tin to reveal a dozen sardines packed head to tail, tail to head.

'Looks like Philadelphia,' Billy said, sitting and leaning far back in his chair.

'I've never been there,' Trinity said.

'Neither have I, but that's how I imagine it.' He wanted nothing to do with the sardines. 'How do they get them packed in that tight?'

'Practice, I guess,' Trinity said. 'It's

all we have at the moment, Billy. Have some?'

Billy studied the small fish again. They still wore their tails and their heads. Small dead, silver fish eyes stared up at him.

'I can't eat nothing that's looking at me,' Billy Raglan said with disgust.

'Then I hope you don't mind if I help myself,' Trinity said and he slid the sardines on to his plate where almost fastidiously he began separating tails and heads from their bodies. Billy watched with ill-restrained disgust.

'How can anybody eat such as that?'

'How can anybody eat nothing? We can't go grazing in the grass.'

'I got me a chicken,' Billy said with subdued truculence. 'And I'm going to invite him to be my guest at an old-fashioned turkey shoot.' So saying he drew his revolver from his holster. 'It's got to be a better meal than fish eyes, even if I blow it to feathers.'

Trinity did not respond. If Billy wanted to go hunting chickens with a pistol, let him. He glanced up as Billy Raglan stomped angrily across the floor toward the front door of the house. Billy opened the door, allowing a thin wedge of sunlight into the empty room.

As he did so, the rifles outside opened up and Trinity dove for the floor, stretching his arm out to recover the two rifles they had left propped in the corner. Billy, on his back, heeled the door shut violently. Trinity tossed him his Winchester. Shots from beyond the house splatted against the walls, rang off the stone fireplace and broke the windows.

'I think you'd best forget about that chicken, Billy.'

2

The rifle shots peppered the house for at least ten minutes, Trinity and Billy keeping their heads down. Now and then they would fire some off-hand shots out into the distance to let whoever was out there know that they were ready should the raiders have thoughts of rushing the house. Billy chanced an occasional peek over the sill from the corner of the broken window, but never spotted a target. When there was a lull in the firing, Trinity sagged back against the wall and reloaded his revolver.

'Spot anything?' he asked Billy, who was risking another look out the window.

'Nothing. No one at all. I once thought I saw a shadow moving over near that big oak tree, but it vanished.' Billy said grimly, 'It's almost like we're fighting an army of ghosts.'

'I've never seen a ghost army,' Trinity said, rising to his knees. 'Not any armed with rifles, anyway.'

'What are we going to do about the horses?' Billy asked, his voice slightly shaky. 'If they get our animals, we're done.'

'My piebald will stand,' Trinity said firmly.

'Well, so will my gray,' Billy said, growing defensive. 'But I don't like having them out in the open like they are.'

'I'm not bringing them into the house,' Trinity said with a smile. 'It sets a bad precedent.'

'I knew a gunny over toward Oklahoma City who always took his horse into the saloon with him.'

'Must have made him welcome there,' Trinity muttered.

'No, it didn't.' Billy Raglan crouched down and replied, 'His name was Toby Shoop. Now old Toby . . . Say, Trinity are there any of those damned sardines left?'

'Only heads and tails,' Trinity said, moving to the window to take a peek outside himself. Shadows were deepening; evening was arriving rapidly.

'I wouldn't feed heads and tails to cats!' Billy grumbled.

'But you'd eat a cat if we had one, I'll wager.'

'Maybe. You know, one time old Carson Browne — '

Trinity interrupted him. 'I hope I never live long enough to gather all of the stories you have about the old times,' Trinity said.

'You learn by living, Trinity. But I ain't ready to check out just yet, are you?'

'They've fallen silent out there. Do you figure that was just a warning or are they trying to figure a way to creep up on the house?'

'I think they were just burning powder, letting us know that we aren't welcome here.'

'You're probably right. I wish this place had a back door.'

'So you could slip out and take a look around?'

'A very cautious look,' Trinity said to the older man. 'I don't much like being pinned down in here.'

'I think that all we can do is wait it out until morning, Trinity. Damn — hear my stomach rumbling. I sure am hungry.'

'Your own fault for being so picky. There's a sackful of salt biscuits in my saddle-bags . . . if we could get to the horses.'

'Oh, we could get to them,' Billy replied drily. 'But I don't know if we could get back after we did. What's your idea, Trinity?'

'There's nothing to try. We'll wait until sunrise.' It was growing very dark beyond the shattered windows.

'Yeah. I don't like it myself, but that's about all we can do.'

'I guess we know now if they meant to give up the ranch or hold out. They don't seemed inclined to want to go anywhere.'

'No, we'll have to give 'em a nudge. We can't ride back to Boss Clark with our tails between our legs.'

'Not and still have a job,' Trinity was forced to admit. 'Look, Billy, I'm going to find a place to sack out. Come back and get me in a few hours.'

'All right,' Billy Raglan agreed. 'You're probably more ready for sleep than I am, what with your stomach being full and all.'

Trinity didn't bother to respond to that.

'Just call me when your eyes start to get heavy, Billy. This isn't the night for us to lose alertness.'

Billy just nodded. Raglan's face, lined and burned brown by the sun, seldom showed much expression. He was a simple man, and a good one to ride the range with. Despite the needling Trinity gave Billy about his age, it was true that his experience had often made the difference between their success and potential failure. They rode now as hired guns for Boss Jefferson Clark because Trinity had no other special skills with which to make a living and Billy was too old for the daily grind of ranch life. No one who has not tried it can understand what a day's work roping and binding calves at branding time or 200 miles of bad trail droving steers through all weather can take from a man. Billy was a bundle of broken bones wrapped up in a tough old hide, although he seldom complained.

There was still a leather-strap bed in one of the back rooms, and after looking under and around it for critters, Trinity stretched out, his pistol near at hand, to watch the night float by.

★ ★ ★

'Are you up yet?' Billy's dry voice asked from the doorway.

'Is it my turn to stand watch already?' Trinity said, swinging heavily from the bed.

'There's silver in the eastern sky, son. You've slept the night away.'

'I told you to wake me if you got sleepy,' Trinity said.

'I started to,' Billy said, 'but I kept myself awake telling old stories that no one else wants to listen to.'

'Funny — those stories always make me sleepy,' Trinity said, rising to stamp into his boots.

'You weren't there when things happened, son. That makes all the difference.'

'I suppose so. No one moving around out there during the night?'

'If you don't count a hoot-owl, it was silent as a grave.'

'I wonder what they're waiting for?' Trinity said, wiping back his dark hair with his hands before positioning his Stetson on top of his head.

'Someone will be watching, waiting for us to pull out,' Billy believed.

'Is that what you're planning to do, Billy?'

'No sir! I'm more a-scared of Boss Clark than of a hundred ghosts. What's your plan, Trinity?'

'Same as yesterday — we've got to find this Polly Travers woman and explain the situation, ask her what she intends to do about it. After all, she took good money from Boss Clark for the Bar-D.'

'Yes, I don't see what else we can do,' Billy agreed. 'The trouble is, it's not as if we had any idea of where she might be.'

'With a herd of cattle, with the natural needs of a human being, I'd say there's only one place she can be — they have to have water, and the only water we know of in this area is along Shamishaw Creek.'

'Do you even know where that is, Trinity?'

'No, but we can take a good guess by watching the sloping of the land. It's got to have its headwaters in those red hills. And when we get close enough, the horses will smell it for sure,'

'It's been a while since our ponies were taken care of properly,' Billy said.

'I know it. We'll make sure they have

plenty of water before we leave. We'll allow them time to graze along the way, even if it's nothing more than those dry oats that seems to have taken over the land.'

'Beats me how they ever maintained a herd of cows on this god-forsaken land,' Billy said, shaking his head.

'I imagine they had good years with sufficient rain and years with a lot of die-offs. You know as well as I do that range cattle are tougher than they're given credit for.'

'Tough . . . and ornery when they can't find water or graze.' Billy rubbed his shoulder; perhaps the thought had brought back some old painful memory.

'I would suppose the lady — Polly Travers — plain got tired of squeezing out a living from the dry land and decided to take Boss Clark's offer when it was made,' Trinity guessed.

'Then changed her mind . . . because?'

'Maybe she got a better offer,' Trinity suggested.

'Or simply because she's a woman.' Billy sniffed.

'The sun's riding higher, Billy. Let's see who's around and then pay some attention to our ponies.'

That seemed the only sensible plan to follow. Neither of them had been able to formulate a long-range strategy. There were too many unknowns. But it was only sensible to have a look around and tend to their horses as well as they could.

Both men had started toward the door to the old house when Trinity halted, crouched slightly and placed a finger across his lips. He had heard something, or thought he had, and in another moment they both heard boot heels clicking across the plank porch toward the front door. Trinity drew back, placing his hand on the butt of his Colt. Billy tightened his grip on his Winchester.

There was a weak rapping at the door and then it swung toward them. The man who entered shakily had dark, thinning hair, a wide mouth and heavy black eyebrows. He had a trembling manner about him. His watery eyes met those of Trinity and he said:

'I was s'posed to tell you . . . ' Then he collapsed, his message undelivered. Billy Raglan hesitated, then stepped forward to crouch and touch the man's throat. He looked up at Trinity and announced:

'The man's dead, Trinity.'

Rolling the stranger over they found two separate gunshot wounds in his back. He had no sort of papers in his pockets, wore no jewelry or other indications of his identity. Only a man with down-at-the-heels boots, ragged trail clothing and a battered hat.

'See if anyone else is outside,' Trinity commanded. Billy worked his way toward the window, crouched down and peered out.

'No one. Nothing,' Billy reported. 'Wonder who this gent was.'

'No one we know, that's for sure. Must have been one of the Bar-D crowd. What in hell do you guess he was supposed to tell us?'

Billy shook his head heavily. 'We'll never know. Could have been sent to tell us to get out, or to say the old owners were pulling out.'

'Either way — why would they kill their own man?' Trinity asked, expecting no answer, receiving none.

Billy stood over the still figure a while longer, then muttered, 'Damn hot day for digging holes.'

And it was. The weather outside was a repeat of the day before, but lacking the occasional gusts of cooler air from the hills left by the passing summer thunderstorm. Hot, dry, with drifting sand, it was tough-going in the dry ground they chose for their grave-digging. They were both bathed in sweat, coated with sand-blow by the time they had finished the job.

They topped-off their canteens with water from the well, filled a trough for the horses to drink from, and scrounged for forage, finding little but a moldering pile of aging straw in the barn which the horses at first refused, then with their hunger urging them on, munched at morosely.

Giving the animals time to let the water and feed settle in their stomachs, they spent another hour searching the ranch and its environs for trespassers. They found none, although Billy came across a dozen spent brass cartridges from the night before in the brush beyond the ranch yard. And the tracks of four hard-ridden westbound horses. The snipers hadn't been in the mood to stay round and judge what damage they might have caused.

Joining Billy, Trinity said, 'They're heading for those hills.' He shaded his eyes with his hand as he looked that way, across the brush-stippled flatlands toward the misty red hills beyond.

'Which way do you think Shamishaw Creek is from here, Billy?'

'I don't know. As you said, it must flow off the hills. Do you think they're heading for the creek?'

'A man needs water in this country,' Trinity reminded him. 'And if they have the herd . . . '

'It'll be the creek they're riding for,' Billy Raglan said. 'I wish we knew this country a little better.'

'It seems,' Trinity said, 'that we're about to learn it some.' Because they still needed to find Mrs Polly Travers, find the missing herd, and track down the men who had tried to kill them the night before. It was that or go back and report to Boss Clark that they had failed. Something neither man was willing to do. They were being paid a fat fifty dollars a month for their work, work which involved no roping, branding, fencing, bronc-breaking, de-horning, castrations or hay-mowing. Neither of them had any likely prospect of finding a better job than the one they had.

Besides, Boss Clark could stand up on his hind legs like a mad grizzly if he was frustrated.

'Let's find that creek,' Trinity said quietly.

They collected their horses. Saddling the piebald was the usual ceremony. The horse was not really obstinate, but always took this opportunity to sort of show off, sidling away, tossing its head when Trinity approached with its bridle. It was indulging in some sort of horse humor. Trinity was used to this and waited until the animal was tired of its games to reach for his saddle.

The piebald was a glossy black for the most part, but it looked as if someone had splashed its body with white paint, patted its muzzle with a paint-covered hand and then wiped his hands on its tail. By the time Trinity had slipped the animal its bit, Billy Raglan had been sitting his patient gray horse for long minutes.

'Why don't you un-teach that maverick some of those tricks?' he asked.

'It doesn't bother me. I'm not that impatient.'

'Maybe other people are waiting on

you,' Billy said with a sniff that was growing chronic with him.

'Maybe, then, they should just go ahead — I'd catch up with them,' Trinity felt obligated to retort.

Within five minutes they were on the trail, the sun already hot on their backs. After passing under the solitary oak they began making their way west, toward the broken red hills. They were looking for tracks — of men, horses, cattle that might guide them on their way. The few tracks they did see were widely scattered and mostly obliterated. Trinity figured that the thunderstorm that had hit them back at Hegler's Canyon had struck the Bar-D as well. Since then the wind, blowing hotly across the land, had lined dust over everything. It would have taken a superior scout to follow what sign remained.

Not a memory of the rain's sudden downpour remained to dampen the trail or cool the air around them. They rode almost aimlessly along a trail leading into a shallow canyon, figuring that the men who had driven the cattle off, the men who had shot at them the day before, would ride the easiest trail they could find. The land grew rocky. Dry willow trees stood along the canyon bottom to their left indicating that there was sometimes water running there. Perhaps this was the 'Shamishaw Trickle' as Billy had called it. The sun grew smaller and hotter as it rose into the sky. The canyon was too shallow for the shadows to reach them.

'You know we're being followed,' Trinity said.

'I seen 'em,' Billy commented.

'Wonder what they want?'

'I couldn't guess,' Raglan answered. 'It seems to me that it's pretty certain that they don't want to talk or they'd have come down.' For their pursuers were riding the canyon ridge to their right. Now and then Trinity had caught a glimpse of color — a man's red shirt or his jeans just visible through the screen of thorny chaparral.

'Other thing is,' Billy continued after pausing for a swallow of water, 'it doesn't seem they want to shoot us, or they'd have tried it by now.'

That was when a rifle shot echoed up the canyon and the canteen was torn from Billy's hand as he raised it to his lips. 'It seems they've changed their minds,' Trinity said, putting his heels to the piebald's flanks. He rode toward the canyon bottom with a dozen rifle shots following him, reached the edge of the parched gray willows and drove his horse on deeper into the thicket, bullets cutting brush all around him.

He pulled the horse to a halt as they reached the rocky bottom of the dry stream bed and looked back for Billy, slipping his Winchester from its scabbard to provide cover for Raglan in case he was being pursued.

Beneath the glaring, burning sun Trinity sat his impatient horse, waiting, watching for Billy, but ten minutes later he had still not appeared. Which way had the old man gone? He would not allow himself to think of the possibility that Raglan had been shot down where he sat his gray. It was still, silent behind the screen of willows. Trinity could hear the swarms of insects that dwelt there. A blue-and-orange dragonfly buzzed past his ear and continued up the creek bottom.

Trinity rode westward, halting now and then to look back for Billy or an approaching gang, listening for any cries of help from Raglan. He felt vaguely guilty for having left Billy alone back there, but what could he have accomplished?

He was halted now as just under his horse's front hoofs a brush rabbit started and made its mad dash for the sheltering gray willow trees. Well, there was some life along the dead creek — or had something, someone, frightened the rabbit into taking flight? He turned abruptly in the saddle and saw the rifle muzzle aimed at him from a clump of deprived creosote growing along the dry watercourse.

'You move, you die,' a voice said.

3

The ambusher rose and stepped from behind the clump of dry bush. Walking toward Trinity who had both hands in the air now, the voice demanded to know:

'Where's my father!'

'Where's my mother?' Trinity shot back at the woman — for it was a young woman who had waylaid him. She was short, slender, with her dark hair worn in a braid from which many strands escaped. Her face was pale and furious.

'What kind of foolish question is that!' she demanded. She neared Trinity, but kept her distance. The rifle in her hands did not waver.

'No more foolish than yours,' Trinity answered, his hands still held high. 'I have about as much idea of where your father is as you have of my mother. I don't know who you are; I don't know who your father is — does that simplify matters?'

'Simplifies the language,' the dark-eyed girl responded, 'but it doesn't do a thing to clear matters up.'

She held her position. Her eyes continued to flash with dark emotion. The hammer on the Winchester rifle she held was drawn back, her fingers remained on the curved trigger of the weapon. 'Are you or are you not working for Jefferson Clark, also known as 'Boss Clark'?' the woman demanded.

'I am,' Trinity admitted with a nod. 'Is that a reason for me to know your father?'

'He was going over to talk to you,' the girl said hotly, 'and he never returned!'

Trinity frowned, 'Tell me what your father looks like.'

With reluctance and hostility the girl did so. There wasn't much doubt in Trinity's mind that the man Billy and he had buried that morning was her father.

'I'm afraid he's dead,' Trinity had to tell her.

'So you just shot him down?' the girl asked hotly.

'No, we did not. He was walking dead by the time he reached the house. Shot in the back. He spoke only a few words, then died. We buried him this morning.'

'So you say!'

'So I say.'

Looking around the girl asked, 'Where's his horse?'

'Never saw one. They must have taken it with them.'

'Who?'

'I can't tell you. We never saw them. Probably the men who came shooting at us yesterday. You'd have a better idea of who they were than I would.'

'No,' she said, her eyes fixed mistrustfully on Trinity, 'no I don't have an idea. Maybe it was an accident.'

'I doubt it — twice in the back? And someone he must have known at that.'

'Why would it be someone who knew my father?'

'Think about it — the Bar-D men are the only ones around. Outside of Billy and me. And we didn't do it.'

'There's only two of you?' the girl said, her forehead furrowing. 'That's all the men Boss Clark sent to run us off?'

'That's all he sent, and we weren't here to run anybody off, only to find out what had gone haywire. Why the deed wasn't delivered to the Culberson County courthouse as promised.'

'My mother would never double-deal. There's some mistake!' the girl protested.

'Polly Travers is your mother?'

'Yes,' she spat, 'and she's the most honest, hardest-working woman you'll ever meet.'

'I guess that's the way she impressed Boss Clark or he would never have done business that way — paying money for the ranch without a deed in hand, I mean.'

'Many people do business on a

40

promise in this country where some-one's word means everything and banks and courts are few and far away.'

'Yes,' Trinity said. All this time he had kept his hands high, his eyes flickering to the brush standing around them. He still did not know where the ambush party had gone. Or where Billy might be.

'That's the truth,' she said firmly. 'We started moving the herd so that if Clark decided to drive in cattle of his own we wouldn't have to waste all that time separating them later. We're on our way to a new section of land up in New Mexico that Mother is buying — of course we can't take possession of it without the money Clark owes us! The check has to clear the bank in Van Horn.'

'He's paid that money, he wants that deed,' Trinity told her.

'The deed was delivered to the county courthouse in Van Horn over two days ago.' She gave a little gasp and the expression in her eyes grew concerned. 'Or at least that's when my brother, Cole, and our foreman, Joe Cordero should have reached it.'

'That's who Polly sent?'

'Yes! Cole took the deed and the check from Clark. There was far too much for her to do around here, preparing the move, to deliver it there herself . . . something must have happened to my brother. Do you think they were held up?'

'Anything is possible, but I wouldn't know, would I?'

'Maybe Cole won't be coming back,' she said, her eyes widening. 'This all seemed like such a good idea at the time. What will happen now?'

'Boss Clark will seize the land and let the court straighten it out later,' Trinity believed.

'But he doesn't need the land, and we have nowhere to take our herd.'

'Whether he needs it or not, he's paid for it and he'll use it. Whatever water there is along the Shamishaw is more than he's got at the moment, and he's got five hundred thirsty steers that won't make it through a hot summer without it.'

'Then . . . we can't go forward and we can't go back!' the girl said in a bewildered voice.

'So it seems. Do you know what your father was sent to tell us?'

'No,' she shook her head heavily. 'That was between him and my mother. I think she was growing frustrated too, needing the money to pay for the property in New Mexico. So, no, I don't know what message she would have wanted to send to you.'

'I think I should have a talk with her,' Trinity said. 'Do you mind if I lower my hands? My shoulders are starting to feel like I'm supporting the sky.'

'All right,' she agreed. 'But sheath your rifle first.'

'What if they come back?'

'I didn't see anyone.'

'No? And I suppose you didn't hear any gunshots either.'

'Just do what I told you,' the girl said.

'I'll get my horse and we'll ride upstream. I guess you should talk to my mother.'

'If she's more sensible than you, I'd be happy to.'

The girl seemed to flush under her tan. Then she made a disgusted sound and headed off toward the rocky river bottom, keeping her eyes on Trinity as she made her way through the river brush. Trinity had no intention of riding off. He had nowhere to go, and besides, a meeting with Polly Travers was what they had had in mind to begin with.

Things were getting a little complicated, though. He wished he had Billy there to talk things over with. But nothing had been seen or heard of Billy since the first rifle shots. The girl came back up out of the stream bed, leading a trim-looking little blue roan. She swung into the saddle now, her eyes still fixed on Trinity as if daring him to make a move. She sidled up beside him, her rifle still pointed in his direction.

'Mind telling me your name?' Trinity asked.

'Why?'

'I don't know — a prisoner kind of likes to know who his jailer is.'

'It's Tamarind, Tamarind Travers.'

'What kind of name is that?' Trinity asked out of idle curiosity.

She sighed. 'Why do people always ask me that? And before you mention it — no, you can't call me Tammy. I hate that.'

'All right, I won't. I think we had better find your mother.'

'So do I. Mister, you ride in front of me if you don't mind. Just keep following the creek bottom. We'll come upon them.'

She gestured with her rifle muzzle and they started on, riding toward the red hills: the Guadalupes as they were called. Cooling shadows began to touch the trail, although the sun was lingering high. As they rode farther on the canyon deepened and the banks rose to block out a portion of the sun's burning glare. Sunlight glinted through the brush along the rim of the narrow canyon and sketched shadows around the rocks in the dry creekbed.

It seemed they must have traveled a mile up the canyon already. It was hot and close there, alive with insects. Trinity looked over his shoulder and asked the stern-faced girl: 'How much farther?'

'Just keep riding.'

After another half a mile or so, Trinity began to see green willow trees. Listening closely he could hear cattle bawling. Tamarind pointed out a trail serving as a creek-crossing and Trinity started the piebald that way. The brush in the bottom was head-high to a horse now. Through it, though, Trinity could make out little, he was sure he saw the figure of a man sitting a sorrel horse.

'We're being watched,' he told the girl.

'I should hope so! Those are Bar-D men, guarding our camp.'

Trinity guided his horse up the sandy far bank of the creek, following a trail which bore the fresh prints of cattle. Ahead he saw sunlight glinting on the murky standing water of a pond. His horse lifted its head expectantly. It had been a long while since the piebald had taken its last drink.

'Which way?' Trinity asked.

'Just keep riding straight ahead.'

Then Trinity began to see cattle, red-and-white and black, all bunched around the small pond as if afraid to leave it. A few men on horseback watched stolidly as the cattle drank. When Tamarind, escorting her prisoner, emerged from the brush, the Bar-D riders turned that way, tensing noticeably.

'Where's my mother?' the girl asked.

'Still at the camp, Miss Travers,' one older man with a faceful of sprouting gray whiskers said, eyeing Trinity closely. 'You need any help?'

'I've made it this far on my own,' the girl answered sharply.

Passing under the gaze of the cowhands, they rode to a small, sheltered camp backed up against a low gray bluff. There were stacks of bedding and a small, barely glowing fire. An older woman crouched down, tending to a coffee pot. Polly Travers, for that must have been who the woman was, looked up and stood, dusting her hands on her jeans. Her eyes were not welcoming.

'What's this, Tammy?' she asked, using the supposedly hated nickname. 'I send you looking for your father and you come back with this . . . '

Polly couldn't find the word she wanted for Trinity.

'He's riding for Boss Clark. I thought you should have a talk with him.'

'I'd as soon shoot him,' answered Polly Travers, a tall, narrow woman with silver-streaked dark hair and flashing dark eyes. She was standing with her hands on her hips. 'What . . . he's still wearing his gunbelt, Tammy!'

'He didn't give me any trouble,' Tamarind Travers said defensively.

'And you led him straight to our camp.' She shook her head in pained wonder. 'Where's your father?'

'This man says he's dead. They buried him back at the ranch.'

'Is that true?' she demanded, turning fiercely shining eyes on Trinity.

'Yes, ma'am. It is, I'm sorry to say.'

'Did you have to kill him! He only wanted to talk, to tell Clark that we were clearing our cows from the land. That we were just waiting for the check to clear,' Polly Travers said, and now there was a sheen of tears over her glittering eyes.

'We didn't kill him,' Trinity said calmly. 'Is it all right if I swing down? We do need to have a talk.'

A small group of wary men had begun to gather around the camp, their expressions cold. Polly Travers approached Trinity, her daughter watching darkly. 'You're right, mister, we need to talk. So swing down and start talking.'

'All I know is that me and my partner, Billy Raglan were sent over to find out if and when you were going to pull off the land so that Boss Clark can make plans on when he means to drive his own cattle on to the parcel. Since then we've been shot at at the house, ambushed on the trail — with my partner possibly dead, and me hauled in here at gunpoint as if this was some sort of tribunal.'

'I see,' Polly said deliberately. 'Clark needs gunmen to just find out what he wanted to know?'

'It seemed prudent — seeing as the situation was unknown. Billy and I, we don't work cattle anyway, so it was a natural job for us.'

'Do you want some coffee, Trinity?' Polly asked out of the blue. Trinity didn't understand her failure to respond, but coffee did sound good. Polly led him to the low-burning campfire and crouched to pour the dark liquid into a tin cup. Tammy, he noticed, had followed along.

'Now, then,' Polly Travers said after Trinity had taken a few sips of dark, bitter coffee. 'It seems that there are opposing points of view as to what's happening. The deed to the ranch is now on its way to the county courthouse, signed, sealed and hope-fully soon delivered. I don't know what Clark is upset about . . . '

'He didn't say he was upset.'

'Of course not, just impatient. He gave me a week to get the deed up to Van Horn, and I'm using it. Meantime, I had to pull my cattle off the ranch in case Clark made another of his hasty decisions and started driving a part of his herd over here. Now I'm sitting with deprived cattle, unhappy men, waiting for the money from Clark to be collected at the bank so I can pay off this man up in Carlsbad before I start my herd that way. The men are getting weary of inaction and going unpaid — I had three of them quit already. Right now my son and my foreman, Joe Cordero, are on their way to deliver the deed and collect the money that Clark is supposed to have there. Clark agreed to give me that much time.

'But when Clark sends men in to push matters, to slaughter my cattle so that I had to move the herd before the deal was firmed up — '

'We didn't slaughter any cattle,' Trinity objected, 'though we did see one dead heifer on our way in.'

'It's not beyond Clark to push hard to get us moving faster,' Polly Travers said. 'I know that.'

'I'm sure he wouldn't do that — in fact I know he didn't, because Billy Raglan and I were the only Clark men in the area.'

'Listen to me, Trinity. The man you're riding for is an abrupt and determined man. I've known Jefferson Clark longer than you've been alive — that's why I never thought he'd do this to me.'

'He didn't, I'm sure of it,' Trinity said. 'After hearing you out it seems to me that this was just one of those deals where both parties were unclear on certain matters of the agreement. Clark wanted the deed before he paid you good money; you thought you had a few more days at least to clear your cattle off the land.'

'That's how it sounds,' Polly agreed. 'But there's more than that — there's a little bit of savagery in all of this. Who killed Luther, if it wasn't you or some other Clark man?'

'Luther?' Trinity asked, puzzled.

'My husband! Luther Travers,' Polly said, growing angry at the memory. 'All he wanted to do was explain things to you. He didn't deserve to die.'

'I was thinking about that. Who might have shot him? I don't know. Who tried to gun down me and Billy on the trail? I'm thinking that there might be a third force involving themselves in this.'

'And who might that be?' Polly asked, her lips tightening.

'I have no idea, This is only my second day on this range.' Trinity tossed the dregs of his coffee into the fire to hiss. He said, 'I think, Mrs Travers, that the best thing we can do now is take care of the obvious problems. Make sure, simply, that you have your money, and Boss Clark receives his deed.'

'That will all be cleared up tomorrow at the latest,' she answered. 'When my son, Cole, gets back from the county seat.'

'Let's hope so.'

'For now you may as well water your horse and find a place to spread your bedroll. The sun is starting to draw long shadows, and it gets dark quickly in this country.'

'All right,' Trinity agreed. He had just started to turn away when a lather-streaked sorrel horse burst from out of the screen of brush, splashed across the shallow pond and its rider, unable to dismount, fell from the saddle to land on his face.

Several cowhands rushed to the man and turned him over. Trinity could see the blood streaking his face.

'Damn all,' one of the men said, looking up at Polly Travers who was hurrying that way. 'It's Joe Cordero, and he's carrying lead!'

4

Joe Cordero the Bar-D foreman, lay ashen-faced, blood streaming from his forehead, purpling his blue jeans.

'The one in his leg don't look good,' one of the examining cowhands said, looking up at Polly Travers. 'Find some clean cloth, Lou, if you can. We'll have to plug it.'

'How's his head?' Polly asked with concern.

'Seems the bullet just grazed him. There's a furrow in his scalp, not too deep, but you never know with that kind of wound. Could be it's addled his brains.'

'He made it back,' Tammy said. 'How confused could he be?'

'More'n likely,' the man called Lou answered, 'it was on account of the horse knowing the way that he made it here.'

But had they been attacked before they reached the county seat, or on their way back? There was no way Cordero could tell them just then.

'Do what you can to fix him,' Polly Travers said, her crisp manner belying the concern that was apparent in her eyes.

'Now what?' Tammy asked her mother in a low voice as they walked away from where the injured man lay against the sand.

'Whoever attacked him . . . we have to find out if they got your brother, too. He may be lying out there in rough country.'

Tammy was more practical — Trinity had the idea that she was not that fond of her brother. 'If Cole didn't make it to the county seat, the check is not deposited, neither is the deed in place for Boss Clark to claim. If they were attacked on the way back, then the money might be missing. We may have nothing at all.' There was fear in Tammy's eyes, but what had caused the fear was not evident to Trinity. Fear for her brother, fear of Boss Clark, the fear of poverty? He couldn't get a read on the girl.

'I'd better head that way,' Trinity said. 'I'll see if I can find Cole, recover the check and the deed, assuming they never reached Van Horn.'

'Why you?' Tammy exploded, whirling toward him.

'I suppose Boss Clark is still interested in that deed, don't you?' Trinity answered. 'It's part of my job to find it.'

'And the money?' Tammy said, almost shrieking so that a few of the men gathered around Joe Cordero glanced that way. 'Clark is determined to have it both ways, isn't he?'

'He doesn't do business that way — running widows off their land.'

'You're such a loyal hand,' Tammy said bitterly. 'You don't even know the trail Cole and Joe were taking.' She let out a small, explosive breath and told her mother, 'I'm going with him, Mom. Someone has to keep an eye on him.'

Polly glanced around nervously as if waiting for assistance. 'I can't let you go riding off with a man we don't even know.'

'Let me take Archie Hagen with me. He's tough enough. Besides, there's nothing for any of the men to do here except sit and watch the cows. If we don't recover Boss Clark's check or the money, we might as well just cut our own throats and die here.'

'Don't talk like that, Tammy!'

'Why not? It's true. We can't go forward and we can't go back — thanks to Mr Jefferson Clark.' Her voice softened a little and she took her mother's hands. 'Mom, we have to have that money to buy the New Mexico land, to pay our debts and our hands. We'll have more of the men riding away if we don't pay them soon. And good men aren't easily replaced out here.'

'You must find Cole,' Polly said in a low, quavering voice. At the moment she was too upset over his fate to be deeply concerned with the practicalities. She knew Tammy was right, but her thoughts were on her son's fate.

'Seems to me they're one and the same,' Trinity said, 'finding Cole and dealing with the legal and financial matters.'

'Oh, shut up!' Tammy said with unexpected vehemence. Trinity just stared at her for a silent moment.

'I'm getting my horse saddled,' he said.

'Don't forget I'm going with you!' Tammy said with only slightly less virulence.

'How could I?' Trinity answered. He touched his hat brim and turned sharply away to find his piebald. The girl was a wildcat, he thought, but then she was frightened. Being frightened can make a man or woman act in ways they would not normally. Or, maybe, he thought with a wry grin, this *was* the way she normally acted.

He had just finished tightening the

cinches on his piebald when a square-faced man with a growth of reddish beard and scowling eyes approached him, sitting a buckskin horse. When Trinity turned to face him, the stranger said:

'I'm Archie Hagen.'

'Pleased to meet you,' Trinity said without being sure that he was all that pleased.

'I'm taking the ride to the Culberson County courthouse with you and Miss Travers.'

'Oh, protection,' Trinity said.

'That's right. If you so much as look at the girl funny, I'll swat you down like a fly.'

'I've got nothing like that in mind.'

'Sometimes men's minds change,' Hagen said, leaning low out of the saddle. 'Just make sure yours doesn't.'

Having cautioned Trinity, Hagen swung his horse back toward the camp. The glow of the firelight could still be seen against the face of the low bluff. Once, Trinity heard Joe Cordero moan

61

in pain. He glanced at the sun which was sagging low. They would not make it far on this evening, but Tammy was eager to get started.

Trinity again found himself wishing that Billy Raglan was riding with him, but Billy was not around any longer. He would have to make it on his own. This job which had never seemed exactly simple had become a dark maze.

Just who had shot at Joe Cordero and Cole Travers? And why? Surely not for profit. No one outside the Bar-D could have known that they were collecting money and delivering the deed to the ranch. Trinity briefly allowed himself the disloyal thought that Boss Clark, annoyed with Polly Travers, had decided to take her ranch and recover his own money, leaving her penniless and homeless. But the idea did not match Trinity's image of Boss Clark. He was a big bull of a man, blustery, bullying and blunt. But he did not, so far as Trinity knew, engage in trickery or deceit to get what he wanted. It was totally out of character.

Besides, if Clark were behind it, why would he have sent Trinity and Raglan off to the Bar-D in the first place? That would only announce his intentions.

Who then?

Trinity thought of the three Bar-D cowhands who had ridden off in disgust after not having been paid. They would have certainly known Cole Travers and Joe Cordero on sight, and known or perhaps guessed that the two were going to see that Clark's bank draft was deposited at the bank in Polly's name and also to transfer the deed of the Bar-D to Boss Clark. Or, Trinity speculated, perhaps they had thoughts of snatching the deed for ransom, asking Boss Clark what it was worth to him.

That would have been a dangerous plan, but they might have managed to convince each other that Boss Clark would pay for the same deed twice if he were given no other choice.

'Are you going to stand there all

day?' Tammy Travers snapped as she rode toward him, the faithful, glowering Archie Hagen just behind her.

'No. No one told me that you were ready to go.'

'Someone has to tell you every move you should make? Let's go — we're burning daylight.'

Trailing out of the camp with Polly Travers watching, her arms folded, Trinity glanced toward the graying, already tinted sky to the west and commented:

'It's a bad time of day to start a long ride.'

'There may not be much time,' Tammy said. She rode beside Trinity now, not behind him. Archie Hagen had taken that position, and he presumably was keeping as close an eye on Trinity as Tammy had.

'Joe Cordero couldn't tell you how far he might have ridden?' Trinity asked. 'Or whether they had already delivered the bank draft and the deed?'

'He couldn't tell us much of

anything. Getting that bullet crease on his skull was the same as getting hit with a sledgehammer. He just said that he and Cole had gotten jumped.'

'He couldn't tell you what happened to Cole?'

'I told you — he doesn't remember anything!'

She heeled her little blue roan and started ahead at a brisk trot, her face furious. After a few minutes of that she held up and waited for Trinity and Hagen. She fell in beside Trinity again, her mouth still tight, but the angry flush gone from her face. They rode silently on across the land that was now yellow sand and scattered igneous rock. Once, a thousand centuries ago, there had been volcanic activity here. Now the land just lay flat and forbidding before them for mile after dreary mile, only occasional clumps of nopal cactus or Spanish bayonets growing. Already, through the screen of color the dying sun had painted across the western sky, Trinity could see the pale, waxing half-moon. Just now it seemed to sit nearly on top of the faintly glowing Venus.

Tammy's eyes darted left and right, searching for some sign of Cole, though surely the two men must have been attacked farther from the camp to keep their shots from being heard. Once Tammy let her dark eyes lift to meet briefly with those of Trinity. She spoke as if she had to wring the words from between her tight lips.

'I'm sorry I'm acting so roughly. I haven't been myself.'

'It's almost as if you blamed me for the ambush,' Trinity said. 'Even though you know that's impossible since you were holding me hostage when it happened.'

'Not you personally,' she answered in a lowered voice. Her horse stumbled slightly and it took her a minute to continue. 'Boss Clark — it had to be him or some of his men.'

'I told you there's none of his men around out here.'

'Yes, and you also told me you have a partner. Billy something.'

'Billy Raglan?' Trinity laughed. 'It's not his style to ambush somebody.'

'Maybe he would, if he thought it would put him in good with the boss. Besides, you told me that the two of you are gunmen. Isn't that what gunmen do?'

'You misunderstand, Tamm . . . arind. It only means that Billy and I carry guns as our tools rather than, say a branding-iron. We protect the other men while they're trying to get their work done, ride the perimeter and chase off interlopers and such. Protect Boss Clark's property.'

'Is that what you really meant?' Tammy asked, her voice dubious, her eyes hidden in the shadows cast by her hat brim.

'That's what I really meant.'

'So you're nothing like hired killers?'

'No. If I gave you that impression, I'm sorry.' They rode silently on for a while, the sky growing darker. They

67

would not make it far on this evening. And traveling in the dark would diminish their chances of spotting Cole Travers.

'We might be able to make Bean's Pasture, Miss Travers,' Archie Hagen called out.

'What's that?' Trinity wanted to know.

'Archie says it's nothing more than a chicken farm masquerading as a ranch.'

Hagen had heard her. 'That's what it is. But they might be able to put us up overnight.'

The moon sank lower. The shadows along the ridges of the hills had now merged and pooled into darkness. 'The trouble between the Bar-D and Boss Clark seems to go back a long way,' Trinity commented.

Tammy sighed before she answered. 'You don't know? Clark didn't tell you?'

'He's not a cozy man. He tells us only what he wants us to know,' Trinity said.

'Well,' Tammy said, growing suddenly more talkative — ahead Trinity could make out the feeble glow of lights which he took for Bean's Pasture. They rode that way down the rough slope of the hill. 'Clark claimed that Cole's father — Polly's first husband — had done him wrong. I can't remember all the details. Mother doesn't talk about those times much. Too many bad memories, I guess.'

'Her first husband?' Trinity asked, trying to clarify things in his own mind.

'Yes, Cole's father; Calvin Dancer. I don't remember him at all, of course, but I've never heard anyone say a word in his defense.'

Dancer. That explained the Bar-D brand. Apparently no one had taken the trouble to register a new one.

'He wasn't a rancher, did not want to be a rancher. It's said he won the ranch in a poker game,' Tammy told Trinity. 'Other people said — when they didn't know I was listening — that he plain stole the place from someone. I don't know which, and it doesn't matter any more.' Tammy hesitated as if on some level it did matter. 'He wasn't my father.'

'What happened?' Trinity asked out of the near-darkness.

'There's different stories — no one talks to me directly about it all. They say that Calvin Dancer was a known badman and something from out of his past was getting too close for comfort.' He saw her shrug her shoulders. 'More likely he just did not like being a rancher . . . or a husband.

'He just rode out, leaving Mother and a four-year-old son alone on a hard-scrabble ranch. When I was growing up I didn't even know who Calvin Dancer was — though Cole had never forgotten. I was told that when Cole was young he still kept vigil at his bedroom window, waiting for his father to return.

'I don't know,' she said with another heavy sigh. 'All I knew was that I had a good, steady father. And if Luther

Travers was not flashy or handsome, he was dependable and honest.'

'I see.'

'Probably not, but my brother and I led different lives though neither was easy. Out here,' she added unnecessarily.

'What about Boss Clark? You were going to tell me how your mother knew him, why it was she who went to talk to Clark about selling the ranch instead of Luther.'

'Was I?'

'I thought so. Polly told me that she has known Boss Clark longer than I've been alive. Is that the reason? Was she asking Jefferson Clark for a favor, rather than making a strictly business deal?'

'I don't understand you.'

Trinity thought she did, but he said, 'Before your brother was even born, before your mother met Calvin Dancer. Say twenty or thirty years ago . . . ' he hesitated, 'do you think there might have ever been something between your mother and Jefferson Clark?'

'Between ... ' Tammy vacillated between anger and laughter. She gave him no answer.

'I mean, it might explain a few things. Like Boss Clark buying a virtually valueless ranch. For its water? The Shamishaw Trickle?' She still refused to answer. Perhaps she was trying to absorb the possibility. Ahead of them now across the stretch of flat ground called Bean's Pasture, they saw a house with lights in the window. Several yard dogs had rushed forward to set up an excited ruckus of welcome or warning.

'If Cole and Joe Corder made it this far on their way back, they might have been seen,' Trinity commented. Again Tammy did not answer. Trinity wondered if he had indeed offended her sensibilities without meaning to. They slowed their horses to a walk and Archie Hagen hallowed the house loudly. Tammy said in a low voice:

'It's a tree — a tamarind, that is — with lovely red-streaked yellow flowers. There was one planted in our yard before drought killed it off. My mother was very fond of that tree.'

They approached the house and were billeted there for the night.

5

Morning arrived without a flourish. Slowly, silver light filtered into the barn where Archie Hagen and Trinity had spent the night in the hayloft. Tammy had been given a spare bedroom in the Bean house — a cozy place overseen by the matronly Mrs Bean. Her pipe-smoking husband, Aaron Bean seemed content to let her be the boss. A man of apparently small ambitions and declining energy, he nevertheless seemed contented with his lot.

Trinity rose earlier than Hagen and walked to the open double doors of the barn, looking out at the summer morning. A yellow dog slunk up to him and decided to take him as a companion on this morning. Trinity took a moment to pet its coarse hair and scratch its back where the tail connected to its body.

Stretching, Trinity looked around. There were chickens there — dozens of them — but also five or six goats, a pair of mules and half a dozen cattle which seemed to be ambling about purposelessly. Trinity could understand why this small, parched place was enough for Aaron Bean. Isolated, quiet, it could be that Bean had accomplished all that he had intended to accomplish with his life. Not everyone quests after riches or power; many seek only quietude and the peace of mind a private life can provide.

If the place were Boss Clark's there would be wells dug, seed planted, cattle driven in, a two-story frame-house structure instead of a stone house. Boss Clark was not unique out here. He was not as rapacious, grasping as many of the big ranchers. But like them, Clark still seemed determined to prove his worth to someone who no longer cared.

Like Polly Travers?

Trinity reflected on that relationship again briefly. A shrewd businessman,

Boss Clark had claimed to covet the water on the Bar-D for his growing herd. After several days on the range, Trinity had not seen enough water to support more than a handful of cattle. The pond at the base of the hills was most probably caused by the recent passing thunderstorm. The Shamishaw Trickle had lived up to its name: a dry waterbed showing signs of only occasional running water. Boss Clark could have had thousands upon thousands of barrels of water freighted in for half the money he had paid for the Bar-D.

No, he had given Polly Travers a gift — Trinity was now sure of that, which reinforced his conviction that Boss Clark was not involved in any sort of double-dealing. Perhaps once, long ago when they were both young, he and Polly . . .

'Who's your friend?'

Tammy Travers stood on the front porch of the Bean house, brushing her hair to a gleaming dark cascade. The sunlight played across her hair and splashed warmth on the shoulders of her white blouse. She indicated the yellow dog with her brush.

'He never did give me his name,' Trinity answered. 'Just seemed happy to show me around the place.' He walked toward the porch. The yellow dog followed and sat watching Trinity. He asked, 'Did you talk to the Beans — ask if they saw your brother and Joe Cordero?'

'No, they didn't,' Tammy said with a small frown. 'They must have skirted the ranch.'

'That makes sense,' Trinity replied. 'No matter if it were the Beans or someone totally unknown, they wouldn't have wanted to take chances considering what they were carrying.'

'I suppose,' Tammy said. 'It would be helpful to know if they'd already been to the bank or not.'

'It would. A lot of things would be helpful,' Trinity responded. 'How much farther is it to Van Horn?'

She glanced skyward, toward the hills

beyond. 'I think we'll be there a little after noon. Maybe Archie can give you a better idea.'

'That's close enough,' Trinity said.

'We'll find Cole along the way — if he stuck to the trail, won't we?' Tammy asked with a modest smile of hope.

'Sure,' Trinity said with a confidence he did not feel. 'He probably just lost his horse and is making his way back on foot.'

Barring the likely possibility — that he had been gunned down and robbed. And a second thought that had occurred to Trinity but which he was not about to share with Tamarind. That was the possibility that Cole had shot Cordero himself taken the money and fled. Was Cole Travers that kind of man? Trinity knew nothing about Cole. Probably his speculation was without substance. But you never knew.

Hagen had already saddled his own horse and Tammy's when Trinity again reached the barn, the dog having taken itself off somewhere. 'Just about ready?' Trinity asked.

'Whenever Tamarind says so,' the rough cowhand replied. He leaned on his saddle and watched as Trinity equipped the piebald with the usual dance and stunts from the horse.

'Ornery, is he?'

'He just likes to play. I suppose I've let it go on too long. Tell me, Archie — I've been giving this some thought — what can you tell me about the three men who quit the Bar-D.'

'Tell you?' Archie looked puzzled.

'I mean, were they always malcontents or did they just get fed up with the lack of wages and the inactivity?'

'I don't understand why it concerns you.'

'Because they went missing at a time when they knew they would soon be paid. Because it was a party of three men that were shooting at me and my partner, Billy. Because they knew that Cordero and Cole Travers would be riding to the county seat soon and returning with a lot of money.'

'You think they ambushed Cole and Cordero?' Archie asked with a deep scowl.

'How many people out this way could have known anything at all about this and waylaid the two?'

'I see what you mean, but it could be that some of the boys from Van Horn got wind of it and followed them out into the desert.'

'Could be, but do you think Cole or Joe were careless enough to talk about what they were doing?'

'No,' Archie admitted, dragging the word out thoughtfully. 'I sure wouldn't. But maybe they started drinking in some saloon and dropped a word or two.'

'It doesn't seem likely, though, does it? Now how about these three men who left the camp?' Trinity asked, slipping the piebald its bit and snugging down the throat latch on its bridle.

'Well,' Archie said hesitantly, 'the truth is all three were friends of mine.

I'd not like to lay blame on men who were innocent.'

'I understand that,' Trinity said, leading his horse toward the barn doors, Archie Hagen beside him, 'but I'd like to solve this thing — find out who was involved. I know it wasn't me and my partner. I can't make myself believe it was Boss Clark. So then who was it? I just wanted to know something about these men who quit the brand only days before they expected to be paid.'

'I see,' Hagen answered. 'Well, Sandy Worth is an old-time brush-popper from down in the Big Thicket country. He was looking for a mite easier job than pushing longhorns out of that tangle. The other two — they were Art Tatum and his younger brother, Walt. They hadn't a lot of skills, but we were looking to push the herd to New Mexico and needed some extra men.'

'They were awful impatient if they couldn't wait to collect their pay,' Trinity said, glancing up as Tammy once again emerged from the house, a small bag in her hand, and paused to hug Mrs Bean and say goodbye.

'Yeah, well, Polly told them that she was sorry to see them go, and they could ride back any time after Cole got back and collect their wages. No one was mad about it or anything — that's just the way it goes with these saddle tramps. Maybe they had another job lined up or had the urge to talk to some people who wear skirts — I wouldn't know. I wasn't that close to them.'

'Was it me, I'd wait for my pay nonetheless,' Trinity said.

'But it wasn't you,' Archie reminded him. They ended their conversation when Tammy walked near, swaying prettily. It was a beautiful morning, the silver-limned clouds etched against the bright-blue sky. It was still cool, with a light breeze stirring.

'Are we ready?' Tamarind asked, looking at each man.

'Ready,' Trinity answered.

'Mrs Bean offered us breakfast, but I

turned her down,' Tammy said. 'Don't get mad at me — it's just that I'm in a hurry. She gave me some hard-boiled eggs and some ham sandwiches that we can eat along the trail,' she said, holding up the sack.

'It's a better breakfast than I've had in some time,' Trinity said. In fact, he had been surviving still on those salt biscuits in his saddle-bags. They swung aboard and walked their horses from the yard. Mrs Bean stood in the doorway, waving after them. Tammy had taken the lead eagerly. Trinity noticed that Archie was riding beside him now, instead of to his rear with a rifle unsheathed.

'Decided to take a chance with me?' Trinity asked with a crooked smile.

'It's sort of that Miss Travers has,' Hagen answered.

'I don't get you,' Trinity said, puzzled.

'You don't?' Archie grinned, showing uneven teeth. 'I thought you were a knowing man, Trinity. Haven't you noticed the way she looks at you now, smiles when you talk to her? You've made a friend of her — if not more.'

'You've got an imagination,' Trinity said, though he was secretly pleased by Hagen's remark.

They started down a rocky slope studded with yucca and barrel cactus. Above, a red-tailed hawk shrieked a comment and dove lower.

And the guns of the ambushers opened up.

Archie Hagen was hit by the first shot. He stood up straight in his stirrups and slapped at the bloody spot on his white shirt. With true puzzlement he glanced at Trinity and fell from his horse to land sprawled and inert against the rocky ground.

Trinity left his rifle in its scabbard for the moment, went to the side of the piebald and heeled it sharply, riding Indian-style as he raced toward Tamarind who had halted, her eyes wide with surprise.

'Get going!' Trinity shouted, although

he was unsure if she could hear him above the roar of the guns and the pounding of the piebald's hoofs. The urgency of the situation seemed to come to her abruptly. Spinning her blue roan on its hind legs, she whipped its flank with the ends of her reins and drove on toward the shadowed ravine ahead of them.

Trinity heard a bullet ricochet off something metallic — probably a cinch ring on his saddle — and whine off into the gray distances. He ran the piebald hard for another half-mile, following Tamarind as she crested a small rocky knoll and guided her nimble little horse down the slope toward the bottom of the ravine.

Trinity followed her. Reaching the bottom, he reined up harshly, startling his horse, and he grabbed his rifle and swung down from the saddle in one clumsy motion. Tammy still sat her heaving horse.

'Get down!' he shouted.

'Surely,' she answered breathlessly,

'we've left them behind?'

'I'm not willing to bet my life on it . . . or yours.'

Tammy swung down and joined Trinity where he had taken up a position behind a group of weather-scoured boulders. 'Shouldn't we see if we can rescue Archie?' she asked, looking up at Trinity's tense face.

'Archie is beyond rescuing,' Trinity said grimly.

'Are you sure?'

'I'm sure.' Trinity held his rifle barrel between a split in the rocks. Behind him the opposite slope of the ravine rose: shadowed, rocky and barren. No one could get at them from up there. 'What do we do now?' Tammy asked in a hoarse, whispered voice.

'Wait. We can probably follow the bottom of the draw to safety. But we don't know that. We may have to wait until darkness settles.'

'It's only mid-morning,' Tammy squeaked.

'I know what time it is,' Trinity told

her. 'Maybe you should get busy cracking a few of those boiled eggs Mrs Bean gave us. We're in for a long siege.'

The sun rose higher, shadows shortened. The micaflecked rock face of the ravine wall behind them became a dully reflecting mirror. Tammy had scooted up to sit against the rocks when Trinity kept watch. There were shadows there, but they did little to cool her. Perspiration trickled down Trinity's forehead into his eyes. An alligator lizard rustled its way past them across dead, brown leaves. Its tread was inordinately loud for such a small creature, so still and silent was the heated day.

'They've gone,' Tammy said, 'I'm sure of it.'

'I'm not, and I'm not standing up to find out.'

She doubled her legs up and sat with her arms encircling her knees, eyes closed. From time to time Trinity studied her face, finding it appealing and deeply charming. Mostly, however, he kept his eyes riveted on the heights of the ravine where their assailants must show themselves if they were intent on finishing their job. Trinity secretly thought that Tammy had been right — they were gone. But he was equally certain that he had been right in refusing to move from where he knelt behind the rocks, although his legs were becoming cramped, his arms stiff, his stomach audibly requesting more food.

It was a small price to pay for staying alive.

The hours staggered past. His rifle was so sun-heated that he could barely touch the steel of it. No one came; the faint shadows of the morning sky flitted here and there as the thin clouds drifted on their course. It was not until the sun had nearly lowered itself behind the wall of the ravine that Tammy roused and spoke again.

'What are we going to do when we reach Van Horn?' She did not say *if* at least.

'The obvious,' Trinity told her. 'Go to the county courthouse and make sure the deed has been transferred, then find out if the bank honored Clark's draft and released the money to your brother.'

Tammy nodded. She had lost faith in their chances of finding her half-brother along the trail. It would soon be dark again, and the raiders — whoever they were — had driven them off their intended course. By now Cole was dead, had somehow made his way back to Polly's camp or he had . . .

'He couldn't have taken the money, could he, Trinity? Cole, I mean.'

'Could he have — I don't know. *Would* he have is the question. I don't know your brother at all. What do you think?'

'I can't conceive of it — he knows it would ruin Mother. With no place left to go, she'd probably have to sell off what was left of the herd . . . if she could find a buyer, and then . . . I don't know! Become a washer-woman or something as dreadful.'

'She'd die of a broken heart before

that happened,' Trinity answered softly. He did not know Polly Travers well, but he could imagine any mother's grief at having all she had worked for, meant to achieve, stolen from her by an ungrateful child.

'It's going to be dark soon,' Tammy said, looking at the western side of the ravine where golden sabers of light splayed skyward as the sun continued to drop.

'Yes, it is,' Trinity answered, but he did not rise or shift position. He returned to an earlier thought: 'Tamarind, you don't suppose that Calvin Dancer is still around.'

'Cole's father!'

'Yes. This whole event seems rather too well organized for three cowhands to have managed, and more than Cole could have thought up on the spur of the moment.'

'You do come up with some! Dancer is long dead. I'm sure of that. The way he lived, outlaw that he was!'

'Well, that's the way I thought it was

— after all, your mother did marry again.'

'After Dancer was gone for years, Mother and Luther Travers had him declared legally dead. My father was that way — he wanted everything on the up and up. No one came forward to say they had seen Calvin Dancer alive all that time. And not since, in perhaps fifteen years. If Dancer has anything to do with this, it must be his ghost who's up to no good.'

Well, Trinity thought, that was that. Tammy sounded completely convinced. He, himself, knew nothing of the details surrounding Calvin Dancer's death or disappearance. But if Dancer were alive he would have a large range of motives for these crimes — money, the deed to his old property, revenge against his former wife and Luther Travers . . .

It *was* getting dark now. The hills were alive with the scent of purple sage; distantly a coyote mourned the dying day. A cottontail rabbit, surprised at coming upon these human intruders skittered away toward its burrow. A ground owl hooted.

'Let's tighten our cinches and get on the trail,' Trinity said, rising creakily from his position like an arthritic old man.

They started up the dark bottom of the ravine before the lazy moon had brightened enough to illuminate their path. There was no sound in the world but the steady clopping of the horses' hoofs. At times the winding trail permitted a view of the lights of Van Horn glittering in the near distance.

Tammy looked hopefully at Trinity and said:

'Well at least we've lost those killers — whoever they are.'

Trinity did not wish to answer her honestly, but he thought she deserved to know what he was thinking. In the purple of dusk his words sounded somehow more ominous.

'I don't think we have. I think the only way we'll ever be rid of them is when they're all lying dead.'

6

The town of Van Horn was wrapped in a twilight haze. Silent, its lights gleaming dully, it did not seem a welcoming place. Trinity asked as they rode slowly up the nearly empty main street: 'Have you enough money for a hotel room?'

'Unless they're exorbitantly high, yes, I think so.'

'Let's find one then, and get you put up for the night. We are going to have a busy day tomorrow.'

'What are you going to do?' Tammy asked.

'After the heat of the day, I'll be just as content to sleep out tonight. I'll stable the horses and then find a place to sleep,' Trinity answered. 'First I'll probably visit some of the local saloons.'

'Just like a man,' Tammy said with some disgust.

'No, it's not like that. I don't like the idea of drinking in a strange town among men I don't know. I just want to see what I can find out about Cole, if anything, and about Art and Walt Tatum, Sandy Worth.'

'You still believe that the three former Bar-D riders are involved?'

'I still believe they *might* be,' Trinity corrected. 'It would be nice to know them on sight, but then I guess they'd know what I look like too. So far they've only seen me the three times they tried to kill me from a distance.'

'If you think it's a good idea to go around asking about them . . . ' Tammy said doubtfully.

'I don't, not particularly, but I'd like to not give them another chance at bushwhacking me. If this keeps up, they're bound to get me sooner or later, even if it's just with a lucky shot.'

Trinity helped Tamarind from her horse in front of a shabby one-storied hotel with a porch awning decorated with broken gingerbread scrollwork. A few men looked with interest from a wooden bench there. Trinity waited on the porch while Tammy went in to inquire about a room.

'They've got one. Affordable,' she said when she emerged.

'All right. I'll see you in the morning. Not too early. These government and bank offices probably don't open early.'

'At least we can look forward to that — clearing this up with the bank.'

'Yes,' Trinity replied. He wasn't sure they would like what they found out. Before Tammy slipped away again, he told her in a low voice, 'Lock your door,' and she nodded grimly.

He waited until she was safely indoors and then mounted, gathering the reins to her little blue roan. He started along the street then, looking for a stable.

With the horses being curried, with feed and water being supplied, he began walking the streets, searching out the many saloons that dotted the small town. What, if anything, he expected to learn, he could not have said, but the effort seemed worth making. Along a side street apparently set aside for and zoned for this purpose, Trinity found eight saloons within a one-block area. They all were clouded with tobacco smoke, all smelling of rank alcohol and stale beer. The only differences were that some were glaringly bright, loud and alive with discordant clamor and others were remarkably drab and silent, as if the men in these were entombed, destined to waste their lives away sitting along a scarred bar under a low, dark ceiling, methodically drinking their way to oblivion.

Which was unlikely to appeal to the ambushers — or to Cole Travers, for that matter — Trinity had not eliminated him from his list of possible culprits. Cole might be the apple of his mother's eye, but not many mothers were capable of seeing or admitting dark tendencies in their children.

Trinity figured each of them for the celebrating kind. They would want the bright lights and entertainment after months on the range. Especially if their pockets were bulging with Polly Travers's money.

The light in the first saloon he entered was bright enough to be nearly blinding after the outside darkness. Trinity winced and waited, letting his eyes adjust as all around him men shouted, cursed, slapped cards down on table tops and called out rudely to the three women evident in the place. Each woman wore a fixed smile and a patience derived solely from knowing how much money these cowboys would spill from their jeans in their haste to give it away to a woman — any woman. They made a lot of money, these saloon girls; how they squared it with their consciences, Trinity did not try to guess.

Making his way toward the bar through the rough-talking men filled with whisky-induced bonhomie, which Trinity knew could turn in an instant to anger and even bloodshed at the wrong jest, he saw himself in the long mirror behind the bar and realized how tired he really was. In his range clothes, wearing a shirt he had torn at the elbow somewhere along the way, stained jeans, and with an unshaven face, he supposed he did not look unique among this mob, but behind his eyes he imagined a different man — barbered, assured and at least somewhat good-looking. Well, they say the mirror doesn't lie. He determined to at least get a shave in the morning before meeting with Tamarind.

Trinity ordered a beer which was slow in coming. Men shouldered each other aside, trying to reach the bar. In the meantime Trinity watched the boisterous men behind him in the saloon's mirror. Outside of the fact that one of the men who had shot at Billy Raglan and him had been wearing a red shirt, he had no description for the men he hunted. And there were at least a dozen men in the saloon wearing red shirts.

Cole was young — that was certain. That might have helped, but the cowboys jostling each other, stumbling about the room were of all sizes and all ages. Was it worth the risk to bring up the names of the Tatum brothers and Sandy Worth? It was dangerous, to be sure, but it was the only way he could think of to begin his hunt.

Archie Hagen had said that Worth was an old 'brush-popper', a cowboy working the dense Big Thicket country of south Texas, pushing out the longhorn cattle, some of which had not seen a human being since before the Civil War. Down in that part of the country the men wore special gear, such as *tapaderos* attached to their stirrups to protect their toes from the thorny brush and cactus which could easily penetrate a man's boot. And leather chaps; always chaps, or the spines of the thicket county under-growth would slash the trousers from your legs. Did Worth cling to that habit? Trinity let his eyes again study the men in the room. There were at least half a dozen cowhands wearing chaps.

As a detective, he decided, he did not make the grade. He was going to have to start talking to people, despite the risk of being found out himself.

He exited the saloon, leaving half a beer behind on the bar. It was cool, quiet outside once he moved away from the doors. It reminded him how much he did like his life on the range despite its occasional difficulties.

It was not at the next saloon he tried, but at the one after that, that he saw the three men in the corner hunched over a round wooden table, speaking in low voices. He did not exchange glances with them as he crossed the room toward the bar, boot heels clicking, but he had seen them well enough. One of them, the youngest wore a red shirt with trail dust on it. Another was a man with a black beard shot with gray. If you could imagine him clean-shaven he bore a strong resemblance to the younger man. The third man, his hat tilted back revealing a receding hairline wore wide Texas chaps.

Trinity could not be sure, but he thought he had found his men — the Tatum brothers and Sandy Worth. Now what? He could hardly approach them directly. Try taking a seat near enough to them to hear what they were talking about? That seemed extremely dangerous. No, it was better just to wait and watch occasionally, maybe follow them when they exited the saloon.

What Trinity was wondering as he idly sipped a beer, was what the three were doing in Van Horn. If they were trying to harass Polly Travers and her herd they should be out there somewhere. They continued to order drinks. The man with the beard whom Trinity took to be Art Tatum laughed recklessly and shouted to a bar girl. They were not short of money, that was for sure.

So why had they come to Van Horn? There was only one possible answer: they had come here to collect their pay.

But who had paid them? The only answer that occurred to Trinity was an unhappy one — Cole Travers was alive and had kept his mother's money after cashing Boss Clark's bank draft. That could be found out with certainty in the morning when the bank was open, but for now it seemed the only reasonable answer.

Hell! When Trinity again glanced toward the table where the three men had been sitting, it was empty. As he had already decided, he was a terrible detective. He had let the three men slip out of the saloon unnoticed. Glancing around to make sure they had not simply relocated, Trinity started toward the batwing doors of the saloon.

The street was empty except for two loud passing cowhands riding their horses slowly along the street, good-naturedly jeering at each other as they rode by. Trinity's quarry had vanished. Which way? He looked up and down the street, seeing no one that resembled them. If they had ridden off, it was an impossible job to find them again, but if, as many drinking men do when out on a night on the town, they had simply decided to try another saloon, he might be able to find them again. Hesitating for a minute, Trinity started toward the nearest, most brightly lit saloon on the street.

It was a mistake, of course. He stepped down off the plankwalk to walk to cross the alley and a hand reached out of the darkness and grabbed his arm, yanking him into the alleyway. Trinity slapped the hand away and reached for his Colt, but there was a second man behind him and this one, large and bearded, pulled the pistol from Trinity's holster before he could grip the butt. Now with both men holding him, a third shadowy figure appeared from the shadows. Trinity could hear the whish-slap of his leather chaps as he came forward and threw a powerful right-hand punch into his belly.

Trinity fought back wildly, trying to wrench his arms free, kicking out with his booted feet at the man in front of him, but it was useless. A heavy blow landed on his ear, a second caught him on the hinge of the jaw, a third drove into his unprotected belly again, driving the wind from him, bringing the raw taste of bile to his throat. His vision began to blur, his head to spin as three, four more heavy punches landed on his face and throat and ribs.

Then the gun went off close beside him, and Trinity fell down into a deep pool of blackness, seeing, hearing, feeling no more.

★　★　★

There was brilliant sunlight piercing the plank walls of the place — whatever it was — striking Trinity's eyes harshly. Where was he? Beneath him was a soft, fluffy bed. It was like sleeping among sheep. That made no sense. None of it did.

He tried to sit up. Failed, but made it on the second attempt. He was in shadow. Outside the day was bright with sunlight. His head thrummed. Trinity buried his head in his hands as he sat, knees drawn up, searching the dark corners of the place. The somehow familiar voice said:

'About time you were coming around. I was set to go looking for a doctor.'

Slowly Trinity's blurred vision cleared and he was able to make out the figure of the man now crouched down beside him.

'*Billy?*'

'It's me, son,' the whiskered gunman said.

'But . . . how?'

'Take a minute to get your head together and I'll tell you all about it.'

'Where am I?' Trinity asked with an exhausted moan.

'It's an old cotton barn I came across. They used to store bales of the stuff here in the old days, before boll weevils wiped out the crops and the farmers around here decided to go to less profitable but more reliable crops.'

Trinity felt around him and now recognized the fluffy stuff he had been sleeping on for what it was. Billy Raglan was saying:

'I hadn't money for a hotel, but I found a few abandoned bales of cotton here. I split them open and made myself a comfortable enough bed.'

'How'd you find me?'

'I was looking. I went over to the stable and there was your ornery, unmistakable, ugly piebald horse looking at me over the stall partition. I didn't know where you'd gone, but I figured to look in the saloons first.'

'And you saw them jump me?'

'That's right. Sorry I couldn't get there quicker, but when I cut loose a shot up in the air, they took to their heels fast enough.'

'Thanks, Billy,' Trinity said, meaning it. 'I think they would have beat me to death.'

'Were they who I think they must have been — our friends from back along the trail?'

'Yes, and I've got names for them now. But, Billy . . . how did you get here?'

'When they tried to ambush us, I hit the ground. I decided to stay there playing possum. I wasn't going to win no gunfight. You were gone, so after they rode on, I got up and circled behind them, then got so's I was flanking them. I seen them start shooting at someone along the way, but I was too far away to tell who it was. I figured it might have been you.'

'It was.'

'I couldn't tell, but they didn't seem all that intent on finishing the job. They went on after a while, and I tagged along all the way to Van Horn. After all that, I lost them in town!'

Billy chuckled at the thought. He could follow men across the desert and the hills and lose them in a small town. 'Tell me, Trinity,' he asked, 'how did you come to be here?'

'After you went down — shot dead, I thought — Tamarind took me to Polly's camp . . . '

'Polly Travers?' Billy Raglan asked with puzzled curiosity.

'That's right. Then Tamarind and I — '

'And who is Tamarind?' Billy asked, still perplexed, so Trinity told him all about it. The sun continued to lance through the gaps in the weathered slats of the old cotton barn and Trinity continued to keep his eyes closed, his head bowed as he spoke. Something occurred to him when he was at an end:

'I wonder how they knew who I was?' Trinity said.

'That's simple. They didn't know you, but they had to have known this Tamarind Travers on sight. They worked for Polly, didn't they? They must have seen you ride into town with her.'

Trinity nodded his understanding. He was staring sullenly at the walls, almost numbly until he realized that the angle of the morning light was all wrong.

'What time is it, Billy!' Trinity asked

suddenly, trying to rise from his bed of cotton.

'Why, it's close on to noon, Trinity. I didn't want to wake you, beat up as you were. Why? What's so important?'

'I was supposed to meet Tammy at the hotel this morning. She'll think I am hurt or dead.'

'Which you are — and almost were,' Billy Raglan answered.

'I don't want her worried,' Trinity said, struggling to get to his feet, 'or alone here.'

'All right,' Billy said, helping Trinity to his feet. 'We'll find her, then. If you're able.'

'I'm able,' Trinity said unconvincingly.

'If you say so.' Trinity held himself only half-erect. Those blows to his body had damaged his ribs enough to make it difficult to straighten up.

'I was going to get a shave before I saw Tammy again,' Trinity said, rubbing his jaw. 'I guess I haven't the time now.'

Billy peered at Trinity through the

shadows of the barn. 'I don't think that would make much difference,' Raglan said.

'That bad, is it?' Trinity asked, trying to grin.

'Oh, you look all right,' Billy replied. 'If you don't count the black eye, the lump on your forehead and the split lip. Plus you smell a little ripe. I had the chance to take a bath yesterday. It cost me fifty cents, but it was worth it.'

'Are you telling me — '

'I'm telling you that you smell like cow, horse, sweat, trail dirt and a little like stale beer. And your face would have children running away screaming. So take your choice — we can either try to find this Tamarind girl or we can take you over to a barber to get you cleaned up.'

'If I'm that bad — look, Billy, would you go looking for her and explain?'

'I don't even know what she looks like.'

'Pretty, dark-haired.'

'That narrows it down, but not much.'

'She'll be at the bank or the county recorder's office. Or, she might have returned to the hotel by now.'

'All right,' Billy agreed reluctantly. 'I'll give it a try then. A courting young man should present himself in the best way he can.' Billy smiled; Trinity flared up.

'Who said anything about courting!'

'It was just in a manner of speaking,' Raglan answered with a blank expression. 'Come on, I'll help you over to that barber I know — the one with a bath in the back. We'll see if he can patch you up some while I go looking for this Miss Tamarind Travers.'

'Thanks, Billy,' Trinity said. 'While you're wandering around, be careful won't you? We've got some unfriendly sorts in this town.'

'I've lasted at least twenty years longer than you have, Trinity, I'm always careful. Take your own advice. These boys are not playing. They want you dead.'

'I know — do you think we should

send a wire to Boss Clark, Billy?'

'And tell him what? Anything we have to tell him is too long for a telegraph message, and I don't know what we know about affairs ourselves.'

'You're right. Let's get started. Have you seen my hat?'

'No. You must have lost it in the alley. Come along now, let's see about getting you cleaned up.'

The bath came first. Trinity soaked and scrubbed and soaked again in the zinc tub in the barber's back room until the water grew cold as Billy Raglan scoured the town looking for Tammy. The hot water eased some of the soreness in Trinity's body — he was at least able to stand up straight. Then the barber shaved him, working around the nicks on Trinity's face. He had leeches in a jar which he advised Trinity to use on his swollen, discolored eye, but somehow Trinity couldn't bring himself to do that. Ice was applied to the large lump on his forehead, and some sort of soothing balm to his split lip. Then briefly, expertly, the barber trimmed Trinity's hair, shaved the back of his neck, splashed some bay rum on his cheeks, dusted off his neck with a soft brush coated with talcum powder, and handed him a hand mirror, declaring him fit again for human civilization.

Trinity didn't look long at himself in the mirror — his face still had a mottled color to it and seemed slightly lopsided, but it was definitely an improvement. He palmed a silver dollar from his scant remaining cash and gave it to the man, who slipped it into the till. He then asked where the nearest dry-goods store was, feeling naked without a hat.

He stepped on to the barber's porch and nearly walked into Art Tatum. He braced himself, but the bearded man pushed past him, not recognizing Trinity, and it was a good thing — Trinity was hardly up to another fight.

What now? Trinity could wait and follow Tatum, hoping to learn something more or he could meet with

Tamarind to see what she had found out. It was not an entirely logical decision that he made. He would find Tammy and talk to her. After a stop at the dry-goods store to purchase a fawn-colored Stetson and a new white-flannel shirt with bone buttons, which used up just about the last of his pocket money, he started back toward the hotel. Glancing back along the street once, he could have sworn that he saw a bearded man watching him go.

It seemed that Art Tatum had recognized him after all, and that meant that all three of them, guns ready for use, would be coming along behind him. The only reason they hadn't shot him down last night, he conjectured, was that they didn't wish to risk being arrested in Van Horn for a murder which could easily be done in the far country.

But they would be coming; they meant to do that murder sooner or later.

7

Trinity saw Tammy before she saw him. She was sitting alone at a little table with a white cloth covering it in the corner of the hotel restaurant, in an area with a sign proclaiming it a 'Ladies' Tea Room'. She was brooding over a cup of tea, stirring it with a small spoon. She was wearing a pink dress and a wide-brimmed white straw hat with a blue ribbon as a tie, looking nearly desolate and quite alone. Trinity, seeing her dressed up like that, was happier that he had taken the time to clean up just a little. He tramped across the hardwood floor toward her table. She lifted sad, expectant eyes toward him and frowned as he seated himself.

'You're some help!' she said. Then noticing his face she blanched, and, chastened, asked in a lower voice: 'What happened to you?' She stretched out a hand almost, but not quite touching his battered face.

'I went looking for them. Found them. Had a fight. They won,' Trinity said. 'Any chance of getting a cup of coffee in here?' he asked, looking around.

'I'm sure there is. Was it . . . were they the men you thought it was? The Tatum brothers and Sandy Worth?'

'It was, and they're splashing a lot of money around. What did you find out?'

'I went to the county recorder's office as soon as it opened at nine o'clock. They didn't even have to check their records. No one's transferred a deed in weeks.'

'Boss Clark will not be a happy man — what did the bank tell you?'

'Oh, that business was taken care of all right! A man came in, said his name was Cole Travers and they cashed the bank draft for him. It didn't matter if it was Cole or not. They tell me those checks are paid to bearer. I asked to see the signature on the back anyway.'

'Was it Cole's?'

'It could have been,' Tammy admitted reluctantly, 'His usual signature has a lot of silly flourishes and curlicues like someone uses to decorate his signature when he's trying to make out that he's someone important. This signature was hastily scrawled — and it appeared to me done a little bit nervously.'

'But you think it was Cole's.'

'I think so,' Tammy said, 'but that doesn't mean he's the man who went into the bank with it, does it?'

'No. Could they give you a description of the man?'

'Young and clean-shaven was all the clerk remembered.'

'That covers a lot of men.'

'Walt Tatum among them,' Tammy said. She was trying to find some way to exonerate her half-brother. 'If they had done something with Cole, had him sign the bank draft, then . . . '

Then what? There was only one *then* after that. They would have had to get rid of Cole to keep him from testifying against them.

'It doesn't look too good, does it?' Tammy asked quietly. 'Either way.'

'It doesn't,' Trinity answered. 'By now those three will be on their way out of town. We won't be getting any answers from them.'

'I don't know what to tell Mother,' Tammy said.

'She probably already knew that finding Cole was a long shot. I could see it in her eyes when we rode out.'

A red-haired, unhappy-looking waitress arrived wearing a black-and-white outfit which Trinity supposed was meant to be the sort women in real tea shops wore. She went away to fetch his coffee and Trinity sat watching Tammy in silence as she stared out the window which was surrounded by flimsy white curtains.

'You sure do look nice this morning,' he managed to say eventually.

'You like this dress?' She smiled with weak gratitude at his compliment.

'After I went to the bank I saw this in a dress-shop window. I went in to avoid having to think about all of this business for a while and ended up buying it. It's been so long since I had a new dress, almost as long since I've had any chance to wear one. Now,' she sighed, 'I guess I'll just have to pack it away. I'll probably never wear it again.'

Trinity nodded his sympathy. 'I guess Billy never did find you, then?'

'Billy?' she asked blankly.

'Billy Raglan — my old partner. He's the one who pulled me out of trouble last night.'

'But I thought he was . . . '

'He's back from the dead,' Trinity told her. 'He followed Worth and the Tatum brothers up here. I asked him to look for you and tell you what happened so that I could wash up a little before I met you.' He smiled. 'It probably doesn't look like I cleaned up, but believe me this is much better than I looked when I got up this morning.'

'I saw your new hat . . . ' she

119

hesitated and repaid the compliment, 'really, Trinity, you're looking quite respectable this morning.'

The waitress delivered the coffee. Tammy got back to business. 'What do we do now, Trinity?'

'What is there to do? I'd be more than surprised to find the Tatum brothers and Worth are still in town. They've collected their pay. They'll have ridden out to avoid us.'

'And there's no hope of finding Cole?'

'Very little if we haven't found him already.'

'Then,' Tammy said, 'I'll just have to ride back and tell Mother that everything's lost. I suppose we can last for a little while if we sell the cattle we still have, but the old house and the new ranch in New Mexico — both gone for good and all.'

Trinity had no ideas to offer the distraught young woman. She was right — if the remaining cattle could be driven, say, to Van Horn and marketed they would have some money. But after the drovers were paid, it would be little enough.

'What about you, Trinity?' Tammy wanted to know. 'What will you do?'

'I've still got a job,' he said. 'I suppose we'll have to do what Billy and I discussed earlier — wire Boss Clark and tell him that both his money and his deed are missing. I'd rather do that than tell him in person. He'll hit the ceiling.'

'And blame my mother.'

'Blame himself for doing business as he never does. For Polly's sake.'

'Are you still clinging to the idea that there was something between them long ago.'

'I don't see any other explanation. Why didn't Luther go over there with the offer to buy the Bar-D? No, your mother went alone.'

'Well, a part of that was because the ranch is in my mother's name. It always has been.'

'I hadn't thought of that. Still, I've

never seen Boss Clark turn over cash money on a promise.'

'I don't suppose it matters now,' Tammy said. She was staring out the window, still deeply distressed. 'I guess I'd better let you go over to the telegraph office. I have to change into riding clothes anyway,' she said, fingering her pretty pink dress with unhappy touches. Her eyes suddenly lit with astonishment and she pointed toward the window. 'Look, Trinity!'

Trinity looked out the window which fronted the street, seeing the usual assortment of idle cowboys and a few passersby, including an old man walking with a cane.

'That's him!' Tammy said breathlessly.

'Who's who?' a deeply puzzled Trinity asked, holding back the sheer curtain to study the people on the street again.

'He's gone now. The man with the cane, didn't you see him?'

'I did. It was no one I know.'

'I think I do.' Her eyes fixed on his holding fear, hope, wonder. 'Trinity — that was Calvin Dancer!'

'The old man?'

'I'm sure of it. There are pictures of him at home. And he looks too much like Cole. It was him. About the right age. He'd be gray by now, wouldn't he? Trinity, I'm positive that was Calvin Dancer.'

Cole's father. Polly's first husband? Here in Van Horn? It was too much to absorb all at once. Maybe there was more to this than simply three disgruntled trail hands robbing their boss. It sure opened up many possibilities. If Tammy was sure. How could she be from a few old pictures? Yet she seemed certain.

'We'd better try to catch up with him,' Trinity said, rising. 'If it's just a mistake, we'll apologize to the man and go on our way. If it is Calvin Dancer, I would say he has a few questions to answer.'

Trinity and Tammy went out quickly.

Just approaching them on foot was Billy Raglan. 'I wondered where you'd got to,' Raglan said, then he took a look at Tammy and nodded to himself as if he had solved the puzzle.

'Tamarind swears that she just saw Calvin Dancer pass by,' Trinity said.

'Is that so?' Billy frowned and squinted into the sun, looking down the street. 'Which way?'

'That way!' Tammy said excitedly.

'Can't see him now. There's not too much down that way, is there?'

'The stable,' Trinity said. 'Let's see if we can catch up.'

Before they had reached the stable they saw a surrey emerge from the shadowed alley beside it and Tammy gulped, pointing at the man driving the rig. 'That's him!' she insisted, 'We can't let him get away.'

'We won't,' Trinity said firmly. 'Let's grab up our ponies, Billy.'

'Wait,' Tammy said, grabbing his arm as they turned away. 'I'm going, too.'

'You're wearing a dress, remember.'

Tammy looked down at herself with dismay. 'I can ride in a dress.'

'Your new dress? Look, Tammy, go back and change. I can't let you hold us up right now, and I know you don't want to do that.'

'No,' she answered with disappointment. 'Go on, then. Hurry up!'

She stood watching as they rushed to the stable, then shook her head unhappily and started back toward the hotel. She muttered, 'I just had to buy the dress!'

Trinity and Billy were quickly saddled. The piebald, perhaps sensing the urgency, performed none of his usual tricks and they were mounted and riding out, ducking to clear the doorway, in minutes. Then they were on to the sun-bright, dusty street riding in the direction the man in the buggy had taken. They did not touch spurs to the horses or hurry them unnecessarily. No buggy was going to outrace them.

Still Trinity eyed the rough country

ahead of them and said, 'We can't lose him now, Billy.'

Billy squinted at Trinity and said without smiling, 'Son, if between the two of us we can't track some four-wheeled buggy across open land, both of us should be considering another line of work.'

The afternoon light was strong enough for them to follow the surrey quickly. They saw no dust ahead of them, but the grooves cut into the dry earth were evident. Besides, they didn't want to ride up on the man too quickly — they wanted to find out where he was going and discover who else might be there.

Then they could have their talk.

If that was Calvin Dancer, alive and well, why hadn't he been reported in the area over the years? Trinity kicked himself mentally. The answer was obvious. The well-known bad man and outlaw had most probably been locked away in prison, only recently reappearing. Maybe he had come back to claim what was his, or thought he owned — the Bar-D ranch, and had seized the opportunity to cheat Boss Clark out of more money. According to Tamarind it was said that Dancer had gotten the ranch through trickery in the first place; why wouldn't he try it again?

All of that made sense even without knowing any of the details, but it only hung together *if* the man ahead of them was really Dancer.

The miles passed. The ground, apparently unsuitable for anything at all, was yellow-dry, rocky and nearly lifeless as it stretched out toward distant Guadalupe Mountains. Nothing grew there but yellow bunch-grass and barrel cactus. Billy rode on with silent intensity, hardly ever lifting his eyes from the tracks they were following, though the carriage was beelining across the flat land and there was no way they were going to lose the sign.

The land began to roll slightly, and now and then they came upon a shallow gulch. Farther along, as the sun

127

switched to the down side of the sky, falling toward evening, the land opened up and a broad valley was revealed.

And on this empty patch of land was a small structure. Someone had thrown up a house here, years ago. It looked as if the hopeful man's dream had not worked out. There was no grass, no cattle on the naked land, Trinity raised his hand toward Billy and halted his piebald. The land was not quite deserted, for standing at the hitch rail in front of the weathered house were four saddle horses.

'That buckskin on the end,' Billy pointed out, 'I've seen that one before.' Trinity nodded, so had he. He thought he recognized two of the others as well, but could not be sure.

'What do you think, Billy?'

'We got to do what we came out here for.'

'There'll be shooting if that's who I think it is down there.'

'Yes,' Billy said, turning his head to spit. 'There will be shooting. Let's go calling. I didn't ride all this way for nothing.'

They started their horses down the rocky bluff. The surrey had used the rough road, but they hoped to make their approach to the house a little less obvious by staying away from the traveled way.

It didn't make much difference. As they drew nearer Trinity saw a man on the porch of the old house raise an arm and call out something they could not distinguish at that distance. Then three other men appeared, looked their way, and bolted for their horses. The four of them spurred their mounts in all directions. Trinity looked at Billy and pointed westward while he himself heeled the piebald and began a pursuit of the man who was riding hard toward the east.

He hoped, but feared, that his man was Cole Travers. He was young, slim. That was all Trinity could tell as the horseman pounded on across the level ground. He needed to find Cole, but did not wish to have to tell Tammy and her mother that Cole was involved in this. Or that he had shot him down.

To the west a pair of shots rang out. In front of Trinity, the man he chased looked around and brought up his revolver, firing wildly across his shoulder, trying to tag Trinity on the run. His shots came nowhere near, but Trinity was able to get a look at the man's face. It was young Walt Tatum. Trinity ducked low across the piebald's withers and unsheathed his long gun.

Slowing his horse, he took the reins in his left hand and shouldered his Winchester. Walt was still a fast-moving, uncertain target. When Trinity triggered off, he also missed, but he saw the unfortunate roan horse the kid rode stumble, falter and begin to fall. It had taken the slug meant for its rider. Trinity charged on and came upon the stunned Walt Tatum as he rose from the ground, shaking his head.

Walt's eyes opened wider, and he looked round in panic. He had lost his handgun in his fall from the roan's back. He got shakily to his fret, but braced himself for a fight. Trinity gave him all he wanted.

Walt was strong, Trinity had to admit that, but he was still a little wobbly on his feet, and as the two men came together Walt's punch whipped past Trinity's ear and caught him on the shoulder, doing little damage. As they briefly exchanged punches, Trinity realized that he himself was still battered from the beating he had taken in the alley the night before. Walt shook off what was Trinity's best left hook. The blow landed solidly on Walt's jaw, but Walt kept his feet. More, his co-ordination and strength seemed to be returning.

Walt blocked Trinity's following right with his left arm and went underneath, digging a right hand shot of his own into Trinity's already battered ribs. Trinity shook his head and backed away, trying to avoid Walt's onslaught. He tripped over one of the dead roan's legs and went down flat on his back.

It was then that Walt spotted his lost revolver glinting in the sunlight. Perhaps figuring he had had enough of fist-fighting, he swept it up and drew back the hammer of the Colt. From his back, Trinity drew and fired as rapidly as he could. He let off two shots, but the second one was unnecessary. Walt Tatum took the first .44 bullet directly to the heart and caved in, dropping his pistol as he fell to the ground.

Panting, Trinity got to his feet and walked to the fallen badman. He cast a long shadow across the dead kid's body. Looking skyward he saw that the buzzards were already gathering. He would have to let them have Walt. There was no way he was going to bury horse and man, no way he was going to carry Walt back on his piebald — not knowing who else he might run into along the way.

There was just nothing else to be done. Stiffly, then, Trinity stepped back into leather and turned his horse away from the still forms of horse and rider as the dark cloud of scavenger birds overhead thickened and waited.

He met Billy Raglan before reaching the house. Billy looked weary; his face was streaked with sweat and dust. He fell in beside Trinity as they rode back toward the house.

'Get your man, did you?' Billy asked.

'It was Walt Tatum. I wish I could have gotten him alive.'

'And do what with him? You think he would have answered any questions you have?'

'I guess not,' Trinity answered. 'How about you, Billy, What happened? I heard shots.'

'Sandy Worth — someone should have told that old brush-popper that he had no business even carrying a gun.'

'That only leaves two of them,' Trinity muttered.

'So far as we know. Just because we chased them off it doesn't mean they won't be coming back.'

'No,' Trinity agreed. 'It doesn't mean

that.' Art Tatum, especially, did not seem to be the sort to just throw up his hands and ride away.

They approached the dilapidated gray house carefully, arriving just as sunset began to color the western skies. Surprisingly, there was the thin glow of a lighted lantern visible through one of the front windows. Trinity mouthed the word 'who' to Billy, but only got a shrug in return. There were no saddle horses in front of the house but behind it, under a solitary oak tree, they saw the two buggy horses nibbling aimlessly at the dead grass.

Carefully, silently, except for the creak of leather, they swung down from their horses at the side of the house and made their way toward the front door, pistols drawn.

Reaching the door without being seen — at least no warning was called out — Trinity stood irresolute for a moment. It could be a trap, he knew. He considered knocking, but did not want to draw forth a hail of bullets from within. Gesturing to Billy Raglan, Trinity stood back and delivered one solid, well-aimed kick at the door, popping the lock. He ducked in, moving quickly to one side, gun leveled.

'That was a new lock,' a tired voice sighed. 'People are so hasty these days.'

'Sorry,' Trinity felt obliged to mutter.

'I suppose it doesn't matter. Way out here, isolated as I am, I've never felt the need for locks . . . until lately.'

8

As Trinity's eyes adjusted to the feeble light cast by the lantern, he was able to make out the bent figure of a man sitting in a wheelchair next to the cold fireplace. A cane was hung from one of the chair's arms. The man's face was craggy but pale, his hands large and gnarled. Whoever he was, he appeared to be a man who had once labored hard but had had his youthful strength cut away from him by time. Trinity wasn't sure how to approach him. Could this truly be the feared Calvin Dancer, or had Tammy's eagerness led her to falsely identify a man whose face even she admitted she did not really know? Billy was more blunt than Trinity.

'Who were those men that went riding off when they saw us coming?'

The old man shifted uneasily in his chair. He shrugged with his hands, 'I can't help you there, partner. I never did learn their names.' His voice sounded truthful, his old face reflected sincerity.

'They were living here and you don't know their names?' Billy Raglan persisted.

'They weren't living here. They came by yesterday and asked to spend the night. They said they'd pay me good money to bunk here. Well,' he said looking around the shabby room, 'as you can see, I haven't much, and little hope of making more.' He slapped his dead leg as he said this. 'They told me they'd be gone by morning, so I let them in. My name, by the way, is Edward Stubblefield. This is my humble house.

'This morning, being relatively flush thanks to my guests,' he said with a weak smile, 'I went to town to take care of some old debts. When I got back they were still here. They said they might have to spend another night. The way they said it indicated that they meant to do whatever they wanted, and I wasn't going to argue with four armed men.

'I suppose it was about an hour after that that you two rode in. One of them shouted and the others scrambled out the door, making for their horses. That's what happened, mister. It's all I can tell you.'

'Did they say where they were going?' Trinity asked.

'All I heard was the big man shout, 'scatter!'.' He attempted a smile again. 'So I guess they just scattered.'

There didn't seem to be any point in trying to get more out of the old man. Either things were as he said, and that was all he knew — or, he *was* Calvin Dancer, and in that case he sure wouldn't be telling them what they wanted to know.

Outside Billy and Trinity led their horses to the trough and let them drink. Now and then they would glance back at the gray house which looked ready to fold its roof and collapse.

'What do you think?' Billy asked at

138

last. Trinity shrugged.

'The truth is, I have no idea. I don't know who he is. Maybe we should have let Tammy come along.'

'And bring her into a gunfight? Besides, she don't even know what the man looks like, I think it might have all been in her head. She wanted something to hang her hopes on.'

'I thought of that, too, but she seemed so damned sure. And, the Tatum boys and Sandy Worth were here.'

'I know,' Billy said, removing his flop hat to scratch at his thinning thatch of hair. 'Coincidence?'

'I wish I knew,' Trinity said with an audible sigh. 'We'd better get back to Van Horn, don't you think, Billy?'

'I suppose. The other two men are long gone, and even if we could track them over this ground, it would be dark before we could find them. Let's go back. There's nothing else we can do.' Billy swung aboard his gray horse before adding, 'At least we've cut the odds down a little.'

'And gotten no nearer to Boss Clark's deed or the stolen money. And we're unlikely to see either again. The men who escaped have them.'

'The money I can understand,' Billy said as they started their horses away. 'But what good is that deed going to do anyone? When Boss Clark finds out, he's going to pay a rough visit to the Bar-D.'

'He may find some rough people waiting,' Trinity answered. 'We're thinking that we've cut down on the odds — but how do we know that? There's plenty of money to hire half a dozen — ten tough men to ride for the Bar-D.'

'I say, let them have it, then. We've seen that place, it can't support more'n a handful of cows. A man would have to be crazy to want it enough to fight for it.'

'Crazy, or determined to teach somebody a lesson,' Trinity said.

'Which leads us back to Calvin Dancer.'

'It does.' Because Calvin Dancer fit both of those profiles.

They reached Van Horn again as night was falling. The haphazardly designed, dusty little town was no more impressive on this evening than it had been the night before.

'I've got to find something to eat pretty soon, Trinity, or you'll have to carry me to a restaurant,' Billy complained as they unsaddled at the stable.

'I'll get Tammy and we can all eat at the hotel.'

'In their Tea Room!' Billy Raglan laughed derisively. 'No, sir — you and Tamarind do what you want, I'm going to find a place that knows what thick steaks and greasy fried potatoes are.'

Trinity was going to correct Billy's mistaken assumption, to assure him that the Ladies' Tea Room was just a small portion of the restaurant, but he stopped short. He had decided that, nothing against Billy, he would rather have dinner alone with Tamarind Travers.

He met her at her room and escorted her down to the restaurant. Tamarind had not changed clothes, or perhaps she had and had decided to put the dress on again for dinner. She had also managed to bathe — there was a scent of some sort of flower soap about her. He tried his best to ignore that and to avoid staring at her: two difficult tasks.

Her eyes were eager and bright as they seated themselves at a cloth-covered table along the wall of the restaurant which was growing crowded at this hour. When she could restrain herself no longer, she asked Trinity excitedly:

'You found him, didn't you? Dancer, I mean.'

'I know who you meant,' Trinity said. 'I just don't know the answer to your question.'

'What do you mean?' she asked, her expression irked and puzzled.

'Well, we found the man you saw — the one with the cane,' Trinity answered, keeping his eyes away from

Tamarind's. 'But he claimed that his name was Stubblefield, and we couldn't prove otherwise.'

'I know he was Calvin Dancer,' Tammy insisted.

'You weren't there,' Trinity replied, 'And you have no way of proving it either.'

'I know what I know,' she said stubbornly.

'Well, we didn't know what you know.'

'So you just left him there?' She looked almost shocked.

'What were we to do? Rough him up? Drag him back to talk to you?'

'You could have done that.'

'I'm sorry, Tamarind, I just don't go around kidnapping people on a notion.'

'Maybe I'll just go out there myself,' she said with a hint of threat.

'Maybe you won't — there are other men down that way, dangerous ones!' Trinity told her firmly.

He had become aware, as the waitress approached their table, that he had somehow torn a hole in the elbow of his new white shirt. He tucked his arm to his side as they ordered ham, sweet potatoes and corn on the cob.

'What are you doing?' Tamarind asked, noticing his odd posture. At least she was smiling faintly now.

'I tore my new shirt,' he explained. 'I don't know why I even bother buying clothes. I might just as well go around naked and save myself the expense.'

Tamarind's cheeks pinkened slightly at his words. She glanced briefly away and told him. 'We can find someone who'll sew it for you. If not, I'll buy needle and thread and do it myself.' Her eyes returned to his, and her conversation to the subject at hand. 'I've been wondering why Dancer is hiding way out there. Do you think that he was in prison . . . maybe he's hiding because he escaped.'

'*If* he's Dancer, that could be.' The old man did have an unhealthy pallor, like a man who's been in prison for many years, but then Stubblefield wouldn't spend much time in the sun, there being little he could accomplish around his tiny ranch with a bad leg. Tamarind seemed to have an idea she was proud of. Her eyes brightened; she leaned across the table, hands tightly clasped together.

'The sheriff would know, wouldn't he? If Calvin Dancer was on the run?'

'I don't think we want to go to the law,' Trinity said, damping her enthusiasm. 'There have been a few men killed lately, and Billy and I have been involved in it. We don't need the sheriff looking into those events.'

Tamarind looked crestfallen, but rebounded quickly. 'We wouldn't have to bring any of that up. I know where the sheriff's office is — I saw it in the courthouse. I could just sort of go in and say, oh . . . perhaps, that Calvin Dancer was my stepfather and I hadn't heard from him for a long time, but someone in Van Horn told me that he might have been seen near here.'

'Same objection,' Trinity said coolly,

145

waiting for the waitress to place their plates on the table before he continued. 'If the sheriff poked around enough he would find that you had come to Van Horn inquiring about a title change in the recorder's office. And at the bank about a stolen check. He would know that something was up, and he might not be satisfied until he found out what it was. I don't feel like wasting my time answering a lot of questions, some of which I'd have to fabricate answers for. Do you?'

'This ham,' Tamarind said, 'is very good.' The idea of going to the sheriff had been suddenly abandoned. This was something they would have to take care of themselves. They had started it; they would see it through.

After eating, Trinity walked back toward the old cotton barn. He took a circuitous route, using the alleyways, not wanting to go past the saloons on this hot, boisterous night. He was fairly certain that Art Tatum and the second man would flee the area, but perhaps not. Not if Dancer, *if* Stubblefield was Dancer, wanted them to stay around for protection or other unguessed at reasons. Too, there might have been other men in Van Horn who wanted to assault or kill him. As he and Billy had discussed, who was to say that those four were all of the men Dancer/ Stubblefield had assembled?

If Dancer meant to take back the Bar-D, possibly running into a fight with Boss Clark in the process, he would need a crew of toughs at his back to have a chance against a big outfit like Clark's.

But why would Dancer even want that waterless range back? Trinity asked Billy Raglan for his thoughts as they settled down for the night.

'He might be plumb crazy,' Billy said. 'Or maybe in his memory the Bar-D is a flourishing place. Maybe he wants to teach Boss Clark some sort of lesson. Maybe it's just because it belonged to him once. Maybe, he holds a grudge against Polly Travers — for what, I couldn't say. Not helping him get out of prison, for marrying Luther Travis, for once, years ago, having liked Boss Clark . . . '

'That's enough!' Trinity said with a grin. 'I just wanted one reason. You're tossing them around like chicken scratch.'

'That's because I don't know,' Billy answered, 'and can't, any more than you can know what the man's thoughts are. You ask me, though,' Billy said, rolling up in his blanket, 'it's the first thought that came into my mind — and yours. The man is plumb crazy.'

Faint moonlight filtered through the cracks between the slats of the old barn. Trinity rolled up on his own bed, still unable to sleep. Billy was probably right, of course. Dancer was crazy. But maybe not. A man could accomplish a lot with enough of Boss Clark's money. New wells could be dug, a new herd of cattle driven on to the Bar-D. And with enough of Boss Clark's money, men could be hired to protect the ranch. Was this Dancer's plan? It seemed to be. All of it hinged on using the money Clark had given to Polly Travers for the land.

Where was that money? Had the man who took the draft to the bank actually been Cole Travers, or someone else? Could they find out who had been spending a lot of money around town?

It was all too much just then, and Trinity was trail-weary. Morning was soon enough to try to formulate a plan of action.

★   ★   ★

Tamarind Travers, asleep on her hotel-room bed, with only a sheet thrown over her on this warm night suddenly awakened. What was that? She glanced toward the window and saw the sheer curtains fluttering in the wind. That was odd — she yawned and sat up in bed. She could have sworn that she had closed the window before retiring.

Then she saw him sitting in the chair across the small room. She started to scream, then immediately stifled the impulse. She knew the man sitting there, knew him well. Or thought she had. She spoke carefully as if afraid to provoke the specter.

'Cole? Is that really you?' she asked.

'It's me,' her stepbrother answered. His voice was raspy, dry.

'We . . . Mother and I, everyone thought you were dead.'

'You did?' the voice was harsh. He rose, walked to the bureau in the corner where pitcher and basin stood and poured himself a glass of water. With his back still turned toward her, he asked, 'Why then did you bother sending men out to kill me?' His sentence ended harshly.

Cole walked back to the chair stiffly. Either he was wounded or very sore, perhaps from riding long miles. He sagged into the chair again.

'I don't know what you mean, Cole. Mother will be so relieved to find out that you are alive.'

'Will she?' He leaned forward,

clasping his hands together, staring at her from out of the near darkness. 'Are you going to tell me that she didn't know that you were sending men after me?'

'We sent men to try to find you, Cole! That's all.'

'And find the money — or was that the primary reason she sent you, money being more important by far to Polly than I am.'

'So you did cash the bank draft, take the money?' Tammy said, not bothering to answer her stepbrother's wild questions.

'Of course,' he said with a dry laugh. 'The money doesn't belong to Mother, does it?'

'Yes, it does,' Tammy said. 'Who else?'

'My father, that's who!' Cole exploded, almost rising to his feet. 'And to me.'

'I don't understand you,' Tammy said to the shadow. 'Mother sold the ranch to Boss Clark, and . . .'

'She sold Calvin Dancer's ranch — and my birthright. I'm left with nothing while Polly moves on to new country! That's the way it's supposed to work, only it won't. We have the money and we have the deed to the Bar-D, and we will build it up finer than it was before, no matter that Polly's stolen the herd as well.'

'*We?*' Polly said, sliding her feet to the floor. 'You mean Calvin Dancer is back?'

'Certainly he's back. I talked to him before Mother went crawling to her old lover to beg for money — Father told me all about what was happening and why we had to stop it. The Bar-D is his and it will be mine. He meant for me to have it one day.'

Cole's voice had descended to a snarl. How Dancer had gotten him to swallow all this nonsense was beyond her. 'Where is he now — Calvin Dancer, I mean?'

'I don't see why you need to know that. Unless you mean to send your gunmen after him.'

'Cole — Mother needs that money to buy the ranch in New Mexico. The Bar-D was her ranch, not Dancer's. I doubt he ever worked on it a day in his life. As for trying to do this for you, he might have thought of that before he rode off and left you all those nights gazing out the window, waiting for him to return. He never did, did he?'

'You don't know what happened — you were just a baby,' Cole pointed out. 'Besides, he couldn't come back. But as soon as he made his . . . as soon as he was able, he returned.'

'The reasonable thing to do would have been to talk to Mother.'

'No! She's the one who's unreasonable, Tammy. Not Father. After she married that lump of dough, Luther Travers, she thought everything would go her way. Father was gone. Luther did whatever she told him.'

'I thought you liked Luther.'

Cole waved a hand, 'Oh, he was all right, I suppose.'

'Why did you shoot him, then!' Tammy asked, growing suddenly heated. 'Why did you murder my father?'

'That wasn't me.'

'It was someone you know.'

Cole didn't respond. Instead he said, 'I've come to warn you, Sis. Just this once. Stay off my trail and stay away from the Bar-D. Tell Polly I've got the money and I'm not coming back. She can always get more money from Boss Clark, I believe.'

'I can't understand you,' Tammy tried, but Cole was already on his feet again, walking to the open window. He swung a leg out and warned her again, 'You go away and take your gunhands with you. We outnumber them and if they keep poking around, something very bad is going to happen to those men.'

Then he slipped out the window and Tamarind was left alone in the darkness of the warm, quite confused and threatening night.

9

'Tell me about it again.' Trinity said in the morning as the three of them sat at a breakfast table in the hotel restaurant drinking coffee. Tammy wore riding jeans and a tan-colored shirt.

'I'm tired of repeating it,' Tammy complained. 'You know all I do.'

'He did say that they outnumber us, didn't he?' Billy asked. 'That means that Dancer is bringing in more guns. He does mean to take the Bar-D back.'

'If so, he's underestimating Boss Clark. The boss won't let him get away with this.'

'What about my mother?' Tammy asked as if both of the men were insensitive to what she had been telling them. 'What can she do; where can she go? What about those loyal men who stayed with her and are expecting their pay. She gave them her word.'

'I've been thinking of them,' Trinity told her sincerely. 'It's Cole who isn't giving them a thought. He has to be caught.'

'He won't have the money or the deed,' Billy Raglan said, sipping at his coffee. 'Dancer will have both.'

'I suppose. Tamarind, did your brother say anything to indicate where Dancer is?' She shook her head negatively. 'Or lead you believe that Stubblefield is really Dancer?'

She shook her head again. 'All he said — or almost let slip — is that Dancer did break out of prison.'

'That doesn't help us much,' Billy said, 'and it will sure give him plenty of reason to fight it out: he won't be wishing to go back there.'

'Well,' Trinity said after a long pause. 'We know that Cole is alive. We don't know where Dancer is, but we know where he's going. All we can do is ride back and tell Polly what we've found out and then head back to the Bar-D. Then we'll have to talk to Boss Clark.'

'He's going to be furious,' Billy said unhappily.

'That's not a strong enough word for it,' Trinity answered. 'But I don't see what else we can accomplish in Van Horn. We've learned everything there is to learn here.'

'And achieved very little,' Billy said morosely.

'We did our best,' Trinity said.

'You try telling that to Boss Clark.'

'I think you two should go back to your original idea of sending him a telegram,' Tamarind said. 'If he's going to be that mad, it will at least give him some time to cool down before you have to talk to him face to face.'

'I suppose she's right,' Billy Raglan said. He sat turning his cup in its saucer. 'How do you want to word it, Trinity? See how much we can fit in, or skip the details and keep it short and sweet?'

'Tell him all we can, but in the shortest way possible. We can fill in the ugly details later.'

'Think he'll get it today?' Billy asked.

'Yes. When they see who the telegram is addressed to, they'll send a man riding out there right away.'

'I'll be sorry to miss it,' Billy said rising from the table.

'What's that?'

'Many times though I've heard the expression, I've never actually seen smoke come out of a man's ears. If there's anything to that, this will do the trick.'

As they stepped out into the sunlight, Trinity halted for a moment on the hotel porch and silently surveyed the town. Aloud, he wondered, 'I wonder how we'll like our next job.'

They started out of town before noon, following the long trail back toward the Shamishaw. They were silent for the most part, the sun beating down, the horses' hoofs stirring up small puffs of dust with each forward stride.

The sky was purpling, cool when they reached the Shamishaw and found

Polly Travers's camp. Polly had been alerted that they were coming, for she stood waiting, looking sleek and slender, her arms crossed. Her face was drawn, faintly hopeful, but resigned to bad news, it seemed.

A pair of cowhands came up from the watering hole which was nearly reduced to mud now, and stood beside their boss. One of them Trinity recognized. The man with the bandage around his head was Joe Cordero, the foreman of the Bar-D who had been sent to ride with Cole Travers to Van Horn and got shot down along the way.

The three incoming riders swung down from their weary mounts. Tamarind rushed to her mother and the two engaged in a lot of women-murmurs and petting while the cowhand who had arrived with Cordero took the reins to their horses and led them down to the water. Trinity removed his hat and walked toward Polly, Billy Raglan following. She studied Billy closely and asked: 'Where's Archie Hagen?' for

159

obviously she had initially mistaken Billy for her own man.

'He didn't make it, Mrs Travers,' Trinity had to tell her. Her mouth tightened and she shook her head. The three traipsed back toward the cliff face where coffee boiled over a low fire.

'I take it,' Polly said, 'that there's a lot to talk about it and not much of it good.'

Met by reluctant silence, she asked her first question directly. 'Cole . . . ?'

'He's alive, Mother. I saw him. We had a talk,' Tamarind said hesitantly.

'A talk,' Polly repeated. 'Does that mean he's not coming back, that he . . . ?'

'It seems he was involved in the theft of your money and the taking of Boss Clark's deed,' Trinity said to save Tamarind the pain of telling her mother.

'Was he?' She paused. 'I see.' Polly sat down on a bare log which had been rolled up toward the fire for that purpose. 'Did he tell you why he did

160

this?' she asked Tammy.

'For . . . oh, he's in it with his father,' Tamarind said, unable to hide her anger and her disappointment.

'You can't mean it? Calvin Dancer is alive? He's come back and the first thing he does is to talk my son into robbing me?'

'So it seems,' Trinity said. He seated himself on the same log, studying Polly's forlorn expression. 'He's determined to reclaim the Bar-D.'

'Now!' Polly laughed but it was a brittle, sarcastic expression. 'Why? The place is worthless, everyone knows that.'

'We think he's a little bit mad,' Billy Raglan told her.

Firelight danced across Polly's face. She poked her silver-streaked dark hair with nervous fingers, took a deep breath and sighed it out. 'Yes, well you're right,' she replied. 'He always was. To tell the truth I was relieved when he left. Then when I met Luther Travers, a gentle steady man, I discovered what a life-partnership is supposed to be like. With Dancer there were always his fits, his ranting and cursing.' She shook her head at unhappy distant memories.

'Cole thinks of him as a hero,' Tammy said in a low voice. 'His father's come back to fix everything, bringing a father's love.'

'Calvin Dancer is incapable of loving anyone but himself,' Polly said bitterly.

'What are we going to do?' Tammy asked anxiously.

'Fight him,' Polly said in a low voice. She did not look up as she spoke. 'Damn the ranch — he can have the Bar-D if he wants it for all I care. But he stole my son away and managed to turn him into a thug!'

'I don't see how we can fight him, Mother,' Tamarind said.

'Maybe we can't, but I am going to try. Didn't you say that you thought they were headed back toward the ranch?' she asked Trinity, who nodded his reply. 'Very well — I am not afraid of Calvin Dancer. I shall be there waiting for him.'

'Mother!' Tamarind was shocked. 'We have other duties to attend to.'

'What duties?' Polly snapped. 'We have nothing to do, nowhere to go. Not now. Someone go find Joe Cordero.'

They waited for Joe to arrive, speaking little. When the foreman reached the fireside, he removed his hat and nodded his bandaged head at Polly. Tamarind was fearful that her mother was going to ask her cowhands to take up guns against Dancer, but Polly had another plan in mind.

'Yes, ma'am?' Joe asked.

'Joe, I want you and the boys to take what's left of the herd and drive it through to Van Horn.'

'Van Horn?' Joe said with surprise.

'That's right, and when you get there, sell the steers for what you can get, I'll write you a bill of sale so you're not taken for rustlers. Take whatever money you make and split it up among the men. They haven't been paid for a long time. Tell them I appreciate their loyalty, but the ranch has folded for good.'

'All right,' Joe said, still hesitant. 'If that's what you want, Mrs Travers.'

'It's what I want. Inform the men tonight and start the herd south in the morning.'

★ ★ ★

Trinity slept that night, but not well. The sunrise bawling of the cattle as they were pushed away from water by the Bar-D cowhands brought him quickly alert. Sitting up in his bed, squinting into the sun he could see the men starting the belligerent cattle southward, heading them out toward Van Horn.

The early risers had started a coffee pot and gathered near it were Polly, Tammy, Joe Cordero, and Billy Raglan. Cordero still seemed to be trying to talk Polly out of the cattle sale, but her mind was made up, her jaw set. Tamarind seemed slightly bewildered;

her expression brightened considerably when she saw Trinity tramping that way. He reached the group just as Joe gave up his pleading, and sorrowfully trudged away toward his horse.

'He was a loyal hand,' Polly said to no one in particular. 'And his reward was being ambushed along the trail and abandoned by the boss's son.'

'What now?' Tammy asked, voicing the question that was in everyone's mind.

'What now?' Polly answered, frowning deeply with determination. 'I'm going back to the ranch to face Mr Calvin Dancer. He might be a dirty rat, but he won't shoot me. As for you, Tammy, I still have a few dollars I've set aside. You can go down to Valentina and stay with Aunt Clara for awhile.'

'I will not!' Tamarind said with unexpected vehemence. 'I don't like Aunt Clara. Besides, you say the Bar-D is still your ranch, and it is. But it's also my home, the only one I've ever known. And if we can't find a new one, I'm going back with you to reclaim what is ours.'

'The two of you alone?' Trinity said. 'I don't think that's very wise.'

'My mind is made up,' Polly said sternly.

'And so is mine,' Tammy said, matching her mother scowl for scowl.

'Well . . . ?' Billy Raglan said, looking a question at Trinity,

Trinity said, 'We'll go along, though I don't think much of the idea. But, after all, the ranch belongs to, is supposed to belong to Boss Clark, and we're still working for the man. I suppose we have an obligation to keep trespassers off his property.'

Billy Raglan stood shaking his head unhappily. It was a damned poor idea all around, but Raglan could understand Trinity's reasons for returning to the ranch — all of them.

After the last of the steers had been bumped unwillingly from the pond and had their noses pointed southward toward Van Horn, they again saddled their horses and started east on a fool's errand.

What satisfactory conclusion Polly hoped to achieve was beyond Trinity's grasp. She could brace Calvin Dancer, perhaps talk his ear off. But scolding a bad man like Dancer was likely to have as much result as talking to a rock. And the four of them were not going to stand up to the force Dancer had probably put together by now. This plan was designed suicide.

'You better come up with some way of talking those women out of this,' Raglan said as the two men rode close together across the dusty land. 'Or they'll get us all killed. For nothing.'

'*You* try talking to them,' Trinity growled. 'Their minds are made up. They will keep what is theirs no matter that it's impossible. Us — we're just along for decoration, it seems.'

'I don't see much future in being decoration for somebody's blood feud,' Billy said, his own voice a near-growl. But there seemed little choice. The women were determined to return home and they could not in good conscience simply ride away and leave them alone. Nor could they envision any sort of scenario that would leave them alive when this was over. Well, men had knowingly marched into death's jaws before. Braver men than they were, perhaps. It sort of goes against a man's grain to give up his blood for utter foolishness.

The land on this day seemed endless as they rose from the dry watercourse of the Shamishaw Trickle and achieved the flats, riding the long miles back toward the Bar-D ranch house. On their own Billy and Trinity would have given the place wide berth and ridden back to take their tongue-lashing from Boss Clark, which he would have ready for them, deserved or not. Trinity could almost visualize Mr Jefferson Clark drawing himself up to his full height of six and a half feet, leveling his cold eyes on them and saying, 'I give you two a simple job — ride over to the Bar-D and see what's holding up this land sale, and what do you do!'

If he didn't fire them out of pure pique, he would make them feel miserable for a good long time. Well, now they wouldn't have to concern themselves with Boss Clark's dressing-down. They would likely not live long enough ever to see the man again.

Ahead now, in the far distance as the shadows grew long, they could see the Bar-D ranch house looking no larger than a die flung against the plains. Without conferring, Trinity and Billy both unsheathed their Winchester rifles and focused honed senses on their surroundings.

Trinity saw no activity near the house, heard nothing, saw no one around them. But you never knew . . . Crossing the yard toward the house, they still saw nothing. No one peered out of the windows.

'Maybe,' Billy suggested, 'it took Dancer longer to round up enough guns for this job than he thought it would.'

It was a hope, but a delay meant nothing to them. Polly was determined to sit and wait for Dancer to arrive. The woman was implacable. Well, she had nothing left to lose, but Trinity thought that she would have made a stronger argument to protect Tammy from any conflict. Maybe, though, Polly knew her daughter better than he did. Perhaps when Tammy said she would not go to her aunt's, her decision was as unbending as her mother's.

Crossing the sad little yard, Trinity noticed as he had not on their first visit, the dead stick of a young tree with white-painted stones circling it. The tamarind tree, he guessed. A small, lost hope now dead like the rest of the ranch. It had been a home, this piece of land, this small house. It had been a home, now it was only a ghost ranch offering nothing further to the living.

Trinity and Billy Raglan gathered the reins to the horses and led them toward the barn as the two women went up the steps to the house and entered — Polly eagerly, Tamarind not so much so. She lagged and shot a look of suffering at Trinity before following her mother into the house.

Billy and Trinity walked the horses through the heat of the dry, dusty day toward the warm shade of the barn. Billy halted in his tracks just before reaching the doors.

'Well,' he said, 'what do you think this means?'

'Find something?' Trinity asked, going forward. Looking down to where Billy's gnarled finger pointed he, too, could make out the tracks of a single shod horse leading away from the barn. His hand dropped nearer to the butt of his holstered Colt.

'Whoever it was, it looks like he's ridden out,' Trinity said. Billy gave him a tolerant scowl.

'You'll never make a tracker, Trinity. You assume too much. This shows that a horse was ridden out. It don't tell us where the man has gotten to. Maybe he saw us coming and just decided he didn't wish to be trapped inside the barn.'

'True,' Trinity replied. 'But if I'm allowed to make guesses, it looks like someone was here checking out the ranch, found no one and went back to report — to Dancer.'

'There's nothing the matter with your thinking,' Billy said. 'And you're probably right. Just mind where you're stepping — we may have a snake around here close by.'

* * *

'Look at all the glass on the floor,' Polly said unhappily. 'Do you know how long it took to get that glass shipped out here?'

'Trinity said that he and Billy had to fort up here. That would be when they were shot out.'

'And look,' Polly said, running her finger along the shattered wood surrounding the small panes. 'They've splintered the sash as well.'

'Yes, Mother,' Tammy answered with a hint of the weariness she was feeling.

What were they doing here? Why had she agreed to come along? No, *demanded* to come along. It was a mistake, she decided, made on the spur of the moment out of emotion. Polly, it seemed, had it in mind to sit here and wait for Calvin Dancer to arrive. Did she mean to scold the outlaw and hope to shame him away, to take Cole by the ear and demand that he stay with her?

Polly Travers could be a willful woman, but even she must see that this could never work. Calvin would simply demand that they leave his ranch. Cole would stay with Dancer — he had already indicated as much. Perhaps Polly was right — Dancer would not harm her or Tammy. But what about Trinity and Billy?

Calvin would not leave them — Boss Clark's men — alive to inform their employer what had happened. Nor would Billy and Trinity just pack up and run. They were of that cadre of men who rode for the brand. They would fight for Jefferson Clark's holdings. That was, after all, the way they had made their living up to this point.

It did no good to think of it; perhaps she could talk to Trinity about the wisdom of this plan later. For the time being she simply walked into the kitchen, and finding dust pan and broom where they had left them, began sweeping the glass from the floor.

Polly stood silently, arms folded under her breasts, staring out the window at the long yellow-grass plains. She glanced at Tammy while she worked, but said nothing until her daughter was finished cleaning up. Then she announced:

'I want to see Luther's grave. Did Trinity tell you where it is?'

'No, Mother. But . . . '

'But nothing. I was married to that man for twenty-two years and he always did his best by us. I can't let him take his leave without at least saying goodbye. It must be lonely enough in that grave.'

Together they went out and circled the house, knowing that Trinity and Billy would have buried him near by. The wind picked up with the lowering of the sun. It tugged at Tammy's hair and flicked at the light fabric of Polly's coat. As the coat flap blew open slightly Tammy saw the butt of a second, concealed pistol tucked into her mother's belt. Why? She still wore her habitual Colt in its belt holster around her waist. Then as they approached Luther Travers's grave and Polly stood over it, her head bowed, her eyes misting, Tammy thought she did understand why Polly was carrying a concealed gun.

Polly meant to say hello and goodbye at the same time to Calvin Dancer.

10

The women had known where a few stores were hidden away and they had started a pot of beans boiling. Coffee was ready within minutes of Trinity and Billy returning from seeing to the tired horses. They said nothing to the women about finding the tracks of a strange horse, but they kept their eyes on the windows at the front of the house until the sun had been fully smothered by night's darkness. Then they listened, listened intently for sounds of approaching riders. It would not be long before Dancer made his move to reclaim the house.

Trinity stalked the front room for a while. Then, noticing Tammy sitting alone at the kitchen table, he went to her and sat opposite the girl.

'What's the matter, Tamarind?' he asked.

'Oh, nothing, really. But I think less

of this plan of action with every passing minute.' She waited for Trinity to say 'I told you so,' or something similar, but he only sat watching her with sympathetic eyes that held some other, deeper emotion. Did he . . . ?

'We could ride out even now,' he said at last. 'Toward Boss Clark's range. I doubt Dancer would wish to follow us.'

'He might,' Tammy responded. 'If he thought he could stop us before we gave Boss Clark the news. Dancer wouldn't know about the telegram you sent, that Clark already knows.'

'I'd still like it better than sitting here, all penned up for Dancer.'

'I think I would too,' Tammy admitted.

'Well, then?'

'Mother is determined to stay and wait for him.' She leaned across the table to whisper, 'I'm pretty sure she's going to try to kill him.'

'That might be her plan at that. But it's surely not a good plan for the rest of us.'

'Trinity . . . ' unexpectedly her small hand touched his and then covered it, 'I can't leave my mother. You and Billy — perhaps you should be the ones to go.'

After a moment's thoughtful silence, Trinity said, 'I'll talk to Billy. Tell him I think he ought to ride for the home ranch.'

'But Trinity! What about you?'

'You can't leave your mother. I can't leave you. It's that simple, Tamarind.'

She looked at him steadily and then let her eyes fall away when she could no longer hold his gaze. There was an odd fluttering in her chest and she felt her mouth go dry. At last Tamarind said:

'I think that you mean that.'

'I think I do, too,' he answered, smiling.

Billy Raglan poked his head around the corner just then. 'I hear somebody coming, Trinity.' Trinity got quickly to his feet, knowing that Billy's warnings were not to be taken lightly. Tamarind's eyes opened wider and if anyone had been looking, they would have seen her hands tremble.

In the front room where it was dark but for the flickering glow of a small fire burning in the hearth, they found Polly peering intently out a window. Her expression, oddly, was a satisfied one. Tamarind noticed that her mother had taken off her holstered Colt and placed the weapon aside.

'It's him,' Polly said without turning her head. 'It's Calvin Dancer.'

'How can you be sure?' Trinity asked, bending to look out the window himself, keeping his body to the side of it.

'We heard the creaking of a buggy, didn't we, Billy?' Polly asked and Raglan nodded.

'Someone in a buggy with a couple of outriders,' Billy told Trinity.

Trinity saw nothing, no one moving in the darkened yard. The moon would be rising within the hour, but that did them no good at the moment.

'What do you think?' Billy asked

Trinity. He was clutching his Winchester tightly.

'Don't know. It doesn't seem they're ready to rush the house just yet.' Had they been a half-dozen, a dozen men with rifles, they would have already been firing at them from out of the darkness.

'I don't think they know who's in here,' Polly said in a low, anxious voice.

'Or how many,' Trinity added. 'It may be they want to have a look first and make a plan after.'

'I don't know how anybody can be so sure that it's Dancer,' Tamarind said with uncertain hope.

'We're going to find out soon enough,' Polly said. They had all heard boots crossing the front porch toward the door. Billy backed out of the room, moving toward the hallway leading to the bedrooms. Trinity started back toward the kitchen, taking Tamarind's wrist, but she shook him off. 'Please — I have to be here,' she told him. Trinity hesitated, locked eyes with her,

180

as someone rapped on the heavy door. Shaking his head, he withdrew into the kitchen. He had learned he was not going to get anywhere arguing with these women.

Polly glanced over her shoulder to fix the set-up in her mind, seemed to glare briefly at Tamarind, who had chosen to stay. Then she walked to the door and boldly swung it open.

'I might have known,' Calvin Dancer — or Edward Stubblefield — moved into the house, his dark eyes alight with triumph. 'Don't you ever give it up, Polly?'

'Do you?' she asked, backing away a little to stand by the fireplace which cast weird moving shadows around the room. Trinity could not see well from where he was concealed, but well enough to see that Dancer carried no cane. He appeared to be as spry as anyone else.

'Why should I?' he asked. 'I always win.'

'I can tell that just by looking at you,'

Polly said scornfully, 'Look at you with your gray hair and lined face, with your shrunken body — what did you win with your life of evil-doing, Cal?'

For a moment it looked as if Dancer might erupt with anger, but when he answered his words were softly spoken. 'What? How about this, dear Polly.' And at a gesture toward the darkness of the porch Cole Travers shuffled in. At least, Trinity assumed it was Cole Travers by the look on Polly's face, by Tammy's reaction. He himself had never seen the rough-looking young man before. Cole's whiskers had sprouted and his hat was torn. His eyes were red-rimmed and sulky as he looked toward his mother.

Polly was obviously pained. 'It didn't take you long to turn him into . . . ' she flipped a hand over and raked Cole with disapproving eyes. 'whatever this is.'

A second man had eased into the house. Art Tatum Trinity did recognize. The bearded man surveyed the room with narrow eyes. Trinity had no doubt that Art had spotted him in the kitchen, for he unbuttoned his coat and stepped to one side. Polly had gone nearer to inspect Cole, who watched her stoically.

'What are you doing to yourself, Cole? Do you really want to end up like Calvin Dancer?'

'Would you have me be like Luther — the husband you deprived of his manhood. Or like Boss Clark who stole everything he has from the Indians and thinks he can continue to run this county like his own kingdom?'

Polly said, 'I see you've been taking your lessons to heart.' Her eyes flickered hotly toward Dancer, who was smiling in a reptilian way.

'Are you telling me none of it's true?' Cole asked, his chin thrust out like a challenging child.

'What do you think? The man who taught you these things has never encountered the truth in his pathetic life.' Dancer remained silent, letting his son argue with Polly. It seemed to be a source of pride to him to let Cole carry the burden, showing Polly plainly who was in control of his son's loyalties.

'When you leave,' Cole Travers said, 'we will build up the Bar-D to a place to be proud of, not like the rundown failure you let it become.'

'You forget — you don't own the Bar-D, neither of you.'

'We say we do,' Cole said, puffing up, glancing at Dancer for approval. 'If anyone tries to run us off, he'll have a surprise waiting for him.'

'I see that you don't know Boss Clark,' Polly said with a small shake of her head.

'No, but you do! Don't you, Mother!' Cole said, unreasonable anger flaring up within him. Polly wondered what Dancer had told her son about Jefferson Clark. She could only imagine; but then, it did not matter.

Calvin Dancer would not be around that much longer.

Trinity saw Polly casually unbutton her coat and reach inside. A split second before Dancer saw it, Trinity recognized the butt of the concealed pistol for what it was. Dancer's eyes opened wide, then settled to amusement. He was about to offer a sneering comment when Polly thumbed back the hammer of the revolver and fired at him at point-blank range.

The roar of the pistol filled the small room and the black powder smoke swept across it, drifted by the breeze through the open door. The sneer was frozen on Calvin Dancer's face. The blood washed from it, and holding his belly, he staggered, placing one heavy foot before the other as he stretched out a clawing hand toward Polly Travers. Then he hit the floor and stayed there, unmoving.

Almost wearily Polly crouched and reached into his bloody jacket to remove the bill of sale for the Bar-D ranch. Then Polly dropped the pistol and spun away. The others were provoked into abrupt action as they saw the title to what they had gambled on taken away. Art Tatum drew his Colt and fired wildly at Trinity — the man who had been responsible for all of his troubles, the man who had likely killed his brother. The bullets whined off a row of heavy pans hung on the kitchen wall and sang off into the woodwork. From the mouth of the hallway Billy Raglan let off an unaimed shot from his Winchester. His hastily fired bullet tagged Art low on the leg, and Tatum turned to hobble toward the door, firing back one wild shot toward the hall.

Two rounds from Trinity's revolver chased after Art Tatum as he fled the house. Cole Travers had drawn his gun but now he stood motionless over his dead father, looking into Polly's eyes with baffled disbelief. Trinity sprinted toward the front door of the house as Tamarind shouted something after him. Billy Raglan followed in Trinity's wake.

'Which way did he go?' Billy asked, his voice a pant.

'I can't tell.' It was dark, very dark

outside. The moon had not yet risen. Listening intently, Trinity heard no sound at all. At last he said, 'Head off that way, Billy.' he jabbed his pistol barrel northward. 'I'll swing the other way.' He nodded toward the Shamishaw.

'Trinity,' Billy warned, 'don't forget that there might be another ten, twelve men out here with guns, if Dancer got his gang assembled.'

'I know it,' Trinity said grimly.

'What about the kid?' Raglan said, nodding toward the house.

'Polly can take care of him. I've no doubt about that.'

Billy shrugged, wiped his hand down his jeans to dry it and then started moving to the north, running in a low crouch. Trinity eased forward more slowly into the darkness. There was no concealment for him, and none for the wounded Art Tatum. Although the wound to Tatum's calf didn't look that terrible, still a man would not be able to run far or fast with the muscle in his leg torn as it must have been. Trinity tried to outthink the bearded gunfighter.

Tatum must have ridden up on a horse, but their mounts and the buggy were still where they had left them, besides they had not heard a horse being ridden off. Where would he go, then? If Tatum felt strong enough, he would obviously try to make it back to camp where presumably Dancer had left the rest of his men. If he were bleeding badly or his leg had been crippled, he would have to go to ground and might lie waiting in the near-darkness for Trinity to walk into his sights.

An hour's cautious search of the yard and surrounding area failed to discover Art Tatum. Crouched, Trinity saw a shadowy figure approaching him, cutting a silhouette against the starlit sky, Trinity softly sounded a mockingbird's whistle and received one in return, It was Billy Raglan, and he rose to meet him.

'Nothing, I take it,' Trinity said.

'No. It's a waste of time to chase a man on a night like this, I was just hoping that he was wounded bad enough so that he couldn't make it far. Trinity?' Billy added as the two started back toward the house. 'We were right about one thing — those three aren't alone. I heard ponies maybe half a mile off. There's men waiting for Dancer to come back and tell them what to do. When Dancer doesn't return, they'll come looking to find out why for themselves.'

'What do we do, then?' Trinity asked. 'Fort up in the house?'

'Too many of them.' Billy guessed. 'The best thing we can do is grab up our horses and spur out of here.'

'If that's the game, we'd better get to it as quick as possible.' Trinity was wondering why Dancer's hired guns weren't already on top of them! If Art Tatum were nearing their camp, wouldn't he have shouted out, even fired a shot to bring help? But they had heard nothing in the night.

Inside the firelit house it was as if the people there had frozen in tableau. No one seemed to have moved. Polly stood to one side, head bowed, Tammy watched the others as if incapable of moving. Cole Travers still clenched his pistol in his dangling hand. His eyes flickered to Trinity as they entered, firelight cast changing shadows across the ceiling and the walls.

Cole — they had not taken his presence into account when they had made their decision to simply flee. Would he try to interfere? Trinity hoped not. He would hate to have to kill Cole in front of his tormented mother. Trinity crossed to where Tammy stood as Billy blocked the doorway, his eyes flickering toward the darkness outside, returning to Cole Travers to see what the young man might have on his mind. Billy could hear Trinity speaking.

'Tammy, we think it's time to get out of here. Your mother's had her meeting with Dancer, and there may be a dozen men or more riding toward the house even now.'

'How many are there, Cole?'

Cole shook his head stubbornly. He would not change sides. He stood silently studying his dead father.

'Why don't you just go if you're going?' the young man said. 'I guess the Bar-D is my ranch now.'

'You're making a mistake in thinking that,' Trinity told him.

'That's not what my father told me.'

'And look where it got him!' Tamarind said with unexpected heat.

'Shut up,' Cole muttered. From the doorway, Billy spoke.

'None of this is getting us anywhere, folks. Speaking for myself, I'm not in the mood to die tonight.'

Cole Travers growled, 'Who says I'll let you just ride off?' He was holding his pistol higher now and there was a new, threatening brightness in his eyes.

Trinity's gaze shifted that way and then locked on Cole's eyes, noticing the uncertainty there. 'Oh, we're leaving,

Cole,' Trinity said. Tamarind's fingers brushed his shoulder as she thought briefly of trying to hold Trinity back. Billy had stepped aside, out of the line of fire. Movement caught Trinity's eye, and he reached for his revolver.

'Don't kill him!' Polly Travers pled, coming out of her shocked silence. 'I couldn't take it if another . . . '

But Trinity was already drawing. Polly screamed and Tamarind yelled 'Don't!', but Trinity had his pistol out of his holster, and was going to one knee for his shot. Cole Travers unleashed a shot from his shakily held gun which racketed off the wall behind Trinity. Trinity fired back accurately, taking down the shadowy figure behind Cole.

Art Tatum hadn't gotten far on his wounded leg, and as he tried to enter the house, he didn't make it far inside. Trinity's more careful shot had taken the bearded gunhand in the middle of the chest. Growling, Tatum tried to aim nearer, but his legs gave out under him and he slumped to the floor, dead, nudging Cole as he fell.

'I thought . . . ' Tamarind said.

Trinity looked at Billy Raglan. 'A fine lookout you are!' He holstered his pistol again and Cole, his eyes as wide as saucers, looked down at the dead man at his feet and did the same.

'You people with all your yammering kind of broke my concentration,' Billy complained, but a weak smile accompanied his words.

'No wonder we couldn't find him,' Trinity said. 'He never left. He was probably hiding in the barn.'

'Now,' Billy asked, 'can we get the hell out of here? If those men outside weren't already on their way, those shots will encourage them to come on in.'

'Let's get moving, Tamarind,' Trinity said. He took the girl's arm and led her toward the door.

Polly still had not moved. 'Cole?' she said in a pleading tone.

'Leave me alone. I'm staying with my

father and the ranch.'

'But you can't abandon us,' Polly said, but it was obvious that Cole already had. She went to Cole and held her son's shoulders briefly, her gaze raised to his, but Cole only shrugged her off. Tamarind took her mother's hand and tugged her toward the door. Tammy mounted the horse Art Tatum had been riding and Polly settled herself in Dancer's buggy as Trinity and Billy rushed to the barn to saddle their own horses.

Within minutes they were off and riding through the darkness of the night. Framed by the doorway, Cole Travers watched them go, his face without expression. The two dead men on the floor behind him cast crooked shadows before the firelight.

11

They were riding directly toward the rising moon, the dull red gold of its face peering across the long horizon at them. Billy and Trinity rode side by side, to the right of Polly's buggy. Tamarind kept her horse close to her mother, whose state of mind was visible even at a distance by the rigidity with which she sat guiding the team of horses across the open prairie land.

Billy swiveled in his saddle now and then, watching their back trail.

'How far back do you figure they are?' he asked Trinity.

'Not far enough. Their ponies should be rested by now, and they can close the distance quickly if they take a notion to.'

'What's in it for them?' Billy Raglan wondered. 'They've already been paid, doubtlessly, and the man who hired them is dead and gone.'

'Cole is still there,' Trinity reminded him. 'He won't let small matters like that deter him. He'll want revenge. The only reason he wasn't more trouble back there was that Dancer's death stunned him. Then with Art Tatum shot down, he sort of lost his confidence in being able to do anything. Now he's undoubtedly shaken off the shock, and he's got a group of hard men to side him.'

'You sure of all that, are you?' Billy asked.

'I'm not sure of a bit of it, Billy. But the man has two choices the way he sees it. Let us ride to Boss Clark and tell our story, or make sure we don't get that far.'

'I suppose,' Billy answered gruffly. 'And what are we supposed to do when we see them coming? The two of us, riding with two women.'

'I haven't an idea in the world, Billy.' Trinity admitted. 'The best we can. But our only choices were to ride or stay at the house and see what came next.'

'I know — no choice at all. Trinity . . . I think I can see someone on our tail.'

Trinity turned his head round and he also saw small, rapidly approaching shadows behind them. Billy was standing in his stirrups now and pointing a finger to their right, toward the south.

'See it?' he asked. Trinity nodded his head. The darker slash of a gully crossing the land which was now faintly burnished by moonlight, stood out starkly. It wasn't much of a shelter, but it beat riding the long flats with a group of rifle-wielding men behind them.

'Head that way. I'll get Tamarind and Polly. If you see anyone getting too close, throw a shot or two their way, let them know we will fight, in case they've got any doubt about it.'

Billy was about to ask a question, but his thought came too late. Trinity had already nudged his piebald into rapid motion and he was driving at a gallop toward the two women.

'What is it?' Tamarind asked, her eyes wide and searching. Her mouth was drawn down; she looked as uncertain and unhappy as Trinity had seen her.

'There's somebody behind us and coming up quick.'

'Why can't he leave us alone and just go on with his rotten life,' Polly muttered.

'Is Cole with them?' Tammy asked.

'There's no way of telling, but he would be, wouldn't he.'

'He's bent on becoming a killer — like his father,' Polly said sharply. Instead of continuing the conversation in Trinity's direction she turned the horses southward, leaving Tammy and Trinity alone in her dust for a few seconds.

'Tammy . . . ' Trinity began.

'Yes?'

Trinity tried to speak, but his mouth had gone dry and his tongue would not work. 'Let's get going,' he said at last, his voice fierce.

They raced on side by side toward

the sear slashed into the dark earth — presumably by the Shamishaw itself in the years past when it had been more than a trickle. They saw Polly halt her buggy abruptly at the rim of the gully. Billy was visible by the pale moonlight leading his reluctant gray horse down the bluff.

Now, behind them they could clearly hear the sounds of onrushing horses. As Trinity took a glance that way the first shots were fired by the bandits. Polly's horse team reared up at the sound of the guns, and she was tossed to the ground from the buggy as she was standing to exit. Tammy gave a little shriek and rode toward her mother, who lay sprawled against the earth. Billy was firing from the rim of the gully at the ranks of onrushing gunmen. He had as much chance of hitting them as he did of being shot at over a half-mile in range, but it might slow them down some, instill some caution in the dark riders.

Tammy was sitting with her mother's

head on her lap. Her eyes turned up to Trinity for help. Polly lifted a hand and waved it toward the gully behind them.

'Leave me,' she said in a cottony voice.

'I don't think so,' Trinity said. 'Tammy — I'll carry your mother. If it looks like I've found an easy path down, try to bring the buggy after me. If it can't be done, leave them behind. We need to get to cover, and now!'

The urgency of his words was punctuated by a dozen shots across the plains. Billy Raglan fired back at targets that were only vaguely discerned under these conditions, but the riders came on, finding their courage in their numbers.

Trinity gathered Polly Travers in his arms, managed to crouch and catch up the reins to the piebald, and headed toward the lip of the gully. Two bullets, perhaps more, whipped past him far too close for comfort on the way. He placed Polly down, and climbed the bluff to go to ground, against the warm grainy earth, at the same time trying to watch Tammy's descent leading the buggy.

A bullet ricocheted off the bright-work on the carriage and he shouted at her. 'Leave them to find their own way!'

Tammy did, slipping and stumbling down into the darkness of the gully. The confused horses, fortunately, followed her. Tammy ran along the bottom of the arroyo and scrambled up to take a position beside Trinity. She lay so near that Trinity could feel the heat of her breath on his neck. Billy Raglan had seen her, too, and he called out:

'Keep spread out folks!'

Of course Billy was right, they should not hunch up. A shot meant for one could as easily tag the other. Billy returned to his slow, methodical shooting. On the moonlit plain now it was easier to see what was happening. Trinity watched one of the horsemen go down. They had the advantage on the badmen now, firing out of the darkness while their foes made clear targets in the moon's glow.

Trinity gave Tammy his Colt revolver, although he cautioned her to not attempt to use it until the attacking men were within its range. She nodded her understanding and with a terrified glance moved farther along the rim of the gully. Polly, Trinity noticed, was seated in the darkness at the bottom of the wash, her knees drawn up, her arms looped around them It seemed that Polly Travers had finally run out of fight.

Billy, Trinity noticed, had slacked the pace of his firing even as the raiders drew nearer. 'Take the one on your left, Billy!' he shouted.

'I see him. I'm letting him get as close as possible! Trinity, I don't have but six rounds left.' Trinity mentally counted his own rifle bullets. He doubted that he had many more cartridges than Billy did.

And the horsemen were drawing nearer.

They were not charging haphazardly toward the gully, but were measuring their approach, feinting one way then sending a man scouting forward in the other. Most of them were simply holding back, loosing off a well-aimed shot from their halted horses. More than one shot grooved the earth within Trinity's reach.

Suddenly from the center of the wolf pack, a lone rider emerged, riding at breakneck speed toward them. Trinity saw instantly what he was up to. 'He's going to try to jump the gully, Billy!' Which would leave them with an enemy behind them, ready to pick them off.

'I'm on him!' Billy shouted back. 'Save your ammunition.'

The rider, in black, was riding a rangy sorrel horse with a white blaze. The man had a trimmed mustache and a short beard. Trinity was able to make out these details as the inrushing rider spurred his frothing sorrel to its best speed. He nearly trampled Trinity down as he reached the edge of the gully. Billy Raglan had been right — for Trinity to shoot the man, he would have to be nearly on his back, firing up at the leaping horse. Billy, down the line, had man and horse silhouetted in front of the moon like a shooting gallery cut-out.

Trinity heard the near explosion of Billy's .44-.40 Winchester, saw the horse begin to tumble, saw the rider's face pale and panicked in the illumination of the moon. The echoes of Billy's rifle still had not died away when man and horse slammed into the opposite bank and tumbled down the gully wall, the horse's legs flailing, the man silent as the animal rolled over him. Both lay still on the bottom of the gully. Trinity took a minute to watch, assuring himself that the raider would not rise again, then turned his attention back to the horsemen on the plain.

They were much nearer now. Trinity sent a bullet twisting down the barrel of his rifle, saw with muted satisfaction that he had tagged one of them.

'I'm thinking they're going to rush us!' Billy shouted. No sooner had he 'said that than the raiders, as if with a single mind, put their horses into rapid motion. 'Here they come!'

But they weren't.

There was chaotic movement out on the plains. The men yanked their horses' heads around and laid on the spurs. The shooting continued in a brief, savage burst. It took Trinity a while to make sense of all of it until he spotted the men rushing from out of the moon, firing as they rode.

'It's Boss Clark!' Billy Raglan shouted, rising to his knees to wave his hat and cheer the men on. On either side horses stumbled, men fell from their saddles, but the former raiders were now in disarray and completely overwhelmed by Boss Clark's men, forty of them at least, who were entering battle riding forward, not trying to turn and twist away as the surprised bad men were.

Tammy was beside Trinity now, her arm around him, her face nestled against his side. She started to rise as the gunfire grew distant, but Trinity held her down.

'Not yet. You can never tell in this sort of random fight. One of Clark's men might even mistake us for the bad men.' Battle chronicles were filled with tales of generals killed accidentally by their own men. And a few not so accidentally.

The night grew still. Either the dispersed raiders had eluded Clark's men or they had simply decided to call it a night.

Trinity looked down to where Billy still held his position and called out, 'Well?'

'Better go out and meet the man,' Billy said in an unhappy tone.

'Why don't you want to see Clark?' Tammy asked.

'We're still afraid that he might not be so happy to see us,' Trinity said as he rose, carefully looking the battleground over. 'We weren't exactly a huge success in carrying out his orders.'

'But he can't blame you!'

'He's the boss; he can blame anybody he wants to.'

'We have to get Mother,' Tammy said.

'Of course. I hope she can walk. I don't want to try to get the buggy up out of here now. I'll come back for it later.'

They found Polly where they had left her seated an hour earlier. Her eyes seemed clear as she watched them walk toward her, but there was some spirit missing in her expression. Perhaps she'd simply been stunned by her fall from the buggy, but Trinity thought it went deeper than that — to her deep disappointment over Cole Travers's betrayal.

Nevertheless, she rose and dusted herself off, and her voice was almost cheerful as she said, 'I was a big help, wasn't I?'

'There wasn't much you could have done,' Trinity told her.

'Did I hear you say that the big boss man was here?' she asked as they started toward the narrow ramp that led up and out of the gully.

'I don't know if he's here personally. I imagine he rode with the men, though.'

'Yes, I imagine that he would,' said Polly with a laugh that seemed very private. Funny, Trinity thought, Polly seemed to know Boss Clark better than anyone. At least she was not intimidated by him, but then she had never been intimidated by anyone.

'I found someone hiding over here, Boss!' a deep voice called out from above, then: 'Well, kiss my pappy! It's Billy Raglan.'

A man sat a horse at the head of the ramp as the three made their way upward. He called out, 'Here's Trinity, Boss. Got a couple of women with him.'

The familiar rumble of Boss Clark's voice yelled back. 'Bring 'em all over here. Someone's got some explaining to do.'

'All right, Boss.'

Clark added: 'You boys set up a night camp, and post some outriders in case those coyotes manage to dredge up

208

enough heart to come back.'

The Clark rider met them at the head of the trail. A slim, energetic man named Poole. 'You heard the boss, Trinity. Man, I'm glad I'm not you right now.'

'Is he still mad?'

'I'd say so. You should have seen him yesterday when he got your telegram! Everyone who crossed his path got a tongue-lashing.'

'Well, we expected as much,' Trinity said. 'Come along, ladies.'

'I can't see why he's so mad,' Tammy said.

'Just because he lost the deed to a ranch he purchased and the money he purchased it with?' Trinity asked.

'Well, he doesn't have to be so mean,' she said. 'Why should you and Billy be blamed?'

'I don't know — I guess he's going to tell us.'

'I'll take all the blame,' Polly Travers said. 'It was my fault. If he wants to tear into someone, let it be me. I've taken it before.'

By the time they reached Boss Clark's bunched outfit, someone had started a campfire. Before it, his arms folded, stood six feet six inches of Jefferson Clark, his face frozen into a glower. That is, until he saw and recognized Polly Travers. Maybe Boss Clark didn't mean to let his guard down, to show emotion, but he did when Polly appeared from out of the darkness. Clark smiled — it must have been a smile although Trinity had never seen the boss smile in his years of working for Clark. His voice rose with pleasure.

'My God, Polly. You were supposed to be in New Mexico by now, settled in and happy with your lot.'

'There were a few problems,' Polly Travers said, brushing back a strand of silver-black hair.

'I've heard of some of them. My boys finally got around to telling me what was happening,' he said frowning, though not especially darkly, at Trinity and Billy Raglan. 'You'll have to tell me all about it. Where's Luther?' he asked, looking across Polly's shoulder.

She shook her head, looked up at Boss Clark and then down again. 'He didn't make it,' she told him.

'I'm sorry. He was a decent hard-working man.' Boss Clark said solemnly. 'I really didn't think that much of your idea in the first place. You could have held on at the Bar-D if you'd just let me help you a little more.'

'Forever?' Polly asked with a tight laugh. 'Jeff, you're all that held that place together for the past five years!'

Boss Clark scuffed the toe of his boot across the dry earth like a schoolboy. Apparently he didn't want what Polly had said to become common knowledge. It seemed that he had been loaning Polly money over the years without Luther knowing about it. Then Polly had decided that her pride would not let her continue to borrow money from him. So she had decided to simply sell the Bar-D to Clark.

Thunder rumbled in the distance,

and everyone glanced eastward, seeing a long low line of clouds moving slowly toward them, skirting the moon. 'If you'd waited, the drought years would have ended,' Clark was saying. 'See those clouds? It will rain. If you got four or five small storms a year, that grass would have come back.'

They didn't hear Polly's answer as the two walked toward the fire where already coffee was boiling. Trinity saw Boss Clark's hand raise as if he would put it on Polly's shoulder, but it fell away before reaching her.

'Coffee?' Trinity suggested and Tammy nodded eagerly. Billy Raglan held back.

'I don't want to be around when Boss's mood changes again,' he told Trinity. 'I'll get our horses undressed.'

Distant lightning arced briefly across the starry sky and thunder rumbled again.

'I guess it just might rain,' Tammy said.

'Looks like it,' Trinity agreed.

'Clark is right, isn't he? I mean if there were three or four rains during our dry season, the grass would come back.'

'Might. But any cattle on the range now would have died before it could have done them any good.'

'I'll just have to bring them on a few at a time, make sure we don't overgraze, don't let the water run completely out before something's done about it.'

They were close enough to the fire for its red, shifting glow to light Tamarind's face. Trinity stopped, turned her by the shoulders and asked, 'What are you thinking, girl? Are you forgetting that you don't even own any land, not a square foot of it.'

'I guess I had forgotten,' she said, her mouth tugged down at the corners. 'It's just that the Bar-D was always there. I was born there — I think I would have been happy to live there until I died.'

They moved nearer the fire and sat on the ground near Clark and Polly Travers. A ranch hand whom Trinity knew, a man called Bodine, brought them each a cup of coffee.

'Where are you headed, Polly?' they heard Boss Clark asking. Tammy's ears perked up, for this question involved her life as well.

'Oh, I don't know, Jeff. I'm too tired to think. My sister, Clara, lives down in Valentina. I suppose she'll let us stay with her for a while.'

Trinity saw Tammy's face screw up into an expression of distaste. Whoever this Aunt Clara was, it was clear that Tamarind had no liking for her.

Boss Clark was silent for a long time. Then, without looking at Polly directly he commented, 'Seems like a long way to go. I've got plenty of room at my house, I've always said you could stay there whenever you wanted.'

Their entire past seemed to pass by, seen only by Boss Clark and Polly. She smiled, touched the back of his hand. 'It would help us out for at least a little while. I hate to descend on Clara without even letting her know we're coming, anyway.'

'It's settled then,' Boss boomed. His eyes fixed on Tammy. 'What do you say, Tamarind?'

'She still wants to go home,' Polly answered for her daughter. 'And do what, I don't know. Considering the fact that the Bar-D has been sold.'

Clark was deep in thought. 'You told me that Calvin Dancer had escaped from prison.'

'So it seems.'

'There might have been a reward posted on him.'

'I couldn't accept such a reward,' Polly replied. 'Nor could Tammy.'

'No?' Boss Clark, who was more perceptive than he seemed, looked at Tammy and Trinity huddled together in front of the fire and said, 'I'll bet Trinity isn't so particular about matters.'

Billy shrugged his agreement. 'He's generally a practical man.'

'Billy,' Boss Clark said, taking Billy's arm in his massive hand. 'I want you to take a couple of men and ride to Van Horn.'

'All right. I'll take Bodine, if that's all right with you. How about Chavez, too?'

Clark exhaled with frustration. 'Billy, you take anyone you like. I'll just look around in the morning and figure that anyone I don't see has gone with you.'

After getting his instructions Billy shambled over to where the hands had huddled around the fire and told Bodine and Chavez that they were taking a little ride with him to Van Horn. 'To an actual town?' Bodine said, expressing pleasure. 'I ain't seen a town in six months, I bet.'

'Well, you're going to see one soon. The thing is, don't either of you get drunk or land in trouble. If you do, Boss Clark will string me up with barbed wire.'

Because Boss Clark had made it more than clear that this time he meant to have the deed to the Bar-D transferred, and this time the job had better be done right.

12

The storm had not moved in any closer, but the air was moist and Trinity found it uncomfortable to breathe. The wind from the east had picked up, and across the long plains the brown grass shuffled in waves. Most of Boss Clark's men had ridden homeward to take care of the day's work. A few had been left behind to take care of the dead.

Polly and Boss himself were sitting on the ground near the morning fire, drinking coffee from tin cups when Trinity approached it. Tamarind walked up from the opposite direction minutes later. No one greeted the others. It was a day unhappy and uncomfortable despite their successes. Polly watched Tammy as she poured her coffee and stood sipping it. Eventually Tammy's mother could hold it in no longer:

'You can't go back to the ranch,

Tammy. There's nothing there for you.'

'I'm going,' Tammy declared.

'But there's no way you can . . . accomplish anything there.'

'Then I won't,' Tammy said simply. 'I just want to live there, to be there, do you understand?'

'No, I don't,' Polly answered.

Trinity had been listening, watching the two of them. 'I think she just wants to say goodbye to the old place in her own way, in her own time,' he offered. 'She won't be in anybody's way,' he added, looking a question at Boss Clark.

'No, of course not,' Clark put in quickly.

'And there is some work to be done,' Trinity reminded them. 'I'll go along with Tammy and see to it.'

Polly frowned at this suggestion, but she realized as well as any of them that the house could not be left with the bodies of Dancer and Art Tatum lying in it. Certainly not in the hot weather they had been having. Still . . .

'How long will you be staying, Trinity?'

'Until that's done and any other work that I might be able to help with — I suppose until Tamarind tells me to be on my way.'

'It's a good idea,' Clark said. 'We can't have Tamarind staying there alone — there still might be some of Dancer's gang around.'

'You don't even have anything to eat!' Polly pointed out.

'I'll knock over a deer,' Trinity said. 'With the cattle gone, now and then there will be one wandering down to the pond where you were camped.'

'Pretty damned primitive way to live,' Polly complained.

'Oh, Mother,' Tamarind said with a smile. 'You have such a short memory. Don't you recall the times we had before Luther arrived — nothing to eat, no wood to burn for warmth, the well running dry?'

'Yes, I do!' Polly said, 'and it hurt me for your sake just as much then as it does now.'

'Mother,' Tamarind said, crouching down. 'I'm not a child any more.'

An hour or so after Billy and his crew had started off toward Van Horn, Trinity and Tammy were on their way back toward the Bar-D ranch house. Trinity was expecting a long, lousy day. He knew what he would find at the house. Flies, possibly wild animals, then the digging in the baked earth. Polly had made him promise one thing:

'Don't bury them near Luther, please. They weren't good enough to walk the same earth with him, and if there were a way I wouldn't let them share the same ground.'

Trinity promised her, although it would only make his job harder than it already was. The sun rose slowly and warmed the morning rapidly. In front of him Tammy sat her pony erectly. Her slender figure was a joy to study. They exchanged few words along the trail.

It was a long hot ride, still Trinity frowned unhappily when the ranch house came into view. The wind was hot flowing past them. The rain clouds they had seen earlier had balked at shifting their shadows toward the plains. The day was going to be long, hot and unpleasant.

'Why don't you unsaddle your horse then sort of poke around the barn, survey the yard?' Trinity suggested to Tamarind as they rode. 'Maybe visit your father's grave.'

'You don't want me to go into the house yet, is that it?'

'That's it. You don't want to, do you?'

'No.'

'Neither do I,' said Trinity. But he was elected to the job. With his kerchief tied over his face he entered the stiflingly hot house, crossed it toward the back door without glancing at his work, flung open the back door and let the breeze stir up the flies that had settled on the bodies of Dancer and Art Tatum. It was loathsome work. Trinity decided that grave diggers did not get paid enough, no matter what they made.

With flies still humming irritatingly around him, Trinity made a quick, cursory search of the bodies. Dancer's pockets were empty except for some silver money. That was odd — where was the money he had stolen? He had paid off a dozen or so gunfighters, but that would not have taken all of it. Oh well, probably he had stashed it somewhere — at the house outside of Van Horn, for instance, meaning to go back for it. Trinity wondered idly how many such small caches were to be found across the frontier, where people were wary of banks.

Art Tatum had three nickels and a twenty-dollar gold piece in his jeans. What was left of his share of the stolen money. Trinity almost left it where he had found it, but that made no sense. It was a pure waste of money, and Tamarind would need whatever they could scrape together soon.

Trinity finished his search, rose, and stepped outside the house to breathe in some clean warm air. The flies followed him in a swarm. He saw Tamarind standing in front of the barn, her arms crossed under her breasts, watching him. She walked away with shuffling steps in the direction of Luther Travers's grave.

Trinity sighed soundlessly. Now for the hard part.

The piebald turned defiant again. This time the animal just refused to go near the front door to the house. Trinity didn't blame the animal, but he needed it for the job. Eventually he uncoiled a fifty-foot lead of rope and returned to the house, tying one end of it to the feet of the dead men. He went back to his horse, threw a dally loop around the pommel of his saddle and swung aboard.

'You're going to earn your keep, darn you,' he snarled at the piebald which still refused to move. Trinity heeled it angrily and the horse backed away, then was turned toward the open land beyond the yard of the house. He made the horse drag its revolting burden a hundred yards or so before he halted it, untied the dally and swung down. As soon as he was out of the saddle, the piebald turned and loped toward the barn. That was something the horse never did normally; it could be counted on to stand, but Trinity couldn't blame it for wanting to get away.

For himself he had only begun. He took the shovel he had brought and tossed it aside, then began swinging his pick against the hard-baked earth as the sun rose higher and the day filled with more stink and a thicker cloud of flies.

★   ★   ★

Tamarind found Trinity at sundown, sitting on the edge of the water-trough beside the barn. He was shirtless, sweat-streaked dust coated his back and chest. His hands were raw and blistered.

'Do you need anything — a bucket, soap, towel?' she asked, gazing at his miserable expression.

'One of each, I suppose,' Trinity answered. 'I don't think the stink is going to wash off, though. It'll just have to wear away.'

'I know.' She sat on the edge of the trough beside him and rested her hand on his bare shoulder. 'I'm sorry.'

'It wasn't your doing,' he said.

'No, but you did it for me, Trinity. I know that.'

He was silent for a while, looking across the long distances where the yellow grass was tinged pink by the light of the dying sun. At last, without looking at the woman, he asked, 'Tammy, how can you hope to make it here, alone?'

Her answer was long in coming. 'I mean to try, Trinity. That's all. Nothing is ever done if you don't at least try. Everything you try to do won't work. But sometimes . . . I mean to try.' She rose and said, 'I'll see if I can find soap and a towel.'

She walked back toward the house. Trinity noticed that she had left both front and rear door open despite the coolness that was settling now.

Trinity refused any food — there was nothing in the house anyway except for the pot of beans Polly had started the day before. He dragged himself early into the barn and spread some hay in the loft for a bed. Then he closed his eyes and let the dark memory of the day pass from consciousness.

It was not a racketing sound, but a sort of distant tapping that awakened Trinity to the dawn. He clambered down the ladder from the loft, walked to the barn doors and opened them wide. It was raining. A soft gentle rain shifted by a gentle breeze, falling from a silver sky. A long, soaking, needful rain this, no gullywasher, crop-damaging downpour. Trinity took his hat from a peg on the wall and walked across to the house. Tamarind was already up, standing in the doorway, leaning against the frame, watching the silver rain. Her eyes were bright and pleased. She smiled as Trinity stepped up beside her.

They stood together in silence, listening to the faint melody of the rainfall, and after a time, Trinity looped his arm around Tamarind's waist and she did not draw away, but looked up at him with a smile.

'Isn't that touching,' a voice from behind them said. 'Isn't that just charming.'

They spun to see Cole Travers standing there, dripping water. He held a revolver in his hand. He had entered through the back door which had been left open all night to air out the house.

'Cole!' Tamarind said. She stuttered a little as she asked, 'What are you doing back here?'

'Me? What are *you* doing here, Tammy — you and the gun hand? This is my property, you know. My house.'

'Not now it isn't,' she said. 'If it ever was.'

'What did you do? Steal the deed from my father?'

'Mother retrieved it and gave it back to Jefferson Clark,' Tamarind said, stepping toward Cole a few paces. Trinity hung back. He had left his pistol in the barn and his rifle was where he had left it yesterday — in the far corner of the room leaning against the wall.

'Dancer told me something like that would happen if Polly were given the chance,' Cole said. 'Said that she had sold herself to Boss Clark and would again.'

'That's not true,' Tammy said. 'She was simply living up to the bargain she had made with him.'

'What was that bargain?' Cole asked with an evil smile. 'Selling Father's ranch out from under him before he could get back and put a halt to it?'

'Cole, you're not reading things right,' Trinity said.

'You shut up!' He waved the muzzle of his gun that way. 'And what are you doing here, anyway? Thought you could polish up Tammy and take over the ranch for yourself — a lesson you learned from Boss Clark.'

'Think what you want, I don't care,'

Trinity said. 'But the best thing you can do for yourself now is to ride back out of here. Clark will never let you stay on the ranch and sooner or later you're only going to get yourself into more trouble if you stay around.'

'Thanks for the advice,' Cole said bitterly. 'Go for your pistol, gunfighting man.'

'You can see I'm not wearing a gun,' Trinity answered, raising his hands.

'Oh, hell, it doesn't matter much, does it?' Cole cocked his weapon. From the corner of his eyes Trinity saw a flitting shadow cross the floor and, as a grinning Cole Travers raised and carefully sighted along the pistol barrel, Tamarind shot him.

The thunder of the Winchester filled the room. Smoke rolled across it. Tamarind dropped the rifle and it hit the floor about the same time as Cole's pistol clattered to the floorboards and Cole himself slumped face down against the rough planking.

Tamarind was on her knees, her

hands covering her face. Trinity went to her. She was wailing: 'Oh, God, I killed my brother. My own brother!'

Trinity knelt beside her and placed his arms around the trembling Tammy. 'He wasn't your brother any more,' he told her gently. 'He was only his father's son.'

That day's work was only slightly better than the previous day's. The rain continued to fall, steadily but so softly that the earth seemed to be soaking it up as fast as it fell. It kept the flies down however, and there was a sweetness to the air. Tamarind and Trinity had a brief conversation about where Cole should be put to rest — beside Luther, making a kind of family plot, or with his father? Neither seemed right to Tammy.

'Put him alone somewhere,' she said. 'I think he always was sort of alone.'

So it was done that way. By the time Trinity was finished it was already mid-afternoon. He and Tammy ate bowls of the beans which were still good. After which Trinity told her, 'The deer will be down in their thickets in this weather; maybe I can get one tomorrow. It's not much, but it'll keep us alive.'

She made no answer. Perhaps her original enthusiasm for staying on at the ranch already seemed foolish. At any rate, Trinity could tell that she wished to be alone for a while, so he stepped out on to the porch to stretch his arms. Rain dipped in strings of beads from the roof, and out on the plains a thin misty curtain had settled. Looking westward, Trinity saw the group of four men approaching the house. He ducked inside and retrieved his rifle. From the kitchen sink, Tammy saw his movement and turned to ask a question.

'What is it?'

'Riders — I don't know who it is.'

'Not again,' he heard Tammy say. 'There has to be an end to this.'

Standing out on the porch again, Trinity watched as one of the riders detached himself from the group and rode toward the house. He was aware of Tamarind standing behind him, just inside the front door. As the incoming rider neared, Trinity frowned. Something seemed familiar about the man — the way he sat the saddle, the gray horse he straddled.

'It's Billy Raglan!' Trinity shouted, though Tammy was nearly at his side. The cry was of relief.

Billy rode directly to the hitch rail, grinning as he came. He swung down, whipped the rain from his hat and stepped up on to the porch.

'Hello,' he said cheerfully and took Trinity's proffered hand. 'How do you like the rain? If this keeps up, you'll have grass before long. We had to cross the Shamishaw — and, believe it or not, there was water running in the bottom.'

'Billy, it's good to see you. Won't you come inside?' Tammy asked.

Trinity stood staring into the distance at the three waiting men. 'Who's with you, Billy?' he wanted to know.

'Them? Oh, that's just Bodine and Chavez — they rode to Van Horn with me.'

'And the other man?'

'Him, we brought him along. Boss said he needed him — it's the preacher, Trinity.'

'Clark and my mother!'Tamarind gasped.

'Tomorrow, it being Sunday. Boss told me that he was danged if he'd lose Polly again. But let's go inside,' he said, swinging an arm to summon the others to the house. The rain had thickened a little.

'This is all so sudden,' Tammy was saying.

'Boss Clark is a sudden man. First things first,' Billy said as they sat at the kitchen table. From his inside pocket he removed the deed to the Bar-D. 'Finally got the title recorded,' Billy commented, glancing at Trinity, 'and hasn't it been a battle?' He slid the deed across the table to Tammy.

'But this is in my name!' She trembled a little. 'And in yours, Trinity,'

233

'What? Let me see that,' Trinity said. He took the title to the land, the Bar-D and just stared at it.

'Boss said that if you two didn't want to split it, that was up to you — he's plain tired of messing with the Bar-D.'

'Of course we will,' Tammy said, her gaze meeting Trinity's, 'but . . . '

'That's another part of it,' Billy Raglan said, looking toward the door where they could hear the men outside talking. 'Polly don't want her daughter living out here without . . . '

The tall man in the dark suit, his collar turned around backwards entered the house, a heavy volume in his hands. 'Come in, Reverend Taylor. This is the young couple,' Billy said. 'Tammy, your mother insisted if you're going to be staying out here.'

'But, Billy! Trinity? What are we to do?'

Trinity said evenly, 'Mind your mother, if you'll have me.' He stood up.

'I guess . . . ' She rose to her feet as well. Now she was trembling strongly.

She held her lower lip clenched between her teeth. 'If you will have *me*!' she said, 'Yes.'

'Reverend?' Billy said, rising. 'I guess it's all up to you now.'

After the ceremony which was held in the front of the fire, three witnesses dripping rainwater on the floor as Tammy and Trinity exchanged vows, they sat at the table again with Billy, drinking hastily boiled coffee. Chavez and Bodine sat in the living room, grateful for the coffee and the fire after a long day riding through the rain. The minister had taken off his boots and fallen asleep in one of the fat leather chairs. Apparently marrying folks was harder work than it seemed. Trinity had a glazed look on his face. Tamarind fidgeted.

'Now then, to business,' Billy said, reaching inside his coat again.

'There's more?' Tammy asked.

'With Boss Clark, there's always more,' Billy replied. 'First thing is that he sent a letter to the town marshal at

Van Horn informing him that Calvin Dancer had been killed in a fight out here. The marshal said that yes, Dancer was an escapee from prison and there was a five-hundred-dollar reward on him. He took Boss Clark's word for the way things had happened. Anyone in Culberson County would. So,' Billy said, producing a sheaf of banknotes with a flourish. 'Here it is.'

Trinity continued to watch like a man stunned. Tamarind was more alert, more pragmatic. 'Billy, this is not five hundred dollars.' The stack was fifty dollars short by her count.

'No, miss . . . I mean *ma'am*, it isn't. Polly said that you two needed to have some vittles around until you could get organized, so we hauled in some flour, potatoes, apples, bacon, coffee, sugar and such. It's out on our horses. It was forty-nine dollars and twelve cents. I can make up the difference.' Billy rose, thrusting a hand into his pocket. It was impossible to tell if he was serious or not, but Tammy took his hand, pulled him down to his chair and laughed.

'That's all right, Billy.'

'Polly said you'd likely have plenty of meat by now.' He looked at Trinity who flushed a little. The past two days had kept him too busy to go deer hunting.

Tamarind shuffled the bills again. 'I hate to tell you, but this still isn't right. I've only got three-hundred and fifty dollars here.'

'That's right,' Billy said. 'I've got the other hundred in my pocket. You have also purchased a mixed herd of twenty cattle from Boss Clark, along with a wagonload of hay. Boss says he doesn't mind taking payments on the ranch property, but he's a cash-only man when it comes to livestock.'

'We didn't ask him for any — '

'Tammy,' Trinity said quietly, taking her hand. 'We can't just sit here and hope. We've got to start running cattle if we hope to make the Bar-D a working ranch again.'

'That's another thing.' Billy said with a grin.

'Another! Doesn't Boss Clark ever run out of thoughts?'

'No, ma'am, I don't think so. I imagine that's a part of what got him where he is today.'

'What's the idea, Billy?' Trinity asked.

'The Bar-D. Boss don't like that brand, seeing the trouble it's caused for him and who it was named after. He wanted me to register a new brand for you while I was in town, but Polly told him that was a personal matter. Boy, does that woman know how to get him to listen.'

'What brand did he suggest?' Tammy asked.

'He was in favor of the Double-T,' Billy said. 'Easy enough iron to forge, a tough one to alter.'

'And appropriate,' Tamarind said, looking a smile at Trinity.

'We'll register it that way — next time we get to Van Horn,' Trinity agreed.

'That's about it then,' Billy said rising. 'The boys and me had better hit the trail if we're going to reach home before sundown.' He was putting on his hat while he used one foot to nudge the sleeping Chavez's boot.

'We traveling?' the cowboy asked, and Billy nodded.

'Soon as you boys bring the rest of those groceries in.'

'Tomorrow then,' Tammy asked in disbelief, 'it's really my mother's wedding day?'

'It is — unless she changes her mind and I don't think Boss Clark in his role as God, will permit that,' Billy tugged down his hat and grinned. 'You two better start early; you can't miss the ceremony. There'll be a barbecue for all the hands and neighbors. Then they're off on their honeymoon.'

'Oh, where are they planning on going, Billy?' Tamarind asked.

'I don't know if it's supposed to be a surprise,' Billy Raglan said, grinning. 'But I suppose it's all right to tell you: Boss Clark's taking his new bride around the world. They're going to

Galveston to catch a ship and just sail off. It'll be a year or so before they get back. Plenty of time for Polly to lose some old memories and gather some new ones to take their place.'

'Around the . . . ' Tamarind was speechless.

'That's incredible,' Trinity said.

Billy was still grinning. 'Isn't it? But tell me, Trinity, have you ever known Boss Clark to do anything in a small way?'

'Well, I suppose we'll see you tomorrow, Billy,' Trinity said as they walked to the door. To the minister he said, 'Thank you,' and gave the cleric a couple of his hideout dollars.

'One last thing, Trinity,' Billy said, pausing to talk to him.

'There *can't* be,' Trinity said.

'Before I left, Boss Clark told me — seeing as you and he are going to be sort of related somehow now, he'd appreciate it if you'd just call him Jefferson, or 'Jeff' if you preferred.'

13

A few days later, Tamarind was busying herself cleaning the kitchen and putting the new supplies away. Trinity, still feeling dazed by the quickness of events, went out to the barn although their horses had already been tended to. A fluttering sound caught his ear above the rainfall. Searching around carefully he found the spotted brown hen that Billy had wanted to eat on their first day here. The hen rushed away from its nest, anxiously squawking, but in her place she had left two brown eggs which Trinity gathered.

Returning to the house by the back way, he squatted, looked, and shook his head in amazement. There was bright-green new grass growing already from the long-suffering arid earth. If the rain drifted in again before the new grass too was parched, they might actually see the ranch return to life.

He glanced at Luther Travers's grave, wondering how many times Tamarind's father had hoped for just such a sign of life on this dead ranch, how many times he had been disappointed.

Upon walking into the kitchen from the rear, he found that Tamarind was gone, the front door standing open. Trinity placed the eggs down on the counter and walked to the door. Outside only a light mist fell. Hatless, Tamarind stood looking upward at the dead twig of a tree that had once been planted here with such optimism.

'Guess what I found,' Trinity began, proud of his egg-scrounging, but Tamarind was not listening.

'Hurry, here!' she said, and Trinity walked to where she stood. She gripped his arm tightly and pointed upward. 'Do you see that?'

Trinity squinted into the falling mist until he saw, on the tip of a tiny branch a small green bud no larger than the tip of Tammy's fingertip.

'It's alive!' she said. 'The Tamarind tree is alive.'

And it was, though not as alive as the light in Tammy's eyes. The tree given up for dead, the land given up for dead was making a comeback and even its many ghosts could not stop the springing toward life.

Tammy showed no inclination to retreat indoors despite the constantly falling rain. She simply clung to Trinity's arm, watching the tiny bud as if it might open and produce a flower at any moment. At last, distantly, she said:

'I wish Mother were here to see it.'

'So do I, but she's probably halfway to Galveston by now.'

'So far — and around the world! Boss Clark does take charge of things in a big way, doesn't he?'

'I suppose he feels he's waited twenty-five years for this moment and isn't about to waste it now.'

'That's right,' Tammy said, turning her eyes down. 'Twenty-five years they waited for this trip, their honeymoon.

It's remarkable.'

'Well, start planning,' Trinity said. 'I'll be taking you around the world in another twenty-five years if you still want to go.'

'That's a long time, isn't it?' She smiled, lifting her eyes to his. 'To wait for a honeymoon?'

'Oh, the honeymoon?' Trinity answered with a grin, 'I don't think we have to wait that long for that.' He turned and led his woman back through the rain to the warmth of the house.

THE END

Other titles in the
Linford Western Library:

BLIND JUSTICE AT WEDLOCK

Ross Morton

When Clint Brennan finds two men kidnapping his wife Belle, he's shot and left for dead. However, though he's been blinded, he realises his wife has gone. So, not giving way, Clint sets out after his wife's abductors, with his dog and astride his donkey. Belle, meanwhile, believes he's dead and when she's rescued by a rich man, she's told it's time to start again . . . All this violence, betrayal and lies will end at Wedlock, amidst flames and bullets.

COLORADO CLEAN-UP

Corba Sunman

Provost Captain Slade Moran arrives from Fort Benson, Colorado, to investigate the disappearance of an army payroll and its military secret. A grim trail has taken him to the empty payroll coach and its murdered escort, with one soldier mysteriously missing. Moran is led to Moundville where he's confronted by desperate men plotting to steal a gold mine. Embroiled in double-cross and mayhem, Moran fears he will fail in his duty. Against all odds, can he succeed?

CANNON FOR HIRE

Doug Thorne

In the autumn of 1897, men flock to the wild Yukon Territory, searching for gold. But Tom Cannon, a one-time cavalry officer, has a different reason for making the hazardous trek north. Hired to find Emmet Lawrence — a greenhorn who'd disappeared seeking his fortune — Cannon searches the icy wastes and snow-capped mountains and draws a blank. No one remembers Lawrence, or knows his whereabouts. Then something happens that Cannon hasn't allowed for — Emmet Lawrence comes looking for him . . .

RYAN'S LEGACY

Bill Williams

Ryan Buchanan is given his father's pistol on the day of his eighteenth birthday, unaware of his legacy and the tragic events that lie ahead. After his uncle refuses to sell his land to a neighbour, Ryan is accused of killing a man, despite not even being able to remember the fight that witnesses say took place. Under the gravest danger, he uncovers secret details from the past that could cost him his life . . .

BATTLE AT
GUN BARREL CANYON

Wolf Lundgren

In Gun Barrel Valley in Montana,
only the law of the gun rules
. . . Joshua Vincent suspects that his
neighbour, Matt Saunders, is cutting
his fence wire and rustling his stock.
A range war threatens when he
sends assassins to kill him. Meanwhile, Polly Vincent, whilst a
prisoner at her own uncle's ranch,
suffers the attentions of her lascivi-
ous cousin. As bullets fly, Matthew
buckles on his trusty Peacemaker.
Can he rescue Polly — and counter
Vincent's overwhelming firepower?

BARRON'S

AP®
Computer Science
Principles

WITH 4 PRACTICE TESTS

Arundel High School

Seth Reichelson

BS Mechanical Engineering
Lake Brantley High School

Published by Kaplan, Inc., d/b/a Barron's Educational Series
750 Third Avenue
New York, NY 10017
www.barronseduc.com

ISBN: 978-1-4380-1262-9

10 9 8 7 6 5 4 3 2 1

Kaplan, Inc., d/b/a Barron's Educational Series print books are available at special quantity discounts to use for sales promotions, employee premiums, or educational purposes. For more information or to purchase books, please call the Simon & Schuster special sales department at 866-506-1949.

Contents

APPENDIX

Preface

This book is aimed at students taking the AP Computer Science Principles exam and is designed to help students prepare for exam topics, regardless of what computer language or method they were taught.

The book provides in-depth instructions on how to complete the Explore Performance Task and the Create Performance Task. We have included sample responses that earn high scores and sample responses that earn low scores. The provided sample responses are intended to serve as guiding resources only. Do NOT copy the sample responses! The College Board does rigorous checks for plagiarism.

The questions and examples all reflect the style of recent exam questions and cover the essential knowledge topics outlined by the College Board. For the benefit of students and instructors, we have included three practice exams, with an extra exam available online.

Acknowledgments

First, I need to thank my wife, Debbie, for her constant encouragement and support. I want to thank my daughter, Lisa, just for being perfect. I would like to thank my dog, Novack III, for his vacant looks and rare kisses. I want to thank the many students I have had the pleasure of teaching, at Lake Brantley High School, Ocoee High School, and Apopka High School, who have inspired me, challenged me, and made me a better teacher and person. Also, I would like to thank Joanne Cohoon, Aaron Fan, and Lisa Reichelson, whose passion and purpose set a high bar that I strive to reach.

—Seth

Introduction

GENERAL INFORMATION ABOUT THE EXAM

The AP Computer Science Principles exam is a two-hour multiple-choice exam with 74 questions covering seven Big Ideas accompanied by two performance tasks containing five submissions (3 for the Create task and 2 for the Explore task). The College Board recommends you submit your performance tasks on April 15, with a due date of approximately April 30. After your teacher sets up your College Board account, you will be able to submit your five performance tasks starting December 3. I recommend you submit your performance tasks well before the April 30 deadline.

Because the College Board is constantly tweaking the dates, check for current dates at *https://apstudent.collegeboard.org/apcourse/ap-computer-science-principles*

Content of Class

Performance task: 40% of AP Grade

  Explore Task: 16%

    Guaranteed 8 hours of classroom time to finish

    Written Responses

    Computational artifact

  Create Task: 24%

    Guaranteed 12 hours of classroom time to finish

    Program Code

    Written Responses

    Video of at least one significant part of your program running

End of Course exam: 60% of AP Grade

  2 hours

  74 multiple-choice questions, paper and pencil exam

    Abstraction 19%

    Data and Information 18%

    Algorithms 20%

    Programming 20%

    The Internet 13%

    Global Impact 10%

Some exam questions may be aligned to more than one learning objective. For example, a question on programming might implement an algorithm and contain an abstraction.

HINTS FOR TAKING THE EXAM
The Multiple-Choice Section

The multiple-choice questions are worth 60% of your score and are administrated at the end of the year. There is no penalty for wrong answers, so answer every question, even if you have to guess.

You have a little more than 1.6 minutes per question. You should have enough time to answer all questions on this test, and you will most likely have enough time at the end to go back to difficult questions.

The 74 questions are fatiguing. You should practice at least one of the sample tests given in one sitting.

Robot and programming questions can be simplified by hand-tracing the code.

People score the performance tasks, while the EOC exam is scored by machine. The test is independent of the computer language used, but there are both text-based programming questions and graphics-based programming questions.

The Performance Tasks

Details on how to create a College Board account and how to submit your performance tasks can be found at *https://apstudent.collegeboard.org/takingtheexam/about-digital-portfolio*

Explore Task

Allow your own interests to drive your choice of computing innovation and computational artifact. This is an individual project, and no collaboration is allowed.

Before you start writing, ensure you have read and understand the questions and how these questions are graded. There are small changes in the question each year, and the newest versions of both the questions and the scoring criteria can be found at *https://apcentral. collegeboard.org/pdf/ap-csp-student-task-directions.pdf*

While grammar is not graded, you still need to support your written analysis of your computing innovation when responding to all the prompts by using details related to the knowledge and understanding of computer science you have obtained throughout the course and your investigation.

Provide evidence to support your claims using inline citations.

To the best of your ability use relevant and credible sources to gather information about your computing innovation.

Provide acknowledgments for the use of any media or program code used in the creation of your computational artifact that is not your own.

The College Board strictly enforces its plagiarism policy. Credit should always be given and cited.

The deadline for submission is April 30. The College Board recommends submitting by April 15.

Create Task

Allow your own interests to drive your choice of computing program.

Before you start writing, make sure you have read and understand the questions and how these questions are graded. There are small changes in the question each year, and the newest versions of both the questions and the scoring criteria can be found at *https://apcentral. collegeboard.org/pdf/ap-csp-student-task-directions.pdf*

Your program code should represent the results of explorations that go beyond the examples presented in class.

Again, the deadline for submission is April 30. The College Board recommends submitting by April 15.

HOW TO USE THIS BOOK

Examples of each section of the Create and Explore Performance Tasks are given in this book. You should not plagiarize examples but instead use them as a model of how to score high on the College Board rubric.

Three complete practice exams are provided in the book. One exam is at the start of the book and may be used as a diagnostic test. It is accompanied by a diagnostic chart that refers you to related topics in the review book. The other two exams are at the end of the book.

Each of the exams has an answer key and detailed explanations for the multiple-choice questions.

Diagnostic Test

The exam that follows has the same format as that used on the actual AP exam. There are two ways you may use it:

1. Use it as a diagnostic test before you start reviewing. Following the answer key is a diagnostic chart that relates each question to sections that you should review. In addition, complete explanations are provided for each solution.

2. You can also use it as a practice exam when you have completed your review.

Diagnostic Test

MULTIPLE CHOICE

> **DIRECTIONS:** Each of the questions or incomplete statements below is followed by four suggested answers or completions. Select the one that is best in each case and fill in the appropriate letter in the corresponding space on the answer sheet.

1. Consider the following code segment, which uses the variables a and c.

   $a \leftarrow 3$
   $a \leftarrow a + 5$
   $c \leftarrow 3$
   $a \leftarrow c + a$
   DISPLAY(a)
   DISPLAY(c)

   What is displayed when running the code segment?

   (A) 3 3
   (B) 3 8
   (C) 11 3
   (D) 3 11

2. When writing a program, what is true about program documentation?

   I. Program documentation is useful while writing the program.
   II. Program documentation is useful after the program is written.
   III. Program documentation is not useful when run speed is a factor.

   (A) I only
   (B) I and II
   (C) II only
   (D) I, II, and III

3. What is true about high-level programming languages?

   I. High-level languages are easier to debug and easier to code than machine code.
   II. High-level languages contain the most abstractions.
   III. High-level languages are translated to machine code when executed on a computer.

   (A) I only
   (B) III only
   (C) II and III
   (D) I, II, and III

4. Hardware is built using multiple levels of abstractions. A computer is an abstraction. By making a computer an abstraction, it hides the complexity of the computer components, allowing the programmer to focus on programming.

   Which of the following lists hardware in order from high- to low-level hardware abstraction?

   (A) Computer, transistor, graphics card
   (B) Logic gate, transistor, graphics card
   (C) Computer, video card, transistor
   (D) Logic gate, video card, transistor

5. Which of the following examples **LEAST** likely indicates a phishing attack?

   (A) An email indicates that a password is expiring and asks you to click a link to renew your password.
   (B) An email from a familiar company, which has the exact look of previous emails from this company, reports that the current credit card information on file has expired, and has a link for you to reenter credit card information.
   (C) An email from the IRS contains the correct IRS logo and asks you to submit your social security number so the IRS can mail an additional tax refund. Additionally, the email contains a warning that if this information is not filled out within 30 days the refund will be lost.
   (D) An email from your credit card company with the correct bank logo indicates that there has been unusual activity on your credit card and to call the number on your card to confirm the purchase.

6. With the lowering of the digital divide and more products using the internet, the world is running out of IP addresses. The current plan is to switch from IPv4, which holds 32 bits, to IPv6, which holds 128 bits.

   With the increase from 32 bits to 128 bits, what is the resulting increase in possible IP addresses?

   (A) 2×96
   (B) 2^{96}
   (C) 96^2
   (D) 96

7. To get their AP scores hours earlier, if not days earlier, than the scheduled release time, students will hide their IP address so they appear to be in a different time zone. What device can students use to hide their IP address?

   (A) Proxy server
   (B) Domain name server
   (C) Distributed denial-of-service (DDoS) attacks
   (D) Phishing attack

8. One reason to use a hexadecimal number is because it takes up less space than the binary representation. Each hexadecimal digit can represent four binary numbers.

   Convert $A7_{HEX}$ to binary.

   (A) 10100111_{BIN}
   (B) 01111010_{BIN}
   (C) 0111_{BIN}
   (D) 11111_{BIN}

9. A computer can use 6 bits to store non-negative numbers. Which of the following will **NOT** give an overflow error?

   I.   64
   II. 63
   III. 54
   IV. 89

   (A) All of the above
   (B) II, III, and IV
   (C) I and III
   (D) II and III

10. Two computers calculate the same equation:

    $$a \leftarrow 1/3$$

    A second computer calculates

    $$b \leftarrow 1/3$$

    If $(a \neq b)$, what error has occurred?

    (A) Roundoff error
    (B) Overflow error
    (C) DDoS attack
    (D) Phishing

Block		Explanation
Oval	(oval shape)	The start or end of the algorithm
Rectangle	(rectangle shape)	One or more processing steps, such as a statement that assigns a value to a variable
Diamond	(diamond shape)	A conditional or decision step, where execution proceeds to the side labeled "True" if the condition is true and to the side labeled "False" otherwise
Parallelogram	(parallelogram shape)	Display a message

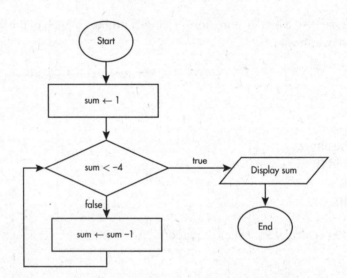

11. What is displayed after executing the algorithm in the flowchart?

(A) 1

(B) 5

(C) −5

(D) −1, −2, −3, −4

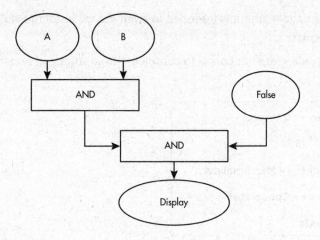

12. What does the above algorithm display?

    (A) True always
    (B) False always
    (C) If A and B are true, the algorithm is true.
    (D) When B is true, the result is true.

13. What error is displayed by the algorithm below?

    $a \leftarrow 8$
    $b \leftarrow 5$
    $c \leftarrow b - 3$ 2
    $d \leftarrow c - 2$ 0
    DISPLAY(a)
    DISPLAY($5/d$)

    (A) Divide by zero error
    (B) Short circuit
    (C) Overflow error
    (D) No error

14. Which of the following is **NOT** true when executing an algorithm?

    (A) All problems can be solved in a reasonable time.
    (B) Every algorithm can be constructed using only sequencing, selection, and
        iteration.
    (C) Different languages are better suited for expressing different algorithms.
    (D) Clarity and readability are important considerations when expressing an algorithm
        in a language.

15. The following code segment is intended to swap the values of the variables Marshmallow and Chocolate.

What can replace <Missing Code> to complete the swapping of Marshmallow and Chocolate?

```
Marshmallow ← 3

Chocolate ← 15

GrahamCracker ← Marshmallow

Marshmallow ← Chocolate

<Missing Code>
```

(A) Chocolate ← Marshmallow
(B) Chocolate ← GrahamCracker
(C) GrahamCracker ← Marshmallow
(D) Marshmallow ← Chocolate

Use the information below to answer questions 16 and 17.

The following question uses two robots in two grids of squares. The robots are represented by triangles pointing in their direction of movement.

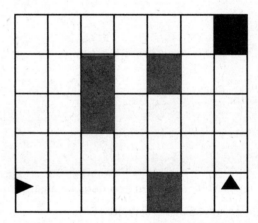

When the robot on the left moves over a light gray square, it sends a message to the robot on the right, causing that robot to move forward.

16. Which of the following code segments will cause the robot on the right to reach the dark gray square?

(A)
```
i ← 4
REPEAT 4 TIMES
{
  REPEAT i TIMES
    MOVE_FORWARD
  ROTATE_LEFT
  i ← i - 1
}
```

(B)
```
i ← 4
REPEAT 4 TIMES
{
  i ← i - 1
  REPEAT i TIMES
    MOVE_FORWARD
  ROTATE_RIGHT
}
```

(C)
```
i ← 4
REPEAT 4 TIMES
{
  i ← i - 1
  REPEAT i TIMES
   MOVE_FORWARD
  ROTATE_RIGHT
}
```

(D)
```
i ←
RE
      AT i TIMES
    MOVE_FORWARD
  ROTATE_RIGHT
  i ← i - 1
}
```

17. Which one of the following grids rearranges the original grid so that the first robot travels four squares before turning and the second robot still reaches the dark gray square?

(A)

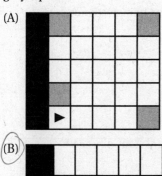

(B)

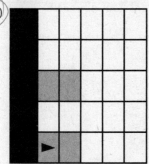

(C)

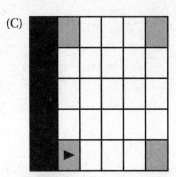

(D)

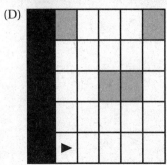

18. Constants are variables that are initialized at the beginning of a program and never change. Which of the following are good uses for a constant?

    I. To represent the maximum number of people that are safely allowed into a movie theater

   II. The score of a ongoing football game

  III. The value of pi

   (A) I and III

   (B) II only

   (C) I only

   (D) I, II, and III

19. What allows users to refer to websites by names, such as hamsterdance.com, instead of IP addresses?

   (A) IP address

   (B) Common protocol packets

   (C) ISP

   (D) Domain name system (DNS)

20. What is the minimum number of bytes needed to store the number 240?

   (A) 1

   (B) 8

   (C) 16

   (D) 24

21. At one of the lowest levels of abstraction, digital data is represented in binary that is a combination of digital zeros and ones.

The number "1001001" in binary is equivalent to what number when converted to base 10? 64 8 1

(A) 45
(B) 37
(C) 86
(D) 73

22. Using a binary search, how many iterations would it take to find the letter *w*?

str ← [a, b, c, d, e, f, g, h, i, j, k, l, m, n, o, p, q, r, s, t, u, v, w, x, y, z]

(A) 3
(B) 2
(C) 23
(D) 24

23. Using a linear search, how many iterations would it take to find the letter *x*?

str ← [a, b, c, d, e, f, g, h, i, j, k, l, m, n, o, p, q, r, s, t, u, v, w, x, y, z]

(A) 3
(B) 4
(C) 23
(D) 24

24. Which of the following statements could be used to describe the role of the Internet Engineering Task Force (IETF)?

 I. Prevents copyrighted material from being illegally distributed
 II. Develops standards and protocols for internet communication
 III. Prevents malware from being distributed

(A) I only
(B) II only
(C) III only
(D) II and III

25. Sequencing, selection, and iteration are building blocks of algorithms. Which of the following is considered selection?

(A) The application of each step of an algorithm in the order in which the statements are given
(B) Using a Boolean condition to determine which part of an algorithm is used
(C) The repetition of part of an algorithm until a condition is met or for a specified number of times
(D) The selection of proper computer languages can be designed to better express algorithms

26. If your algorithm needs to search through a list of unsorted words, what type of search would you use?

    (A) Linear search
    (B) Binary search
    (C) Bubble sort
    (D) Insertion sort

27. The code segment below is a test program intended to diagnose the disease held by a young child based on a user's entry of `fatigue_present` and `has_cough`.

```
IF fatigue_present AND has_cough
     DISPLAY "Flu"
IF has_cough
     DISPLAY "Cold"
DISPLAY "Healthy"
```

    If all variables have the value `true`, what is displayed as a result of running the segments as shown?

    (A) Flu
    (B) Cold
    (C) Flu Healthy
    (D) Flu Cold Healthy

28. Which of the following trade-offs is **TRUE** when representing information as digital data?

    I. There are trade-offs in using lossy and lossless compression techniques for storage and transmitting data.
    II. Reading data and updating data have different storage requirements.
    III. Lossy data compression reduces the number of bits stored or transmitted at the cost of being able to reconstruct only an approximation of the original.

    (A) I and II
    (B) II and III
    (C) I and III
    (D) I, II, and III

29. Colors can be represented by a hexadecimal number. It is made up of three two-digit hexadecimal numbers representing the red, green, and blue components. For example, a color with Red 1, Green 2, and Blue 3 would have the hexadecimal code #010203. Which of the following is the hexadecimal code for a color with Red 160, Green 80, and Blue 60?

    (A) #39825A
    (B) #A0503C
    (C) #38225A
    (D) #398050

30. This is a web of devices connected through the fault-tolerant redundant internet.

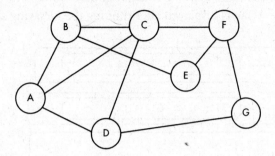

What is the minimum number of other devices that device C must connect with to communicate with E?

(A) 1
(B) 2
(C) 3
(D) 4

31. This is a web of devices connected through the internet.

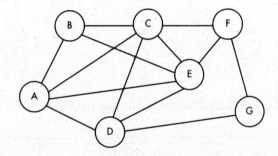

What is the minimum number of connections that must be broken or removed in the network so that computer G can no longer communicate with computer A?

(A) 1
(B) 2
(C) 3
(D) 4

32. The following code segment is intended to create list3, which is initially empty. The algorithm uses an abstraction, isFound(list, number), which returns true if the number is found in the list. What is displayed after running the following algorithm?

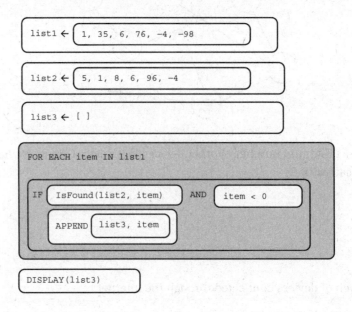

```
list1 ← [ 1, 35, 6, 76, -4, -98 ]

list2 ← [ 5, 1, 8, 6, 96, -4 ]

list3 ← [ ]

FOR EACH item IN list1

    IF  IsFound(list2, item)  AND  item < 0

        APPEND  list3, item

DISPLAY(list3)
```

    (A) [−4, −98]
    (B) [−4]
    (C) [ ]
    (D) [5, 1, 8, 6, 96]

33. What is displayed after running the following algorithm?

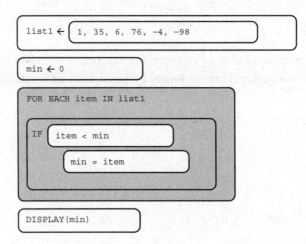

```
list1 ← [ 1, 35, 6, 76, -4, -98 ]

min ← 0

FOR EACH item IN list1

    IF  item < min

        min = item

DISPLAY(min)
```

    (A) 0
    (B) −4
    (C) −98
    (D) 76

34. What is displayed after running the following algorithm?

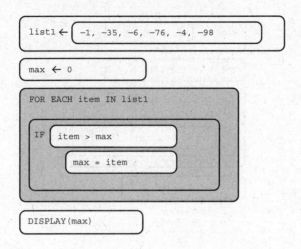

```
list1 ← -1, -35, -6, -76, -4, -98

max ← 0

FOR EACH item IN list1

    IF  item > max

            max = item

DISPLAY(max)
```

(A) 0
(B) -76
(C) -98
(D) -1

35. What is displayed after running the following algorithm?

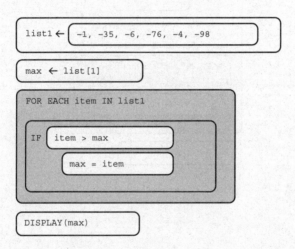

```
list1 ← -1, -35, -6, -76, -4, -98

max ← list[1]

FOR EACH item IN list1

    IF  item > max

            max = item

DISPLAY(max)
```

(A) 0
(B) -76
(C) -98
(D) -1

36. What is displayed after running the following algorithm?

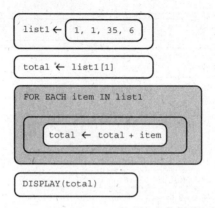

(A) 0

(B) 43

(C) 44

(D) 54

37. What is displayed after running the following algorithm?

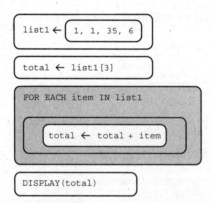

(A) 43

(B) 35

(C) 73

(D) 78

38. What is displayed after running the following algorithm?

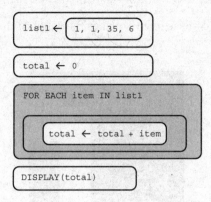

(A) 43
(B) 35
(C) 68
(D) 73

39. The following question uses a robot in a grid of squares. The robot is represented as a triangle, which is initially in the bottom-left square and facing right.

Which of the following code segments places the robot in the gray goal?

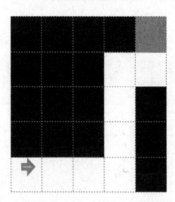

PROCEDURE MoveForward (int y)	PROCEDURE TurnRight (int x)
{	{
REPEAT y TIMES	REPEAT x TIMES
{	{
MOVE_FORWARD( )	TURN_RIGHT ( )
}	}
}	}

(A) MoveForward(4)
    TurnRight(1)
    MoveForward(4)
    TurnRight(1)
    MoveForward(1)
    TurnRight(1)
    MoveForward(1)

(B) MoveForward(4)
    TurnRight(3)
    MoveForward(4)
    TurnRight(1)
    MoveForward(1)
    TurnRight(3)
    MoveForward(1)

(C) MoveForward(3)
    TurnRight(3)
    MoveForward(3)
    TurnRight(1)
    MoveForward(1)
    TurnRight(3)
    MoveForward(1)

(D) MoveForward(3)
   TurnRight(3)
   MoveForward(3)
   TurnRight(3)
   MoveForward(1)
   TurnRight(3)
   MoveForward(1)

40. A smartphone stores the following data for each picture taken using the phone.

   The location where the photo was taken
   The number of photos taken
   The date and time the photo was taken
   The filename of the photo

   Which of the following can be determined using the metadata described above?

   I.   How many photos were taken at Disney World
   II. The name of the person who took the most recent photo
   III. Whether people tend to take more photos on the weekend than during the week

   (A) I only
   (B) III only
   (C) I and III
   (D) I, II, and III

41. What is displayed after running the following algorithm?

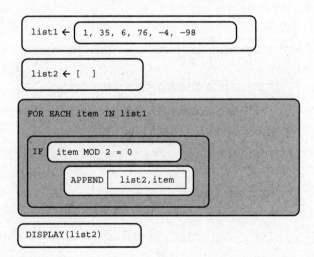

```
list1 ←  1, 35, 6, 76, −4, −98

list2 ← [  ]

FOR EACH item IN list1

    IF   item MOD 2 = 0

         APPEND   list2,item


DISPLAY(list2)
```

   (A) [ ]
   (B) [−4, −98]
   (C) [1, 35, 6, 76, −4, −98]
   (D) [6, 76, −4, −98]

42. What is displayed after running the following algorithm?

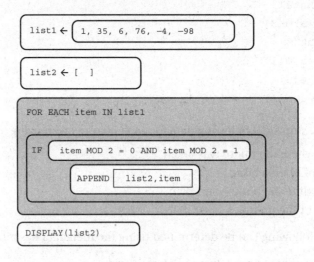

list1 ← [1, 35, 6, 76, −4, −98]

list2 ← [ ]

FOR EACH item IN list1

IF [item MOD 2 = 0 AND item MOD 2 = 1]

APPEND [list2,item]

DISPLAY(list2)

(A) [ ]
(B) [−4, −98]
(C) [1, 35, 6, 76, −4, −98]
(D) [6, 4, 98]

43. What is displayed after running the following algorithm?

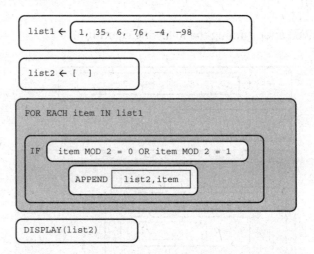

list1 ← [1, 35, 6, 76, −4, −98]

list2 ← [ ]

FOR EACH item IN list1

IF [item MOD 2 = 0 OR item MOD 2 = 1]

APPEND [list2,item]

DISPLAY(list2)

(A) [ ]
(B) [−4, −98]
(C) [1, 35, 6, 76, −4, −98]
(D) [6, 4, 98]

44. In a computer, text is represented by numbers, which are converted into characters using an encoding standard. Two common examples are the American Standard Code for Information Interchange (ASCII) and Extended Binary Coded Decimal Interchange Code (EBCDIC), which correspond the same character to different numbers. A sample of the encoding standards is provided below.

Decimal number	ASCII character	EBCDIC character
74	J	¢
75	K	.
76	L	<
77	M	(
78	N	+
79	O	|
80	P	&

Convert the hexadecimal array {50, 4F, 4B, 4C} to a list of ASCII characters and a list of EBCDIC characters.

(A) ASCII: {"P", "N", "K" , "L"}
    EBCDIC: {"|", "+", ".", "<"}
(B) ASCII: {"P", "O", "K" , "L"}
    EBCDIC: {"&", "|", ".", "¢"}
(C) ASCII: {"P", "O", "L" , "K"}
    EBCDIC: {"&", "|", "<", "."}
(D) ASCII: {"P", "O", "K" , "L"}
    EBCDIC: {"&", "|", ".", "<"}

45. Using the table in question 44, convert the ASCII character "M" to a binary number.

(A) 1001100
(B) 1001101
(C) 1001110
(D) 1010000

46. What will the following program display?

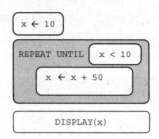

```
x ← 10
```
```
REPEAT UNTIL   x < 10
     x ← x + 50
```
```
DISPLAY(x)
```

(A) 10
(B) 50
(C) 100
(D) An infinite amount

47. Errors in Microsoft Windows are often displayed with hexadecimal error codes. If this number is converted into a decimal, it can be used by certain utilities to diagnose the problem with the computer.

   If a stop error (i.e., a "Blue Screen of Death") returns the error code 0x0000008F, what is the error? (Ignore the "0x" at the start; this is a signal that the number is in hexadecimal.)

Decimal error code	Error type
138	GPIO_CONTROLLER_DRIVER_ERROR
139	KERNEL_SECURITY_CHECK_FAILURE
140	STORAGE_DEVICE_ABNORMALITY_DETECTED
141	VIDEO_ENGINE_TIMEOUT_DETECTED
142	VIDEO_TDR_APPLICATION_BLOCKED
143	PP0_INITIALIZATION_FAILED
144	PP1_INITIALIZATION_FAILED
145	SECURE_BOOT_VIOLATION
147	ABNORMAL_RESET_DETECTED
149	REFS_FILE_SYSTEM
150	TCPIP_AOAC_NIC_ACTIVE_REFERENCE_LEAK

(A) TCPIP_AOAC_NIC_ACTIVE_REFERENCE_LEAK
(B) PP1_INITIALIZATION_FAILED
(C) PP0_INITIALIZATION_FAILED
(D) VIDEO_TDR_APPLICATION_BLOCKED

48. How is a string stored in a computer's memory?

    (A) It is a set of hexadecimal numbers representing each letter.
    (B) It is a set of binary numbers representing each letter.
    (C) It is a single binary number representing the string as a whole.
    (D) It is a set of characters that cannot be broken down any further.

49. A programmer is proposing to have her debugging program report errors in hexadecimal numbers rather than decimal numbers. Which of the following is a good reason for doing so?

    (A) Hexadecimal easily converts into binary, which is more useful for determining system-level errors.
    (B) Hexadecimal is easier to understand for typical end-users.
    (C) Hexadecimal makes it harder for hackers to hijack debugging reports.
    (D) Hexadecimal numbers are longer than binary numbers, which provides more detail.

50. A programmer is planning to make a program that allows a company to organize its employees by name, ID number, and salary. Suppose the programmer is making an abstraction called `newEntry` that takes in this data to create a new entry.

    Which of the following would be a good header for the abstraction?

    (A) `newEntry(int name, String idNo, int salary)`
    (B) `newEntry(String n, int i)`
    (C) `newEntry(String name, int idNo, int salary)`
    (D) `newEntry(String name, int idNo)`

51. Why is it best to use an iterative and incremental process of program development?

    (A) It is easier to find errors because any error-causing code is usually in the last change.
    (B) It is faster because it requires less testing.
    (C) It always produces the desired output regardless of the point in the development cycle.
    (D) It requires less processor time at all stages of development.

52. How many times does the inner loop iterate in the following?

```
REPEAT x TIMES
{
    REPEAT y TIMES
    {
        <Program statement>
    }
}
```

    (A) $2xy$
    (B) $y * (x - 1)$
    (C) $2x$
    (D) $x * y$

53. The figure below uses a robot in a grid of squares. The robot is represented as an arrow, which is initially in the bottom-right square of the grid and facing toward the right of the grid. Which of the following algorithms will place the robot in the gray square?

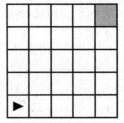

(A) ROTATE_LEFT()
    MOVE_FORWARD()
    MOVE_FORWARD()
    MOVE_FORWARD()
    MOVE_FORWARD()
    ROTATE_LEFT()
    MOVE_FORWARD()
    MOVE_FORWARD()
    MOVE_FORWARD()
    MOVE_FORWARD()

(B) ROTATE_LEFT()
    REPEAT 4 TIMES
    {
      MOVE_FORWARD()
    }
    ROTATE_LEFT()
    REPEAT 4 TIMES
    {
      MOVE_FORWARD()
    }

(C) ROTATE_LEFT()
    REPEAT 4 TIMES
    {
      MOVE_FORWARD()
    }
    ROTATE_LEFT()
    ROTATE_LEFT()
    REPEAT 4 TIMES
    {
      MOVE_FORWARD()
    }

```
(D) REPEAT 4 TIMES
    {
      MOVE_FORWARD()
    }
    ROTATE_LEFT()
    REPEAT 4 TIMES
    {
      MOVE_FORWARD()
    }
```

54. What percentage of the time will the following program display an even number?
    DISPLAY(RANDOM(1,10))

    (A) 0%
    (B) 10%
    (C) 40%
    (D) 50%

55. Where is cloud data stored?

    (A) Data centers of computers that can keep your information accessible
    (B) Electrical currents of nimbus clouds
    (C) The computer's software
    (D) The computer's hardware

56. In general, which of the following is **NOT** an advantage of using computer simulations?

    Select two answers.

    (A) Simulations are more costly to companies when changes to the simulation are needed.
    (B) The parameters of a simulation can be altered easily to test varying circumstances.
    (C) Simulations can run faster than real-time experiments and thus save time.
    (D) Information gathered by simulations is more accurate than that gathered by real-world experiments.

57. Which of the following describes a lossy transformation of digital data?

    I. Compressing an image file into a smaller resolution image so the image can easily be emailed
    II. Inverting the colors of an image by subtracting each RGB value from 255
    III. Converting an image by averaging its RGB values and assigning the new value to a shade of gray ranging from white to black

    (A) I only
    (B) II only
    (C) I and II
    (D) I and III

58. Which of the expressions are equivalent to the Boolean expression NOT (num < 13)?

    (A) num > 13 OR num = 13
    (B) num > 13
    (C) num < 13 AND num = 13
    (D) num > 13 AND num = 13

59. The following are steps data takes as it travels across the internet.

    I. Data is chopped into chunks called packets.
    II. Packets are reassembled into a coherent message.
    III. Packets are routed throughout the internet.
    IV. Packets go through internet service providers (ISPs) to access the internet.

    Which of the following is the correct path data takes when it travels from one device to another device through the internet?

    (A) IV –> II –> I –> III
    (B) I –> III –> IV –> II
    (C) I –> IV –> II –> III
    (D) I –> IV –> III –> II

60. An algorithm has n number of steps. Which of the following would NOT be considered a reasonable number of steps?

    (A) n
    (B) $4n + 8n^2$
    (C) $100\ n^4$
    (D) 3^n

61. A student was unable to connect to a website by entering its URL into her web browser. However, she successfully accessed the website by entering its IP address. Which of the following systems was most likely the one that failed when trying to access the website?

    (A) Domain name server (DNS)
    (B) Data source name (DSN)
    (C) File transfer protocol (FTP)
    (D) Hypertext transfer protocol (HTTP)

62. Which of the following are benefits to having information be easy to access?

    I. Information can be easily found by researchers, which can improve experimental and investigational findings.
    II. Information can be easily found by students, who can use it to improve their understanding of a topic.
    III. Information can be easily checked by third parties, which ensures that it is always correct and up-to-date.

    (A) I only
    (B) I and II
    (C) II only
    (D) I, II, and III

63. Most coding languages enable programmers to include a source file in the form of abstractions. For example, in C++, the command #include <iostream> grants the program access to basic input/output commands. Why would such a feature be useful in a language?

(A) It enables programmers to increase the level of complexity of the program and just focus on the current program.

(B) It ensures programmers can modify the language's functions.

(C) It enables features to be used in multiple programs, which reduces the complexity of the code by allowing for reuse.

(D) It is a useful reminder to copy the entire source file at a later time.

64. Why would a heuristic analysis be useful in an antivirus program?

(A) Heuristic solutions are only needed when exact solutions are needed and the program can be run in a reasonable amount of time.

(B) It enables the program to flag files that it needs to fully inspect, which ensures it does not need to fully scan the entire computer.

(C) It is able to pick out viruses without selecting false positives and without requiring a full file scan at all.

(D) It is more capable of separating dangerous viruses from simple adware.

65. "Boids" is a flocking algorithm that is used to determine the direction of objects in a moving population. It is built on three principles:

   I. Separation: steer to keep local flock mates at a certain distance
   II. Alignment: steer toward the average heading
   III. Cohesion: steer toward the center of the flock

Suppose that a programmer is creating a method called findBoidHeading that calculates the heading of an individual boid in the flock. findBoidHeading takes in a data structure of the other boids in the program.

The following commands are used on Boid objects. Assume that the name is representative of the function. Which might be useful in findBoidHeading?

Select two answers.

(A) getVelocity
(B) getDate
(C) getShape
(D) getHeading

66. A simulation for a coin flip should result in 50% heads and 50% tails. Select two answers that could replace the missing condition.

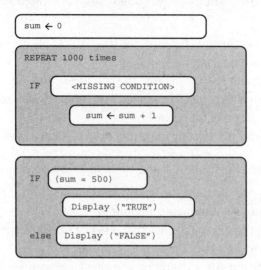

```
sum ← 0

REPEAT 1000 times

    IF      <MISSING CONDITION>

                sum ← sum + 1


    IF   (sum = 500)

                Display ("TRUE")

    else   Display ("FALSE")
```

Select two answers.

(A) RANDOM(1,5) < 2
(B) RANDOM(1,10) < 6
(C) RANDOM(1,2) = 2
(D) RANDOM(6,10) < 6

67. A program for children is designed to display a math problem and let the user input what he or she believes to be the answer. What data transformations are undergone at the most basic level of the program?

Select two answers.

(A) The keyboard number entry is converted from number to machine code.
(B) The keyboard entry is converted from text to number to hexadecimal.
(C) The problem is converted from decimal to text.
(D) The solution is converted from machine code to decimal.

68. Why is it more effective to use abstractions in a program than to repeat code?

Select two answers.

(A) Abstractions make it harder to edit because every extraction is saved on a distinct file.

(B) Abstractions simplify editing by requiring only one edit to the abstraction rather than to every instance of the code.

(C) Using abstractions takes up less space than repeating code, which makes the program easier to read.

(D) Abstractions are guaranteed to work in every instance, and if they work once, they are used.

69. Which of the following is NOT possible using the RANDOM(a, b) and DISPLAY(expression) abstractions?

Select two answers.

DISPLAY (RANDOM(1, 4) + RANDOM(2, 5))

(A) 6

(B) 10

(C) 1

(D) 5

70. The algorithm below displays TRUE 60% of the time.

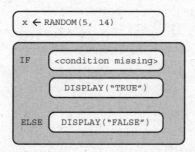

```
x ← RANDOM(5, 14)

IF   <condition missing>
        DISPLAY("TRUE")

ELSE    DISPLAY("FALSE")
```

What is the missing condition?

5 6 7 8 9 10 11 12 13 14

Select two answers.

(A) x > 8

(B) x <= 10

(C) x > 10

(D) x >= 10

71. Which of the following are examples of collaborations that have been created through crowdsourcing?

    Select two answers.

    (A) Small teams and businesses can collaborate with the general public to receive financing for projects.

    (B) A moderately-sized development team can have members of the general public edit and improve a beta's source code.

    (C) A development team can invite a small amount of potential users to give comments on a current beta build.

    (D) A project that had been abandoned can be remade and finished by another group made up of members of the general public.

ANSWER KEY
Multiple Choice

1. **C**	19. **D**	37. **D**	55. **A**
2. **B**	20. **B**	38. **A**	56. **A, D**
3. **D**	21. **D**	39. **C**	57. **D**
4. **C**	22. **A**	40. **C**	58. **D**
5. **D**	23. **D**	41. **D**	59. **D**
6. **B**	24. **B**	42. **A**	60. **D**
7. **A**	25. **B**	43. **C**	61. **A**
8. **A**	26. **A**	44. **D**	62. **B**
9. **D**	27. **D**	45. **B**	63. **C**
10. **A**	28. **D**	46. **A**	64. **A**
11. **C**	29. **B**	47. **C**	65. **A, D**
12. **B**	30. **A**	48. **B**	66. **B, C**
13. **A**	31. **B**	49. **A**	67. **A, D**
14. **A**	32. **B**	50. **C**	68. **B, C**
15. **B**	33. **C**	51. **A**	69. **B, C**
16. **A**	34. **A**	52. **D**	70. **A, B**
17. **C**	35. **D**	53. **D**	71. **A, B**
18. **A**	36. **C**	54. **D**	

ANSWERS EXPLAINED
Multiple Choice

1. **(C)** When answering program questions, a trace table is helpful in keeping track of variables.

a	c
3	3
8	
11	

   (A) While the initial value of a is 3, it updates to 8, then 11.

   (B) Variable c is initialized at 3 and is not updated in this problem.

   (C) Correct. Variables a and c follow the above trace table, and the DISPLAY method displays the value contained in a followed by a space, then the value contained in c followed by a space.

   (D) While the value of a and c follow the trace table, the order of the DISPLAY method is a first, then c.

2. **(B)** Program documentation is always useful in all stages of programming before, during, and after. Documentation before programming helps with planning the algorithms. Documentation during the development of the program helps with organization and collaboration. Documentation after programming helps the coder update the program after completion.

(A) Program documentation is useful while writing the program, and is also useful before and after the program is written.

(B) Correct.

(C) Program documentation is useful after writing the program, and is also useful before and during the program development.

(D) Program documentation does not affect the run speed of programs.

3. **(D)** Different programming languages offer different levels of abstraction. High-level programming languages provide more abstractions for programmers and make it easier for them to read and write a program, thus reducing the level of complexity. Abstractions can hide the details from specific examples to generalize functionality.

The lowest-level programming languages contain no abstractions and are in machine code, which is all 0's and 1's.

Code written in a high-level programming language is often translated into code in another (lower-level) language to be executed on a computer.

(A) I is a true statement. Higher-level programming languages somewhat indicate where a program needs debugging. Some lower-level programming languages do not indicate where debugging is needed.

(B) III is also a true statement. Computers can only understand machine code (zeros and ones). So programs written in a high-level programming language like COBOL need to be converted from COBOL to machine code.

(C) II and III are both true statements, making (C) a correct choice, but not the best choice. High-level programming language includes abstractions, which reduce the level of complexity of program.

(D) Correct.

4. **(C)** Hardware is built using multiple levels of abstractions, such as transistors, logic gates, chips, memory, motherboards, special purpose cards, and storage devices. Like software abstractions, hardware abstractions reduce the level of complexity when using a computer. Hardware component can be low level, like a transistor, or high level, like a video card.

The correct order from high to low is computer, video card, and transistor.

(A) Transistors are the lowest hardware abstraction that a computer is built on.

(B) While logic gates are above transistors, graphics cards are higher.

(C) Correct.

(D) The correct order here from low to high would be transistor, logic gate, and video cards.

5. **(D)** Phishing, viruses, and other attacks have human and software components and can have potentially devastating effects.

   (A) This is likely a phishing attack. Hackers can use the entered password to gain access to personal accounts.

   (B) The format of a company's email can be imitated. Hackers can use credit card information to purchase things and not pay for them.

   (C) The format for an IRS email can be imitated. The promise of an additional tax refund is used to motivate victims to reply with the correct information.

   (D) Correct. The credit card company is asking you to call a number already printed on your card.

6. **(B)** The number of devices that could use an IP address has grown so fast that a new protocol (IPv6) has been established increasing the bits used to store an IP address from 32 bits to 128 bits.

   Bits can hold $2^{(number\ of\ bits)}$ values. For example, 3 bits can hold 2^3 values, $2^3 = 2 \times 2 \times 2 = 8$ values.

   Increasing 32 bits to 128 bits would increase the size of the possible values by $2^{128} - 2^{32} = 2^{96}$.

   Calculating the value of 2^{96} is beyond the scope of this class, but for the curious it is equal to $7.922816251426434e_{28}$.

   (A) $2 \times 96 = 192$, which is considerably smaller then 2^{96}.

   (B) Correct.

   (C) $96^2 = 9,216$, which is considerably smaller then 2^{96}.

   (D) 96 is considerably smaller then 2^{96}.

7. **(A)**

   (A) Correct. Anonymity in online interactions can be enabled through the use of proxy servers.

   (B) Domain name server (DNS) translates domain names to IP addresses.

   (C) Distributed denial-of-service (DDoS) attacks compromise a target by flooding it with requests from multiple systems.

   (D) Phishing attacks have human and software components and can have potentially devastating effects.

8. **(A)** Hexadecimal is a base 16 system and is used to simplify how binary is represented. Each digit in hex (hexadecimal) is equal to four digits in binary.

$A7_{HEX}$

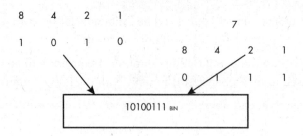

(A) Correct.

(B) $0111 = 7_{HEX}$; $1010 = 10$ or A_{HEX}; $7A_{HEX}$ is not equal to $A7_{HEX}$.

(C) $0111 = 7_{HEX}$; 7_{HEX} is not equal to $A7_{HEX}$.

(D) $11111 = 1F_{HEX}$; $1F_{HEX}$ is not equal to $A7_{HEX}$.

9. **(D)** Six bits can store 2^6 numbers.
$2^6 = 2 \times 2 \times 2 \times 2 \times 2 \times 2 = 64$

Six bits can store 64 numbers from 0 to 63.

An overflow error is an error that occurs when trying to store too large a number. Since the largest number stored using 6 bits is 63 (II), III, which is less than the cutoff number, will NOT cause an overflow error.

(A) 64 and 89 = overflow error

(B) 89 = overflow error

(C) 64 = overflow error

(D) Correct.

10. **(A)**

(A) Correct. A roundoff error occurs when computers round fractions to different decimal places. For example, one computer can round 1/3 to .33333333. A second computer can round 1/3 to .3333. .3333 and .333333333 do not equal each other.

(B) Overflow error is an error that occurs when trying to store too large a number.

(C) Distributed denial-of-service (DDoS) attacks compromise a target by flooding it with requests from multiple systems.

(D) Phishing attacks have human and software components and can have potentially devastating effects.

11. **(C)**

sum	true/false	Display
1	false	
0	false	
−1	false	
−2	false	
−3	false	
−4	false	
−5	true	−5

(A) While the initial value of sum is set to 1, it does not leave the loop until the value is less than −4.

(B) For every iteration on the loop it will subtract 1 from sum. It will not add 1 to sum. The highest value of sum is 1.

(C) Correct.

(D) There is no display abstraction in the loop. The value of sum will only be displayed after it leaves the loop, not in the loop.

12. **(B)** Any value AND False will always result in a False.

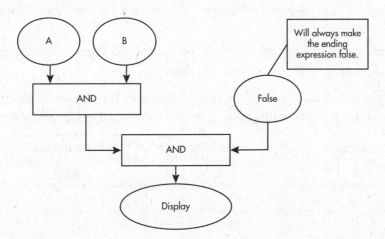

(A) Since any value AND False evaluates to False, there is no need to check A or B. This is called short circuiting.

(B) Correct.

(C) False AND False evaluates to False. True AND False evaluates to False. Since any value AND False evaluates to False, there is no need to check A or B.

(D) False AND False evaluates to False. True AND False evaluates to False. Since any value AND False evaluates to False, there is no need to check A or B.

13. **(A)**

a	b	c	d
8	5	5 − 3 = 2	2 − 2 = 0

DISPLAY 8

DISPLAY 5/0

(A) Correct. A divide by zero results from 5/0.

(B) A short circuit is not an error. A short circuit will occur if the computer will skip part of a logical Boolean.

(C) When the language is compiled, 5/0 would be caught.

(D) An error is caused by 5/0, but 0/5 would not cause an error.

14. **(A)**

(A) This is the FALSE statement. Some problems cannot be solved in a reasonable time, even for small input sizes. Reasonable time means the number of steps the algorithm takes is less than or equal to a polynomial function. Exponential growth is not considered reasonable growth. For example $n^4 + n^{10}$ would be considered reasonable growth, but 4^n would not be considered reasonable growth.

(B) Sequencing, selection, and iteration are building blocks of algorithms, so this is a true statement.

(C) This is also true; different programming languages are better suited for expressing different algorithms.

(D) Clarity and readability are important considerations when expressing an algorithm in a language, which makes this statement true as well.

15. **(B)** Putting actual numbers in for a tracing algorithm is a consistent strategy. Keeping the question abstract without adding numbers increases the difficulty of the problem.

Marshmallow	Chocolate	GrahamCracker
3	15	3
15		
	3	

(A) Chocolate ← Marshmallow
Marshmallow 15/Chocolate 15

(B) Correct.
Chocolate ← GrahamCracker
Marshmallow 15/Chocolate 3

(C) GrahamCracker ← Marshmallow
Marshmallow 15/Chocolate 15

(D) Marshmallow ← Chocolate
Marshmallow 15/Chocolate 15

16. **(A)** For the robot on the right to hit all four gray squares, the robot on the left needs to hit all four lightly shaded squares. MOVE_FORWARD 4 times then ROTATE_LEFT. This algorithm is iterated four times with the MOVE_FORWARD one less time after every pass of the loop. (B), (C), and (D) will not work because the robot is rotating right (clockwise), which will result in the robot leaving the grid.

17. **(C)**

```
REPEAT 4 TIMES
{
    REPEAT i TIMES
      MOVE_FORWARD
    ROTATE_LEFT

}
```

The robot needs to MOVE_FORWARD forward 4 times then ROTATE_LEFT. This algorithm needs to be repeated 4 times. Answer (A) would not hit the last gray square. Answer (B) would have to MOVE_FORWARD, TURN_LEFT, then MOVE_FORWARD twice. (D) also does not reach all four gray squares.

18. **(A)** Both I and III remain constant while the score of a football game is constantly changing. Constants are numbers that are not supposed to vary throughout the program.

19. **(D)**

(A) Everything connected to the internet has an IP address.

(B) For computers from different manufacturers to communicate, there needs to be a common protocol.

(C) The ISP is the internet service provider. Most computers do not directly connect to the internet, but rather connect to their ISP, which then connects to the internet.

(D) Correct. The domain name system (DNS) translates domain names to IP addresses. Without DNS, users of the internet would have to look up the IP address of targeted sites. With the switching between IPv4 to IPv6 the longer IP addresses make DNS even more vital.

20. **(B)** A bit can hold two numbers, 0 and 1.

2^n where $n = 1$

$2^1 = 2$

Two bits can hold four numbers, 0 to 3.

2^n where $n = 2$

$2^2 = 4$

(A) 2^1 can store 2 numbers.

(B) Correct. The max 8 bits can hold is $2^8 = 2 \times 2 \times 2 \times 2 \times 2 \times 2 \times 2 \times 2 = 256$ numbers from 0 to 255.

(C) 2^{16} can fit 65,536 numbers.

(D) 2^{24} can fit a significantly larger amount then needed.

21. **(D)**

64	32	16	8	4	2	1
1	0	0	1	0	0	1

$1 \times 1 + 8 \times 1 + 64 \times 1 = 1 + 8 + 64 = 73$

(A) 45 in base 10 = 101101 in binary

(B) 37 in base 10 = 100101 in binary

(C) 86 in base 10 = 1010110 in binary

(D) Correct.

22. **(A)** A binary search needs to be performed with a **sorted list**. A binary search starts from the middle and reduces the number of elements to check by ½ every pass.

In the first list, the binary search would start at the 13th letter.

[a, b, c, d, e, f, g, h, i, j, k, l, m, n, o, p, q, r, s, t, u, v, w, x, y, z]

The letter w is being searched; therefore, the first half of the list is left off. The new list has 13 objects.

Dividing 13 in half yields 6.5 (13/2 = 6.5), which is rounded to 7.

[n, o, p, q, r, s, t, u, v, w, x, y, z]

Again, because the letter *w* is being searched, the first half of the list is eliminated. The new list has seven objects.

6/2 = 3

[u, v, w, x, y, z]

A binary search in a sorted list, therefore, requires three passes to find the letter *w*.

(A) Correct.

(B) Two passes of the binary search would result in the letter *t*.

(C) If a linear search was being done, 23 would be correct. A linear search starts from the left end of the data structure and checks every letter in order from left to right.

(D) Every pass in a binary search reduces the number of searchable items by half. The worst-case scenario would be five in this data structure.

23. **(D)** In a linear search, the data structure **does not have to be sorted**. A linear search starts at the first letter and checks each consecutive letter from left to right.

[a, b, c, d, e, f, g, h, i, j, k, l, m, n, o, p, q, r, s, t, u, v, w, x, y, z]

Using this data structure, it would take 24 passes to find the correct letter.

(A) The third pass using a linear search would result in the letter *c*.

(B) The fourth pass using a linear search would result in the letter *d*.

(C) The 23rd pass using a linear search would result in the letter *w*.

(D) Correct.

24. **(B)**

(A) The Digital Millennium Copyright Act prevents material from being illegally distributed.

(B) Correct. The IETF (Internet Engineering Task Force) is the body that defines standard internet operating protocols such as TCP/IP.

(C) There is no standard to prevent malware from being distributed.

(D) II is true, but III is incorrect.

25. **(B)**

(A) The order in which statements are given is sequencing.

(B) Correct. A Boolean statement can be used for selection ("If" statements).

(C) Loops and repetition are iteration.

(D) Most computer languages can perform sequencing, selection, and iteration.

26. **(A)**

(A) Correct. A linear search can be performed on an unsorted list.

(B) While a binary search is generally faster than a linear search, a binary search can only be performed on a sorted list.

(C) Bubble sort is a sort, not a search.

(D) Insertion sort is a sort, not a search.

27. **(D)** The result of running the program segment would be:

Flu Cold Healthy. All "If" statements are true, so all answers will be displayed. Since Healthy is outside the "If" statement, it will always be displayed.

Fatigue_present is set to true.

Has_cough is set to true.

Healthy will always display.

```
        IF fatigue_present AND has_cough
            DISPLAY "Flu"
If (true AND true) → evaluates to true so "FLU" is displayed.
        IF has_cough
            DISPLAY "Cold"
If (true) → evaluates to true so "Cold" is displayed.
DISPLAY "Healthy"
Display "Healthy" will display "Healthy"
Combining all the strings results in "Flu Cold Healthy"
```

(A) While fatigue_present AND has_cough is true, displaying "Flu" does not end the program.

(B) While "Cold" is displayed, "Flu" and "Healthy" also display.

(C) While "Flu" and "Healthy" are displayed, "Healthy" is not in an "If" statement, so it will be displayed for all values of fatigue_present AND has_cough.

(D) Insertion sort is a sort, not a search.

28. **(D)** When using lossy compression, some data will be lost and can never be restored. The advantage with lossy compression is that the file size is smaller and can be emailed and stored easier. The data that is lost results in files with less resolution.

Lossless compression loses no data. The file size is larger than using lossy compression, but the data can be restored to the original resolution.

Reading data requires less data storage than updating data.

29. **(B)**

(A) Red 160   Green 80   Blue 60

$39_{HEX} = 9 \times 16^0 + 3 \times 16^1$ $82_{HEX} = 2 \times 16^0 + 8 \times 16^1$ $5A_{HEX} = 10 \times 16^0 + 5 \times 16^1$

$= 9 + 3 \times 16 = \cancel{57}$ $= 2 + 8 \times 16 = \cancel{130}$ $= 10 + 5 \times 16 = \cancel{90}$

(B) Correct.

$A0_{HEX} = 0 \times 16^0 + 10 \times 16^1$ $50_{HEX} = 0 \times 16^0 + 5 \times 16^1$ $3C_{HEX} = 12 \times 16^0 + 3 \times 16^1$

$= 0 + 10 \times 16 = 160$ $= 0 + 5 \times 16 = 80$ $= 12 + 3 \times 16 = 60$

(C)

$38_{HEX} = 8 \times 16^0 + 3 \times 16^1$ $22_{HEX} = 2 \times 16^0 + 2 \times 16^1$ $5A_{HEX} = 10 \times 16^0 + 5 \times 16^1$

$= 8 + 3 \times 16 = \cancel{56}$ $= 2 + 2 \times 16 = \cancel{34}$ $= 10 + 5 \times 16 = \cancel{90}$

(D)

$39_{HEX} = 9 \times 16^0 + 3 \times 16^1$ $80_{HEX} = 0 \times 16^0 + 8 \times 16^1$ $50_{HEX} = 0 \times 16^0 + 5 \times 16^1$

$= 9 + 3 \times 16 = \cancel{57}$ $= 0 + 8 \times 16 = \cancel{128}$ $= 0 + 5 \times 16 = \cancel{80}$

30. **(A)** The internet is designed to be fault tolerant. If one node is disconnected, the data traveling will pick a different path. This fault-tolerant nature requires multiple paths.

The shortest path from C to E would involve one additional device.

(A) Correct. There are two paths from computer C to computer E: C–B–E and C–F–E.

(B) There is no path from computer C to E that has two additional devices.

(C) There is no path from computer C to E that has three additional devices.

(D) There is no path from computer C to E that has four additional devices.

31. **(B)** The minimum number of connections needed to be cut to isolate G is two.

(A) Node A has four paths to G. If one line is cut, it leaves three paths from A to G.

(B) Correct. Cutting both GD and GF would isolate G.

(C) Node A has four paths to G. If three lines are cut, it leaves one path from A to G.

(D) Cutting four connections would isolate A, but the question asks for the least amount of connections to be cut to isolate G.

32. **(B)**

FOR EACH item IN list1

1,   35,   6,   76,   -4,   -98

First pass item = 1, second pass item = 35, third pass = 6...

Text: `condition1 AND condition2` Block: (condition1) AND (condition2)	Evaluates to `true` if both `condition1` and `condition2` are `true`; otherwise, evaluates to `false`.

For a number from list1 to be appended into list3, the IsFound and the item must be < 0.

Text: `APPEND (list, value)` Block: (APPEND [list, value])	The length `list` is increased by 1, and `value` is placed at the end of `list`.

(A) The −4 works; it hits on both conditions. However, while −98 is < 0, the IsFound is false.

(B) Correct. This works: −4 hits on both conditions, and −4 is in both lists and is less than 0.

(C) Here, −4 hits both sides of the "AND" statement and should be appended to list3.

(D) Only −4 fits both conditions.

33. **(C)**

item	min	Is item < min? (true/false)	min
1	0	F	0
35	0	F	0
6	0	F	0
76	0	F	0
−4	0	T	−4
−98	−4	T	−98

The correct answer is −98.

34. **(A)**

item	max	Is item > min? (true/false)	max
−1	0	F	0
−35	0	F	0
−6	0	F	0
−76	0	F	0
−4	0	F	0
−98	0	F	0

The correct answer is 0. While this program runs and returns a value, that value is logically incorrect. This is a case where initializing the value of max will lead to a runtime error. To prevent this error, always initialize max to the first element of the list. This also applies to finding the minimum number in a list.

35. **(D)**

item	max	Is item > min? (true/false)
−1	−1	F
−35	−1	F
−6	−1	F
−76	−1	F
−4	−1	F
−98	−1	F

The correct answer is −1.

When trying to find the max of min in a data structure always set the initial value equal to the first element in the list. This will work for all test cases.

36. **(C)**

list1	1	1	35	6

Total = list1 [1] = 1 // total is not set to 0, but instead is set to the first number in the list, which is 1. When iterating through the list it will add the first element of the list twice. To prevent this logical error, when finding the sum of a list initialize the total equal to 0.

Item

1	1	35	6
Total = 1 + 1 = 2	Total = 2 + 1 = 3	Total = 3 + 35 = 38	Total = 38 + 6 = 44

The correct answer is 44.

37. **(D)** The correct answer is 78.

list1	1	1	35	6
index	1	2	3	4

Total = list1[3] = 35

Item

1   1   35   6

Total = 35 + 1 = 36   Total = 36 + 1 = 37   Total = 37 + 35 = 72   Total = 72 + 6 = 78

38. **(A)** The correct answer is 43.

list1	1	1	35	6
index	1	2	3	4

total = 0

Item

1   1   35   6

Total = 0 + 1 = 1   Total = 1 + 1 = 2   Total = 2 + 35 = 37   Total = 37 + 6 = 43

39. **(C)**

Text: MOVE_FORWARD () Block: (MOVE_FORWARD)	The robot moves one square forward in the direction it is facing.

(A) `MoveForward(4)` puts the robot off the grid in the first move.

(B) `MoveForward(4)` puts the robot off the grid in the first move.

(C) Correct.

```
MoveForward(3)
TurnRight(3)(270 degrees clockwise)
MoveForward(3)
TurnRight(1)(90 degrees clockwise)
MoveForward(1)
TurnRight(3) (270 degrees clockwise)
MoveForward(1)
```

(D) `MoveForward(3)`

    `TurnRight(3)(270 degrees clockwise)`

    `MoveForward(3)`

    `TurnRight(1)(270 degrees clockwise)`

    `Off of grid`

40. **(C)** Using the metadata only the number of photos taken at Disney can be determined (I). The amount of photos taken at a certain time can also be determined (III). What cannot be determined is who took the pictures (II).

I is true. Using the location data you can determine how many pictures were taken at Disney World; however, III is also true. Using the metadata, date, and time, you can determine when the most photos were taken. Therefore, (C) is the best, and correct, answer.

II cannot be determined using the metadata.

41. **(D)**

list1	1	35	6	76	−4	−98
index	1	2	3	4	5	6

Item MOD 2 will equal 0 when the item is even. To reach the APPEND list2 the Boolean condition item MOD 2 must be true.

42. **(A)** [ ] No numbers will be appended to list2.

list1	1	35	6	76	−4	−98
index	1	2	3	4	5	6

To reach the APPEND list2 the Boolean condition item MOD 2 = 0 must be true and item MOD 2 = 1 must also be true. If item MOD 2 = 0 then the number is even. If item MOD 2 = 1 the number is odd. A number cannot be both odd and even at the same time. Since the conditional statement blocks all numbers, no numbers will be appended to list2.

43. **(C)** All numbers [1, 35, 6, 76, −4, −98] will appear in list2.

list1	1	35	6	76	−4	−98
index	1	2	3	4	5	6

To reach the APPEND list2 the Boolean condition item MOD 2 = 0 must be true or item MOD 2 = 1 must be true. If item MOD 2 = 0 the number is even. If item MOD 2 = 1 the number is odd. A number will be either even or odd. The conditional statement will be true for all numbers.

44. **(D)** Convert:

| 50 | 4F | 4B | 4C |

$0 \times 16^0 + 5 \times 16^1 =$ $15 \times 16^0 + 4 \times 16^1 =$ $11 \times 16^0 + 4 \times 16^1 =$ $12 \times 16^0 + 4 \times 16^1 =$

$0 + 80 = 80$ $15 + 64 = 79$ $11 + 64 = 75$ $12 + 64 = 76$

Using the table:

ASCII: {"P", "O", "K", "L"}

EBCDIC: {"&", "|", ".", "<"}

45. **(B)** Convert 77 to binary.

128	64	32	16	8	4	2	1
1	1	0	0	1	1	0	1

$77 - 64 = 13$

$13 - 8 = 5$

$5 - 4 = 1$

$1 - 1 = 0$

46. **(A)**

x	Output
10	
50	50
250	250

The condition $x < 10$ will never hit as x will only get bigger. This will result in the loop never executing, and the program will display the unchanged value 10.

47. **(C)** Convert 8F:

| 8 | F |

8×16 15

$128 + 15 = 143$

143 is PP0_INITIALIZATION_FAILED

48. **(B)** Strings are stored the same way any type of data is stored on a computer, using binary numbers. Generally, a letter is stored as an 8-bit combination of binary numbers. For example, the letter *A* in some computers is stored as 01000001 or 65 in decimal.

(A) Hexadecimal numbers are used to describe memory locations and colors. Hexadecimal is also an easier way of expressing binary numbers because each hexadecimal number represents four binary numbers.

(B) Correct. Strings are made up of letters. Letters are represented by eight binary numbers.

(C) Single binary number can only store two values.

(D) Computers can only store binary numbers. Everything stored on a computer including videos, numbers, audio, and pictures is stored as binary numbers.

49. **(A)** For example, 4B hex → binary would be

$$4 \qquad\qquad\qquad 11$$
$$0100 \qquad\qquad 1011 = 4B$$

(A) Correct. Hex to binary is convenient.

(B) Hex is not easier to understand than decimal.

(C) Hackers can also count in hex.

(D) Hex cannot provide more details.

50. **(C)** The method/procedure parameters need to match what is given. The procedure needs to take in a name (String), ID number(int), and salary(int).

(A) Name is a String, and idNo should be an int.

(B) This procedure is missing the second number salary. While not producing an error, the variable names *n* and *I* could be more descriptive.

(C) Correct. The correct parameters are there and are in the correct order.

(D) This procedure is missing the second number salary.

51. **(A)** When programming, it is better to test your code in small chunks as you write it. If your code is correct and you then add a section that generates an error, the search for the new error would be in the code you just added. If you do not check for errors as you code but wait, a significant amount of errors could pile up. Determining where the error originated would be difficult.

(A) Correct. The error is likely in the newest section coded.

(B) It probably requires more testing but saves time in the long run.

(C) Nothing *always* produces desired output on Earth.

(D) It is independent of processor time.

52. **(D)** If the inner loop executes three times but that inner loop must repeat two times, the program statement would execute 3×2 times.

If the inner loop executes four times but that inner loop must repeat five times, the program statement would execute 4×5 times.

53. **(D)**

(A) ROTATE_LEFT( ) rotates the robot counterclockwise. The second ROTATE_LEFT( ) would send the robot off the grid.

(B) ROTATE_LEFT( ) rotates the robot counterclockwise. The second ROTATE_LEFT( ) would send the robot off the grid.

(C) This code would result in the robot moving off the grid.

(D) Correct. REPEAT 4 TIMES would result in the robot moving 4 spaces to the right along the bottom of the grid. ROTATE_LEFT( ) would rotate the robot counterclockwise facing upward. The final REPEAT 4 TIMES would move the robot forward 4 spaces to the goal.

54. **(D)** DISPLAY (RANDOM(1,10)) will display the numbers 1, 2, 3, 4, 5, 6, 7, 8, 9, 10 with equal probability. The numbers 2, 4, 6, 8, and 10 are even numbers. 5 out of 10 numbers is 50%.

55. **(A)** Cloud data is stored in data centers around the world. These data centers keep your data sets safe if your personal computer receives damage. Cloud centers are not actual clouds, but you do need the internet to access your data. One of the advances of cloud computing is it takes the responsibility of handling your application and memory away from your personal computer. The physical storage can span multiple servers (sometimes in multiple locations), and the physical environment is typically owned and managed by a hosting company.

56. **(A), (D)** Simulating situations can potentially save money. For example, car manufacturers don't have to crash test as many cars as they would before simulations. (D) is a correct nonexample because simulations can never have all the real-world variables as the actual world. Answers (B) and (C) are both valid reasons for using a simulation. However, this question is asking for what is NOT an advantage.

57. **(D)** When compressing data using lossy compression some data is lost and cannot be retrieved. II is incorrect. No data is lost, so this is lossless compression. By adding the new number by 255 the original number can be found. III is incorrect. Data is lost in averaging pixels, which is lossy compression. By averaging pixels the original pixel values are lost.

58. **(D)** NOT (num < 13) is everything that num <13 is not, which is num = 13 or greater than 13.

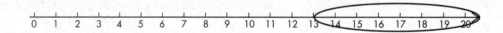

(A) Correct. (num < 13) is true when num is less than 13 exclusive. NOT (num < 13) is the opposite of (num < 13). Therefore, NOT (num < 13) is true when num is greater than or equal to 13 inclusive.

(B) num > 13 does not include the number 13.

(C) num < 13 is not included in the num > 13 or num = 13 subset.

(D) A number cannot be both greater than 13 and equal to 13 at the same time.

59. **(D)**

(A) Before data travels through the internet, it must first be broken down into packets.

(B) Computers usually are not directly connected to the internet. Instead they are connected to the internet by an ISP.

(C) Packets are reassembled after traveling to the designated computer.

(D) Correct. First your data will be chopped up into small packets. The packets then enter the internet through your internet service provider (ISP). Those packets are then routed throughout the internet. Finally the packets will be reassembled into a coherent message.

60. **(D)** Polynomial growth is acceptable. Exponential growth is not acceptable.

61. **(A)** The domain name server (DNS) converts the name of the website to the IP address. For example, Facebook could have the IP address of 66.220.159.255.

(B) Data source name is an incorrect term.

(C) File transfer protocol (FTP) breaks the rules of how computers communicate using the internet. Without FTP no communication on the internet would work.

(D) Hypertext transfer protocol (HTTP) is the protocol that web browsers and web servers use to communicate with each other over the internet.

62. **(B)** I and II describe uses for information, and making that information easier to access improves both of these effects. III is incorrect because information is not always checked, and checks made do not necessarily lead to changes to articles.

63. **(C)** Abstractions should reduce the level of complexity of a program.

A programmer can override existing code to extend or change abstractions.

While abstractions should be designed to be used in multiple programs, they do not guarantee fewer lines of code are used. The user of the program will care about runtime and memory space; the lines of code should not be a factor.

Abstractions are built to be in the background and hidden. While the source code can be potentially seen, abstractions are designed to be in the background.

64. **(A)** A heuristic solution is a "rule of thumb." For example, if you are checking to see if a supermarket sells bananas, a heuristic solution would be to check if the supermarket has a produce section. An exact solution would be to check every item in the supermarket for bananas. Since (A) does not check every file on the computer, it is a heuristic solution. Heuristic solutions are designed to save time or memory. Taking bits out of files would not make the solution heuristic.

65. **(A), (D)** A good abstraction name is designed to reduce the level of complexity of the program by hinting the function of the abstraction by the name. The heading of the Boid is relevant to the velocity and heading, so either should be useful. The date and shape are unrelated to the heading of the Boid. (B) and (C) are incorrect because getDate and getShape would not be useful in finding the Boid heading.

66. **(B), (C)** will result in the "If" statement resulting in true 50% of the time. (A) is true 20% of the time, while (D) is true 0% of the time.

67. **(A), (D)** Anything used by a computer needs to be converted into machine code. The solution to the problem will be a number. For the computer to understand the value of the number, it would first have to be converted into machine code. When the number needs to go back to the user, it must first be converted back from machine code to decimal. (B) is not correct because hexadecimal is not the lowest level of abstraction that computers use. (C) is not correct because text-to-decimal conversion is not done.

68. **(B), (C)** Abstractions reduce the level of complexity of a program. They allow for the programmer to write the abstraction one time but use the code many times. They also encapsulate where errors appear. For example, if a coder writes an abstraction for finding the maximum number in a data structure, and the maximum number is not correct, the error probably is in the maximum abstraction.

    (A) is incorrect because abstractions make it easier to edit.

    (D) is incorrect because nothing is guaranteed to work.

69. **(B), (C)** (B) and (C) are not possible.
    The range of numbers at the low end is $1 + 2 = 3$.

    The range of numbers at the high end is $4 + 5 = 9$.

    Anything outside the range of 3 to 9 is not possible.

70. **(A), (B)** There are 10 numbers between 5 and 14. For the program to return true 60% of the time, 6 numbers must be included.

    (A) 9, 10, 11, 12, 13, 14

    (B) 5, 6, 7, 8, 9, 10

    (C) 11, 12, 13, 14

    (D) 10, 11, 12, 13, 14

71. **(A), (B)** Crowdsourcing refers to aspects of the project coming from the public, and in both of these cases some aspect is from the public (financing and the source code). (C) Inviting a small amount of potential users to give comments on a current beta build is not crowdsourcing because the testers were specifically picked. (D) Remaking and finishing a project is not crowdsourcing because the original project was not specifically put up for the purposes of editing.

DIAGNOSTIC TABLE MATCH

Question	Diagnostic Chapter
1	Algorithms
2	Programming
3	Abstraction
4	Abstraction
5	The Internet
6	The Internet
7	Global Impact
8	Abstraction
9	Abstraction
10	Abstraction
11	Programming
12	Algorithms
13	Algorithms
14	Algorithms
15	Programming
16	Programming
17	Programming
18	Programming
19	The Internet
20	Abstraction
21	Abstraction
22	Programming
23	Programming
24	The Internet
25	Algorithms
26	Programming
27	Programming
28	Data and Information
29	Abstraction
30	The Internet
31	The Internet
32	Programming
33	Programming
34	Programming
35	Programming

Question	Diagnostic Chapter
36	Programming
37	Programming
38	Programming
39	Programming
40	Data and Information
41	Programming
42	Programming
43	Programming
44	Abstraction
45	Abstraction
46	Programming
47	Abstraction
48	Abstraction
49	Abstraction
50	Data and Information
51	Programming
52	Programming
53	Programming
54	Algorithms
55	Abstraction
56	Global Impact
57	Global Impact
58	Algorithms
59	The Internet
60	Algorithms
61	The Internet
62	Data and Information
63	Programming
64	Programming
65	Algorithms
66	Programming
67	Abstraction
68	Abstraction
69	Algorithms
70	Programming
71	Global Impact

Explore Performance Task

1

"While many explorers like to endure hardship by traveling to remote inhospitable parts of the world, I prefer to explore from the comfort of my own home."

—Steven Magee

Chapter Goals

- General information
- Choosing a potential computing innovation
- Positive and negative effects on society, culture, or economy
- Checking references by date
- Acceptable references
- Software versus hardware

- Explore task 2a
- Explore task 2b
- Explore task 2c
- Explore task 2d
- Explore task 2e
- Rubric scoring
- Computational artifact

GENERAL INFORMATION

This performance task is designed to explore a computing innovation of your choice. A computing innovation is an innovation that includes a computer or program code as an integral part of its functionality.

You are NOT required to invent your computing innovation. However, you ARE required to explore a current computing innovation, create a computing artifact, and answer written responses in 700 words or less. This innovation does not have to be new, but the innovation must be current enough to have at least two references created since the last day of the previous school year.

Your teacher is required to provide a minimum of eight hours of classroom time to develop, complete, and submit this performance task. Although the eight hours are required, you can work on this performance task at home. Students in nontraditional classroom environments should consult a school-based AP coordinator for submission instructions.

This task is NOT a collaborative project. Care must be taken to give proper credit to all references used. Do not plagiarize, use a practice Explore task, or submit an Explore Performance Task used by a previous year student.

The recommended completion date is April 15th, but you are allowed to submit this performance task earlier.

CHOOSING A POTENTIAL COMPUTING INNOVATION

No points will be earned for any section if the identified innovation is not a computing innovation.

Computing innovations may be physical computing innovations, such as Google glasses or self-driving cars; nonphysical computer software, like a cell phone app; or computing concepts, such as e-commerce or social networking, which rely on physical transactions conducted on the internet.

Your computing innovation can have hardware components, like a self-driving car, but the answers to the prompts must be about the software, not the hardware.

Examples:

Software	Hardware
Operating systems	Motherboard
Driverless vehicle software to avoid crashes	Self-driving car
Dual-monitor programs for Windows	Monitor
Java compiler	Transistor
Graphics card driver	Graphics card

A perfectly written report on a noncomputing innovation will not be awarded a single point. Selecting a computing innovation is of high importance.

Some examples of computing innovations:

Snapchat
Facebook
WhatsApp
Software that enables drones and cars to drive/fly autonomously
GPS systems
Cloud services
ATMs
Instagram
Twitter
YouTube
Sound Cloud
Uber
Pandora
LetGo
Google Maps
Amazon
Food Apps
Find My iPhone
Spotify
Netflix
Hulu

Quizlet
Remind
Banking apps
Google Docs

Your choice of a computing innovation must have both a beneficial and a harmful effect on society, culture, or economy. An effect may be an impact, a result, an outcome, and so on. Beneficial and/or harmful effects are contextual and interpretive; identification includes both the classification of the effect as beneficial or harmful and justification for that classification.

Effects need to be societal, economical, or cultural and need to be connected to a group or individuals. Examples include, but are not limited to:

The impact of social media online access varies in different countries and in different socioeconomic groups.

Mobile, wireless, and networked computing have an impact on innovation throughout the world.

The global distribution of computing resources raises issues of equity, access, and power.

Groups and individuals are affected by the "digital divide."

Networks and infrastructure are supported by both commercial and governmental initiatives.

No points will be awarded if the identified effect is not a result of the use of the innovation as intended (e.g., a self-driving car is not intended to crash; therefore, its exposure to hacking is not an effect of its intended use).

Your computing innovation must consume, produce, and transform data.

Your computing innovation must raise at least one data-storage concern, data-privacy concern, or data-security concern.

CHECKING REFERENCES BY DATE

At least two of the three required references must have been created after the end of the previous academic year.

Filtering Search Results by Date Using Google

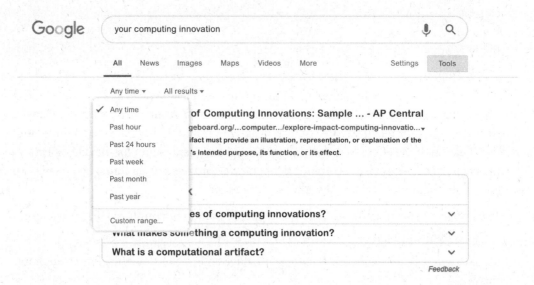

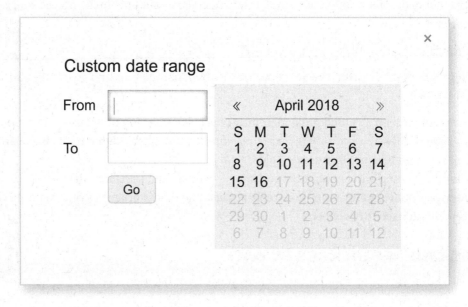

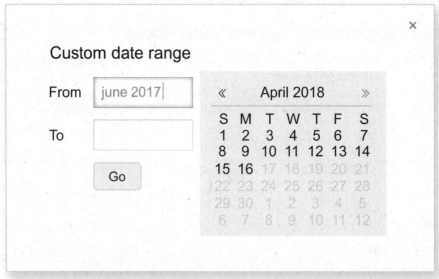

Select Custom Range

Enter the date of the last day of school for the previous school year.

Before moving on to the next step, make sure you can answer "yes" to all of the following questions.

Is your innovation a computing innovation?	yes / no
Is your innovation meaningful to you?	yes / no
Can you find at least three credible resources, with two being "new"?	yes / no
Does your innovation have a beneficial and harmful effect on society, culture, or economy?	yes / no
Does your innovation consume, produce, and transform data?	yes / no
Does your innovation have at least one data-storage concern, data-privacy concern, or data-security concern?	yes / no

COMPUTATIONAL ARTIFACT

In this section, you will be required to create a computational artifact that identifies a specific computing innovation AND illustrates, represents, or explains your computing innovation's intended purpose, function, or effect. A computational artifact is something created by a human using a computer including, but not limited to, a program, an image, an audio, a video, a presentation, or a webpage file. The computational artifact could solve a problem, show creative expression, or provide the viewer with new insight or knowledge.

The computational artifact must not simply repeat the information supplied in the written responses and should be primarily nontextual. In creating your computational artifact, you can create your own original work, including video, music, text, images, graphs, and program code. If you use external work to integrate into your computational artifact, you must acknowledge, attribute, and/or cite sources and include a bibliography with your submission. External work that should be acknowledged includes videos, music, texts, images, graphs, and program code that are used in the creation of your computational artifact.

This section can be completed by using a range of computer tools, from a word processing program to complex video-editing tools to simply the camera on your phone.

A high-scoring computational artifact will identify the computing innovation and provide an illustration, a representation, or an explanation of the computing innovation's intended purpose, function, or effect.

The following will not receive ANY credit:

(A) There is no artifact.
(B) The artifact is not a computational artifact.
(C) The artifact does not match the innovation described in the written report.
(D) The artifact does not identify the innovation clearly.
(E) The artifact does not illustrate or explain the innovation's intended purpose, function, or effect.
(F) Self-identification will result in disqualification.

Examples of Self-Identification

"Hello, my name is Aubrey, and my computing innovation is Twitter..."

Do not just repeat what is in the written response, and make sure to comprehensively explain how your computational artifact explains the innovation's intended purpose, function, or effect.

Note that artifacts that showcase a feature of the innovation instead of the purpose, function, or effect of the artifact will not earn the computational artifact point.

Video

(A) Acceptable multimedia file types include .mp3, .mp4, .wmv, .avi, .mov, or .aif [1].

    1. Record computing innovation running with digital camera/cell phone.
    2. Record computing innovation running with screen-capture software.

(B) Your video needs to be less than or equal to one minute in length.

(C) File size must be less than or equal to 30 MB.

Use file compression software such as PowerPoint or shareware software.

Directions on how to compress video using PowerPoint can be found at *https://www.youtube.com/watch?v=i_VCHFvniYI*

Use phrases such as:

"The name of my innovation is..."

"The purpose of my innovation is..."

"My innovation functions by..."

If possible, show the innovation running. Record the computing innovation running on your computer using screen-capture software or using your personal phone. If your application is a phone innovation, use a second phone to record your innovation running.

Examples of Video Artifacts

https://www.youtube.com/watch?v=tq9mcYux2Vc&feature=youtu.be

https://www.youtube.com/watch?v=sNsvT_rlzNQ&feature=youtu.be

https://www.youtube.com/watch?v=mFNWJ_zlhL4&feature=youtu.be

Info-Graph

Info-graphs should be primarily nontextual. Do not simply repeat what is in the written report.

Example:

Written Response

Response 2a

Provide information on your computing innovation and computational artifact.

Prompts:

Name the computing innovation that is represented by your computational artifact.

Describe the computing innovation's intended purpose. Purpose means the desired goal or objective of the innovation.

Describe the computing innovation's intended function. Function refers to how the innovation works (e.g., consumes and produces data).

Describe how your computational artifact illustrates, represents, or explains the computing innovation's intended purpose, function, or effect.

Must not exceed 100 words.

The following will not receive ANY credit:

(A) The innovation is not a computing innovation.
(B) The written statement is not answering the correct question.

Sample One:

My computing innovation is Bitcoin transactions.

Bitcoin transactions' purpose is to serve as a network of financial transfers that is decentralized and keeps users anonymous. This is done by replacing real-world currency in the transaction with a virtual substitute.

Bitcoins function much like an exchangeable currency: "Bitcoins (or fractions of Bitcoins known as satoshis) can be bought and sold in return for traditional currency on several exchanges" [1]. Users can then transfer Bitcoins between each other through client software.

My computational artifact illustrates the purpose of Bitcoin transactions by highlighting the issues with official currencies that Bitcoin avoids through its decentralized design.

Sample Two:

The name of my innovation is Twitter.

The purpose of my computing innovation is "to give everyone the power to create and share ideas and information instantly, without barriers" [4]. It is a place where people can share their opinions and thoughts with the world instantly, and it allows people to spread their message quickly and easily to many people.

Its function is that it allows users to post a short message of only 140 characters to their own Twitter account. People can then "follow" other users and see whatever that person tweets. It's used by many people, including celebrities, to share what they think on different events using a "hashtag" to group messages with a similar idea so that they can be searched for more efficiently.

My video represents my innovation's purpose by showing how people can share what they are doing throughout the day and post their thoughts.

Response 2b

Describe your development process, explicitly identifying the computing tools and techniques you used to create your artifact. Your description must be detailed enough so that a person unfamiliar with those tools and techniques will understand your process. If music or pictures were used, citations should be used. Steps used to refrain from self-identification in the video must be used. This section is used to provide credit for any tools used in creating your artifact.

Sample One:

I used a program called Adobe Premiere to make my computational artifact. I was able to use it to edit my video, and I used Open Broadcast Studio to screen record. Lastly, I used my phone to record a voiceover for my video; this way I could do many takes on the voiceover, without needing to redo the video as well. Then I put it all together in Adobe Premiere, and I edited it to keep the parts with any personal information out. Then I was able to export my video in a file form that was small enough to be submitted.

Sample Two:

I filmed my video using my iPhone 6S. First, I accessed the GoFundMe webpage on a desktop computer and showed their homepage, a campaign page [4], a login page, and a donation page. I showed binary code using an online binary code converter. This illustrated the conversion from unstructured to structured data. Once I filmed the video using the script I wrote, I loaded the video onto Google Drive through the app on my phone and saved it onto the desktop computer.

Response 2c

Explain at least one beneficial effect and at least one harmful effect the computing innovation has had, or has the potential to have, on society, economy, or culture.

Definition of Society:

1. a voluntary association of individuals for common ends; *especially*: an organized group working together or periodically meeting because of common interests, beliefs, or profession
2. an enduring and cooperating social group whose members have developed organized patterns of relationships through interaction with one another
3. community, nation, or broad grouping of people having common traditions, institutions, and collective activities and interests

Definition of Culture:

1. the customary beliefs, social norms, and material traits of a racial, religious, or social group; *also*: the characteristic features of everyday existence (such as diversions or a way of life) shared by people in a place or time
2. the set of shared attitudes, values, goals, and practices that characterizes an institution or organization

Definition of Economy:

1. the structure or conditions of economic life in a country, area, or period; *also*: an economic system

The following will not receive ANY credit:

(A) The innovation is not a computing innovation.
(B) The response is missing the adjectives *harmful* or *beneficial* (or synonyms thereof).
(C) The response is missing a plausible beneficial effect.
(D) The response is missing a plausible harmful effect.
(E) The identified effect is not a result of the use of the innovation as intended (e.g., a self-driving car is not intended to crash; therefore, its exposure to hacking is not an effect of its intended use).
(F) The explanation does not connect one of the effects to society, economy, or culture.

Sample One:

One beneficial effect GoFundMe has on society is that the website facilitates fundraising for the needy. GoFundMe allows organizations to raise money for donations to charity. Organizations can raise money for victims of violence or disaster. This benefits society because it improves the status of the needy by providing them with money for recovery. For example, fundraisers like Equality Florida raised money to benefit victims of the Pulse Nightclub shooting. According to the *Orlando Sentinel*, "The largest GoFundMe page for Pulse Nightclub shooting fallout and victims has broken records on the website, nearing $5 million on Thursday" [3]. GoFundMe allowed donations for the victims to break records.

One harmful effect of GoFundMe on society is that the fundraising site can facilitate the growth of fraudulent organizations. Because money is transferred online, users cannot confirm their money is going to legitimate causes. GoFundMe is unable to effectively prevent fraud, and the growth of fraudulent organizations harms society because it prevents money from going to those with true need. For example, individuals can set up accounts claiming to donate to a charity but use the money for themselves. This happened in the case of donations collected for Justin Owens's funeral. His friend, Justin Racine, created the account and likely kept the money for himself. According to *The Denver Channel*, "It was very easy for him to set up this bogus account with GoFundMe and then be able to take all the grieving friends' money, not to mention the grieving parents" [1].

Sample Two:

One beneficial effect that Twitter can have on society is that it can help spread awareness of an issue or a cause. It is an easy way for groups to reach millions of people, and making an account is free. An example of this is when the Memphis VA was concerned with the number of veterans committing suicide, and they started a Twitter campaign using the hashtag #BeThere on Twitter [1]. With this campaign they were able to reach out to their community and help stop suicides thanks to Twitter's service. This not only helped the veterans but also helped to create a more caring, concerned, and charitable society.

A harmful effect that Twitter can have on society is that it makes it easy for terror groups to spread their message. If it is easy to spread a good message, it is almost equally as easy to spread a bad message. So far Twitter has suspended 360,000 terror-related Twitter accounts in this year alone, and there are still many popping up every day [2]. The ability for terrorists to spread their message and recruit new members is alarming, especially because of just how easy Twitter makes it. These messages also make our society feel afraid for their safety and well-being.

Response 2d

Using specific details, describe:

(A) The data your innovation uses;

(B) How the innovation consumes (as input), produces (as output), and/or transforms data; and

(C) At least one data-storage concern, data-privacy concern, or data-security concern directly related to the computing innovation.

In this response, you must identify the data your chosen computing innovation uses AND explain how that data is consumed, produced, or transformed. Data types include images, text, audio, video, numbers, integers, signals, and Booleans. Large data sets include data such as measurements, texts, sounds, images, videos, and transactions. Make sure you specifically state the name of the data (don't simply say "data"), and make sure you understand that *data collection devices are NOT data (e.g., sensors, cameras, etc.)!*

Computing innovations use data such as audio, text, images, numbers, and video. To send the data on the internet or to another device, the data must be **transformed** into binary. Computers use binary because at the lowest level of abstraction all computers use tiny transistors as memory storage. A transistor is a miniature electronic switch with two distinct states:

an on position and an off position. The binary number 0 is "off" and the binary number 1 is "on." A modern computer can have billions of transistors. These 0's and 1's combine to form data that computing innovations use.

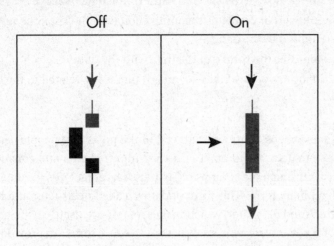

Examples: A computer transforms the letter a to 01100001. (We say that the letter a is an abstraction for the binary number 01100001.)

The binary conversion for a purple pixel is 10101010000000001010101010.

Data gets converted into binary when traveling through the internet. Most of the internet uses fiber optics. There are still parts of the country that use copper wire to transport data on the internet.

Example

English	Binary
Computer Science Rocks!	01000011011011110110110101110000011101010110100
	01100101011100100010000001010011011000110101101001
	01100101011011100110001101100101001000000101001 0
	01101111011000110110101011011001100100001

Some computing innovations' business model is to sell user information to targeted advertisers. This requires another data transformation in order to make the user data organized and ready to sell. The data will be converted from unsorted to sorted data. This sorted data is sold to advertisers to better target users with more personalized advertisements. The binary data is then transformed back from binary into its original format (audio, text, images, numbers, and video).

A computing innovation's metadata can have the effect of reducing the privacy of the user. Metadata can include geolocation, time, date, filename, etc.

Many computing innovations continue to collect data but never delete old data. This requires an increasing storage requirement. Companies can predict their increasing cost by using Moore's law (the size of transistors doubles every year, while the cost halves every two years).

The follow will not receive ANY credit:

(A) The described innovation is not a computing innovation.

(B) The response does not state the specific name of the data or simply says "data."

(C) The response confuses or conflates the innovation with the data; the response fails to explain what happens to the data.

(D) The response confuses the source of the data with the data.

(E) The response identifies or describes a concern that is not related to the data.

Sample One:

Twitter uses pictures, videos, numbers, and text in the posts that people can make.

Twitter must store data. Twitter takes the user-inputted data and converts it into binary so that it can transfer through the computer. Twitter's server receives the date as binary where it is stored—still in binary form. This form of data is called unstructured data; this data can be turned into structured data later, which makes it far more useful to the consumer. This is also easier to use for advertisers, who analyze your tweets in order to provide you with advertisements that are more suited to you as an individual. This data accumulation can be concerning to a user because it allows advertising companies to use their data to try and find out as much about them as possible, so they can give them targeted ads.

Sample Two:

GoFundMe operates using data such as text, pictures, videos, and numbers.

Users input their credit card number and personal information to set up fundraising campaigns and transfer money to charities. The numbers and text are transformed into binary numbers for the computer to process the data. The binary numbers allow the data to be transformed from unstructured to structured data at various servers, which "provides a well-defined way for applications to manage data in a [database]" [6]. From there, the structured data, still transferred as binary numbers, is transformed back into text, pictures, videos, and numbers that are used to set up accounts and facilitate the transfer of money.

One privacy concern caused by GoFundMe is the publicizing of information about individuals by others despite the individual potentially not wanting that information made public. For example, a friend of someone with health issues may set up a campaign for the one in need without consent. Data such as text and pictures is used in an instance like this to provide background on the campaign, but the data also compromises the privacy of the individual the money is being raised for. According to the *Simon Fraser University News*, funding sites like GoFundMe increase user risk through "participation in fraudulent campaigns and privacy loss" [2].

Response 2e

Provide a list of at least three online or print sources used to create your computational artifact and/or support your responses to the prompts provided in this performance task.

- At least two of the sources must have been created after the end of the previous academic year.
- For each online source, include the permanent URL. Identify the author, title, source, the date you retrieved the source, and, if possible, the date the reference was written or posted.
- For each print source, include the author, title of excerpt/article and magazine or book, page number(s), publisher, and date of publication.
- If you include an interview source, include the name of the person you interviewed, the date on which the interview occurred, and the person's position in the field.
- Include citations for the sources you used, and number each source accordingly.
- Each source must be relevant, credible, and easily accessed.

Your resources must have identified relevant, credible, and easily accessible sources to support your creation of the written responses to the College Board prompts. You can search for print or nonprint sources as part of your investigation. You can refer to a journal, a webpage, or an expert that is being quoted as part of your written responses. Avoid plagiarism by acknowledging, attributing, and/or citing sources throughout your responses.

Generally, crowdsourced sites such as Wikipedia should be avoided.

The following will not receive ANY credit:

(A) The response contains a list of sources only, **no in-text citations;**
(B) The response contains less than three in-text citations; or
(C) There are fewer than three sources cited, even if there are three or more in-text citations.

Sample One:

[1] Allen, Jaclyn. "Family Alleges GoFundMe Account Fraud after $3,500 Meant to Pay for Funeral Disappeared." *The Denver Channel*. N.p., 15 June 2016. Web. 18 Oct. 2016. <http://www.thedenverchannel.com/news/local-news/family-alleges-gofundme-account-fraud-after-3500-meant-to-pay-for-funeral-disappeared>.

[2] Beaulieu, Halimah. "Turning Unmet Medical Needs into Big Business: How Ethical Is Crowdfunding?" *Simon Fraser University News*, 13 Oct. 2016. Web. 20 Oct. 2016. <https://www.sfu.ca/sfunews/stories/2016/turning-unmet-medical-needs-into-big-business.html>.

[3] Brinkmann, Paul. "Pulse Fund on GoFundMe Nears $5M, Breaks Records." *Orlando Sentinel*. N.p., 16 June 2016. Web. 17 Oct. 2016. <http://www.orlandosentinel.com/business/brinkmann-on-business/os-fundraising-gofundme-record-20160616-story.html>.

[4] Gestal, Laurie. "Lucky Pup Oliver's Vet Bills." GoFundMe.com. N.p., 22 Oct. 2016. Web. 25 Oct. 2016. <https://www.gofundme.com/luckypupoliver>.

[5] GoFundMe. "About Us." GoFundMe. N.p., n.d. Web. 17 Oct. 2016. <https://www.gofundme.com/about-us>.

[6] Primmer, Robert. "Robert Primmer." Structured vs. Unstructured Data. N.p., n.d. Web. 20 Oct. 2016. <http://www.robertprimmer.com/blog/structured-vs-unstructured.html>

Sample Two:

[1] McKenzie, Kevin. "Memphis VA Promotes Suicide Prevention with Comedy, Fashion." The Commerical Appeal. *USA Today,* 7 Sept. 2016. Web. 9 Sept. 2016.

[2] Rutkin, Aviva. "Extremists Are Turning Twitter and Facebook into Theatres of War." *New Scientist,* 7 Sept. 2016. Web. 9 Sept. 2016.

[3] Heath, Sara. "How Social Media Can Improve Public Health, Patient Education." Patient Engagement HIT, 10 Oct. 2016. Web. 18 Oct. 2016.

[4] "It's What's Happening." Twitter, 30 June 2016. Web. 18 Oct. 2016.

Scoring Checklist

2a Computational artifact	Name of innovation Shows innovation running States the purpose Shows the function
2b	Not graded but can reinforce 2a. State the steps used to not self-identify. Cite any music used.
2c Beneficial effect and at least one harmful effect	Beneficial effects on society, culture, or economy. Harmful effects on society, culture, or economy.
2d Data	The data your innovation uses; How the innovation consumes (as input), produces (as output), and/or transforms data; At least one data-storage concern, data-privacy concern, or data-security concern directly related to the computing innovation.
2e References	At least three online or print sources

Create Performance Task

2

"It always takes longer than you expect, even when you take into account Hofstadter's Law."

— Hofstadter's Law

Chapter Goals

- **The Create Performance Task: 24% of grade**
- **Programming**
- **General requirements**
- **Program requirements**
- **Programming planning**
- **Sample algorithms**
- **Create sample program high scoring**
- **Program checklist**

- **Create sample program low scoring**
- **Create sample program medium scoring**
- **Submission requirements**
- **Recording video**
- **Compressing video**
- **Sample 2a**
- **Sample 2b**
- **Sample 2c**
- **Sample 2d**

The Create Performance Task is worth 24 percent of your AP exam. If careful attention is paid to the prompts and rubric, no points should be lost on this section. The current prompts and rubric can be found on *apcentral.collegeboard.org*. Make sure you are using the most current version of the rubric as it can change.

Programming is a collaborative and creative process that brings ideas to life through the development of software. Programs can help solve problems, enable innovations, or express personal interests. In this performance task, you will be developing a program of your choice. Your development process should include iteratively designing, implementing, and testing your program. You are strongly encouraged to work with another student in your class for parts of this program.

WARNING: You are NOT allowed to work collaboratively on any part of this performance task that is graded.

You are guaranteed at least **12 hours** of class time and unlimited out of class time to complete and submit the following:

A video of at least one significant feature of the program running

Written responses about your program and development process

Marked program code

GENERAL REQUIREMENTS

This performance task requires you to develop a program on a topic that interests you or one that solves a problem. It is strongly recommended that a portion of the program involve some form of collaboration with another student in your class. Your program-development process must involve a significant portion of work completed independently that requires a significant level of planning, designing, and program development.

Parts of this task can be collaborative, but a significant part must be completed independently.

The marked abstraction for grading is NOT a collaborative section.

The marked algorithms for grading is NOT a collaborative section.

The written portion is NOT a collaborative section.

PROGRAM REQUIREMENTS

Your program must demonstrate a variety of capabilities and implement several different language features that, when combined, produce a result that cannot easily be accomplished without computing tools and techniques. Your program should draw upon a combination of mathematical and logical concepts, such as use of numbers, variables, mathematical expressions with arithmetic operators, logical and Boolean operators and expressions, decision statements, iteration, and collections.

Your program can be written in ANY language. There is NO designed programming language for AP Computer Science Principles. The difficulty level of the program language is not considered in the scoring of this performance task.

Your program must demonstrate:

- Use of several effectively integrated mathematical and logical concepts from the language you are using
- Implementation of an algorithm that integrates other algorithms and integrates mathematical and/or logical concepts
- Development and use of abstractions to manage the complexity of your program (e.g., procedures, abstractions provided by the programming language, APIs)

The recommended completion date is prior to April 15th.

Your independently developed algorithms need to be fundamental for your program to achieve its intended purpose.

There is NO designed programming language for AP Computer Science Principles. Students may choose a programming language learned while taking the course to complete the task, or they may select a different programming language that they are familiar with outside of class.

Sample languages that can be used for the Create Performance Task:

JAVA	Python	SNAP	Scratch
MobileCSP	ALICE	C++	Pascal
COBOL	Machine Code	LISP	C

Programming Planning

When selecting a programming language and the program focus, students should ensure that their program will be sophisticated enough to integrate mathematical and logical concepts, develop abstraction, and implement algorithms.

A 500-line program will not necessarily score higher than a 30-line program. In fact, a 500-line program that does not have abstractions (called procedures, functions, or methods) and an algorithm that contains two algorithms will score lower than the 30-line program if the 30-line program contains all the correct elements.

The programming topic is completely up to you and should be something that interests you. However, you need to account for the limited number of classtime hours. If you want to write the new version of *Halo*, go for it. However, *Halo* will not be able to be written in the provided 12 hours. Think of the scope of your program before diving in. Still write the new version of *Halo*, just do it on your non-AP time.

While writing the program you should be aware that your end program requires an abstraction, two algorithms that combine to make one algorithm, and the development process of two distinct points of difficulties or opportunities when programming. At least one of these difficulties must have been resolved independently.

Your algorithms do not have to be physically next to each other in the code.

Examples of Starting Algorithms

Approximate counting algorithm
Correlation coefficient
Digital signature encryption algorithm
Card games
Dice games
Physics
Doomsday algorithm
Statistical algorithms
Easter algorithm
ElGamal asymmetric encryption algorithm
False position method in finding roots
Lesk algorithm
Parity error-detection technique
Pooled standard error
Projectile motion
Range
Standard deviation
Stemming algorithm
Total Energy = Kinetic Energy + Potential Energy
Variance
Zeller's congruence

SAMPLE CODE

Example One

Sample One Statistics

> Create an empty data structure and fill it with a large amount of random numbers. Once the data structure is filled with random numbers it opens up your program to contain statistics algorithms.

Text-Based **LOW SCORING**

```
1    import java.util.Random
2    public class MySample
3    {
4      public static void main (String args[])
5      {
6        Random rand = new Random();
7        int[] nums = new int[100];
8        for( int x = 0 ; x < nums.length ; x++)
9        {
10         nums[x] = rand.nextInt(100) + 1;
11       }
12     }
13   }
```

Score	This program will score LOW because there is NO abstraction. The program
LOW	also only contains the single algorithm num[x] = rand.nextInt(100) + 1. Loops do not count as an algorithm.

Graphical-Based **LOW SCORING**

Score	This program will score LOW because there is NO abstraction. The program
LOW	also does not contain an algorithm. Loops do not count as an algorithm.

Text-Based MEDIUM SCORING

```
1    import java.util.Random
2    public class MySample
3    {
4      public static void main(String args[])
5      {
6        int[] numbers = fillArray(100);
7      }
8
9      public static int[] fillArray(int length)
10     {
11       Random rand = new Random();
12       int[] nums = new int[length];
13       for( int x = ; x < nums.length ; x++)
14       {
15         nums[x] = rand.nextInt(100) + 1 ;
16       }
17       return nums;
18     }
19   }
```

Score	This program will score MEDIUM because it does contain the abstraction
MEDIUM	fillArray. The program contains a single algorithm nums[x] = rand. nextInt(100) + 1. Loops do not count as an algorithm.

Graphical-Based MEDIUM SCORING

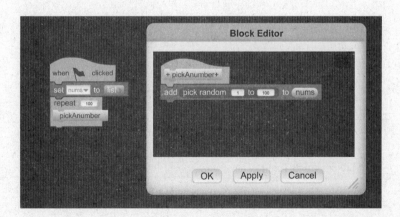

Score	This program will score MEDIUM because it does contain the abstraction
MEDIUM	pickAnumber. The program does not contain an algorithm. Loops do not count as an algorithm.

```
1    import java.util.Random
2    public class MySample
3    {
4      public static void main(String args[])
5      {
6        int[] nums = fillArray;
7        int range = getMax(nums) - getMin(nums);
8        System.out.println(range);
9      }
10
11     public static int[] fillArray(int num)
12     {
13       int[] nums = new int[num];
14       Random rand = new Random();
15       for(int x = 0 ; x < nums.length; x++)
16       {
17         nums[x] = rand.nextInt(100) + 1
18       }
19       return nums;
20     }
21
22     public static int getMax() (int[] nums)
23     {
24       int max = nums[0];
25       for(int x = 0 ; x < nums.length; x++)
26       {
27       if( nums[x] > max)
28         max = nums[x];
29       }
30       return max;
31     }
32     public static int getMax() (int[] nums)
33     {
34       int min = nums[0];
35       for(int x = 0 ; x < nums.length; x++)
36       {
37         if( nums[x] < min)
38           min = nums[x];
39       }
40       return min;
41     }
42
43   }
44
```

Score	This program will score HIGH because contains an abstraction. Actually, it contains the getMax, getMin, and fillArray abstractions. The program also contains the algorithm range, which uses two other abstractions, getMax and getMin.
HIGH	

Graphical-Based HIGH SCORING

The following program draws two line segments and then applies the line-line intersection algorithm, which finds the point where two nonparallel lines intersect.

$$(P_x, P_y) = \left(\frac{(x_1 y_2 - y_1 x_2)(x_3 - x_4) - (x_1 - x_2)(x_3 y_4 - y_3 x_4)}{(x_1 - x_2)(y_3 - y_4) - (y_1 - y_2)(x_3 - x_4)}, \right.$$

$$\left. \frac{(x_1 y_2 - y_1 x_2)(y_3 - y_4) - (y_1 - y_2)(x_3 y_4 - y_3 x_4)}{(x_1 - x_2)(y_3 - y_4) - (y_1 - y_2)(x_3 - x_4)} \right)$$

Once the x and y intersection points are determined, the program then determines if that point lies on one of the lines.

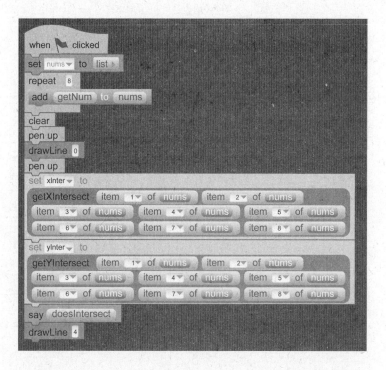

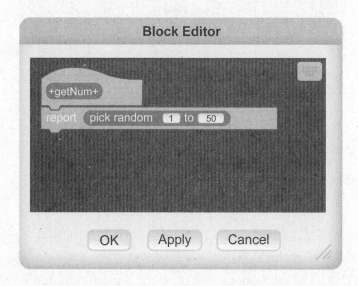

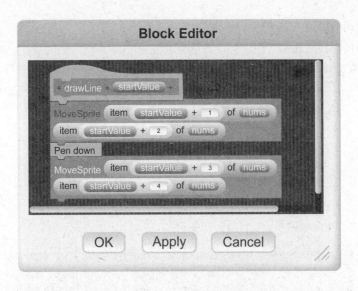

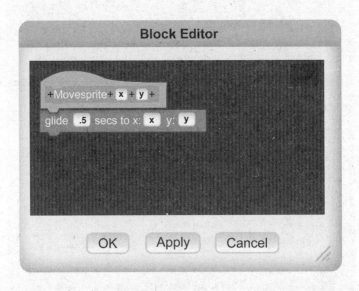

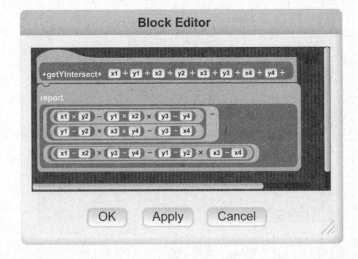

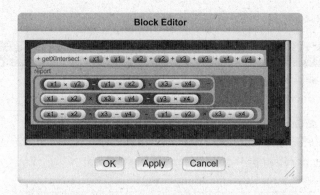

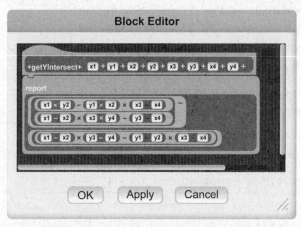

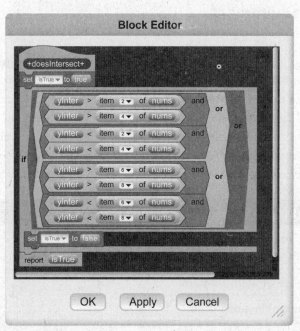

Score	This program will score HIGH because it contains an abstraction. Actually, it contains the doesIntersect, getXIntersect, getYIntersect, MoveSprite, drawLine, and getNum abstractions. The program also contains the algorithm doesIntersect, which contains both a logical algorithm along with a mathematical algorithm.
HIGH	

Checklist for High-Scoring Programming

Question	Yes	No
Does your program contain at least one INDEPENDENTLY DEVELOPED abstraction?		
Does your program contain one difficulty and/or opportunity that you encountered and resolved? Was development described as collaborative or independent (at least one of the difficulties must be resolved independently)?		
Does your program contain another difficulty and/or opportunity that you encountered and resolved? Was the development described collaborative or independent (at least one of the difficulties must be resolved independently)?		
Does your program contain two INDEPENDENTLY DEVELOPED algorithms?		
Does your program contain an INDEPENDENTLY DEVELOPED algorithm that combines the two algorithms?		
Does at least one part of your program run?		

Submission Requirements

Video

Submit one video in .mp4, .wmv, .avi, or .mov format that demonstrates the running of at least one significant feature of your program. **Your video must not exceed one minute in length and must not exceed 30 MB in size.**

There are many free screen-recording software options. PowerPoint Mix can be used to record your program running using screen recording. To record sound, a microphone is required. If your school blocks screen recorders or you do not have access to microphones, consider recording your program with a cell phone or external video recorder.

High-Scoring Video	Yes	No
Show and narrate your program compiling and running.		
Describe the purpose of your program.		
Identify the computer language used.		
Do not self-identify.		
Under 1 minute		

If you record your program running using your phone, most likely your video will exceed 30 MB. The College Board will not accept a video over 30 MB, so you will have to compress your video.

You can find an example video at *https://youtu.be/w8bJgXgOIPA*

Prompt 2a: *Program Purpose and Development*

Provide a written response or audio narration in your video that:
  Identifies the programming language.
  Identifies the purpose of your program.
  Explains what the video illustrates.

(Approximately 150 words)

The programming language I used was Java and I used the Java IDE environment Dr. Java.

The purpose of my program is to help people perform operations using numbers. It is meant to be used as a tool that can quickly do what would ordinarily be difficult for a person to do, like finding distance on a coordinate plane, finding missing values in functions, finding missing sides of triangles, and many more things. These types of functions are very useful when doing different types of math.

The video illustrates all five components of this program running, showing distance, triangle measurements, range, mass/density/volume, and time/speed/distance methods running. My video illustrates running the range for a 100-element array. It then shows the same range program running with 10 numbers in the data structure along with a 10,000 d=number data structure.

2b

Describe the incremental and iterative development process of your program, focusing on two distinct points in that process. Describe the difficulties and/or opportunities you encountered and how they were resolved or incorporated. In your description clearly indicate whether the development described was collaborative or independent. At least one of these points must refer to independent program development. *(Must not exceed 200 words)*

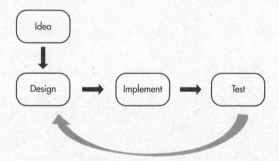

Your two points can be two opportunities or two difficulties or one opportunity and one difficulty. At least one of those points must have been resolved independently. Use the term "I" when referring to the independent process and "we" when referring to the collaborative process. The second point described can be either independent or collaborative.

While the process may have been collaborative, ALL writing must be done independently. When answering 2b take the reader through the entire development process. Don't just state the difficulty or opportunity.

I needed to fill up an array with randomly generated numbers. I created an abstraction called fillArray to compartmentalize the code and a while loop to access each element of the data structure. My difficulty is I tried to use the Random() method but it was giving me an error. I resolved this error by independently researching on Google "how to generate a random number in java." I discovered the website stackoverflow. It instructed me to import java.util. Random, then create a random object and use the method nextInt(50)+ 1. I implemented the code and it worked! I did have to change the 50 to a 100 because I wanted 100 random numbers, not 50.

I also had a difficulty in creating abstractions. I wanted to create an abstraction to return the maximum number in the array. When I compiled the program I got the following error.

2 errors found:

File: C:\Users\seth_\Documents\MySample.java [line: 17]

Error: nums cannot be resolved to a variable

File: C:\Users\seth_\Documents\MySample.java [line: 19]

Error: nums cannot be resolved to a variable

From the error I determined that the data structure I called nums scope is not covered by the abstraction. To fix this I looked at old code on codingbat.com and determined that I should pass nums as a formal parameter. My excitement was short lived as I got the following error.

1 error found:

File: C:\Users\seth_\Documents\MySample.java [line: 12]

Error: Cannot make a static reference to the non-static method getMax(int[]) from the type MySample

By looking at the error and noticing the words non-static method I changed my method header to include static as the second word of the method header. Success! The method now works as intended.

2c

Capture and paste a program code segment that implements an algorithm (marked with an **oval** in **section 3** below) and that is fundamental for your program to achieve its intended purpose. This code segment must be an algorithm you developed individually on your own, must include two or more algorithms, and must integrate mathematical and/or logical concepts. Describe how each algorithm within your selected algorithm functions independently, as well as in combination with others, to form a new algorithm that helps to achieve the intended purpose of the program. *(Must not exceed 200 words)*

```
178    public static void findRange()
179    {
180      range = findMax() - findMin()
181    }
182
183    public static int findMax()
184    {
185      int max = rangeNumbers[0]
186      for (int x=0; x<rangeNumbers.length; x++)
187      {
188        if ( rangeNumbers[x] > max)
189          max = rangeNumbers[x];
190      }
191      return max;
192    }
193
194    public static int findMIN()
195    {
196      int min = rangeNumbers[0]
197      for (int x=0; x<rangeNumbers.length; x++)
198      {
199        if ( rangeNumbers[x] < min)
200          min = rangeNumbers[x];
201      }
202      return min;
203    }
```

This algorithm's purpose is to find the range in a set of numbers previously inputted by the user. The method findRange() is called if the user selects the option 3. This algorithm first calls findMax(), which returns the maximum value in the set of numbers the user previously inputted. Next it calls findMin(), which returns the minimum value in the set. Individually, findMax() finds the largest number in the set by setting max equal to the first value then checking each following value, replacing max if the number is larger. Individually findMin() finds the smallest number in the set by setting min equal to the first value and checking every other value, replacing min if the number is smaller. Together, these two algorithims are used to make findRange() work by doing findMax() minus findMin() and prints the range value. This accomplishes the task of this algorithmic method to find range, an integral part of the entire function of the program to help with number functions.

Written Response 2d

Capture and paste a program code segment that contains an abstraction you developed individually on your own (marked with a rectangle in section 3). This abstraction must integrate mathematical and logical concepts. Explain how your abstraction helped manage the complexity of your program. *(Must not exceed 200 words)*

```
109    public static void findDistanceBetweenTheTwoPoints()
110    {
111      distance = Math.sqrt(xValuesSquared() * xValuesSquared());
112    }
113
114    public static int xValuesSquared()
115    {
116      int squaredx = (firstX - secondX) * (firstX-secondX);
117      return squaredx
118    }
119    public static void int yValuesSquared()
120    {
121      int squaredy = (firstY-secondY) * (firstY-secondY);
122      return squaredy;
123    }
124
```

The purpose of the abstraction findDistanceBetweenTheTwoPoints() is to take the two points that were inputted by the user in a previous abstraction and find the distance between them on the coordinate plane. This abstraction is called if the user selects option 1 when given their choices, which finds coordinate plane distance. After the method to collect the points has run, findDistanceBetweenTheTwoPoints() is called. Within this abstraction the formula for distance is used. However, to further manage the complexity, two more abstractions are called, both of which return integer values back to findDistanceBetweenTheTwoPoints(). The first method, xValuesSquared(), takes the first and second x values, subtracts them, then squares the difference. The second method, yValuesSquared(), is identical but uses y values. These values are returned to findDistanceBetweenTheTwoPoints(), where they are used as needed in the formula—added and then square rooted. This manages complexity because it allows anyone reading the program to see much more clearly what is going on. findDistanceBetweenTheTwoPoints() also manages complexity since it lets me more easily change my program if I wanted to move which option number I wanted distance to be. Were the method findDistanceBetweenTheTwoPoints() not in the program it would not properly function when the user chose option 1 to find distance as it serves to use the user's input to output the distance that they are looking for.

Abstraction

3

BIG IDEA 2: ABSTRACTION

"We are so much the victims of abstraction that with the Earth in flames we can barely rouse ourselves to wander across the room and look at the thermostat."

—Terence McKenna

Chapter Goals

- What is an abstraction?
- Machine code
- Binary sequences
- Software abstractions
- Converting numbers to decimal
- Overflow errors
- Models and simulations
- Programming levels
- Hardware abstractions
- Abstraction examples
- Converting numbers from decimal
- Roundoff errors
- Abstraction questions

What Is an Abstraction?

In computer science, an abstraction is a way to represent essential features without including the background details or explanations. Abstractions reduce complexity and allow efficient design and implementation of complex software systems. Abstraction become a necessity as systems become more complex. For example, any time you check your stories on Instagram you are using a bunch of processes in the background that you have no control over. Without these abstractions it would be difficult to send a message to a friend. With the use of abstractions you can focus on content, not the technical details of how the application works.

Programmers also use abstractions. Rarely will programmers deal directly in machine code. Machine code is a base language where no abstractions are implemented. Programmers have worked to hide details by using abstractions. This allows the user to focus on the problem. Think of it as comparable to a problem of driving. A user's job is to navigate a course at speed. Abstraction keeps the details "under the hood" so that the "driver can drive." The driver has his/her job and does not need to worry about what makes the engine run; abstraction allows the machine to run and the driver or user to navigate his or her challenge.

Programming Language Levels

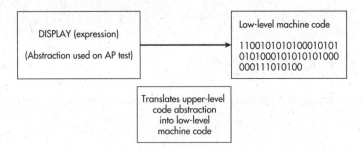

Abstractions find common features to generalize the program. This can also help shrink the code if you are planning to use a method/procedure more than once in a program. Instead of repeating the code lines you can reference a prior set of directions—to repeat the outcome without having to rewrite the lines of code. By reducing the number of lines of code, chances for errors are also reduced.

For example:

Adding the number 1234 + 4321 in an upper-level language with abstractions could look something like this for the language of JAVA: int $x = 1234 + 4321$. In Python it would look something like $x = 1234 + 4321$. Without abstractions and using just machine code the same math example would look like 10111001 11010010 0000011 100001001 00001110 00000000 00000000 10111001 11100001 00010000 10001001 00001110 00000010 00000000 10100001 00000000 00000000 1001011 00011110 00000010 00000000 00000011 11000011 10100011 00000100 00000000.

High-level languages contain the most abstractions and allow for easier coding and easier debugging.

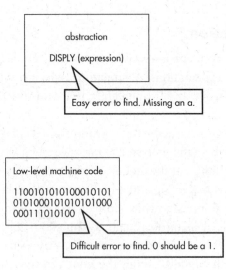

Hardware Abstractions

At the lowest level, computers are built on transistors. Transistors are tiny switches that have two settings: on and off. A binary off is represented by 0, and a binary on is represented by 1.

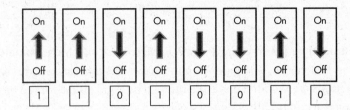

The current size of a transistor is approximately 10 nm long. More than 30,000 million transistors can fit on a single computer chip. The details of how semiconductors work is beyond the scope of this class.

To program a computer, we would have to feed it all 0's and 1's if not for abstractions. These low-level languages are extremely difficult to program and debug. To make programming easier, multiple layers of abstractions are used. Abstractions hide details, allowing the programmer to focus on solving problems.

At the lowest level, all digital data are represented by bits. For example, the letter *A* is an abstraction for 01000001. At a higher level, bits are grouped to represent abstractions, including but not limited to numbers, colors, characters, audio, and pictures.

BINARY SEQUENCES

A variety of abstractions built on binary sequences can be used to represent all digital data. Binary sequences can represent color, Boolean logic, lists, and so on. Anything that can be stored on a computer can be represented by binary sequences.

A pixel of light red can also be represented as binary numbers at the lowest level. For example, the maximum red value of a pixel is an abstraction for the binary number 1111 1111 0011 0011 0110 0110.

Abstraction Examples

The process of developing an abstraction involves removing detail and generalizing functionality. Different program languages offer different levels of abstractions. High-level programming languages provide more abstractions than lower-level languages. Coding in a programming language is often translated into code in another low-level language that the computer can execute.

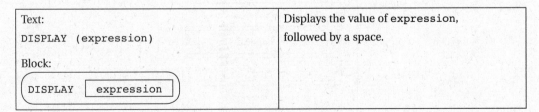

DISPLAY(expression) is an abstraction that is used on your AP test to display a value of expression followed by a space. The input parameter for the DISPLAY abstraction is expression.

Text: RANDOM (a, b) Block: RANDOM a, b	Evaluates to a random integer from a to b, including a and b. For example, RANDOM (1,3) could evaluate to 1, 2, or 3.

Another abstraction used on your AP test is RANDOM(*a*, *b*), which evaluates to a random number from *a* to *b* inclusive. The input parameters in this abstraction are *a* and *b*.

Both abstractions were coded one time but can be used an unlimited amount of times without rewriting the code. This code reuse saves time and can prevent errors when writing code.

An abstraction generalizes functionality with input parameters that allow software reuse. Being aware of and using multiple levels of abstractions in developing programs helps to more effectively apply available resources and tools to solve problems.

A way to handle complex tasks and ideas is to "chunk" them into smaller, more manageable concepts/sections. This allows us to address each term itself, rather than all the supporting components.

Software Abstraction Levels

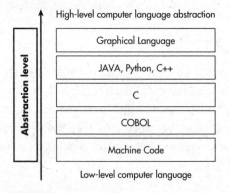

Hardware Abstraction Levels

Hardware also has levels of abstractions.

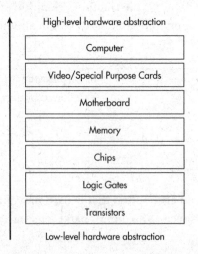

Converting Numbers

Number bases, including binary, decimal, and hexadecimal, are used to represent and investigate digital data.

Part of the AP test is converting numbers from any base to any other base. We will focus on the more popular conversions where the rules can apply to any conversion.

Decimal	Hexadecimal	Binary
0	0	0000
1	1	0001
2	2	0010
3	3	0011
4	4	0100
5	5	0101
6	6	0110
7	7	0111
8	8	1000
9	9	1001
10	A	1010
11	B	1011
12	C	1100
13	D	1101
14	E	1110
15	F	1111

Example One

Converting Binary (BIN) Numbers to Decimal (DEC)

$11011_{BIN} = ?_{DEC}$

Step 1. A five-column table is needed because 11011 has five numbers. Start by putting a 1 in the upper-right box of the five-column table.

				1

Step 2. Fill in the remaining first row by continually multiplying by the base. Because the base number is in binary, fill the columns by continually multiplying the product by 2.

$8 \times 2 = 16$	$4 \times 2 = 8$	$2 \times 2 = 4$	$1 \times 2 = 2$	1

Step 3. Place the numbers to be converted in the second row.

16	8	4	2	1
1	1	0	1	1

Step 4. Add the result of multiplying row one with row two.

$$16 \times 1 + 8 \times 1 + 4 \times 0 + 2 \times 1 + 1 \times 1 = 27_{DEC}$$

Example Two

$110_{BIN} = ?_{DEC}$

Use a three-column table and multiply the top row by the base number starting with 1 in the upper-right box.

4	2	1
1	1	0

Add the result of multiplying row one with row two.

$$4 \times 1 + 2 \times 1 + 1 \times 0 = 6_{DEC}$$

Example Three

$11011011_{BIN} = ?_{DEC}$

Use an eight-column table and multiply the top row by the base number starting with 1 in the upper-right box.

128	64	32	16	8	4	2	1
1	1	0	1	1	0	1	1

Add the result of multiplying row one with row two.

$$128 \times 1 + 64 \times 1 + 32 \times 0 + 16 \times 1 + 8 \times 1 + 4 \times 0 + 2 \times 1 + 1 \times 1 = 219_{DEC}$$

Hexadecimal (base 16)

Example Four

Converting Hexadecimal (HEX) Numbers to Decimal (DEC)

$12_{HEX} = ?_{DEC}$

Step 1. A two-column table is needed because 12 has two numbers. Start by putting a 1 in the upper-right box of the two-column table.

	1

Step 2. Fill in the remaining first row by continually multiplying by the base. The base number is in HEX, so fill the columns by continually multiplying the product by 16.

$1 \times 16 = 16$	1

Step 3. Place the numbers to be converted in the second row.

16	1
1	2

Step 4. Add the result of multiplying row one with row two.

$16 \times 1 + 1 \times 2 = 18_{DEC}$

Decimal (base 10) goes from 0 to 9, which contains 10 numbers.
Binary (base 2) goes from 0 to 1, which contains two numbers.
Hexadecimal (base 16) goes from 0 to 15, which contains 16 numbers. To represent the numbers 10 through 15 the letters A to F are used.

0	1	2	3	4	5	6	7	8	9	10	11	12	13	14	15
										A	B	C	D	E	F

Example Five

$2B_{HEX} = ?_{DEC}$

Use a two-column table and multiply the top row by the base number starting with 1 in the upper-right box.

16	1
2	11

Add the result of multiplying row one with row two.

$16 \times 2 + 1 \times 11 = 43_{DEC}$

Example Six

$AD_{HEX} = ?_{DEC}$

Use a two-column table and multiply the top row by the base number starting with 1 in the upper-right box.

16	1
10	13

Add the result of multiplying row one with row two.

$16 \times 10 + 1 \times 11 = 171_{DEC}$

Example Seven

Octal (base 8)
Converting Octal (OCT) Numbers to Decimal (DEC)

$28_{OCT} = ?_{DEC}$

Step 1. A two-column table is needed because 28 has two numbers. Start by putting a 1 in the upper-right box of the two-column table.

	1

Step 2. Fill in the remaining first row by continually multiplying by the base. Since the base number is in octal, fill the columns by continually multiplying the product by 8.

$1 \times 8 = 8$	1

Step 3. Place the numbers to be converted in the second row.

8	1
2	8

Step 4. Add the result of multiplying row one with row two.

$8 \times 2 + 1 \times 8 = 24_{DEC}$

Example Eight

$127_{OCT} = ?_{DEC}$

Use a three-column table and multiply the top row by the base number starting with 1 in the upper-right box.

64	8	1
1	2	7

Add the result of multiplying row one with row two.

$64 \times 1 + 8 \times 2 + 1 \times 7 = 87_{DEC}$

Example Nine

Converting Numbers from Decimal

$46_{DEC} = ?_{BIN}$

Step 1. Create a flexible table with enough columns until the number in the upper row is just bigger than the number you are converting to.

(64 is bigger than 46)

64	32	16	8	4	2	1

Step 2. Start with the largest number that is still smaller than the target number.

64	32	16	8	4	2	1
		1				

Subtract the table number from the base number.

$46 - 32 = 14_{DEC}$

Can 16 fit into 14? No, it cannot.

64	32	16	8	4	2	1
		1	0			

$14 - 0 = 14$

Can 8 fit into 14? Yes, it can.

$14 - 8 = 6$

64	32	16	8	4	2	1
	1	0	1			

Can 4 fit into 6? Yes, it can.

$6 - 4 = 2$

64	32	16	8	4	2	1
		1	0	1	1	

Can 2 fit into 2? Yes, it can.

$2 - 2 = 0$

64	32	16	8	4	2	1
		1	0	1	1	1

Can 1 fit into 0? No.

64	32	16	8	4	2	1
	1	0	1	1	1	0

Answer: 101110_{BIN}.

Example Ten

$30_{DEC} = ?_{BIN}$

Step 1. Create a flexible table with enough columns until the number in the upper row is just bigger than the number you are converting to.

32	16	8	4	2	1

Step 2. Start with the largest number that is still smaller than the target number.

$30 - 16 = 14$

32	16	8	4	2	1
	1				

$14 - 8 = 6$

32	16	8	4	2	1
	1	1			

$6 - 4 = 2$

32	16	8	4	2	1
		1	1	1	

$2 - 2 = 0$

32	16	8	4	2	1
	1	1	1	1	

0

32	16	8	4	2	1
	1	1	1	1	0

Answer: 11110_{BIN}.

Example Eleven

$130_{DEC} = ?_{HEX}$

Step 1. Create a flexible table with enough columns until the number in the upper row is just bigger than the number you are converting to.

256	16	1

$120 - (16 \times 8) = 2$

256	16	1
	8	

$2 - (1 \times 2) = 0$

256	16	1
	8	2

Answer: 82_{HEX}.

Example Twelve

$163_{DEC} = ?_{HEX}$

Step 1. Create a flexible table with enough columns until the number in the upper row is just bigger than the number you are converting to.

256	16	1

$163 - (16 \times 10) = 3$

256	16	1
	A	

$3 - (1 \times 3) = 0$

256	16	1
	A	3

Answer: $A3_{HEX}$.

Binary numbers can be conveniently represented by hexadecimal numbers, where one hexadecimal number represents four binary numbers.

Example Thirteen

Converting Hexadecimal to Binary

Convert BD_{HEX} to $_{BIN}$

B					D			
11					13			

8	4	2	1		8	4	2	1
1	0	1	1		1	1	0	1

Answer: $BD_{HEX} = 10111101_{BIN}$.

Example Fourteen

Convert $A9_{HEX}$ to $_{BIN}$

10					9			

8	4	2	1		8	4	2	1
1	0	1	0		1	0	0	1

Answer: $A9_{HEX} = 10101001_{BIN}$.

Example Fifteen

Convert EE_{HEX} to $_{BIN}$

15					15			

8	4	2	1		8	4	2	1
1	1	1	1		1	1	1	1

Answer: $EE_{HEX} = 11111111_{BIN}$.

Overflow Errors

In many programming languages a fixed number of bits is used to represent characters or integer limits. For example, in JAVA integers have a range from $-2,147,483,648$ to $2,147,483,647$. These limits can result in overflow or other errors.

Example One

What is the largest value stored using two bits?

2	1

The largest number would be 11_{BIN}.

2	1
1	1

$2 \times 1 + 1 \times 1 = 3$

The smallest number would be 0.

Two bits can store numbers from 0 to 3, which is 4 numbers, or 2^2.

If you try to store the number 4 or greater in a two-bit system, you will get an overflow error.

Example Two

Using a two-bit system, what would result in add $5 + 3$?

Answer: To store the number 8 would require a four-bit system, so this is an overflow error.

Example Three

What is the largest value stored using three bits?

4	2	1
1	1	1

Largest number: $4 \times 1 + 2 \times 1 + 1 \times 1 = 7$

Smallest number: 0

Two bits can store numbers from 0 to 7, which is 8 numbers, or 2^3.

If you try to store the number 9 or greater in a three-bit system, you will get an overflow error.

Example Four

What is the largest value stored using four bits?

8	4	2	1
1	1	1	1

Largest number: $8 \times 1 + 4 \times 1 + 2 \times 1 + 1 \times 1 = 15$

Smallest number: 0

Two bits can store numbers from 0 to 15, which is 16 numbers, or 2^4.

Example Five

What is the largest value stored using eight bits?

The largest number is 255: $2^8 = 256$ numbers from 0 to 255.

For every additional bit the amount of numbers stored is squared.

Roundoff Errors

A roundoff error occurs when decimals are rounded. One computer might calculate $\frac{1}{3} = .333333$. Another computer might calculate $\frac{1}{3} = .3333333333$. In this case $\frac{1}{3}$ on one computer is not equal to $\frac{1}{3}$ on a second computer.

At a higher level, bits are grouped to represent abstractions, including (but not limited to) numbers, colors, characters, audio, and pictures. Computer hard drives contain many bits of storage. For example, a computer with eight gigabytes of memory has 8,589,934,592 bits.

MODELS AND SIMULATIONS

Models and simulations use abstractions to generate new understanding and knowledge.

Models and simulations are tools frequently used to represent objects or phenomena that could not easily be replicated on a similar scale. Simulations are often used to test safety features or changes in business models without affecting customers while testing. The benefit of using a computer program to test a car crash, for example, rather than physically crashing a car is clear—it is less expensive and significantly less dangerous. The real crash, however, is affected by more variables than can be coded into a simulation and is more accurate as a result. Simulations require more abstractions as they become more complex; a simulation of a car crash will require more abstractions than one of a simpler task, such as dropping a ball from a given height.

The use of models and simulations allows for the user to gain insight on the workings of a particular object or phenomenon. The outcomes of each simulation or model accumulate to allow the formation of a hypothesis, or a proposed explanation of a phenomenon that serves as a starting point for further simulations. Testing a hypothesis through simulations is speedier and more easily done in comparison to testing a hypothesis through the real world. It allows testing in conditions that may not be possible on Earth, like that of a vacuum. The more detail put into testing a hypothesis, the more time and equipment required to run the program.

Generally, the more variables considered in a simulation, the more accurate the simulation is.

DIRECTIONS: Each of the questions or incomplete statements below is followed by four suggested answers or completions. Select the one that is best in each case.

1. Convert 100001_{BIN} to a decimal number.

   (A) 29
   (B) 33
   (C) 31
   (D) 63

2. Convert 111111_{BIN} to a decimal number.

   (A) 29
   (B) 33
   (C) 31
   (D) 63

3. Convert $2D_{HEX}$ to a decimal number.

   (A) 29
   (B) 33
   (C) 31
   (D) 45

4. Convert $1F_{HEX}$ to a decimal number.

   (A) 29
   (B) 33
   (C) 31
   (D) 45

5. Convert 1101_{BIN} to a decimal number.

   (A) 11
   (B) 1
   (C) 13
   (D) 1101

6. Convert 48_{HEX} to a decimal number.

   (A) 44
   (B) 54
   (C) 72
   (D) 89

7. Convert 8_{HEX} to a decimal number.

   (A) 44

   (B) 54

   (C) 72

   (D) 8

8. Convert AD_{HEX} to a decimal number.

   (A) 44

   (B) 54

   (C) 87

   (D) 173

9. Convert 48_{OCT} to a decimal number.

   (A) 40

   (B) 55

   (C) 80

   (D) 89

10. Convert AA_{HEX} to a decimal number.

    (A) 170

    (B) 180

    (C) 190

    (D) 200

11. Order the numbers from lowest to highest.

    I. 12_{HEX}

    II. 12_{DEC}

    III. 12_{OCT}

    (A) I, II, and III

    (B) III, II, and I

    (C) II, III, and I

    (D) I, III, and II

12. Order the numbers from lowest to highest.

    I. A_{HEX}

    II. 11_{DEC}

    III. 1111_{BIN}

    (A) I, II, III

    (B) III, II, I

    (C) II, III, I

    (D) I, III, II

13. Order the numbers from highest to lowest.

    I. AA_{HEX}
    II. 99_{DEC}
    III. 1111_{BIN}

    (A) I, II, III
    (B) III, II, I
    (C) II, III, I
    (D) I, III, II

14. Order the numbers from highest to lowest.

    I. AA_{HEX}
    II. 99_{DEC}
    III. 77_{OCT}

    (A) I, II, III
    (B) III, II, I
    (C) II, III, I
    (D) I, III, II

15. Convert 48_{DEC} to a binary number.

    (A) 110001_{BIN}
    (B) 110000_{BIN}
    (C) 110111_{BIN}
    (D) 111111_{BIN}

16. Convert 63_{DEC} to a binary number.

    (A) 110001_{BIN}
    (B) 110000_{BIN}
    (C) 110111_{BIN}
    (D) 111111_{BIN}

17. Convert 17_{OCT} to a binary number.

    (A) 10001_{BIN}
    (B) 1111_{BIN}
    (C) 10111_{BIN}
    (D) 11111_{BIN}

18. Convert AC_{HEX} to a binary number.

    (A) 10101100_{BIN}
    (B) 11001010_{BIN}
    (C) 11110000_{BIN}
    (D) 11111111_{BIN}

19. Convert 2A $_{HEX}$ to a binary number.

    (A) 00101010 $_{BIN}$

    (B) 11001010 $_{BIN}$

    (C) 11110000 $_{BIN}$

    (D) 11111111 $_{BIN}$

20. Convert 16_{HEX} to a binary number.

    (A) 10101_{BIN}

    (B) 10110_{BIN}

    (C) 11110_{BIN}

    (D) 11111_{BIN}

21.

Text: RANDOM (a, b) Block: RANDOM `a, b`	Evaluates to a random integer from a to b, including a and b. For example, RANDOM (1, 3) could evaluate to 1, 2, or 3.
Text: DISPLAY (expression) Block: DISPLAY `expression`	Displays the value of expression, followed by a space.

Which of the following is NOT possible using the RANDOM(a, b) and DISPLAY(expression) abstractions?

DISPLAY(RANDOM(2, 5))

    (A) 2

    (B) 4

    (C) 5

    (D) 6

22. Which of the following is NOT possible using the RANDOM(a, b) and DISPLAY(expression) abstractions?

DISPLAY(RANDOM(1, 4) + RANDOM(2, 5)

    (A) 6

    (B) 9

    (C) 1

    (D) 5

23. Which of the following will result in an overflow error in a three-bit system?

    (A) 3

    (B) 4

    (C) 6

    (D) 8

24. Which of the following will result in an overflow error in a four-bit system?

    (A) 6
    (B) 9
    (C) 15
    (D) 16

25. Which is the largest number that will NOT result in an overflow error in a five-bit system?

    (A) 30
    (B) 34
    (C) 32
    (D) 33

26. Which math solution could result in a roundoff error?

    (A) 1/3
    (B) 2 * 6
    (C) 6 − 2
    (D) 3 + 5

27. Many older computers were only designed to handle 8-bit systems, meaning that all numbers that the computers used could not exceed 8 bits in length. Which of the following hexadecimal numbers would NOT be viable in an 8-bit system?

    (A) 14_{HEX}
    (B) 34_{HEX}
    (C) 84_{HEX}
    (D) 100_{HEX}

28. Many computing languages store an integer in 4 bytes, limiting the range of numbers to from 2,147,483,648 to −2,147,483,647. Given that numbers can be of infinite size, why is this limitation put in place?
    Select two answers.

    (A) Programmers need numbers to be as small as possible because that limits rollover errors.
    (B) Most computed numbers are within this range, so 4 bytes is a reasonable size for most purposes.
    (C) Making an integer infinite would require so much space that it would be impractical for most uses.
    (D) No programmer ever needs a number outside of this range, so there's no point in extending the limit.

29. A programmer working for an architect needs to create a program to describe several properties with given names, areas, and images. Assume that the properties behave in an identical manner. What would be a benefit of creating an abstraction that uses these three as parameters?

(A) The parameters would allow all the objects to hold their own properties without requiring each to be coded separately.

(B) The abstraction would be able to account for every difference in the way the objects behave.

(C) The abstraction would make them harder to include in the code, which makes stealing and editing the program code more difficult.

(D) The use of an abstraction would ensure that each object's files can be edited.

30. Find the error in the following low-level programming code.

10111001 11010010 0000011 100001001 00001110 00000000 00000000 10111001 11100001 00010000 10001001 00001110 00000010 00000000 10100001 00000000 00000000 1001011 00011110 00000010 00000000 00000011 11000011 10100011 00000100 00000000 100001001 00001110 00000000 00000000 10111001 11100001 00010000 10001001 00001110 00000010 00000000 10100001 00000000 00000000 1001011 00011110 00000010 00000000 00000011 11000011 10100011

(A) The 17th 1 needs to be changed to a 0.

(B) This is too difficult. To determine errors, it would be considerably easier to use an upper-level language.

(C) The 34th 0 should be a 1.

(D) The 84th digit should be a 1.

31. Order the following programming languages from low-level language to high-level language.

* COBOL
* Python
* Machine code

(A) COBOL, Python, and machine code

(B) Python, machine code, and COBOL

(C) Machine code, COBOL, and Python

(D) All languages have equal level language.

32. Order the following hardware from low-level abstraction to high-level abstraction.

* Video card
* Transistor
* Computer

(A) Video card, transistor, and computer

(B) Transistor, computer, and video card

(C) Transistor, video card, and computer

(D) Hardware does not have abstraction levels.

33. Why is it usually easier to read code written in a high-level language than compared to a lower-level language?

    (A) High-level languages tend to be written by smarter people.

    (B) High-level languages tend to be closer to basic computer code, which makes it easier to translate them.

    (C) High-level languages tend to be written for more experienced programmers to use, which implicitly makes them easier to read.

    (D) High-level languages tend to be closer to natural language by utilizing simplified abstractions with descriptive names.

34. The abstraction Draw(magnitude, direction) is used to draw line segments at a given magnitude and direction (north, south, east, or west) starting at the tip of the first vector to the tail of the second vector. Consider the following program, where the vector starts in the upper-left corner of a grid of dots.

    Draw(2, south)
    Draw(1, east)
    Draw(2, east)
    Draw(1, north)

    Which of the following represents the figure that is drawn by the program?

    (A)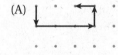

    (B)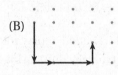

    (C)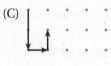

    (D)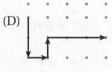

35. Taken as a whole, is a physical computer low-level or high-level?

    (A) Low-level, because the computer processes the lowest-level form of software

    (B) High-level, because the computer contains many lower-level components, such as the CPU

    (C) High-level, because the computer is capable of utilizing higher-level programming languages

    (D) Neither, as it is not software

36. Logic gates are physical hardware that are used to determine Boolean functions such as AND and OR. Given this, are Boolean functions abstractions?

   (A) Yes, they represent the activity of these gates in a manner that can be coded.
   (B) Yes, they represent the physical presence of the gates.
   (C) No, they are performed by processors; logic gates are merely a way to visualize this.
   (D) No, they are not abstractions because they deal with things at the bit level.

37. A theme park wants to create a simulation to determine how long it should expect the wait time at its most popular ride. Which of the following characteristics for the virtual patrons would be most useful? **Select two answers.**

   (A) Ride preference—denotes whether a patron prefers roller coasters, other thrill rides, gentle rides, or no rides.
   (B) Walking preference—denotes how far a patron is willing to walk in between rides.
   (C) Food preference—denotes the type of food that a patron prefers to eat (e.g., chicken, burgers, salads).
   (D) Ticket type—denotes whether the patron has a single-day pass, a multi-day pass, or an annual pass.

38. A programmer has created a program that models the growth of foxes and rabbits. Which of the following potential aspects of the simulation does NOT need to be implemented?

   (A) A representation of grass that rabbits must eat frequently to survive.
   (B) Each rabbit may only have a certain amount of children per litter.
   (C) Each fox must eat a rabbit frequently to survive.
   (D) Each rabbit can only live to a certain age, assuming that they are not eaten.

39. When the FAA investigates plane crashes, they often have high-level pilots replay the scenario to see if the situation could have been avoided. This is typically done using a moving simulator, as opposed to an actual airplane. Why?

   (A) A simulator is much clumsier to pilot than a real airplane, so the pilots' being successful is proof that an amateur pilot would be successful as well.
   (B) A simulator is much easier to pilot than a real airplane, so the pilots' failing is proof that any pilot would be unsuccessful.
   (C) If the crash could not be properly avoided, it would be much more expensive to replace a simulator than an actual airplane.
   (D) If the crash could not be properly avoided, this would put the pilots (and potentially others) in mortal danger.

40. The heavy use of chemicals called chlorofluorocarbons (CFCs) has caused damage to the Earth's ozone layer, creating a noticeable hole over Antarctica. A scientist created a simulation of the hole in the layer using a computer, which models the growth of the hole over many years. Which of the following could be useful information that the simulation could produce?

   (A) The approximate length of time until the hole would be refilled (due to various atmospheric processes)
   (B) The exact size of the hole at any given point in time
   (C) The exact length of time until the hole would be refilled (due to various atmospheric processes)
   (D) The exact depth of the hole at any point in time

41. Suppose that an environmentalist wanted to understand the spread of invasive species. What would be a benefit of doing this with a simulation, rather than in real life?

   (A) The species used in the simulation could be designed to mimic many different species at once.
   (B) The species created could be quickly tested in multiple environments to better understand how its spread is affected by environmental factors.
   (C) The simulation could be run much more quickly than in real life.
   (D) All of the above

42. A program is being created to simulate the growth of a brain based on randomly determined environmental factors. The developer plans to add a feature that lets the user quickly run several hundred simulations with any number of factors kept constant. Why would this be useful? **Select two answers.**

   (A) It would allow the user to gather data without taxing the computer's hardware.
   (B) It would allow the user to see the effect of specific variables by ensuring that the others do not change.
   (C) It would quickly provide the user with a large amount of data.
   (D) It would make simulations more detailed.

43. Which of the following computer languages have the highest level of abstractions?

   (A) COBOL
   (B) Machine code
   (C) Python/JAVA
   (D) All of the above

44. Which of the following has the lowest level of hardware abstraction?

   (A) Transistors
   (B) Computer chips
   (C) Motherboard
   (D) Computer

45. What number system has the lowest abstraction level?

   (A) Binary
   (B) Octal
   (C) Decimal
   (D) Hexadecimal

ANSWER KEY

1. **B**	13. **A**	25. **A**	37. **A, B**
2. **D**	14. **A**	26. **A**	38. **A**
3. **D**	15. **B**	27. **D**	39. **D**
4. **C**	16. **D**	28. **B, C**	40. **A**
5. **C**	17. **B**	29. **A**	41. **D**
6. **C**	18. **A**	30. **B**	42. **B, D**
7. **D**	19. **A**	31. **C**	43. **C**
8. **D**	20. **B**	32. **C**	44. **A**
9. **A**	21. **D**	33. **D**	45. **A**
10. **A**	22. **C**	34. **B**	
11. **B**	23. **D**	35. **B**	
12. **A**	24. **D**	36. **B**	

ANSWERS EXPLAINED

1. **(B)** Use a table for binary numbers.

32	16	8	4	2	1
1	0	0	0	0	1

$32 \times 1 + 1 \times 1 = 33$

2. **(D)** Use a table for binary numbers.

32	16	8	4	2	1
1	1	1	1	1	1

$32 \times 1 + 16 \times 1 + 8 \times 1 + 4 \times 1 + 2 \times 1 + 1 \times 1 = 63$

3. **(D)** Use a table for hexadecimal numbers.

16	1
2	D (13)

$16 \times 2 + 13 \times 1 = 45$

4. **(C)** Use a table for hexadecimal numbers.

16	1
1	F (15)

$16 \times 1 + 1 \times 15 = 31$

5. **(C)**

8	4	2	1
1	1	0	1

$8 \times 1 + 4 \times 1 + 1 \times 1 = 13$

6. **(C)**

16	1
4	8

$16 \times 4 + 1 \times 8 = 72$

7. **(D)**

1
8

$1 \times 8 = 8$

8. **(D)**

16	1
10	13

$16 \times 10 + 1 \times 14 = 174$

9. **(A)**

8	1
4	8

$8 \times 4 + 1 \times 8 = 40$

10. **(A)**

16	1
10	10

$16 \times 10 + 1 \times 10 = 170$

11. **(B)**

16	1
1	2

$16 \times 1 + 1 \times 2 = 18$ (highest)

$12_{DEC} = 12$ (middle)

8	1
1	2

$8 \times 1 + 1 \times 2 = 10$ (lowest)

12. **(A)**

1
10

$1 \times 10 = 10$ (lowest)

$11_{DEC} = 11$ (middle)

8	4	2	1
1	1	1	1

$8 \times 1 + 4 \times 1 + 2 \times 1 + 1 \times 1 = 15$ (highest)

13. **(A)**

16	1
10	10

$16 \times 10 + 1 \times 10 = 170$ (highest)

$99_{DEC} = 99$ (middle)

8	4	2	1
1	1	1	1

$8 \times 1 + 4 \times 1 + 2 \times 1 + 1 \times 1 = 15$ (lowest)

14. **(A)**

16	1
10	10

$16 \times 10 + 1 \times 10 = 170$ (highest)

$99_{\text{DEC}} = 93$ (middle)

8	1
7	7

$8 \times 7 + 1 \times 7 = 63$ (lowest)

15. **(B)**

$48 - 32 = 16$

$16 - 16 = 0$

64	32	16	8	4	2	1
	1	1	0	0	0	0

110000

16. **(D)**

64	32	16	8	4	2	1
	1	1	1	1	1	1

$63 - 32 = 31$

$31 - 16 = 15$

$15 - 8 = 7$

$7 - 4 = 3$

$3 - 2 = 1$

$1 - 1 = 0$

111111

17. **(B)**

8	1
1	7

$8 \times 1 + 1 \times 7 = 15$

32	16	8	4	2	1
	0	1	1	1	1

1111

18. **(A)**

10   12

8	4	2	1	8	4	2	1
1	0	1	0	1	1	0	0

10101100

19. **(A)**

2   10

8	4	2	1	8	4	2	1
0	0	1	0	1	0	1	0

00101010

20. **(B)**

1   6

8	4	2	1	8	4	2	1
0	0	0	1	0	1	1	0

00010110

21. **(D)** The RANDOM abstraction returns a value from *a* to *b* inclusive. The only number that is outside of the range is 6. RANDOM will pick a number from 2 to 5 inclusive. So 2, 3, 4, 5 are all equally possible.

22. **(C)** Low case $1 + 2 = 3$

High case $4 + 5 = 9$

The range of numbers is from 3 to 9 inclusive.

The only answer outside the range of 3 to 9 is 1.

23. **(D)** An overflow error occurs when trying to save a number too large for the bit storage in a three-bit storage system.

4	2	1
1	1	1

The largest number possible in a three-bit system is $4 \times 1 + 2 \times 1 + 1 \times 1 = 7$.

Anything greater than 7 will cause an overflow error.

24. **(D)** An overflow error occurs when trying to save a number too large for the bit storage in a four-bit storage system.

8	4	2	1
1	1	1	1

$8 \times 1 + 4 \times 1 + 2 \times 1 + 1 \times 1 = 15$.

Anything greater than 15 will cause an error.

25. **(A)** The largest number that will not result in an overflow error in a five-bit storage system is 30.

16	8	4	2	1
1	1	1	1	1

$16 \times 1 + 8 \times 1 + 4 \times 1 + 2 \times 1 + 1 \times 1 = 31$

Any number greater than 30 will cause an overflow error.

26. **(A)** A roundoff error occurs when computers round the final decimal place to different values.

For example, 1/3 could be equal to .3333333333333 or, depending on the second computer, .33333333333333333333333333. The two are not equal.

27. **(D)** Each digit in a hexadecimal number represents 4 bits. Since (D) is three digits long, it would need 12 bits to be sustained. The other three are only two digits, so they would work in an 8-bit system.

28. **(B), (C)** Most numbers are within the range of 2 to −2 billion. At the same time, a programmer does not want a number to take up an infinite space.

If a programmer wants a number outside the range he can use special large integers such as longs, but the number should not default to longs. A truly infinite integer would take an infinite number of bits to store, regardless of its value.

(A) is incorrect in its reasoning; while programmers need small numbers, this is to ensure that there is enough space for the millions of involved variables. (Also, smaller numbers make rollover errors more likely since there is less wiggle room.)

(D) is incorrect because there are reasons for having high limits, as evidenced by the existence of larger integer types.

29. **(A)** Parameters allow each object to be given certain properties, including the three listed in the question.

(B) is incorrect because the objects are specifically stated to behave in the same manner, making the purpose given unnecessary.

(C) is incorrect because abstractions, by design, make it easier to code by simplifying aspects.

(D) is incorrect because the edit-ability of variables is dependent on the way that the abstraction is coded (private variables within an abstraction cannot be edited).

30. **(B)** Lower-level machine code is extremely difficult to code and extremely difficult to debug, while an upper-level language is easier to code and debug. However, an upper-level language needs to be translated into a lower-level language before the computer can understand and run the code. So, upper-level languages still need to work with the lowest-level hardware abstractions, which can only understand 0's and 1's.

31. **(C)** The more abstractions in a language, the higher the order of the language. Machine code has no abstractions. COBOL, while a big step up from machine code, has some abstractions. Python, JAVA, and SNAP! all have a high number of abstractions and are the highest-level programming languages.

32. **(C)** Hardware, like software, has abstraction levels. The highest level is the complete computer itself. The lowest-level abstraction is the transistor, which is just an on/off switch. The middle abstraction levels are video cards or motherboards.

33. **(D)** High-level languages use enough abstractions to keep the text used close to English, which naturally makes them much easier to read. (Low-level languages tend to use blunt commands that are not particularly close to English.)

(A) is incorrect because the creator's intelligence rarely determines ease of use.

(B) is incorrect because making code close to computer code would make it much harder to read (see: Assembly).

(C) is incorrect because many high-level languages (C++, for one) are designed for adults to use. (However, most children's languages, such as NXT-G, are high-level because that makes them easier to use.)

34. **(B)** Following the order of commands, (B) follows the instructions.

35. **(B)** A computer is a high-level abstraction for all of the parts that encompass it.

(A) incorrectly links its abstraction level to the type of software that it processes, which is irrelevant.

(C) also states that the computer processes high-level languages, which it does not. (Compilers exist to translate high-level language.)

(D) is incorrect because hardware can still be abstracted.

36. **(B)** Boolean functions are abstractions for the commands that access and get the result from logic gates.

    (A) suggests that abstraction level is based on the number of parts, which is false.

    (B) is correct because using the physical presence alone would not determine a result. It also suggests that the abstraction level is based on the level of technology used, which is false.

    (C) is incorrect because logic gates are used in processors.

    (D) is incorrect because "at the bit level" only refers to the software, which is merely instructions for the lower-level hardware, and it suggests that chips are low-level, which is false because there are components within. The chip is high-level both before and after the new transistor is used.

37. **(A), (B)** A person's ride preferences and willingness to walk have the most effect on what they ride first (willingness to walk via distance to the ride from the gate), which has the most effect on lines. While the variables in (C) and (D) may have some effect (people may go to rides near the places they eat, and annual passholders may be more likely to try for less popular rides), they have a small enough effect that they can be ignored if necessary.

38. **(A)** Rabbits are capable of eating most plants, so the likelihood of them, realistically, running out of food is low. Implementing this would only make the simulation more needlessly complex.

    While (C) features a similar principle, requiring a fox to eat rabbits is a necessary complexity since the fox's food is far more limited.

    (B) is important for ensuring that the rabbit population grows at a natural rate, while (D) is simple enough to implement that it shouldn't be overlooked.

39. **(D)** A plane crash would endanger pilots and many other people, so using a simulator ensures that plane crashes do not actually harm the pilots.

    (A) and (B) suggest massive, intentional differences between a simulator and real life, which would distort the FAA's findings too much.

    (C) suggests that simulators are damaged and destroyed in a simulated crash, which is false.

40. **(A)** Measurements have been used for atmospheric simulations, which predict that the hole will be closed in about 2070. This is incredibly useful for atmospheric scientists and the public at large. (B), (C), and (D) all state that the information described is *exact*, which is not possible due to the fact that a model will never imitate such a large system perfectly.

41. **(D)** All three are true. The simulated species could be designed to show specific traits, be easily tested in multiple environments, and be run faster than a real-life experiment.

42. **(B), (D)** More efficient simulations mean more results, which can be used both to refine simulations and to create more detailed data.

(A) is incorrect because simulations are more efficient when there are as few variables and decisions as possible (and that means that the final code is faster).

(C) is incorrect because more efficient simulations work better on lower-end hardware because they require fewer resources.

43. **(C)** The higher the level of programming language, the more abstractions are used.

(A) is an upper-level language but does not contain as many abstractions as new programming languages such as Python or JAVA.

(B) Machine code has no abstractions and can be used directly by the computer.

44. **(A)** Hardware similar to software is built on abstractions. The lowest level is the transistor, which is the logic that all data on the computer is stored. Computer chips, motherboards, and computers contain transistors.

45. **(A)** The lowest-level number system is binary. Binary is 0 or 1, which in a computer is on or off voltage in a transistor. (B), (C), and (D) are all built off of binary.

Data and Information

4

BIG IDEA 3: DATA AND INFORMATION

"Information is the oil of the 21st century, and analytics is the combustion engine."

—Peter Sondergaard, senior vice president, Gartner

Chapter Goals

- Generating data
- Data visualization
- Data storage
- Privacy concerns
- Lossy and lossless compression
- Big data

- Predicting algorithms
- Processing data
- Collaboration
- Metadata
- Writing versus reading data

Generating Data

People generate significant amounts of digital data daily. Some always-on devices are collecting geographic location data constantly, while social media sites are collecting premium data based on your usage.

People can use computer programs to process information to gain insight and knowledge. Gaining insight from this valuable data involves the combination of statistics, mathematics, programming, and problem solving. Large data sets may be analyzed computationally to reveal patterns, trends, and associations. These trends are powerful predictors of future behavior. Investors are constantly reviewing trends in past pricing to influence their future investment decisions. However, sometimes trends can be misinterpreted and result in business disasters.

Big Data

Big data is data that is collected from traditional and nontraditional sources. Data collections can include data from product transactions, financial records, behavior, and social network interactions. Digital data can contain extremely large data sets that may be analyzed computationally to reveal patterns and trends. Computational tools are used to gain insights that can be drawn from large data sets.

Data can get too large for traditional data-processing applications. Social media activity generates an enormous amount of data. In the absence of a data-processing application, much of this data will go unexamined. This data is too large to examine all of the information by hand in real time. Tools such as spreadsheets, word processors, accounting software, and databases can sort and filter data to gain insight and knowledge. Data filtering is a strategy to take out data that is useless to the user. Data filtering can also be used to remove sensitive data like social security data before releasing data to third parties. Data filtering can increase privacy for the user of an application while still allowing the sale of that data to third parties.

Visualization of Data

Using appropriate visualizations when presenting digitally processed data can help one gain insight and knowledge. While big data is a powerful tool, the data will lose its value if it cannot be presented in a way that can be interpreted. Visualization tools can communicate information about data. Column charts, line graphs, pie charts, bar charts, XY charts, radar charts, histograms, and waterfall charts can make complex data easier to interpret.

For example, the following table plots users versus profit. Looking at the trends from this graph, it looks like a direct relationship exists between the number of users and profit. The company might want to invest in drawing more members or spending on advertisers to draw new members in.

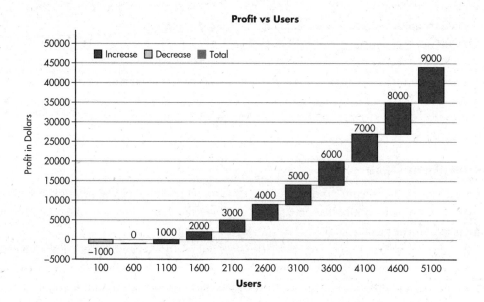

Predicting trends is not a guarantee of future usage. For example, the diagram above cannot predict an innovation that could make this current innovation obsolete. It can be dangerous to draw conclusions based on good data and assume that those conclusions apply across the board or that past patterns will remain consistent.

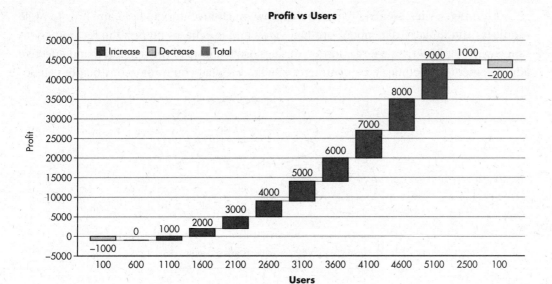

Profit vs Users

Predicting algorithms use historical data to predict future events. This data is used to build a mathematical model that encompasses trends. That predictive model is then used on current data to predict what will happen next.

Example Question:

What can be learned from the following data table kept in a pet store?

Date	Pet Food	City	Number of Times Purchased
7/2018	Kibbles	Orlando	10
7/2018	Bill-Jackson	Orlando	2
7/2018	Science Food	Altamonte Springs	23
7/2018	Bill-Jackson	Maitland	37
7/2018	Kibbles	Altamonte Springs	1

- The date when a certain dog food was purchased the greatest number of times
- The total number of cities in which a certain food was purchased
- The total number of foods purchased in a certain city during a particular month

Predicting Algorithms

Predicting algorithms can have an effect on our daily lives. For example:

- A credit card company can use purchasing patterns to identify when to extend credit or flag a purchase for possible fraud.
- Social media sites can use these patterns to target advertising based on viewing habits.
- An online store analyzing customers' past purchases can suggest new products the customer may be interested in.
- An entertainment application may recommend an additional movie to watch based on your interests.
- The algorithms can be used to prevent crimes by identifying crime "hot spots." The police then step up patrols in those areas.

e-commerce sites use data to determine how much inventory to hold and how to price products. Additionally, data about product views and purchases powers the recommendation engine, which drives a large portion of sales. Data allows for personalized and effective advertisement. Sometimes an e-commerce site knows what you want to buy before you do.

Example:

A high school principal is interested in predicting the number of students passing a state-level exam. She created a computer model that uses data from third-party software showing an increasing student pass rate for the exam. The model provided by the software company predicts a 90% student pass rate. The actual percentage of students passing the state exam was 74%. Which of the following is likely to provide a more accurate prediction?

- Refine the model to include data from more sources other than the third-party software due to the financial interest in the software being used.
- Refine the model to compare data for years when the new testing software was not used.
- Refine the model to include information about the community, such as redistricting.

Processing Data

Computing facilitates exploration and the discovery of connections in information.

Computers process data iteratively and interactively when processing digital information to gain insight and knowledge.

Iterative means that computers can go through all data in large data sets to filter, clean, and convert the unsorted data into sorted data.

Interactive means that people can gain insight and knowledge from translating and transforming digitally represented information.

Small chunks of incremental code are developmental and are integrated based on their completion. Interactive users give feedback to modify the development to refine programs. This process is then repeated for the life of the program.

Data Storage

The storing, processing, and curating of large data sets is challenging simply because of the amount of data it is now possible to obtain.

Large data sets are valuable to companies, and the storage of this data can result in significant costs. These costs are related to the increasing volume of data generated by people and the value of keeping all that data. Storage options can include cloud storage, mainframes, or local servers.

Historically it has been observed that computer processing speeds tend to double every two years, with the cost reduced at the same rate. This law, called Moore's law, can be helpful when companies predict their future storage costs.

With the rise of big data, storage concerns have also grown. There are trade-offs when deciding where to save your data. Cloud computing (not a real cloud but a remote server) can provide online storage and online resources, such as spreadsheets, word processing, email, and so on.

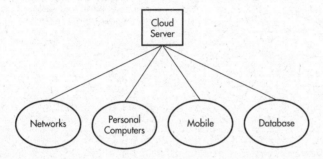

Sample Question:

The following is a list of how cloud computing has affected data storage:

- Cloud computing has reduced the need to store data on personal computers.
- Cloud computing has enhanced collaboration.
- Cloud computing has increased the need for internet connection.
- Cloud computing has introduced new security concerns.

If something physically breaks on your computer, your data is still safe on the cloud server. However, if internet access were not available in your area or there were a temporary loss of connection of your internet, your information stored on the cloud would not be available. Inexpensive computers can use the cloud to store data and run applications that would normally be accessible with high-priced equipment.

Collaboration

Current computing tools allow for people to collaborate by sharing data. Collaboration when processing information can help one gain insight and knowledge by applying multiple perspectives, experiences, and skill sets.

Collaboration with others can make the programmer more self-aware. Group programming can match up your weaknesses with someone else's strengths, which results in a better product and leads to insight and knowledge not obtainable when working alone.

Collaboration facilitates solving computational problems by applying multiple perspectives and skill sets by combining resources, talent, and experience. This knowledge gained by the group increases learning experiences for the entire group.

Privacy Concerns

Privacy concerns arise through the mass collection of data. The content of the data may contain personal information and can affect the choice in storage and transmitting.

Anything done online is likely to lead to an invasion of privacy. Using Gmail to order a pair of shoes from Clarks could result in ads for shoes showing up in your search engine. Geolocation is an API that, when used within a program, helps you find the approximate geographic location of an IP address along with some other useful information, including ISP, time zone, area code, state, and so on. The high volume of e-commerce makes it difficult to determine if you are dealing with a legitimate site or an illegal phishing site. Identity theft has become common and more significant. The trade-off for the convenience of online shopping is the risk of violating privacy.

Metadata

Metadata is data that describes your data—for example, a picture of you standing in front of a waterfall. The picture itself is the data. The information about the picture is the metadata. Where you took the picture, the time you took the picture, and who took the picture can all be considered metadata.

Metadata can increase the effective use of data or data sets by providing additional information about various aspects of that data.

Data: Picture of Dog (Novack 3rd) playing in the snow (Aspen)

Example Question:

A photo album contains metadata for each photo. The metadata is intended to help a search feature locate the popularity of geographic locations. All of the following are metadata:

- The picture's filename
- The location where the picture was taken
- The date the picture was taken
- The author of the picture

Lossy and Lossless Compression

There are trade-offs when representing information as digital data.

Digital data representations often involve trade-offs in quality versus storage requirements. Lossy compression can significantly reduce the file size while decreasing resolution. Traditionally, lossy compression is used to reduce file size for storage and transmitting (email). The trade-off of using lossy data is that you will not recover the original file. Some data will be lost.

Lossless and Lossy data compression

In lossless data compression, no data is lost. After compression the original file can be reproduced without any lost data. The trade-off of lossless data compression is larger files that can be difficult to store, transfer, and handle.

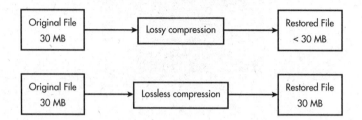

The choice of media storage affects both the methods and costs of manipulating the data it contains. Examples of storage devices are floppy disks, USB flash drives, memory cards, and cloud storage.

Writing versus Reading Data

Writing data is also known as storing data. Reading data is when you are retrieving the stored data. Writing data has a higher storage requirement rather than just reading the data. A file that is read-only requires assets currently being or about to be used. An updated file, however, requires the entire file to be saved in memory as the hard drive's copy is being rewritten so that the information is not lost.

1. Computers are described as processing data iteratively. What is the order in which a computer will process the following program?

   Line 1: $a \leftarrow 38$
   Line 2: $b \leftarrow 54$
   Line 3: $a \leftarrow b + a$
   Line 4: DISPLAY$(a + b)$

   (A) A computer will process all lines of code at once.
   (B) Computers process the metadata before pure data.
   (C) A computer will process data one step at a time in the given 1, 2, 3, 4 order.
   (D) A computer will display the value 92 while processing lines 1, 2, 3, and 4 at the same time.

2. An Alaskan biologist is tracking a pod (group) of whales. For the whales the following geolocation data is collected at frequent intervals.

   - Time
   - Data
   - Geological location of the sea mammals

   Which of the following questions about a whale could NOT be answered using only the data collected from the tracking collars?

   (A) Approximately how many miles did the animal travel in one week?
   (B) Does the animal travel in groups with other tracked animals?
   (C) Do the movement patterns of the animal vary according to the weather?
   (D) In what geographic location does the animal typically travel?

3. Large data sets are useful in finding patterns in the data that can predict future usage. Which of the following is used to predict future usage?

   (A) Calculating the monthly bill charged
   (B) Using past purchases to recommend products for possible purchase
   (C) Identifying the largest spending addresses
   (D) Identifying the time at which most purchases are made

4. Suppose that a company is creating an algorithm that matches people to advertisements that they might have an interest in. The company is basing its algorithm on a data source accumulated from data bought from social media. Which of the following sources would be useful for the algorithm?

(A) Information about a person's video-watching preferences (whether they watch viral videos, reviews, animations, etc.)
(B) A social network's information on what sites a person likes and follows
(C) Information on a person's previous purchases
(D) All of the above

5. Short message service (SMS) can be sent from one phone to another phone. Once the message is converted into binary form it is sent by radio waves to the control tower. Once the SMS travels through the control tower it arrives at the short message service center to be stored or sent immediately. In addition to sending the SMS, the cell phone carrier sends metadata.

Which of the following is NOT metadata?

(A) The time the message was sent and received
(B) The content of the SMS
(C) The geographic location of both the sender and the receiver
(D) The phone number of both the sender and the receiver

6. Spotify is a music streaming service that uses metadata collected to suggest future playlists. The metadata contains the album name, the genre, the tags describing the music, the mood of the music, and the time and date the music was played.

Which of the following CANNOT be determined using only the information contained in the metadata?

(A) The most popular current album
(B) The time when the streaming service is used
(C) Whether the streaming service is used more during inclement weather
(D) The least common mood of the audience

7. An online e-commerce site maintains a database containing the following information:

- Price
- Colors
- Quantity available
- Customer comments from the purchasing public

Using only the database, which of the following CANNOT be determined?

(A) How some of the buying public feel about their purchases
(B) The popularity of a color depending on the season
(C) When a color sold the most product
(D) When the most product was sold for a color

8. Google Trends is a website by Google that analyzes the popularity of top search queries in Google Search across various regions and languages. The large number of searches make Google Trends one of the world's largest real-time data sets. The data can be filtered so no one is personally identified, categorized, and grouped together.

Which of the following is Trends data most likely to answer?

(A) Whether the public is concerned about incoming weather
(B) What date is the cheapest date to book a hotel room
(C) The cost of a gas-powered chainsaw
(D) The length of the Iditarod

9. In 2000, the Chicago Public Schools set up a computing algorithm to detect teachers who had changed their students' answers on standardized tests. The algorithm would look at students' answers, with letters representing correct answers, a 0 representing a blank answer, and other numbers representing an incorrect answer. Which of the following is a way that the algorithm could have used this data?

(A) To look for consecutive answer patterns shared by students in the same class
(B) To look at the number of correct answers on harder questions
(C) To look for consecutive correct answers shared by students in the same class
(D) To look at the percentage of students who passed the test

10. A large data set contains information on students about to take the College Board's SAT test, including the following:

The student's parents' highest education level
The student's grade point average (GPA)
The student's intended college major
The college that the student is interested in
The student's current address
The student's high school name and location

Which of the following could NOT be answered by analyzing only information in the student data set?

(A) The number of students accepted to a college
(B) The number of students interested in a college major
(C) The average GPA for a college
(D) The college with the most interest from a high school

11. Suppose a team is creating a program that contains several different data-based algorithms. Which of the following would be the most effective strategy for creating the algorithms?

(A) Each algorithm is created and implemented by the entire group before the next one is started.
(B) Each algorithm is created by a different member, and one member tries to implement them as they are completed.
(C) Each algorithm is created by a different member and is implemented by the entire group after all algorithms are completed.
(D) Each algorithm is created and implemented by a different member based on particular strengths and experiences that the group agrees on at the start of programming.

12. Why might it be more beneficial to create processing algorithms with a team rather than alone? **Select two answers.**

   (A) Different team members will have different understandings of the concepts used, which can create stronger algorithms through their incorporation.
   (B) Team members will be able to socialize, which can speed up the development process by reducing fatigue.
   (C) Team members will compete with each other, resulting in the best algorithm being chosen.
   (D) Different team members will be skilled in different areas, so each part of the algorithm can be made by the most skilled in the necessary area.

13. What predictions can be made by using only the data provided in the following table?

Mass of object (kg)	Time it takes an object to fall one meter in a vacuum (s)
2	4.9
4	4.9
8	4.9
16	4.9
32	4.9
64	4.9

   (A) Doubling the mass results in half the time required to fall 1 meter.
   (B) Doubling the mass results in twice the time required to fall 1 meter.
   (C) Mass has no effect on time for an object to fall one meter in a vacuum.
   (D) Increasing the mass results in increasing the time to fall 1 meter in a vacuum.

14. The following data shows growth of companies (series 1 to series 4) versus time.

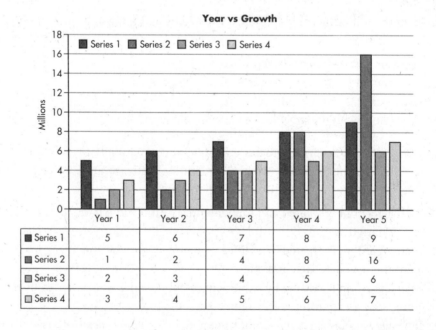

	Year 1	Year 2	Year 3	Year 4	Year 5
Series 1	5	6	7	8	9
Series 2	1	2	4	8	16
Series 3	2	3	4	5	6
Series 4	3	4	5	6	7

Which of the following series will show the greatest growth in year 6?

(A) Series 1
(B) Series 2
(C) Series 3
(D) Series 4

15. Which of the following **CANNOT** be determined using only the information in the database?

Date	Types of Cake	City	Number of Times Purchased
02/01/2015	Chocolate	New York City, New York	3
02/01/2015	Vanilla	Houston, Texas	2
02/01/2015	Marbled	Chicago, Illinois	4
02/01/2015	Red Velvet	Wichita, Kansas	1
02/03/2015	Chocolate	Orlando, Florida	2

(A) The date when a certain type of cake was purchased most
(B) The total number of times chocolate cake was purchased
(C) The total number of times a bakery sold a certain type of cake
(D) The total amount a certain type of cake was purchased in a city over a given month

16. A programmer is writing a program that is intended to process large amounts of data. Which of the following is likely to affect the ability of the program to process larger data sets?

(A) How well the program is documented
(B) The order in which the data is put into the data set
(C) How much memory the program requires to run
(D) How many program statements the program contains

17. Which of the following **CANNOT** be found using the provided table?

Date	Movie Title	State	Number of Times Rented
May 1, 2018	Movie A	Florida	10
June 15, 2018	Movie B	New York	11
August 15, 2018	Movie C	California	12
April 7, 2018	Movie A	Georgia	10
June 23, 2018	Movie C	Illinois	13
August 27, 2018	Movie B	Washington	14
July 3, 2018	Movie B	Maine	13
September 19, 2018	Movie A	Michigan	12

(A) The average number of rented movies for a given month
(B) The movie that was rented the most overall
(C) The number of times an individual person rented a movie
(D) The movie that was most popular

18. Some computer science companies have certain rules that members must meet face-to-face or over video chat a certain amount of times per week. Some companies have physical robots with screens for faces. What is the importance of these face-to-face meetings?

(A) Face-to-face interaction makes it easier to share and discuss information used in the project, compared to impersonal methods such as messaging.
(B) Face-to-face interaction is more convenient than any other form of communication.
(C) Impersonal methods such as messaging are more expensive than face-to-face methods.
(D) Face-to-face methods are more time efficient than impersonal methods.

19. Why do most data-analyzing programs include options for creating graphs?

(A) Graphs are less taxing on the computer's graphics card than a plain spreadsheet.
(B) Graphs make it easier to interpret data values, trends, and proportions, so they are an incredibly useful feature.
(C) It is easier to code a graph-based data analyzer than a spreadsheet-based one.
(D) It is harder to make spreadsheets properly display because the resulting file is not an image.

20. When the findings from a project are presented, they are typically presented using a graph as opposed to a table or raw data. Why might this be? **Select two answers.**

(A) Graphs can be easily placed into a slideshow or document, while tables cannot.
(B) Graphs can show trends that might not be easily seen with raw data.
(C) Graphs are able to show all the detail necessary to understand data.
(D) Graphs are easier to read and interpret at a glance.

21. Google's website Trends provides information about the frequency of searches made using the search engine. Why might this be more useful than a similar tool offered by smaller search engines? **Select two answers.**

    (A) Google is the largest search engine, so its results are guaranteed to be accurate.
    (B) Google is a more popular search engine; therefore, it will have a larger data set, creating more accurate data.
    (C) Google's competitors might primarily be used by certain demographics (scholars, politicians, etc.), distorting the data in comparison to the broad reach of Google.
    (D) Google tracks the popularity of websites present in its search results, so it can show more accurate data about its responses.

22. Which of the following is a uniquely useful feature of search engines?

    (A) The ability to distinguish between different versions of something (e.g., differentiating a 1984 film from its 2005 remake)
    (B) The ability to find and filter information from a large variety of sites
    (C) The ability to find basic information such as creators or release dates
    (D) The ability to find information originally released in print form

23. Suppose that a team was creating an online registry of the books in a library system. The purpose of the registry is to make it easier to find a certain book by using both filters and searches. Which of the following would NOT be a useful way for a user to filter the entries?

    (A) The genre of the book
    (B) The library/libraries in the system that have a copy of the book
    (C) The author of the book
    (D) The number of letters in the book's title

24. A small business needed a way to keep track of their profit and expenses daily. The following are features of the spreadsheet application. Which of the following would be of most use to the business? **Select two answers.**

    (A) The ability to easily create a graph of the data
    (B) The ability to create and add map charts
    (C) The ability to have specified rows (such as total profit) update automatically
    (D) An error checker that finds errors in advanced formulas

25. Which of the following is an example of metadata that serves to be descriptive of the content of a file?

    (A) User-selected tags (e.g., "Vacation," "Personal Work")
    (B) File size
    (C) Date created
    (D) Program used to read the file

26. Which of the following can metadata use to improve the use of actual data?

    (A) Files can be sorted by date of creation to make finding an old file easier.
    (B) The Author and Organization fields in documents can be used to keep track of the source of a document.
    (C) The length of a set of videos can be used to determine the way that those videos should be presented.
    (D) All of the above

27. Why might it be far harder for companies to maintain the privacy of larger data sets than smaller ones? **Select two answers.**

    (A) Large data sets are more insecure simply by nature of their size.
    (B) Large data sets have more opportunities for attacks because there tend to be more access channels.
    (C) Large data sets are bigger targets for hackers, so they are more likely to receive attacks more sophisticated than security protocols can handle.
    (D) Large data sets are easier for thieves to navigate.

28. Why is it important that online systems with large data sets be scalable?

    (A) If the workload placed on the system increases, the resulting decrease in performance can be mitigated.
    (B) If the workload placed on the system increases, the resulting increase in performance can be mitigated.
    (C) If a system is scalable, all future programs will run faster.
    (D) If a system is scalable, all future programs are guaranteed to run properly.

29. Which of the following is an example of a way to improve the **transmission** of large data sets?

    (A) Encryption—uses a public key to scramble the code and requires a specific private key for it to be reassembled properly.
    (B) Compression—files are made smaller by utilizing an algorithm and then must be uncompressed by the receiver.
    (C) SMS—a client and server periodically send small messages to each other to ensure that the connection between them has not been severed.
    (D) Emulation—a computer runs a program that allows it to behave like another machine.

30. Which of the following is a trade-off inherent in lossy compression ease of handling?

    (A) Smaller file size (bytes)
    (B) Viewing ability
    (C) Image quality
    (D) Image size (pixels)

31. Which of the following is a way to protect data containing personal information?

    (A) Encryption—uses a public key to scramble the code and requires a specific private key for it to be reassembled properly.
    (B) Compression—files are made smaller by utilizing an algorithm and then must be uncompressed by the receiver.
    (C) SMS—a client and server periodically send small messages to each other to ensure that the connection between them has not been severed.
    (D) Emulation—a computer runs a program that allows it to behave like another machine.

ANSWER KEY

1. **C**	9. **A**	17. **C**	25. **A**
2. **C**	10. **A**	18. **A**	26. **D**
3. **B**	11. **D**	19. **B**	27. **B, C**
4. **D**	12. **A, D**	20. **B, D**	28. **A**
5. **B**	13. **C**	21. **B, C**	29. **B**
6. **C**	14. **B**	22. **B**	30. **C**
7. **B**	15. **C**	23. **D**	31. **A**
8. **A**	16. **C**	24. **A, C**	

ANSWERS EXPLAINED

1. **(C)** "Iterative" refers to a repeated process, which is how computer code is processed. Each piece of data is put through a process, which is repeated for every piece.

   (A) would require multiple lines of code to be evaluated at once. To correctly calculate line 3, lines 1 and 2 would have needed to be evaluated first.

   (B) is dependent on the program in question (most don't even require metadata).

   (D) is the value of $a + b$ without changing the value of a.

2. **(C)** Searching for patterns in big data can be used in careers other than strictly computer science. Tracking whales is one such example. Because this data is tracking multiple whales, it would be possible to know if this whale was traveling with other whales, the typical travel patterns, and how many miles the animal travels weekly.

   (A), (B), and (C) can be determined using strictly the data. While (C) can be determined by matching up the whale data with weather data, it would require the addition of another data set. Since the question was what can be determined by just using the one data set the answer would be (C). That was a whale of a question.

3. **(B)** Companies use computer programs to process information to gain insight and knowledge. Large data sets provide opportunities and challenges for extracting information and knowledge. Past purchases can be used to suggest future purchases. For example, if a puppy is purchased from Amazon, the next time the customer visits Amazon the site might suggest dog food. Choices (A), (C), and (D) do not make predictions, but instead make calculations based on the actual data.

4. **(D)** Combining data sources, clustering data, and data classification are all part of gaining insight and knowledge of customer preferences. There is little data that is not filtered and cleaned for use in targeted advertisements. A person's viewing habits might show interests or where the user is likely to view ads. Which sites a user follows and likes can lead to sales in products related to those sites. Previous purchases like buying a pet would be valuable to pet food companies.

5. **(B)** Metadata is data about the data. The actual data in this example is the content of the SMS message. Metadata is descriptive data and can provide additional information about various aspects of that data. Time (A), geographic location (B), and phone numbers (C) are all metadata.

6. **(C)** Combining data sources is part of the process of using computers to process information. To determine if the streaming service is used more during a hurricane would require an additional data set that includes weather.

Choices (A), (B), and (D) are all data about the data (metadata). Spotify uses this metadata to suggest music to the user to increase his or her positive experience with Spotify so the customer will continue using their product.

7. **(B)** Summaries of data analyzed computationally can be effective in communicating insight and knowledge gained from digitally represented information. An additional data set containing date and location would be needed to determine season.

(A), (C), and (D) can be determined by examining the data set only.

8. **(A)** Google Trends looks up what people search, but not the content contained on the searched websites. When the public is concerned about a topic they tend to search to find resources to examine the situation. People searching for a flight will not indicate the price of the flight. While people may search for a gas-powered chainsaw, the search itself will not indicate the price. Searching for hurricanes indicates interest/concern, but not the path of a hurricane.

9. **(A)** The algorithm was set up to look for patterns in the data, whether that was a string of correct answers shared by many students or the same incorrect answer being shared by many students. (For example, in one instance, 15 of 22 students shared a string of seven identical answers. Six of these were correct answers for the hardest questions, with no comparable string in the easier sections.)

(B) and (D) are both too broad and would likely catch teachers with a large number of prepared students.

(C) leaves out the search for incorrect answers, which can be even more telling because students rarely reach the *wrong* conclusion at the same time.

10. **(A)** The College Board collects data to gain insight on students taking College Board tests. While the College Board collects significant data, that data does not include if a student was accepted into and attended a college. The College Board will combine the data to gain insight and knowledge, but it has no access to the students nor college decisions on acceptance from this data set.

11. **(D)** Splitting up the group work enables multiple algorithms to be worked on at once and allows group members to play to their strengths. Creating specifications is likely to make the finished work easier to implement and more cohesive.

(A) would only create one algorithm at a time, which would likely be too slow to be effective.

(B) would force the person tasked with implementing to wait for work, and the final workload would likely be difficult to handle.

(C) would require group members to wait for all algorithms to be completed if they finish early and still requires the implementation to be done one at a time, slowing work.

12. **(A), (D)** Different team members approach problems with different ways of viewing them and different skill sets, so having multiple team members means that all of these differences can be put to use in development.

(B) does correctly state that teamwork can speed up development, but the way that this is proposed is incorrect, as socializing is a distraction.

(C) might occur, but that is dependent on the structure of the team, so the use of "will" is not appropriate.

13. **(C)** The table only includes data on mass and time. Since time does not change with a changing mass, it can be assumed that mass and time are unrelated for objects in a vacuum.

(A), (B), and (D) cannot be supported based on the table alone because time is not changing.

14. **(B)** Series 2 has an exponential growth.

(A), (C), and (D) start higher and the growth rate is slower than the growth rate of series 2. Exponential growth gets very large very quickly.

15. **(C)** The bakery name is not included in the table. The data, type, location, and quantity of cake is recorded. If the question is asking for information using only the database, no predicting is allowed. Just state what you can determine is in the table.

16. **(C)** If the computer does not have enough memory it will not be able to run the program. With very large data sets memory is a factor.

(A) Program documentation enables team members to discuss work made in the suite, which enables members to share understanding without erasing original work. The amount of documentation does not affect runtime of a program as documentation is ignored by the computer.

(B) As long as the data is in the format expected it will not make a difference in what order the data was entered.

(D) The user does not care if the program was written in 10 lines or 200 lines. While the programmer strives to make her program the shortest amount of steps, what type of loop used has little effect on runtime.

17. **(C)** The person renting the movie is not included in the data table. Date, movie name, state, and quantity are recorded. If the question is asking for information using only the database, no predicting is allowed. Just state what can be determined from the table.

18. **(A)** Face-to-face interaction enables the presence of emotions, back-and-forth discussion, and the use of physical items such as a whiteboard. These are also present when using a video chat program such as Skype or FaceTime or similar applications.

(B) Face-to-face interaction is not more convenient than other forms of communication, as both people must be able to work at the same time (while messaging works with a gap between responses).

(C) Impersonal methods tend to be cheaper (face-to-face needs transportation to a common area, while video chat often charges like a phone plan).

(D) Face-to-face discussions can include emotional tangents and arguments that can eat up time.

19. **(B)** Graphs are useful for summarizing and finding trends in data, so a quick way to create them makes it easier to find abnormalities or reach conclusions.

(A) The inherently graphical nature of graphs makes them more taxing than the formatted text of a basic spreadsheet.

(C) Coding a graph-based analyzer requires graphical aspects, which are harder to code.

(D) Spreadsheets can be easily displayed regardless of the file with decent coding and design.

20. **(B), (D)** Graphs can illustrate trends in a manner that is easier to digest than the numbers that make up raw data.

(A) Tables can be added to an office suite's applications easily.

(C) Different types of graphs can only show specific aspects of data (e.g., a line graph only shows trends, while a pie chart only shows proportions).

21. **(B), (C)** Google is by far the most popular search engine, so it has a large data set and a broad range of users. This would create the most general (and therefore most accurate) trends and connections. (A) makes a poor assumption (**never** assume that a single source is always correct!), while (D) discusses the popularity of websites, which is not the goal of Google Trends.

22. **(B)** The benefit of a search engine is that it consolidates all available websites, which may provide different information or perspectives (e.g., fan reactions versus critical analysis).

(A) and (C) can be done in online encyclopedias and databases (through filtering and differentiating text).

(D) could be found on online archives (e.g., *The New York Times's* website has many pre-internet articles in their online archive).

23. **(D)** The length of a book's title, while it can be easily used as a filter, would have little use as such. The length of a title is not something most people would be able to utilize, as they likely do not know the title of the book (much less the length of the title) they are looking for. (A) would be useful for finding books of a certain genre, which is a common need in searches.

(B) would be useful for people to determine which books they can find in their local library (and which ones they will have to place a hold request for).

(C) would be useful for finding works by an author someone admires.

24. **(A), (C)** Creating a graph like (A) would help the business observe changes in its profits and expenses, suggesting reasons for sudden changes to the bottom line. (C) would make the spreadsheet easier to edit by requiring fewer changes for all information to be accurate.

(B) is incorrect because map charts (which demonstrate relationships between various entities) would be of little use to a simple finance-management scheme.

(D) is incorrect because it is unlikely that a simple scenario such as this would require the advanced formulas that would make use of the error checker.

25. **(A)** Tags can be attached to a file by a user to describe the content within, which makes it easier to find and sort files. Their purpose is specifically to describe content.

(B), (C), and (D) are used to describe the file itself, as opposed to the content (subject, format, etc.) of the file.

26. **(D)** All of these are legitimate uses.

(A) can be utilized in most environments as long as the date of creation is known.

(B) can be used as long as the fields are filled out (which is often done automatically).

(C) could be used to determine the videos usable in a time crunch or the order in which they should be displayed (in case people might be leaving early, for example).

27. **(B), (C)** Large data sets are a gold mine for information thieves, so attackers are more likely to be chasing a way in. Large sets also tend to have more ways in (to accommodate the large amount of information requests), which means that there are more chances for a broken or weak channel to be exploited.

(A) assumes that the only determination of security is the information involved, when the determination is primarily the protocols used to try to prevent breaches.

(D) More data would actually make data sets harder to navigate because the organization scheme can be made more complex and hackers would need to sift through more data to find specific information. (Note, however, that this isn't a huge deal for most hackers, who merely want a volume of information as opposed to information about a specific user.)

28. **(A)** Scalable systems demonstrate improved performance when additional hardware is added to the system. The benefit here is that the potential workload can be increased without damaging overall performance.

(B) suggests that an increased workload would lead to better performance, which is false.

(C) Improvements to the system don't come automatically.

(D) is incorrect because performance is not guaranteed to make all programs work; some do not work due to software factors such as architecture.

29. **(B)** Large files can take time to transmit, so compressing them makes the amount of data that must be transmitted smaller so that they can be sent in less time (and, in some instances, with fewer restrictions).

(A) is used to improve privacy, (C) is used to ensure connectivity, and (D) is used to ensure compatibility.

30. **(C)** Lossy compression creates a lower-quality image than lossless, and the decrease in quality cannot be undone.

The smaller size in (A) is actually a benefit of lossy, while the factors in (B) and (D) do not change with the style of compression.

31. **(A)** Encryption is utilized when storing data on servers to ensure that the data cannot be read if it was illegitimately received. This serves to protect data.

(B) improves communication ability.

(C) ensures connectivity.

(D) ensures compatibility.

Algorithms

5

BIG IDEA 4: ALGORITHMS

" *An algorithm must be seen to be believed.*"

—Donald Knuth

Chapter Goals

- Mathematical operators
- Modulus
- Display operators
- Relational and Boolean operators
- Logical operators
- Boolean logic
- The swap

- Order of operations
- Assignment operators
- Input operators
- Numeric procedures
- Random
- Robot
- Examples

Mathematical Operators Used on the Exam

Operator	Meaning	Example
+	Addition	$5 + 7 = 12$
−	Subtraction	$2 - 1 = 1$
*	Multiplication	$3 * 3 = 9$
/	Division	$3/2 = 1.5$
MOD	Modulus	$3 \text{ MOD } 2 = 1$

Order of Operations

a. Parentheses

b. MOD

c. *, /

d. +, −

Example One

$3/2 = 1.5$

As there is only one operation in this example, simply divide 3 by 2 for a final answer of 1.5.

Example Two

$6 + 3 * 5 = 21$

In accordance with the order of operations, first multiply 3 by 5 to get a product of 15. Then, add 6 to 15 for a final answer of 21.

Example Three

$8/2 \times 10 = 40$

When operators have the same precedence, the equation should be evaluated left to right. For instance, this equation contains both division and multiplication. In this case, first divide 8 by 2 to get a quotient of 4. Then multiply 4 by 10 for a final answer of 40.

Example Four

$17 - 5 + 12/4 = 15$

3
12

In this example, first divide 12 by 4 to get a quotient of 3. Then, since addition and subtraction have the same precedence, evaluate the problem from left to right—subtract 5 from 17 for a difference of 12, then add 3 for a final answer of 15.

How to Solve Modulus (MOD)

Although "modulus" may be a new term for beginning programmers, the actual operation is one that should be familiar to those who know long division. A **modulus** is a mathematical operation that returns the remainder after an initial number (the **dividend**) is divided by another number (the **divisor**). Moduli are often used to determine whether a number is even or odd.

Example Five

10 MOD 3

1. When solving, understanding which number is the dividend and which number is the divisor is crucial. It is important to note that when in a modulus operation, the number to the left of MOD is always the dividend and the number to the right of MOD is always the divisor. In this case, the dividend is 10 and the divisor is 3. A trick to remember this is to say: "Put the first number in the house."

1ˢᵗ number goes in the house!

2. Once you determine which number is the dividend and which is the divisor, set the problem up as a long-division equation. Make sure to place the dividend inside the long-division bracket (in the house) and the divisor outside the long-division bracket.

3 | 10

3. Then, solve the long-division equation and find the integer remainder, which is the modulus answer.

$$
\begin{array}{r}
3 \\
3 \overline{\smash{)}\, 10} \\
-\ 9 \\
\hline
1 \ \text{(Remainder is 1)}
\end{array}
$$

4. Thus, the answer to 10 MOD 3 = 1.

NOTE

1. If the divisor is a multiple of the dividend, it will divide evenly with no remainder, resulting in a modulus calculation of 0.
2. If the dividend is less than the divisor, the resulting modulus calculation will equal the value of the dividend.
3. A zero to the right of MOD results in a DIVIDE BY ZERO error.
4. A zero to the left of MOD is feasible and results in a modulus calculation of 0.

Example Six

The modulus is the integer remainder when two numbers are divided.
4 MOD 3

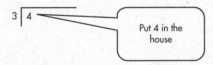

The dividend is 4, and 3 is the divisor. Three goes into 4 one time. Write a 1 on top and multiply it by the divisor. One multiplied by 3 is 3, and then 3 is subtracted from 4. Four minus 3 is 1, which is the remainder. The remainder is the answer.

Example Seven

8 MOD 2

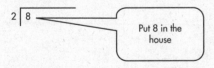

The dividend is 8, and 2 is the divisor. Two goes into 8 four times. Write a 4 on top and multiply it by the divisor. Four multiplied by 2 is 8, and then 8 is subtracted from 8. Eight minus 8 is 0, which is the remainder. The remainder is the answer.

Example Eight

6 MOD 2

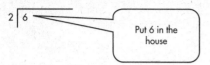

The dividend is 6, and 2 is the divisor. Two goes into 6 three times. Write a 3 on top and multiply it by the divisor. Two multiplied by 3 is 6, and then 6 is subtracted from 6. Six minus 6 is 0, which is the remainder. The remainder is the answer.

Example Nine

5 MOD 2

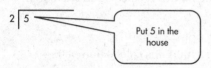

The dividend is 5, and 2 is the divisor. Two goes into 5 two times. Write a 2 on top and multiply it by the divisor. Two multiplied by 2 is 4, and then 4 is subtracted from 5. Five minus 4 is 1, which is the remainder. The remainder is the answer.

Example Ten

13 MOD 2

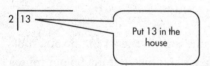

The dividend is 13, and 2 is the divisor. Two goes into 13 six times. Write a 6 on top and multiply it by the divisor. Six multiplied by 2 is 12, and then 12 is subtracted from 13. Thirteen minus 12 is 1, which is the remainder. The remainder is the answer.

Example Eleven

4 MOD 6

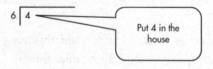

The dividend is 4, and 6 is the divisor. Six goes into 4 zero times. Write a 0 on top and multiply it by the divisor. Zero multiplied by 4 is 0, and then 0 is subtracted from 4. Four minus 0 is 4, which is the remainder. The remainder is the answer.

Example Twelve

3 MOD 4

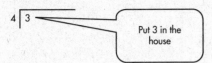

The dividend is 3, and 4 is the divisor. Four goes into 3 zero times. Write a 0 on top and multiply it by the divisor. Zero multiplied by 4 is 0, and then 0 is subtracted from 3. Three minus 0 is 3, which is the remainder. The remainder is the answer.

Assignment Operators

Text: a ← expression Block: a ← expression	Evaluates expression and assigns the result to the variable *a*.

NOTE

- First, the expression is evaluated, which then sets the value to the appropriate variable.

Examples

What is the value of *a* after the expression is evaluated?

a ← 3	a = 3

a is equal to 3.

a ← 4 * 5 + 6	a = 26

First multiply 4 by 5 to get 20, then add 6 to get 26.

a ← 26 MOD 2	a = 0

Two goes into 26 13 times, so 26 minus 26 is 0. *a* is equal to 0.

a ← 17 MOD 2	a = 1

Two goes into 17 8 times, so 16 minus 17 is 1. *a* is equal to 1.

a ← 33 MOD 1	*a* = 0

1 goes into 33 33 times, so 33 minus 33 is 0. *a* is equal to 0.

Display Operators

Text: DISPLAY (expression) Block: ``` DISPLAY expression ```	Displays the value of expression, followed by a space

What will the following program display?

a ← 3

Since *a* is equal to 3, the program will display 3.

b ← 17

Since *b* is equal to 17, the program will display 17.

a ← *b*

Since *a* is equal to the value of *b* and the value of *b* is 17, the program will display 17.

DISPLAY (*a*)

As shown by the following chart, all variables must be initialized before *a* can be printed. *a* is initialized to the value of 3, and *b* is set to 17. The next step sets *a*'s value to *b*'s, which is 17.

	a		*b*
3	17		
17			

Answer: 17

Example Thirteen

What will the following program display?

a	*b*	I
3	14	5
5	5	

$a \leftarrow 3$
$b \leftarrow 14$
$c \leftarrow 5$
$a \leftarrow c$
$b \leftarrow a$
DISPLAY (a)
DISPLAY (b)
DISPLAY (c)
Answer: 5 5 14

Example Fourteen

What will the following program display?

$a \leftarrow 5 + 4 * 2$

$b \leftarrow 4 \text{ MOD } 5$

DISPLAY $a + b$

a	b	DISPLAY
5 + 8 = 13	4 MOD 5 = 4	13 + 4 = 17

Answer: 17

Input Operators

Text: INPUT ( ) Block: INPUT	Accepts a value from the user and returns it.

Example Fifteen

What will the following program display if the INPUT function reads an even number such as 4?
$a \leftarrow$ INPUT ( )
$a \leftarrow a \text{ MOD } 2$
DISPLAY (a)
For 4 (or any even number) divided by 2, the remainder will always be 0 …
Answer: 0

Example Sixteen

What will the following program display if the INPUT function reads an odd number such as 5?

$a \leftarrow$ INPUT ( )

$a \leftarrow$ a MOD 2

DISPLAY (a)

An odd number will always have a remainder of 1 when divided by 2.

Answer: 1

Relational and Boolean Operators

Text and Block:	The relational operators $=, \neq, >, <, \geq$, and $\leq$ are used to test the relationship between two variables, expressions, or values.
$a = b$	For example, $a = b$ evaluates to true if a and b are equal; otherwise, it evaluates to false.
$a \neq b$	For example, a not equal to b evaluates to true if a and b are not equal; otherwise, it evaluates to false.
$a > b$	For example, a greater than b evaluates to true if a is greater than b; otherwise, it evaluates to false.
$a < b$	For example, a less than b evaluates to true if a is less than b; otherwise, it evaluates to false.
$a \geq b$	For example, a greater than or equal to b evaluates to true if a is greater than or equal to b; otherwise, it evaluates to false.
$a \leq b$	For example, a less than or equal to b evaluates to true if a is less than or equal to b; otherwise, it evaluates to false.

Example Seventeen

What will the following program display?

$a \leftarrow 3$

$b \leftarrow 3$ MOD 5

DISPLAY ($a = b$)

a	b	DISPLAY
3	3 MOD 5 = 3	3 = 3 (true)

a is initialized to 3; b is initialized to the remainder when 3 is divided by 5. Since 3 is equivalent to 3, the program will display true.

Answer: true

Example Eighteen

What will the following program display?

$a \leftarrow 4 * (3 + 6)$

$b \leftarrow 4 * 3 + 6$

DISPLAY $(a \leq b)$

a	b	DISPLAY
36	18	false

Using the order of operations, a will be initialized to 36, and b will be initialized to 18. Because 36 is not less than or equal to 18, this program displays false.

Answer: false

Numeric Procedures

Text: RANDOM (a, b)	Evaluates to a random integer from a to b, including a and b.
Block: RANDOM $\boxed{\text{a, b}}$	For example, RANDOM (1, 3) could evaluate to 1, 2, or 3.

Example Nineteen

What is the percentage of times a would display false?

$a \leftarrow$ RANDOM $(1, 2)$

DISPLAY $(a = 1)$

Answer: RANDOM can pick number 1 or 2. The chance of 1 being picked is 1/2 or 50%.

Answer: 50%

Example Twenty

What is the percentage of times a would display false?

$a \leftarrow$ RANDOM $(1, 4)$

DISPLAY $(a = 3)$

Answer: 1, 2, 3, and 4 are all possible selections. The chance of 3 being selected is 1/4 or 25%. The chance of 3 not being selected is 3/4, which is 75%.

Answer: 75%

Example Twenty-One

What is the percentage of times a would display true?

$a \leftarrow$ RANDOM $(1, 10)$

DISPLAY $(a \leq 3)$

Answer: 1, 2, 3, 4, 5, 6, 7, 8, 9, and 10 can all be selected. $a \leq 3$ includes 1, 2, and 3; $3/10 = 30\%$.

Answer: 30%

Instruction	Explanation
Text: NOT condition **Block:** NOT [condition]	Evaluates to true if condition is false; otherwise evaluates to false.
Text: condition1 AND condition2 **Block:** [condition1] AND [condition2]	Evaluates to true if both condition1 and condition2 are true; otherwise, evaluates to false.
Text: condition1 OR condition2 **Block:** [condition1] OR [condition2]	Evaluates to true if either condition1 is true or condition2 is true or if both condition1 and condition2 are true; otherwise, evaluates to false.

Boolean Table

Condition One	Logical Operator	Condition Two	Evaluation	Result
True	AND	True	Both arguments are true	True
True	AND	False	One argument is false	False
False	OR	True	One argument is true	True
False	OR	False	Both arguments are false	False
True	AND	True or False	When evaluating an "AND" logical operation, if at least one condition is false...	False
False	OR	True or False	When evaluating an "OR" logical operation, if at least one condition is true...	True

Example Twenty-Two

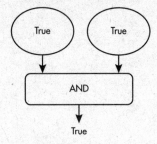

Example Twenty-Three

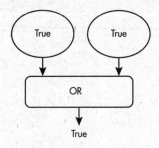

Example Twenty-Four

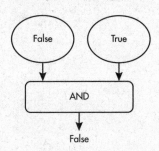

Example Twenty-Five

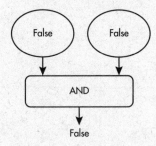

Example Twenty-Six

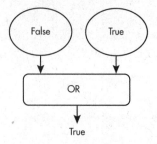

Example Twenty-Seven

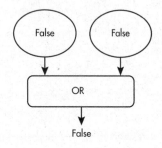

Example Twenty-Eight

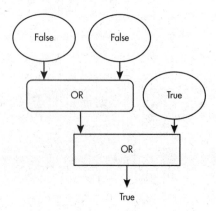

Example Twenty-Nine

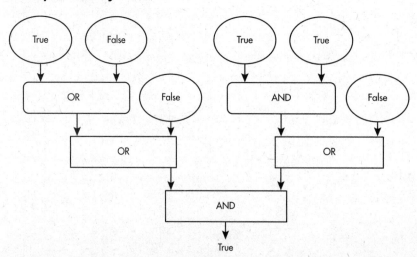

The Robot

Instruction	Explanation
Robot	
If the robot attempts to move to a square that is not open or is beyond the edge of the grid, the robot will stay in its current location, and the program will terminate.	

Text:
`MOVE_FORWARD ()`
Block:
`MOVE_FORWARD`
	The robot moves one square forward in the direction it is facing.

Text:
`ROTATE_LEFT ()`
Block:
`ROTATE_LEFT`
	The robot rotates in place 90 degrees counterclockwise (i.e., makes an in-place left turn).

Text:
`ROTATE_RIGHT ()`
Block:
`ROTATE_RIGHT`
	The robot rotates in place 90 degrees clockwise (i.e., makes an in-place right turn).

Text:
`CAN_MOVE (direction)`
Block:
`CAN_MOVE` `direction`
	Evaluates to `true` if there is an open square one square in the direction relative to where the robot is facing; otherwise evaluates to `false`. The value of direction can be `left`, `right`, `forward`, or `backward`.

The robot on the AP test has both a direction and location. The direction can be facing left, facing right, facing up, or facing down. The location of the robot is what row and column the robot is currently sitting in the grid.

The robot will end any program if the robot is asked to move off the grid.

The robot can change its direction and location by using the four listed abstractions in the table below.

The robot questions can contain procedures and loops, which are coded in graphical and text-based programming language.

ROTATE_RIGHT will rotate the robot 90 degrees clockwise.

▲	ROTATE_RIGHT( )	▶
▶	ROTATE_RIGHT( )	▼
▼	ROTATE_RIGHT( )	◀
◀	ROTATE_RIGHT( )	▲

ROTATE_LEFT will rotate the robot 90 degrees counterclockwise.

▲	ROTATE_LEFT( )	◀
▶	ROTATE_LEFT( )	▲
▼	ROTATE_LEFT( )	▶
◀	ROTATE_LEFT( )	▼

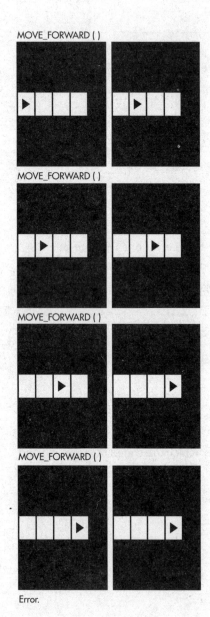

MOVE_FORWARD ( )

MOVE_FORWARD ( )

MOVE_FORWARD ( )

MOVE_FORWARD ( )

Error.

CAN_MOVE ( ) = FALSE   CAN_MOVE ( ) = TRUE

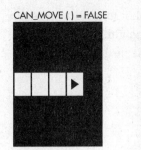 

Line 1: REPEAT_UNTIL (CAN_MOVE = false)
Line 2: {
Line 3:   MOVE_FORWARD ( )
Line 4: }

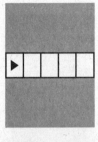 

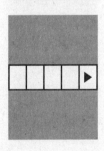

For the following grid, the program below is intended to move the robot to the gray square. The program uses the procedure Goal_Reached ( ), which returns true if the robot is in the gray square and returns false otherwise. Use the following code for the next five maps.

```
REPEAT UNTIL (Goal_Reached ( ))
{
  IF (CAN_MOVE (right))
  {
    ROTATE_RIGHT ( )
  }
  ELSE
  {
    IF (CAN_MOVE (left))
    {
    ROTATE_LEFT( )
    }
  }
  IF (CAN_MOVE (forward))
  {
    MOVE_FORWARD ( )
  }
}
```

Starting Map

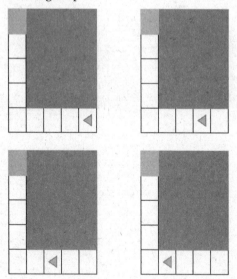

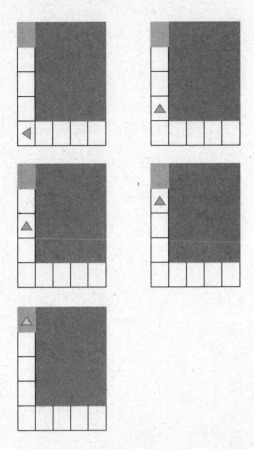

For the following grid, the program below is intended to move the robot to the gray square. The program uses the procedure Goal_Reached ( ), which returns true if the robot is in the gray square and returns false otherwise. Use the following code for the next five maps.

```
REPEAT UNTIL (Goal_Reached ( ))
{
  IF (CAN_MOVE (right))
  {
    ROTATE_RIGHT ( )
  }
  ELSE
  {
    IF (CAN_MOVE (left))
    {
      ROTATE_LEFT( )
    }
  }
  IF (CAN_MOVE (forward))
  {
    MOVE_FORWARD ( )
  }
}
```

Starting Map

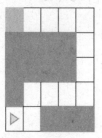

Ending Map

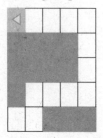

Starting Map with same code

Trace: Same as previous problem up to current spot

Ending Spot: Goal never reached

```
REPEAT (RANDOM(0,2))
{
  ROTATE_LEFT ( )
}
  REPEAT (RANDOM(0,2))
{
  MOVE_FORWARD( )
}
```

Starting

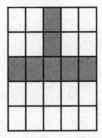

Answer:

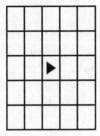

Starting

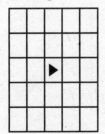

```
REPEAT (RANDOM( 1,3))
{
  ROTATE_LEFT ( )
}
  REPEAT (RANDOM( 1,2))
{
  MOVE_FORWARD( )
}
```

Rotate clockwise once, twice, or three times.

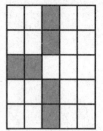

The Swap

Animals

A common algorithm is the swap. In the above animal data structure, we want to swap the sheep with the frog.

animals[1] = sheep
animals[2] = bear
animals[3] = frog

If the swap is successful, the animals' data structure would swap the sheep with the frog.

Animals

animals[1] = frog
animals[2] = bear
animals[3] = sheep
Step one: temp = animals[1]

Step two: animals[1] = animals[3]

Animals

Step three: animals[3] = temp

DIRECTIONS: Each of the questions or incomplete statements below is followed by four suggested answers or completions. Select the one that is best in each case.

1. What will the following algorithm display?

```
a ← 13
b ← 17
a ← a + 1
c ← a / 7
DISPLAY(c)
DISPLAY(a)
DISPLAY(b)
```

(A) 2 14 17

(B) 13 17 5

(C) 2 12 2

(D) 14 17 2

2. What will the following algorithm display?

```
a ← 13
a ← 17
a ← a + 1
DISPLAY(a)
```

(A) 13

(B) 17

(C) 18

(D) 19

3. What will the following algorithm display?

```
a ← 11
a ← a + 35
a ← a + 6
b ← a MOD 2
b ← a × b
DISPLAY(b)
```

(A) 0

(B) 42

(C) 84

(D) 126

4. What will the following algorithm display?

```
a ← "Milk"
a ← a + "Cookies Soda"
a ← a + "Chips"
b ← a + "put them in a bag so you know they stay crisp"
DISPLAY(b)
```

(A) Milk

(B) Milk Cookies Soda

(C) Put them in a bag and they stay crisp

(D) Milk Cookies Soda Chips put them in a bag so you know they stay crisp

5. What is the value displayed after the program is run?

```
a ← 8
b ← 3
c ← 2
a ← b * c
c ← c + 4
DISPLAY ("a")
DISPLAY (c)
```

(A) a 8

(B) a 6

(C) 8 6

(D) 16 4

6. What is the value displayed after the program is run?

```
a ← 8
b ← 3
c ← 2
a ← b * c
c ← c + 4
DISPLAY ("a")
DISPLAY ("c")
```

(A) a 8

(B) a c

(C) 8 6

(D) 16 4

7. What will the following algorithm display?

```
a ← 26 MOD 2
```

DISPLAY (a)

(A) 26

(B) 13

(C) 0

(D) 1

8. What will the following algorithm display?

```
a ← 5 MOD 2
```

DISPLAY (a)

(A) 26

(B) 13

(C) 0

(D) 1

9. What will the following algorithm display?

```
a ← 8 MOD 26
```

DISPLAY (a)

(A) 26

(B) 13

(C) 8

(D) 1

10. What will the following algorithm display?

```
a ← 13 MOD 26
```

DISPLAY (a)

(A) 26

(B) 13

(C) 8

(D) 0

11. What will the following algorithm display?

```
a ← 26 MOD 13
```

DISPLAY (a)

(A) 26

(B) 13

(C) 8

(D) 0

12. What will the following algorithm display?

```
a ← 26 MOD 3
b ← 7 MOD a
DISPLAY (b)
```

(A) 26

(B) 13

(C) 0

(D) 1

13. What will the following algorithm display?

```
a ← 2 MOD 3
b ← 7 MOD a
DISPLAY (b)
```

(A) 26

(B) 13

(C) 0

(D) 1

14. What will the following code segment display?

```
a ← 13
b ← 5
temp ← a
a ← b
b ← temp
DISPLAY(a)
DISPLAY(b)
```

(A) 13 5

(B) 5 13

(C) a b

(D) 13 13

15. What is the percentage that this algorithm displays true?

```
DISPLAY(RANDOM(1, 10) = 6)
```

(A) 9%

(B) 10%

(C) 60%

(D) 100%

16. What is the percentage that this algorithm displays true?

```
DISPLAY(RANDOM(5, 9) = 6)
```

(A) 10%

(B) 20%

(C) 60%

(D) 100%

17. What is the percentage that this algorithm displays true?

```
DISPLAY(RANDOM(5, 9) = 4)
```

(A) 0%

(B) 20%

(C) 60%

(D) 100%

18. What is the percentage that this algorithm displays true?

```
DISPLAY(RANDOM(5, 9) ≤ 9)
```

(A) 0%

(B) 20%

(C) 60%

(D) 100%

19. What is the percentage that this algorithm displays true?

```
DISPLAY(RANDOM(5, 9) > 9)
```

(A) 0%

(B) 20%

(C) 60%

(D) 100%

20. What is the percentage that this algorithm displays true?

```
DISPLAY(RANDOM(1, 10) ≤ 6)
```

(A) 9%

(B) 10%

(C) 60%

(D) 100%

21. What is the percentage that this algorithm displays true?

```
DISPLAY(RANDOM(1, 5) = 5 OR RANDOM(1, 5) = 9)
```

(A) 20%

(B) 40%

(C) 60%

(D) 100%

22. What is the percentage that this algorithm displays true?

```
DISPLAY(RANDOM(1, 5) = 6 AND RANDOM(1, 5) ≤ 5)
```

(A) 0%

(B) 40%

(C) 60%

(D) 100%

23. What is the percentage that this algorithm displays `true`?

```
DISPLAY(RANDOM(1, 5) = 6 OR RANDOM(1, 5) ≤ 5 )
```

(A) 0%

(B) 40%

(C) 60%

(D) 100%

24. The algorithm below displays TRUE 60% of the time.

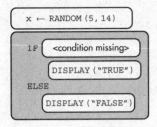

What is the missing condition?

(A) x < 10

(B) x ≤ 10

(C) x > 10

(D) x ≥ 10

25. What is the value displayed after the algorithm is run?

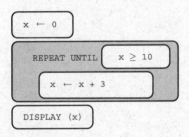

(A) 0

(B) 1

(C) 10

(D) 12

26. What is the value displayed after the algorithm is run?

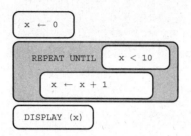

(A) 0

(B) 1

(C) 10

(D) 12

27. What is the value displayed after the algorithm is run?

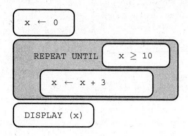

(A) 0

(B) 1

(C) 9

(D) 12

28. What is the value displayed after the algorithm is run?

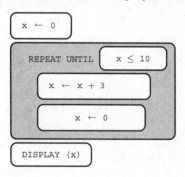

(A) 0

(B) 1

(C) 10

(D) Nothing is printed due to an infinite loop.

29. What is the value displayed after the algorithm is run?

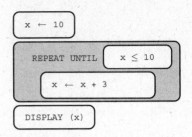

(A) 0

(B) 1

(C) 10

(D) 12

30. What is the value displayed after the algorithm is run?

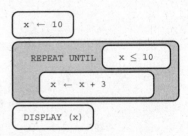

(A) 0

(B) 1

(C) 10

(D) 12

31. What is the value displayed after the algorithm is run?

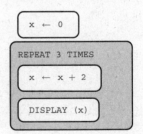

(A) 2 4 6

(B) 0 2 4 6

(C) 6

(D) 8

32. What is the value displayed after the algorithm is run?

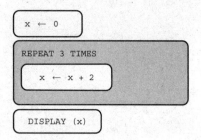

```
x ← 0

REPEAT 3 TIMES
    x ← x + 2

DISPLAY (x)
```

(A) 2 4 6

(B) 0 2 4 6

(C) 6

(D) 8

33. What is the value displayed after the algorithm is run?

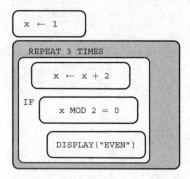

```
x ← 1

REPEAT 3 TIMES
    x ← x + 2
    IF
        x MOD 2 = 0
            DISPLAY ("EVEN")
```

(A) Nothing will be displayed.

(B) EVEN EVEN EVEN EVEN

(C) ODD ODD ODD

(D) 2 4 6

34. What is the value displayed after the algorithm is run?

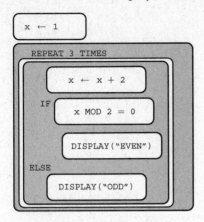

(A) Nothing will be displayed.
(B) EVEN EVEN EVEN EVEN
(C) ODD ODD ODD
(D) 2 4 6

35. What is the value displayed after the algorithm is run?

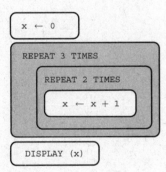

(A) 0
(B) 2
(C) 5
(D) 6

36. What is displayed after the algorithm is run?

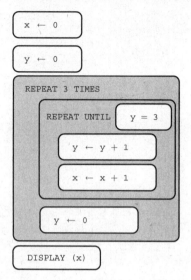

```
x ← 0

y ← 0

REPEAT 3 TIMES
    REPEAT UNTIL   y = 3
        y ← y + 1
        x ← x + 1
    y ← 0

DISPLAY (x)
```

(A) 0

(B) 3

(C) 9

(D) 12

37. What is displayed after the algorithm is run?

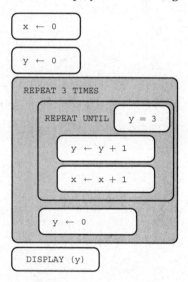

```
x ← 0

y ← 0

REPEAT 3 TIMES
    REPEAT UNTIL   y = 3
        y ← y + 1
        x ← x + 1
    y ← 0

DISPLAY (y)
```

(A) 0

(B) 3

(C) 9

(D) 12

38. How many numbers will the following algorithm display?

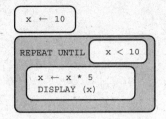

```
x ← 10

REPEAT UNTIL   x < 10

   x ← x * 5
   DISPLAY (x)
```

(A) 0

(B) 10

(C) 100

(D) An infinite amount

39. What will be printed when this algorithm is run?

```
x ← 4
y ← 8
z ← x
IF (x < 2)
{
  DISPLAY ("Pineapple")
}
IF (z < y)
{
  DISPLAY ("Kumquat")
}
ELSE (x < z)
{
  DISPLAY("Star Fruit")
}
```

(A) Pineapple

(B) Kumquat

(C) Star Fruit

(D) Pineapple Kumquat Star Fruit

40. How many times will "fish" be displayed?

```
a ← 1
REPEAT 5 TIMES
{
  IF (a > 3)
  {
    DISPLAY ("fish")
  }
  a = a + 1
}
```

(A) 4

(B) 3

(C) 2

(D) 1

41. What is displayed at the end of the algorithm?

```
IF (TRUE = TRUE AND 7 < 6)
{
  DISPLAY ("Elephant")
}
IF (8 > 4 OR TRUE = FALSE)
{
  DISPLAY ("Alligator")
}
IF (3=3)
{
  DISPLAY ("Ostrich")
}
```

(A) Elephant

(B) Alligator Ostrich

(C) Alligator

(D) Elephant Alligator Ostrich

42. A user inputs 5 for the value of *a.* What is a possible value of *c?*

$a \leftarrow$ INPUT( )

$b \leftarrow$ RANDOM(a, 6)

$c \leftarrow b - 6$

(A) −3

(B) −1

(C) 1

(D) 3

43. The following is a truth table for all possible values of *A* and *B*.

A	B	\<missing condition\>
T	T	T
T	F	F
F	T	F
F	F	F

Which of the following can replace the missing condition?

(A) (A AND B)
(B) (A OR B)
(C) (A OR NOT(A))
(D) (A AND NOT(A))

44. The following is a truth table for all possible values of *A*.

A	B	\<missing condition\>
T	T	T
T	F	T
F	T	T
F	F	F

Which of the following can replace the missing condition?

(A) (A AND B)
(B) (A OR B)
(C) (A OR NOT(A))
(D) (A AND NOT(A))

45. Which of the following statements describe the major building blocks of algorithms?

   I. Sequencing—statements execute in a given order
  II. Selection—Boolean conditions determine an algorithm's path
 III. Iteration—the repetition of parts of an algorithm

(A) I only
(B) I and II
(C) II and III
(D) I, II, and III

46. A programmer is writing code to display the difference of the squares of two user-inputted numbers (i.e., $a^2 - b^2$). The following lines represent parts of the code. What order should they be placed in?

```
1. DISPLAY (a - b)
2. b ← INPUT( )
3. a ← a * a
4. a ← INPUT( )
5. b ← b * b
```

(A) 1, 2, 3, 4, 5
(B) 1, 2, 4, 5, 3
(C) 2, 4, 3, 5, 1
(D) 4, 2, 5, 1, 3

47. An algorithm compares the user-inputted number `picked` to the randomly selected number `drawing` and calls the method `victoryJingle ()` if the two are the same. What should replace `<Missing Code>` in the following algorithm?

```
<Missing Code>
{
  victoryJingle()
}
```

(A) IF(picked AND drawing)
(B) IF(picked = drawing)
(C) IF(picked ≠ drawing)
(D) IF(picked NOT drawing)

48.

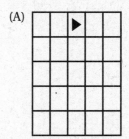

```
REPEAT 3 TIMES
    MOVE_FORWARD( )
    ROTATE_LEFT( )
    ROTATE_RIGHT( )
```

(A)

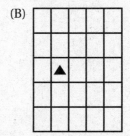

(B)

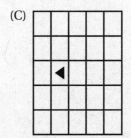

(C)

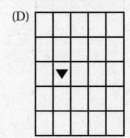

(D)

49.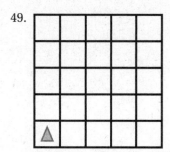

```
Line 1:  move ← INPUT( )
Line 2:  REPEAT move TIMES
Line 3:  {
Line 4:    MOVE_FORWARD( )
Line 5:    ROTATE_RIGHT( )
Line 6:  }
```

Which of the following are possible landing spots for the robot?

(A)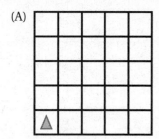

(B)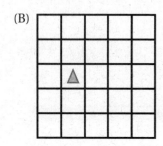

(C)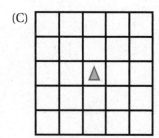

(D)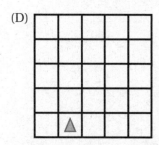

50.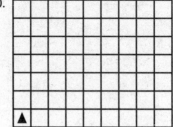

```
Line 1: y ← RANDOM ( 1, 10000)
Line 2: {
Line 3: n ← RANDOM (0, 3)
Line 4: REPEAT n TIMES
Line 5: {
Line 6:    if CAN_MOVE FORWARD ; MOVE_FORWARD ( )
Line 7:    }
Line 8:    p ← RANDOM (0, 1)
Line 9:    REPEAT p TIMES
Line 10:    {
Line 11:    TURN_LEFT ( )
Line 12:    }
Line 13: }
```

What are the possible landing spots for the robot?

(A)

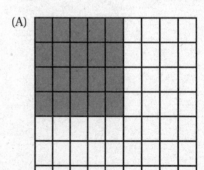

(B)

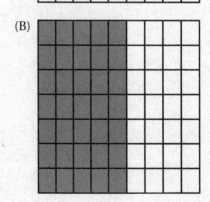

(C)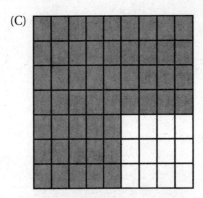

(D)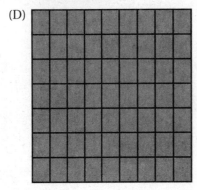

```
51. IF (TRUE = TRUE OR 7 < 6)
    {
      MOVE_FORWARD( )
      MOVE_FORWARD( )
      MOVE_FORWARD( )
    }
    IF (4 > 4 AND TRUE = FALSE)
    {
      MOVE_FORWARD( )
    }
    IF (3=3)
    {
      MOVE_FORWARD( )
      MOVE_FORWARD( )
      MOVE_FORWARD( )
    }
```

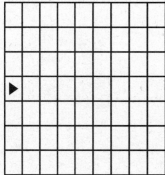

(A)

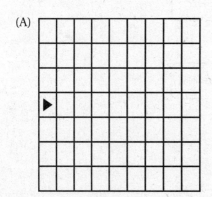

(B)

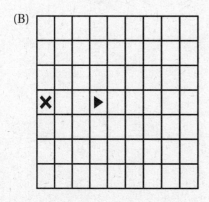

(C)

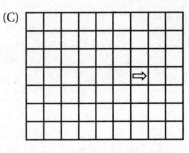

(D)

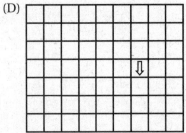

52. A programmer is creating an algorithm that doubles the square root of an inputted number and prints "small" if the result is less than 100. Which of the following would be an appropriate way to express it?

```
input number n1
root square n1
multiply n1 by 2
is n1 < 100?
yes -> print "small"
no -> do nothing
```

(A)

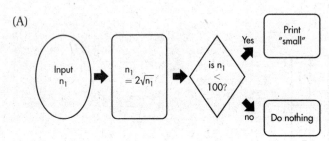

(B)

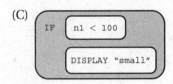

(C)

```
IF   n1 < 100

     DISPLAY "small"
```

(D) All of the above

53. Which of the following MUST an algorithm be written or be converted into to be executed by a computer?

(A) Natural language
(B) Pseudocode
(C) High-level language
(D) Low-level machine language

54. Suppose that a programmer has created an algorithm using a low-level assembly language. If the algorithm is translated exactly into a higher-level language such as Python, will the solution utilized still work? Why?

(A) Yes, because an exact translation of an algorithm only affects the way that it is read.
(B) Yes, because an algorithm will always work regardless of the language.
(C) No, because the readability of a language affects how complex algorithms can be.
(D) No, because an algorithmic solution can only exist in the language it is written in.

55. Why is it important that algorithms be executed in a reasonable time?

(A) An algorithm that does not execute in a reasonable time will break the computer it is running on.
(B) An algorithm that does not execute in a reasonable time will be rejected by the compiler.
(C) This ensures that the algorithm is capable of handling the data sets it will be given.
(D) This ensures that the algorithm is capable of finding an exact answer.

56. An algorithm has n number of steps. Which of the following would NOT be considered a reasonable number of steps?

(A) n
(B) $4n + 8n^2$
(C) $100 \, n^4$
(D) 3^n

57. Why might a programmer decide to make a portion of an algorithm heuristic?

(A) Heuristics are more accurate, so adding them makes for a stronger algorithm.
(B) While heuristics are not as accurate, they are much faster to run, which would make the ultimate algorithm more efficient.
(C) Heuristics are always easier to add into a program.
(D) Heuristics make an algorithm much harder to copy.

58. Which of the following would be considered a heuristic solution?

(A) A file-organizing algorithm determines the content of a file based on a certain number of bytes in the beginning of the file.
(B) A sorting algorithm passes every value, swapping two values where the first is lower. This repeats until there are no more swaps left.
(C) An antivirus program scans the entirety of every file on the hard drive.
(D) A searching algorithm determines the bit-level location of a text string in a document.

ANSWER KEY

1. **A**		16. **B**		31. **A**		46. **C**
2. **C**		17. **A**		32. **C**		47. **B**
3. **A**		18. **D**		33. **A**		48. **C**
4. **D**		19. **A**		34. **C**		49. **A**
5. **B**		20. **C**		35. **D**		50. **D**
6. **B**		21. **A**		36. **C**		51. **C**
7. **C**		22. **A**		37. **A**		52. **D**
8. **D**		23. **D**		38. **D**		53. **D**
9. **C**		24. **B**		39. **B**		54. **A**
10. **B**		25. **C**		40. **C**		55. **C**
11. **D**		26. **A**		41. **B**		56. **D**
12. **D**		27. **D**		42. **B**		57. **B**
13. **D**		28. **A**		43. **A**		58. **A**
14. **B**		29. **C**		44. **C**		
15. **B**		30. **A**		45. **D**		

ANSWERS EXPLAINED

1. **(A)** When tracing an algorithm, a trace table makes keeping track of your variables easier. Notice the display is *c* then *a* then *b*. Don't assume the order is always *a*, *b*, and *c*. Always evaluate the right-hand side of the equation first, then set the value to the variable on the left.

a	*b*	*c*	Output
~~13~~	17	2	2
14			14
			17

2. **(C)** When tracing an algorithm, a trace table makes keeping track of your variables easier. While *a* was initially set to 13, it is overwritten in the second line setting *a* equal to 17.

a	Output
~~13~~	18
~~17~~	
18	

3. **(A)** MOD is the remainder when two numbers are divided. Always put the first number in the "house." For example, in this problem, the fourth line is 52 MOD 2. Putting 52 in the "house" we have $2/52 = 26$ with a remainder of 0. Since 52 MOD 2 equals 0, b is set to 0. As a side note, if a number is even when you MOD 2 it will equal zero. If the number MOD 2 is equal to 1 then the number is odd.

a	b	Output
~~11~~	~~0~~	0
~~46~~	0	
52		

4. **(D)** Variables can hold strings (words). Adding strings is called *concatenation*.

a	b	Output
Milk	Milk Cookies Soda Chips put them in a bag and they stay crisp	Milk Cookies Soda Chips put them in a bag and they stay crisp
Milk Cookies Soda		
Milk Cookies Soda Chips		

5. **(B)** In this example, by putting "*a*" it will output the literal letter "a," not the value contained in *a*.

a	b	c	Output
~~8~~	~~3~~	~~2~~	a
24		6	6

6. **(B)** In this example, by putting "*a*" it will output the literal letter "a," not the value contained in *a,* and "*c*" would display the literal letter "c."

a	b	c	Output
~~8~~	~~3~~	~~2~~	a
24		6	c

7. **(C)** MOD is the remainder when two numbers are divided. Always put the first number in the "house." For example, in this problem, 26 MOD 2 putting 26 in the "house" we have $2/26 = 13$ with a remainder of 0. Since 26 MOD 2 equals 0, a is set to 0. As a side note, if a number is even when you MOD 2 it will equal zero. If the number MOD 2 is equal to 1 then the number is odd.

a	Display
0	0

8. **(D)** MOD is the remainder when two numbers are divided. Always put the first number in the "house." For example, in this problem, 5 MOD 2 putting 5 in the "house" we have $2/5 = 2$ with a remainder of 1. Since 5 MOD 2 equals 1, a is set to 1. As a side note, if a number is even when you MOD 2 it will equal zero. If the number MOD 2 is equal to 1 then the number is odd.

a	Display
1	1

9. **(C)** MOD is the remainder when two numbers are divided. Always put the first number in the "house." For example, in this problem, 8 MOD 26 putting 8 in the "house" we have $8/26 = 0$ with a remainder of 8. Since 8 MOD 26 equals 8 a is set to 8. As a side note, if a number is even when you MOD 2 it will equal zero. If the number MOD 2 is equal to 1 then the number is odd.

a	Display
8	8

10. **(B)** MOD is the remainder when two numbers are divided. Always put the first number in the "house." For example, in this problem, 13 MOD 26 putting 13 in the "house" we have $13/26 = 0$ with a remainder of 13. Since 13 MOD 26 equals 13, a is set to 13.

a	Display
13	13

11. **(D)** MOD is the remainder when two numbers are divided. Always put the first number in the "house." For example, in this problem, 26 MOD 13 putting 26 in the "house" we have $26/13 = 2$ with a remainder of 0. Since 26 MOD 13 equals 0, a is set to 0.

a	Display
0	0

12. **(D)** MOD is the remainder when two numbers are divided. Always put the first number in the "house." For example, in this problem, 26 MOD 3 putting 26 in the "house" we have $26/3 = 8$ with a remainder of 2. Since 26 MOD 3 equals 2, a is set to 2. In the second step we have 7 MOD a, which is 7 MOD 2. Since 7 is an odd number, we know that when MOD 2 if the number is odd the answer will be 1.

a	b	Display
2	1	1

13. **(D)** MOD is the remainder when two numbers are divided. Always put the first number in the "house." For example, in this problem, 2 MOD 3 putting 2 in the "house" we have $2/3 = 0$ with a remainder of 2. Since 2 MOD 3 equals 2, a is set to 2. In the second step, we have 7 MOD a, which is 7 MOD 2. Since 7 is an odd number, we know that when MOD 2 if the number is odd the answer will be 1.

a	b	Display
2	1	1

14. **(B)** This problem swaps the values of a and b. It is a "swapping" algorithm. A trace table simplifies the problem.

a	b	Temp	Display
~~13~~	5	13	5
5	13		13

15. **(B)** The random method, as seen in the reference page included with the AP test, picks a random number from the first parameter to the second parameter inclusive. RANDOM (1, 10) will randomly pick one of the following numbers: 1, 2, 3, 4, 5, 6, 7, 8, 9, 10. The chance of 6 being picked is 1 out of 10, which is $(1/10) \times 100 = 10\%$.

16. **(B)** The random method, as seen in the reference page included with the AP test, picks a random number from the first parameter to the second parameter inclusive. RANDOM (5, 9) will randomly pick one of the following numbers: 5, 6, 7, 8, 9. The chance of 6 being picked is one out of five, which is $(1/5) \times 100 = 20\%$

17. **(A)** The random method, as seen in the reference page included with the AP test, picks a random number from the first parameter to the second parameter inclusive. RANDOM (5, 9) will randomly pick one of the following numbers: 5, 6, 7, 8, 9. The chance of 4 being picked is 0 because it is not in the range of the random method.

18. **(D)** The random method, as seen in the reference page included with the AP test, picks a random number from the first parameter to the second parameter inclusive. RANDOM (5, 9) will randomly pick one of the following numbers: 5, 6, 7, 8, 9. The chance of a number being less than or equal to 9 is 100% because all the numbers in the range are less than or equal to 9.

19. **(A)** The random method, as seen in the reference page included with the AP test, picks a random number from the first parameter to the second parameter inclusive. RANDOM (5, 9) will randomly pick one of the following numbers: 5, 6, 7, 8, 9. The chance of a number being greater than 9 is 0 because all numbers greater than 9 are outside the range of possible numbers.

20. **(C)** The random method, as seen in the reference page included with the AP test, picks a random number from the first parameter to the second parameter inclusive. RANDOM (1, 10) will randomly pick one of the following numbers: 1, 2, 3, 4, 5, 6, 7, 8, 9, 10. The chance of a number being 1, 2, 3, 4, 5, or 6 is $(6/10) \times 100 = 60\%$.

21. **(A)** For an "OR" to be true, one side of the equation needs to be true.

a	b	Result
True	True	True
True	False	True
False	True	True
False	False	False

The random method, as seen in the reference page included with the AP test, picks a random number from the first parameter to the second parameter inclusive. RANDOM (1, 5) will randomly pick one of the following numbers: 1, 2, 3, 4, 5. The chance of a 5 being picked is $(1/5) \times 100 = 20\%$. The chance of a 3 being picked is also $(1/5) \times 100 = 20\%$. Because only one side needs to be true, the lowest percentage will be the percentage the "OR" statement will be true. Because both sides are 20% the answer is 20%.

22. **(A)** For an "AND" to be true, both sides of the equation need to be true.

a	b	Result
True	True	True
True	False	False
False	True	False
False	False	False

The random method, as seen in the reference page included with the AP test, picks a random number from the first parameter to the second parameter inclusive. RANDOM (1, 5) will randomly pick one of the following numbers: 1, 2, 3, 4, 5. The chance of a 6 being picked is $(0/5) \times 100 = 0\%$. Because both sides need to be true, the computer will short circuit and not check the second side as the answer is false.

23. **(D)** For an "OR" to be true, one side of the equation needs to be true. RANDOM (1, 5) will randomly pick one of the following numbers: 1, 2, 3, 4, 5. The chance of a 6 being picked is $(0/5) \times 100 = 0\%$. For the second side, RANDOM (1, 5) will randomly pick one of the following numbers: 1, 2, 3, 4, 5. The chance of the number being less than or equal to 5 is $(5/5) \times 100 = 100\%$. A false OR true will equal true.

24. **(B)** RANDOM (5, 14) will randomly pick one of the following numbers: 5, 6, 7, 8, 9, 10, 11, 12, 13, 14. The chance of a true being 60% of the time would be 6 of the 10 numbers need to be selected. If x is less than or equal to 10 it would include 6 numbers. $(6/10) \times 100 = 60\%$.

25. **(C)** A REPEAT UNTIL loop will keep on looping until the condition is true. This algorithm does not DISPLAY the value until after the loop has finished. If the Display was inside the loop the algorithm would display 10 numbers.

x	Is $x \geq 10$?	Display
0	No	
1	No	
2	No	
3	No	
4	No	
5	No	
6	No	
7	No	
8	No	
9	No	
10	Yes	10

26. **(A)** A REPEAT UNTIL loop will keep on looping until the condition is true. In this algorithm the loop ends before the first pass due to x initialized to 0, which is less than 10.

x	Is x less than 10?	Display
0	Yes	10

27. **(D)** A REPEAT UNTIL loop will keep on looping until the condition is true.

x	Is x greater than or equal to 10?	Display
0	No	
3	No	
6	No	
9	No	
12	Yes	12

28. **(A)** A REPEAT UNTIL loop will keep on looping until the condition is true.

x	Is x less than or equal to 10?	Display
0	Yes	0

29. **(C)** A REPEAT UNTIL loop will keep on looping until the condition is true.

x	Is x less than or equal to 10?	Display
10	Yes	10

30. **(A)** A REPEAT UNTIL loop will keep on looping until the condition is true.

x	Is x greater than or equal to 10?	Display
0	Yes	0

31. **(A)** A REPEAT 3 TIMES will repeat the loop three times. Notice the DISPLAY command is in the loop so three numbers will be displayed.

x	Repeat	Display
~~0~~		
~~2~~	1	2
4	2	4
6	3	6

32. **(C)** A REPEAT 3 TIMES will repeat the loop three times. Notice the DISPLAY command is outside the loop so one number will be displayed.

x	Repeat	Display
~~0~~		
~~2~~	1	
4	2	
6	3	6

33. **(A)** A REPEAT 3 TIMES will repeat the loop three times. Notice the DISPLAY command will only execute when the "If" statement is true. If a number MOD 2 is equal to 0 the number must be even.

x	Repeat	Is x MOD 2 = 0?	Display
~~1~~			
~~3~~	1	No	
5	2	No	
7	3	No	

Since the values of x are always odd, nothing will be displayed.

34. **(C)** A REPEAT 3 TIMES will repeat the loop three times. Notice the DISPLAY "EVEN" command will only execute when the "If" statement is true. If the "If" statement is false the else statement will DISPLAY "ODD." If a number MOD 2 is equal to 0 the number must be even else the number is odd.

x	Repeat	Is x MOD 2 = 0?	Display
1			
3	1	No	ODD
5	2	No	ODD
7	3	No	ODD

35. **(D)** The outer loop will repeat three times. The inner loop will loop two times for every iteration of the outer loop. The inner loop will execute $3 \times 2 = 6$ times.

x	Repeat	Display
0		
1	1	
2	1	
3	2	
4	2	
5	3	
6	3	6

36. **(C)** The outer loop will repeat three times. The inner loop will repeat until y is equal to 3.

x	y	Repeat	Is y = 3?	Display
0	0			
1	1	1	No	
2	2	1	No	
3	3	1	Yes	
	0	1		
4	1	2	No	
5	2	2	No	
6	3	2	Yes	
	0	2		
7	1	3	No	
8	2	3	No	
9	3	3	Yes	9

37. **(A)** The outer loop will repeat three times. The inner loop will repeat until y is equal to 3.

x	y	Repeat	Is y = 3?	Display
0	0			
1	1	1	No	
2	2	1	No	
3	3	1	Yes	
	0	1		
4	1	2	No	
5	2	2	No	
6	3	2	Yes	
	0	2		
7	1	3	No	
8	2	3	No	
9	3	3	Yes	
	0			0

38. **(D)** A REPEAT UNTIL will loop until x is less than 10. Because x starts at 10 and in the loop, x will only increase. The REPEAT UNTIL will never be false, so it is an infinite loop.

39. **(B)** The first "If" statement is false, so Pineapple will not be displayed. The second "If" statement is true, so Kumquat is displayed. Because the second "If" statement is true, the else will not be executed.

x	y	z	Is x less than 2?	Is z less than y?	Display
4	8	4	No	Yes	Kumquat

40. **(C)** The loop will execute five times. Fish will only be displayed when a is greater than 3.

a	Repeat	Is a greater than 3?	Display
1	1	No	
2	2	No	
3	3	No	
4	4	Yes	fish
5	5	Yes	fish

41. **(B)** The first "If" statement will evaluate as false and will not display "Elephant."

TRUE = TRUE AND 7 < 6 will reduce to TRUE AND FALSE, which is FALSE.

The second "If" statement will evaluate to true, so "Alligator" will display.

8 > 4 OR TRUE = FALSE will reduce to TRUE OR FALSE, which is true.

The third "If" statement will evaluate to true, so "Ostrich" will also display.

42. **(B)**

a	b	c
5	Random (5, 6) will randomly choose 5 or 6	5 − 6 = −1 Or 6 − 6 = 0

The only possible answer is −1 or 0.

43. **(A)**

A	B	A AND B	A OR B	NOT A	A OR NOT A	A AND NOT A
T	T	T	T	F	T	F
T	F	F	T	F	T	F
F	T	F	T	T	T	F
F	F	F	F	T	T	F

A AND B matches up to choice (A).

44. **(C)**

A	B	A AND B	A OR B	NOT A	A OR NOT A	A AND NOT A
T	T	T	T	F	T	F
T	F	F	T	F	T	F
F	T	F	T	T	T	F
F	F	F	F	T	T	F

A AND NOT(A) matches up to choice (C).

45. **(D)** All three are the basic building blocks of algorithm-making. Sequencing ensures that algorithms execute in order. Selection is used to determine results and some in-between steps. Iteration is used to repeat parts that need to be performed a certain number of times.

46. **(C)** The INPUT commands must come first so that the values are usable, while the commands squaring the variables (a * a and b * b) must come after so that the subtraction involves the correct numbers. This makes the order 2, 4, 3, 5, 1 (with 2 and 4 interchangeable and 3 and 5 interchangeable). (A) and (B) place DISPLAY before any INPUTs, while (D) places DISPLAY before one of the square commands.

47. **(B)** The computer plays the victory jingle if the two numbers are the same. With (B)'s line ahead of it, the jingle call would only be called if the condition were true, which happens if both numbers are the same.

(A) and (D) would not work because `picked` and `drawing` are integers, while `AND` and `NOT` require Boolean values.

(C) would have the opposite effect of what is intended.

48. **(C)**

```
MOVE_FORWARD()
ROTATE_LEFT( )
```

```
MOVE_FORWARD()
ROTATE_LEFT( )
ROTATE_LEFT( )
```

```
MOVE_FORWARD()
ROTATE_LEFT( )
ROTATE_LEFT( )
```

```
ROTATE_RIGHT()
```

Answer

49. **(A)** Other possible landing spots are listed below.

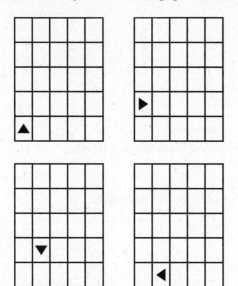

50. **(D)** With such a large number of trials the entire grid is a possible landing spot.

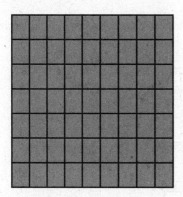

51. **(C)** Because TRUE = TRUE the "OR" statement will execute as true.

```
IF (TRUE = TRUE OR 7 < 6)
{
  MOVE_FORWARD( )
  MOVE_FORWARD( )
  MOVE_FORWARD( )
}
```

The above algorithm will result in the robot moving forward three times.

```
IF (4 > 4 AND TRUE = FALSE)
```

The above algorithm will execute as false, so the robot will not move.

```
IF (3=3)
{
  MOVE_FORWARD( )
  MOVE_FORWARD( )
  MOVE_FORWARD( )
}
```

The above algorithm will execute as true, so the robot will move forward an additional three spaces for a total of six.

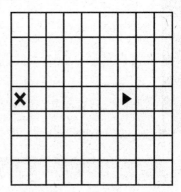

52. **(D)** All of these are valid ways to display the given algorithm. (A) is pseudocode (notice "is n1 < 100?"), (B) is a flowchart containing pseudocode, and (C) is a series of "block" programming statements.

53. **(D)** At the lowest abstraction level a computer only reads low-level machine language, which is binary code.

    (A) and (B) are not programming languages; they are merely ways to articulate a program's content to others.

    (C) needs to be placed through a compiler, which converts it into a language low-level enough for the computer.

54. **(A)** High-level languages are more clear and readable, which makes it much easier to understand an algorithm and fix errors in it.

(B) This is untrue because low-level languages still allow for commenting (as comments are merely sections ignored by the assembler/compiler).

(C) This is incorrect because a low-level program can have its actions rearranged (though it may be harder to find alternate orders due to the language's more procedural nature).

(D) This choice is incorrect because a low-level language is far easier to turn into machine code (since it is essentially as close as humanly possible to machine code), which results in more lightweight programs.

55. **(C)** Algorithms must execute in a reasonable time frame because that ensures that they are capable of providing answers efficiently with a data set of the necessary size. A reasonable amount of time on this AP test is not exponential growth.

(A) An algorithm can run forever without causing hardware damage (so long as it does not overly tax the system).

(B) Compilers only check for errors in syntax and missing files, not efficiency.

(D) Efficiency has little to do with exactness (in fact, some efficient programs are only as such because they are NOT exact).

56. **(D)** An unreasonable amount of time is an exponential increase. Polynomials are acceptable.

57. **(B)** Heuristics only look for approximate solutions, which tend to take less time than exact solutions. This makes the resulting program more efficient.

(A) Heuristics are less accurate, so this choice is incorrect.

(C) A heuristic may be somewhat harder to write in determining the bounds of acceptability, so this is not a true statement.

(D) A heuristic has no effect on the ability to copy a program.

58. **(A)** A heuristic searches for an approximate solution, and this choice describes this; the file approximates the content of a file based on a certain amount of data from the beginning. (Scanning entire files to determine content would take longer, and the heuristic approach could be fairly accurate depending on the files it's used on.)

(B) This describes a bubble search, which is not a heuristic because it leads to the lists being fully organized.

(C) The described antivirus program is not a heuristic because the program uses the entire file rather than a portion to approximate.

(D) This is not a heuristic because the result is not approximate; the location is accurate to the bit level.

Programming

6

BIG IDEA 5: PROGRAMMING

"Programming is the art of the algorithm design and the craft of debugging errant code."

—Ellen Ullman

Chapter Goals

- Creative expression
- Programming design steps
- Flowcharts
- Assigning lists
- Removing an item from a list
- Traversing a list
- Finding average
- Finding minimum
- Sample questions

- Programs can be flexible
- Programming documentation
- Lists
- Appending an item from a list
- Length of a list
- Procedures
- Finding maximum
- Searching

Programming

Programs can be developed for creative expression, to satisfy personal curiosity, to create new knowledge, or to solve problems (to help people, organizations, or society).

Advances in computing have generated and increased creativity in other fields. For example, new computer tools are being used to track dolphins and to decode their vocalization. Understanding complex dolphin behavior would not have been possible without the ability to data mine the acoustic dolphin database (searching through large databases of information to pinpoint relevant data).

Sometimes programs that are developed for personal use can be adapted to serve a larger audience and purpose. In 2004, Mark Zuckerberg created Facebook, a local platform for Harvard students to use to connect with each other. Before adapting his program to apply to a larger audience, it totaled about 1 million users by the end of 2004. Only eight years later, that number had increased to over a billion active users. This widespread distribution was made possible by changes to the program in its development.

Programs Can Be Flexible

When it was targeted to a smaller, local audience simply to satisfy Zuckerberg's personal curiosity and enjoyment, Facebook was held to much different standards in its development. When it was made for billions of people to use, changes had to be made to accommodate so many people and to target it toward a wide market of people that might use it—making it appealing to a wider audience.

The technologies and programs that are applied to Facebook could also be applied to other fields. As well as inspiring the age of social media, the data-mining programs used to understand and process the data that is "harvested" from Facebook is the same type of program that allows researchers to make sense of data gathered from the acoustic dolphin database.

Programming Design Steps

The first step in programming is planning and identifying programmer and user concerns that can affect the solution. This consultation and communication with program users are important aspects of program development to solve problems.

When designing a large program an iterative process helps with correctly coding. Checking for errors in small chunks can make isolating errors more efficient. Once a small chunk of the program is error free, it can be combined with already checked programs to help create a larger correct program. This process of designing, implementing, testing, debugging, and maintaining programs is repeated until the entire program is completed.

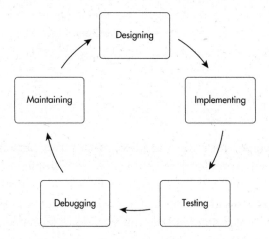

Program Documentation

Program documentation is helpful in all stages of program development. Documentation does not slow down run speed and is necessary when collaborating or programming alone. Documentation is useful during initial program development and when modifications are made.

Flowcharts

A flowchart is a way to visually represent an algorithm. The flowchart below uses the following building blocks.

Block	Explanation
Oval ⬭	The start or end of the algorithm
Rectangle ▭	One or more processing steps, such as a statement that assigns a value to a variable
Diamond ◇	A conditional or decision step, where execution proceeds to the side labeled `true` if the condition is true and to the side labeled `false` otherwise
Parallelogram ▱	Displays a message

Example One

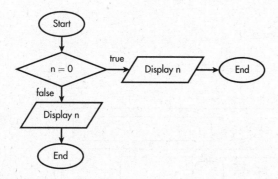

Step 1: Start the program
Step 2: Set num = 0
Step 3: Is *n* equal to 0 evaluates to true
Step 4: Display 0
Step 5: End the program

Example Two

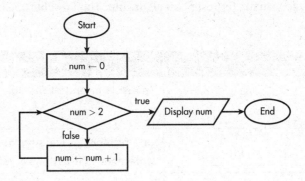

Step 1: Start the program
Step 2: Set num = 0
Step 3: Is 0 greater than 2—evaluates to false
Step 4: Set num equal to 0 + 1, which equals 1
Step 5: Is 1 greater than 2—evaluates to false
Step 6: Set num equal to 1 + 1, which equals 2
Step 7: Is 2 greater than 2—evaluates to false
Step 8: Set num equal to 2 + 1, which equals 3
Step 9: Is 3 greater than 2—evaluates to true
Step 10: Display 3
Step 11: End the program

Example Three

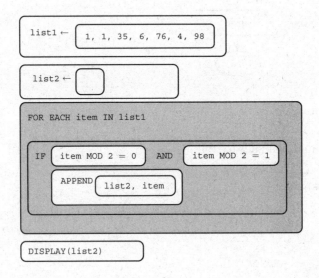

Step 1: Puts the following numbers [1, 1, 35, 6, 76, 4, 98] into a data structure called list1

Step 2: The data structure called list2 is set to empty

Step 3: This is a FOR EACH loop which will loop through each item contained in list1.

Step 4: If the item is both even AND odd it will add the number to the end of list2.

- Item MOD 2 = 0 will evaluate to true if the number is even
- Item MOD 2 = 1 will evaluate to true if the number is odd

Step 5: Since a number can never be both even AND odd no numbers will be appended to the end of list2.

Step 6: Since list2 remains empty there is nothing to DISPLAY

Lists

Lists are an organized and formatted way of storing and retrieving data. Each element in a list can be accessed by its index.

Example Four

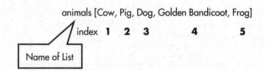

Unlike some common programming languages, indexes start at 1, not 0.

animals[1] = Cow

animals[2] = Pig

animals[3] = Dog

animals[4] = Golden Bandicoot

animals[5] = Frog

Example Five

scores [11, 35, 6, 75, 37]

scores[1] = 11

scores[2] = 35

scores[3] = 6

scores[4] = 75

scores[5] = 37

For all list operations, if a list index is less than 1 or greater than the length of the list, an error message is produced and the program terminates.	

Text:
`list[i]`
 	
Block:
`list i`
	Refers to the element of `list` at index i. The first element of list is at index 1.

Text:
`list[i] ← list[j]`
 	
Block:
`list i ← list j`
	Assigns the value of `list[j]` to `list[i]`.

Text:
`list ← [value1, value2, value3]`
 	
Block:
`list ← value1, value2, value3`
	Assigns `value1`, `value2`, and `value3` to `list[1]`, `list[2]`, and `list[3]`, respectively.

Example Six

words ← ["The", "Little", "Frog", "Jumping"]

words[2] = "Little"

words[4] = "Jumping"

Text:
`INSERT (list, i, value)`
 	
Block:
`INSERT list, i, value`
	Any values in `list` at indices greater than or equal to i are shifted to the right. The length of list is increased by 1, and `value` is placed at index i in `list`.

Text:
`APPEND (list, value)`
 	
Block:
`APPEND list, value`
	The length of `list` is increased by 1, and `value` is placed at the end of `list`.

Example Seven

```
words ← ["The", "Little", "Frog", "Jumping"]
INSERT (words, 3, "Green")
```
words["The", "Little", "Green", "Frog", "Jumping"]

Example Eight

```
words ← ["The", "Little", "Frog", "Jumping"]
INSERT (words, 2, "Green")
APPEND (words, "Fox")
```
words["The", "Green", "Little", "Frog", "Jumping", "Fox"]

Example Nine

```
words ← ["The"]
INSERT (words, 1, "Green")
APPEND (words, "Fox")
APPEND (words, "Pig")
APPEND (words, "Rhino")
INSERT (words, 1, "Elephant")
```
words["Elephant","Green", "The", "Fox", "Pig", "Rhino", "Fox"]

Text:
`INSERT (list, i)`
 	
Block:
`REMOVE` `list, i`
	Removes the item at index `i` in `list` and shifts to the left any values at indices greater than `i`. The length of `list` is decreased by 1.

Text:
`LENGTH (list)`
 	
Block:
`LENGTH` `list`
	Evaluates to the number of elements in `list`.

Example Ten

Line 1: words ← ["Elephant","Green", "The", "Fox", "Pig", "Rhino", "Fox"]
Line 2: DISPLAY (LENGTH (words)) // answer 7
Line 3: REMOVE (words, 1)
Line 4: DISPLAY (LENGTH (words)) // answer 8

Traversing a List

Traversing a list means that you are checking all the elements of the list one by one.

```
Text
FOR EACH item IN list
{
    <block of statements>
}
```

Block:

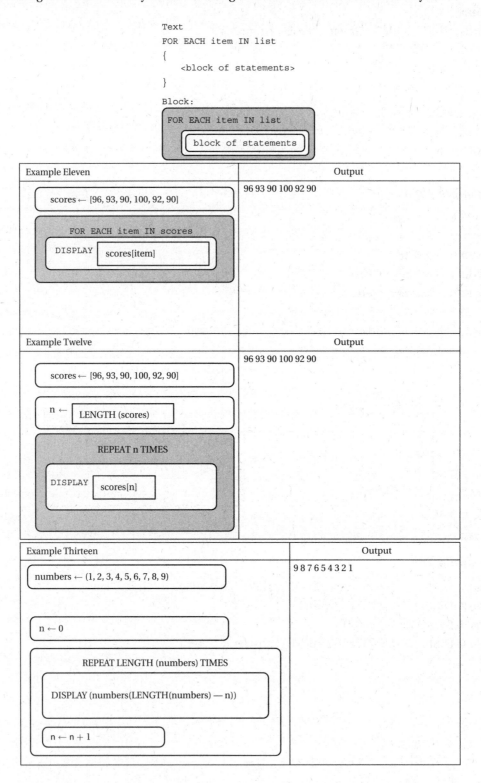

Example Eleven	Output
scores ← [96, 93, 90, 100, 92, 90] FOR EACH item IN scores DISPLAY scores[item]	96 93 90 100 92 90

Example Twelve	Output
scores ← [96, 93, 90, 100, 92, 90] n ← LENGTH (scores) REPEAT n TIMES DISPLAY scores[n]	96 93 90 100 92 90

Example Thirteen	Output
numbers ← (1, 2, 3, 4, 5, 6, 7, 8, 9) n ← 0 REPEAT LENGTH (numbers) TIMES DISPLAY (numbers(LENGTH(numbers) — n)) n ← n + 1	9 8 7 6 5 4 3 2 1

Procedures

A **procedure** is a set of code that is referred to by name and can be called (invoked) at any point in a program simply by utilizing the procedure's name. In other languages, a procedure could be called a *method* or *subroutine*. In the Create Performance Task, a procedure is referred to as an *abstraction*.

Example Fourteen

Line 1: num ← 7

Line 2: DISPLAY (addThree (num))

Line 3: Procedure addThree (num)

Line 4: RETURN num + 3

Output
10

Example Fifteen

Line 1: scores ← [90, 89, 98, 100, 90]

Line 2: total ← findTotal (scores)

Line 3: DISPLAY (total)

Line 4:

Line 5: PROCEDURE findTotal (scores)

Line 6: {

Line 7: sum = 0

Line 8: FOR EACH item IN scores

Line 9: {

Line 10: sum ← sum + item

Line 11: }

Line 12: RETURN sum

Output
467

Example Sixteen

Finding Average Text-Based Coding

Line 1:   PROCEDURE findAverage (list)
Line 2:   {
Line 3:   sum ← 0
Line 4:   count ← 0
Line 5:   n ← LENGTH (list)
Line 6:   REPEAT n TIMES
Line 7:   {
Line 8:   sum ← sum + list(count)
Line 9:   count ← count + 1
Line 10:   }
Line 11:   RETURN (sum / n)
Line 12: }

Lines 3 and 4: Initialize the variables sum and count and set them equal to zero.

Line 5: Set the variable n equal to the number of items in the list.

Line 6: Repeat the next segment n times (for every item in the list).

Line 8: Add the item in position count from the list to the sum.

Line 9: Increment, count by one (so that the next time you loop through you will add the item in the next spot in the list).

Line 11: Take the sum of all the items and divide by n, the number of items in the list.

Example Seventeen

Finding Maximum Number in a Text-Based Coding List

Line 1:   PROCEDURE findMaximum (list)
Line 2:   {
Line 3:   max ← list[1]
Line 4:   n ← LENGTH (list)
Line 5:   count ← 1
Line 6:   REPEAT n TIMES
Line 7:   {
Line 8:   if(list[count] > max)
Line 9:   max = list[count]
Line 10:   count ← count + 1
Line 11:   }
Line 12:   RETURN (max)
Line 13: }

Line 3: Initialize the variable max to the first element in the list.

Line 4: Initialize the variable n to the number of items in the list.

Line 5: Initializes count to 1.

Line 6: Repeats the loop n number of times.

Lines 7–9: If the current value is greater than max then the current value is set to max.

Line 10: Increases the value of count.

Line 12: Returns the maximum value in the data structure.

Example Eighteen

Finding Minimum Number in a Text-Based Coding List

Line 1:   PROCEDURE findMinimum (list)

Line 2:   {

Line 3:   min ← list[1]

Line 4:   n ← LENGTH (list)

Line 5:   count ← 1

Line 6:   REPEAT n TIMES

Line 7:   {

Line 8:   if(list[count] < min)

Line 9:   min = list[count]

Line 10:   count ← count + 1

Line 11:   }

Line 12:   RETURN (min)

Line 13:   }

Line 3: Initialize the variable min to the first element in the list.

Line 4: Initialize the variable n to the number of items in the list.

Line 5: Initializes count to 1.

Line 6: Repeats the loop n number of times.

Lines 7–9: If the current value is greater than min then the current value is set to min.

Line 10: Increases the value of count.

Line 12: Returns the minimum value in the data structure.

Example Nineteen

Searching for a Word in a Text-Based Coding List

Line 1:   PROCEDURE findNumber (list, word)

Line 2:   {

Line 3:   index ← 1

Line 4:   FOR EACH item IN list

Line 5:   {

Line 6:   if (item = word)

Line 7:   {

Line 8:   RETURN index

Line 9:   }

Line 10:   index ← index + 1

Line 11:   }

Line 12:   RETURN ("Word not in list")

Line 13:   }

Line 3: Initialize the variable index to equal one, since that is where to begin the search for "word."

Line 4: This For Each loop will loop for every item in the array. Each iteration then looks at the next object in the array, calling it item.

Line 6 to Line 9: If the current item is the same as the word being searched for, it will return that given index.

Line 10: If the word did not match with the item, continue with the program and increment the index.

Example Twenty

Searching for a Word in a Text-Based Coding Alternate-Solution List

```
Line 1:    PROCEDURE findNumber (list, word)
Line 2:    {
Line 3:      index ← 1
Line 4:      FOR EACH item IN list
Line 5:      {
Line 6:        if (item = word)
Line 7:        {
Line 8:          RETURN index
Line 9:        }
Line 10:     else
Line 11:     {
Line 12:       index ← index + 1
Line 13:     }
Line 14:   }
Line 15:   RETURN ("Word not in list")
Line 16: }
```

Line 3: Initialize the index equal to 1 because that is the starting point.

Line 4 to Line 7: Make a For Each loop to look at every item in the list.

Line 8: If the item being looked for is the same as the word, it will return the index currently being looked at.

Line 12: Otherwise, add one to the index for the next iteration.

DIRECTIONS: Each of the questions or incomplete statements below is followed by four suggested answers or completions. Select the one that is best in each case.

1. What will the following program display?

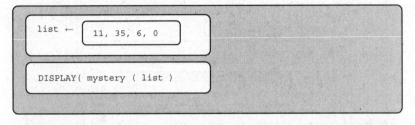

```
list ←   11, 35, 6, 0

DISPLAY( mystery ( list )
```

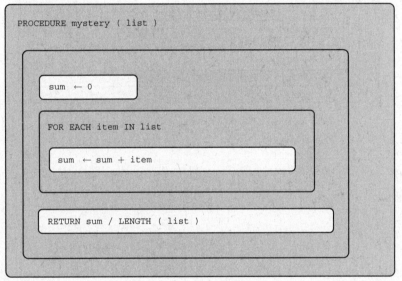

```
PROCEDURE mystery ( list )

    sum ← 0

    FOR EACH item IN list

        sum ← sum + item

    RETURN sum / LENGTH ( list )
```

(A) 0
(B) 4
(C) 13
(D) 35

2. What will the following program display?

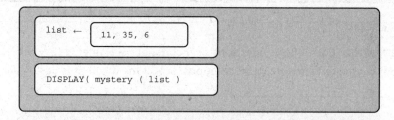

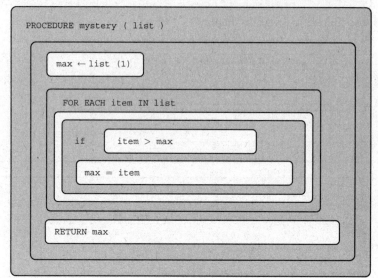

(A) 0

(B) 12

(C) 16

(D) 35

3. What will the following program display?

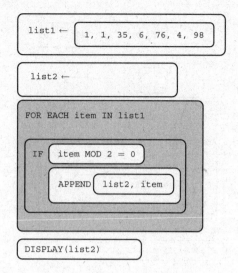

```
list1 ←   1, 1, 35, 6, 76, 4, 98

list2 ←

FOR EACH item IN list1

    IF   item MOD 2 = 0

        APPEND   list2, item


DISPLAY(list2)
```

(A) [6, 76, 4, 98]

(B) [1, 1, 35]

(C) [1, 1, 35, 6, 76, 4, 98]

(D) [ ]

4. What will the following program display?

Line 1:   list ← [11, 35, 6, 2]
Line 2:   DISPLAY (mystery (list))
Line 3:
Line 4:   PROCEDURE mystery (list)
Line 5:   {
Line 6:   sum ← list [1]
Line 7:   count ← 1
Line 8:   n ← LENGTH (list)
Line 9:   REPEAT n TIMES
Line 10:   {
Line 11:   sum ← sum + list (count)
Line 12:   count ← count + 1
Line 13:   }
Line 14:   RETURN (sum / count)
Line 15:   }

(A) 0

(B) 13

(C) 16

(D) 35

5. What will the following program display?

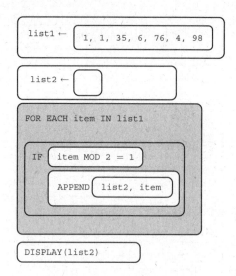

(A) [6, 76, 4, 98]

(B) [1, 1, 35]

(C) [1, 1, 35, 6, 76, 4, 98]

(D) [ ]

6. What will the following program display?

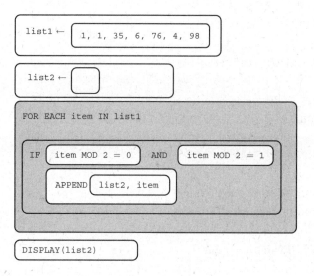

(A) [0]

(B) [−11]

(C) [−35]

(D) [ ]

7. What will the following program display?

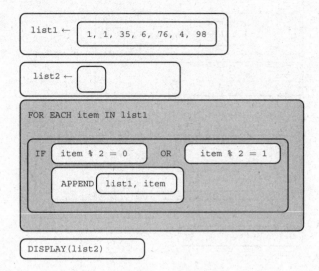

(A) [6, 76, 4, 98]
(B) [1, 1, 35]
(C) [1, 1, 35, 6, 76, 4, 98]
(D) [ ]

8. What will the following program display?

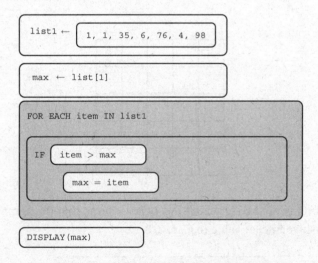

(A) 1
(B) 98
(C) 0
(D) 76

9. What will the following program display?

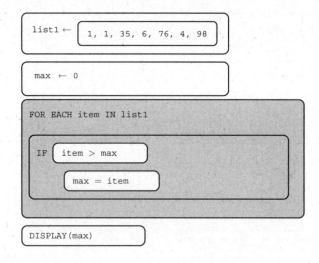

```
list1 ← [ 1, 1, 35, 6, 76, 4, 98 ]

max ← 0

FOR EACH item IN list1

    IF item > max

        max = item

DISPLAY(max)
```

(A) 0

(B) 98

(C) 1

(D) −98

10. The following question uses a robot in a grid of squares. The robot is represented as a triangle, which is initially in the top-left square of the grid and facing toward the top of the grid.

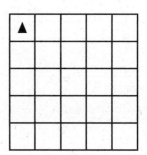

Code for the procedure Mystery is shown here. Assume that the parameter p has been assigned a positive integer value (e.g., 1, 2, 3, …).

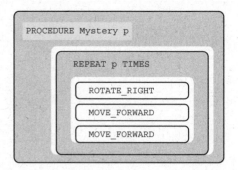

```
PROCEDURE Mystery p

    REPEAT p TIMES

        ROTATE_RIGHT
        MOVE_FORWARD
        MOVE_FORWARD
```

Which of the following shows a possible result of calling the procedure?

(A)

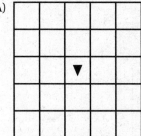

(B)

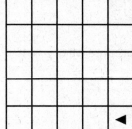

(C)

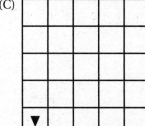

(D)

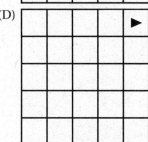

11. The following question uses a robot in a grid of squares. The robot is represented as a triangle, which is initially in the top-left square of the grid and facing toward the top of the grid.

Code for the procedure Mystery is shown below. Assume that the parameter p has been assigned a positive integer value (e.g., 1, 2, 3, ...).

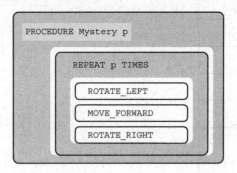

```
PROCEDURE Mystery p

    REPEAT p TIMES

        ROTATE_LEFT
        MOVE_FORWARD
        ROTATE_RIGHT
```

Which of the following shows the result of calling the procedure when $p = 4$?

(A)

(B)

(C)

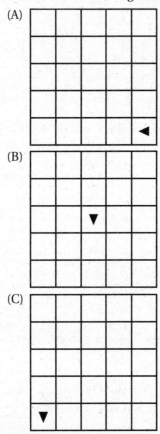

(D) Error. The robot will be out of the grid.

12. The following question uses a robot in a grid of squares. The robot is represented as a triangle, which is initially in the top-left square of the grid and facing toward the top of the grid.

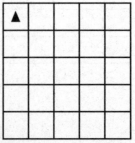

Code for the procedure Mystery is shown below. Assume that the parameter p has been assigned a positive integer value (e.g., 1, 2, 3, ...).

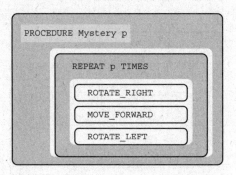

```
PROCEDURE Mystery p
    REPEAT p TIMES
        ROTATE_RIGHT
        MOVE_FORWARD
        ROTATE_LEFT
```

Which of the following shows the result of calling the procedure when $p = 4$?

(A)

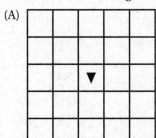

(B)

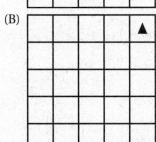

(C)

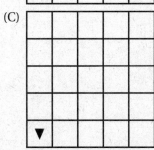

(D)

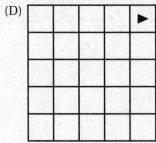

13. The program below is intended to find the highest non-negative number in list.

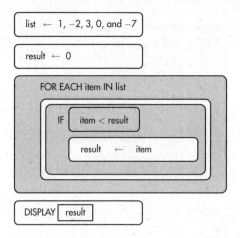

Does the program work as intended? If so, what is the result? If not, why?

(A) Yes, the program works as intended; it displays 1.
(B) No, the program does not work as intended; result starts at 0.
(C) Yes, the program works as intended; it displays 3.
(D) No, the program does not work as intended; the if conditional should be "item > result."

14. The following program is intended to find the lowest number in list.

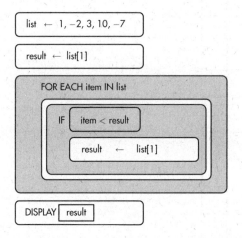

Does the program work as intended? If so, what is the result? If not, why?

(A) Yes, the program works as intended; it displays −7.
(B) No, the program does not work as intended; result is always list[1].
(C) Yes, the program works as intended; it displays 1.
(D) No, the program does not work as intended; runtime error.

15. The following program is intended to find the lowest number in list.

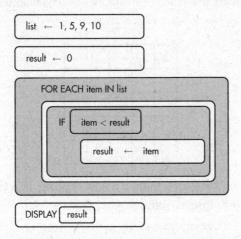

Does the program work as intended? If so, what is the result? If not, why?

(A) Yes, the program works as intended and returns 10.
(B) No, the program does not work as intended; while this code will run, it would return a logical error of the value 0.
(C) Yes, the program works as intended and would return the value 1.
(D) No, the program does not work as intended and would result in a runtime error not returning a number.

16. The following program is intended to find the greatest number in list.

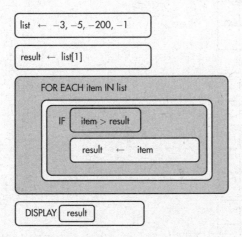

Does the program work as intended? If so, what is the result? If not, why?

(A) Yes, the program works as intended, returning −200.
(B) No, the program does not work as intended; result never changes and returns −3.
(C) Yes, the program works as intended and returns −1.
(D) No, the program does not work as intended; runtime error.

17. The following question uses a robot in a grid of squares. The robot is represented as a triangle, which is initially in the top-left square of the grid and facing toward the top of the grid.

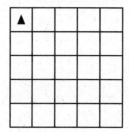

Code for the procedure Mystery is shown below. Assume that the parameter p has been assigned a positive integer value (e.g., 1, 2, 3, …).

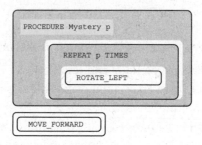

```
PROCEDURE Mystery p

    REPEAT p TIMES

        ROTATE_LEFT


MOVE_FORWARD
```

Which of the following shows the result of calling the procedure when $p = 6$?

(A)

(B)

(C)

(D)

18. The following question uses a robot in a grid of squares. The robot is represented as a triangle, which is initially in the top-left square of the grid and facing toward the top of the grid.

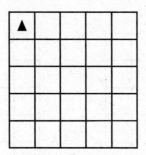

Code for the procedure Mystery is shown below. Assume that the parameter p has been assigned a positive integer value (e.g., 1, 2, 3, . . .).

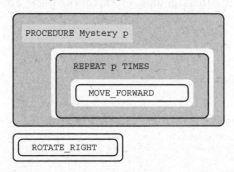

```
PROCEDURE Mystery p

    REPEAT p TIMES

        MOVE_FORWARD


ROTATE_RIGHT
```

Which of the following shows the result of calling the procedure when $p = 6$?

(A)

(B)

(C)

(D) Error. The robot moves off the grid.

19. The following question uses a robot in a grid of squares. The robot is represented as a triangle, which is initially in the bottom-left square of the grid and facing toward the top of the grid.

Start

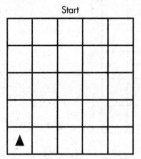

Finish

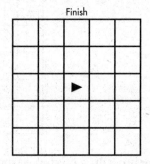

Which of the following code segments produces the result above?

(A) n ← 2

REPEAT n TIMES{

  ROTATE_RIGHT

  MOVE_FORWARD

  ROTATE_LEFT

  MOVE_FORWARD

}

(B) MOVE_FORWARD

MOVE_FORWARD

ROTATE_RIGHT

MOVE_FORWARD

(C) n ← 2

ROTATE_RIGHT

REPEAT n TIMES

{

  MOVE_FORWARD

}

ROTATE_LEFT

MOVE_FORWARD

(D) n ← 2

REPEAT n TIMES

{

  ROTATE_RIGHT

  MOVE_FORWARD

  ROTATE_LEFT

  MOVE_FORWARD

}

ROTATE_RIGHT

20. The following question uses a robot in a grid of squares. The robot is represented as a triangle, which is initially in the top-left square of the grid and facing toward the top of the grid.

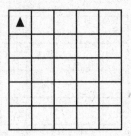

Code for the procedure Mystery is shown below. Assume that the parameter p has been assigned a positive integer value (e.g., 1, 2, 3, …).

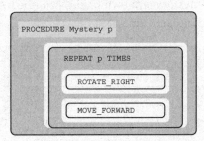

```
PROCEDURE Mystery p

    REPEAT p TIMES

        ROTATE_RIGHT

        MOVE_FORWARD
```

Which of the following shows the result of calling the procedure for any value of p?
Select two answers.

(A)
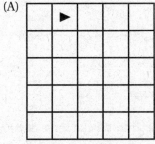

(C)
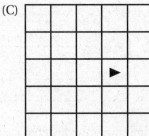

(B)

(D)

21. The following question uses a robot in a grid of squares. The robot is represented as a triangle, which is initially in the top-left square of the grid and facing toward the top of the grid.

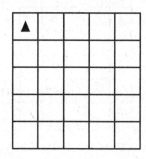

Code for the procedure Mystery is shown below. Assume that the parameter p has been assigned a positive integer value of either 0 or 1.

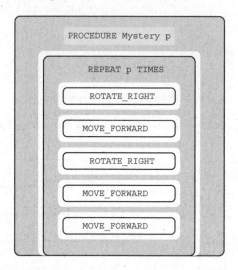

```
PROCEDURE Mystery p

    REPEAT p TIMES

        ROTATE_RIGHT

        MOVE_FORWARD

        ROTATE_RIGHT

        MOVE_FORWARD

        MOVE_FORWARD
```

Which of the following shows the result of calling the procedure for the value of p equal to 0 or 1?

Select two answers.

(A)

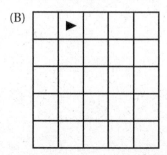

(B)

(C)

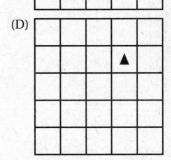

(D)

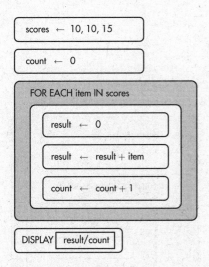

22. The following program is intended to find the average of a class's scores.

```
scores  ←  10, 10, 15

count  ←  0

FOR EACH item IN scores
    result  ←  0
    result  ←  result + item
    count  ←  count + 1

DISPLAY  result/count
```

What does the code segment display?

(A) 0

(B) 5

(C) Nothing, runtime error

(D) 20

23. The following code segment is intended to find the maximum.

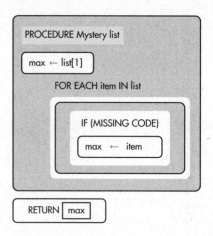

Which of the following code segments can replace MISSING CODE to make the procedure work as intended?

(A) max > item

(B) max = item

(C) item > max

(D) max >= item

24. What does the following code segment return?

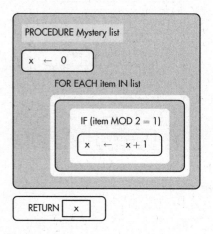

(A) The number of even items in list

(B) The number of items in list

(C) The number of odd items in list

(D) Nothing, runtime error

25. The following procedure is intended to find the amount of numbers in list that are divisible by 5 and 2.

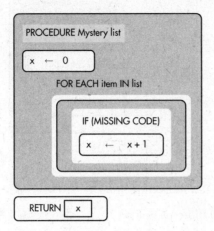

PROCEDURE Mystery list

x ← 0

FOR EACH item IN list

IF (MISSING CODE)

x ← x + 1

RETURN x

Which of the following code segments can replace MISSING CODE to make the procedure work as intended?

(A) item MOD 5 = 0 OR item MOD 2 = 1
(B) item MOD 2 = 1 AND item MOD 5 = 1
(C) item MOD 5 = 0 AND item MOD 2 = 1
(D) item MOD 2 = 0 AND item MOD 5 = 0

26. The following code segment is intended to switch the values of x and y (assume x and y have already been initialized).

x ← y

y ← x

What can be done to make the code segment work as intended?

(A) Add "temp ← x" above "$x ← y$" and replace $y ← x$ with $y ←$ temp
(B) Nothing, the code works as intended
(C) Add "temp ← x" below "$x ← y$"
(D) Add "temp ← y" above "$x ← y$"

27.

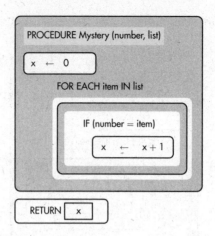

What is the purpose of the procedure above?

(A) To find the amount of items in list
(B) To find the amount of items in list that are equal to number
(C) To find the amount of items in list that do not equal number
(D) Nothing, compile-time error

28.

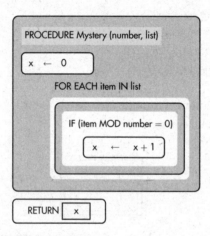

What is returned by the procedure above?

(A) Nothing, compile-time error
(B) To find the amount of items in list that equal number
(C) To find the amount of items in list that are divisible by number
(D) Nothing, runtime error

29. The following procedure is intended to find the amount of values divisible by 15 in list.

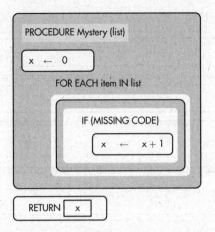

What can replace MISSING CODE to make the function work as intended?

(A) item MOD 15 = 0
(B) item / 15 = 1
(C) item MOD 15 = 1
(D) item / 15 = 0

30. What will the following program display?

```
x ← 10
arr ← ["I", "Love", "Puppies"]
DISPLAY (arr[(x - LENGTH(arr)) MOD 4])
```

(A) I
(B) Love
(C) Puppies
(D) ArrayOutOfBoundsException

31. What does the following program display?

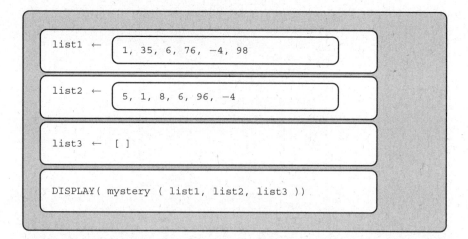

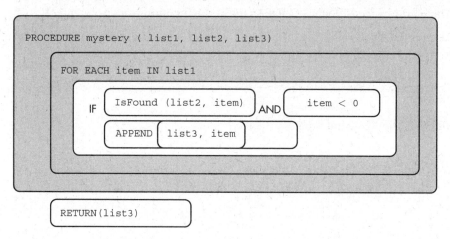

RETURN(list3)

(A) [−4, −98]

(B) [1, 6, −4]

(C) [−4]

(D) [1, 35, 6, 76, 4, 98, 5, 1, 8, 96, −4]

32. What does the following program display?

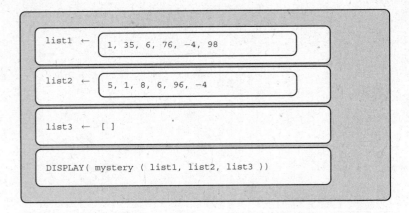

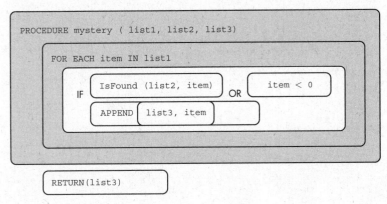

(A) [−4, −98]

(B) [1, 6, −4]

(C) [−4]

(D) [1, 35, 6, 76, 4, 98, 5, 1, 8, 96, −4]

33. In the following program, which chart displays the ways in which the variables are changed?

$x \leftarrow 5$
$y \leftarrow 10$
$z \leftarrow 15$
$z \leftarrow x - y$
$x \leftarrow z - 15$
$y \leftarrow y + x$
$x \leftarrow x + y + z$

(A)

x	y	z
~~5~~	~~10~~	~~15~~
~~-5~~	-5	0
-10		

(B)

x	y	z
~~5~~	~~10~~	~~15~~
~~0~~	10	0
10		

(C)

x	y	z
~~5~~	~~10~~	~~15~~
~~5~~	10	15
5		

(D)

x	y	z
~~5~~	~~10~~	~~15~~
~~-20~~	-10	-5
-35		

34. A programmer is curious about the accuracy of a new touchpad. To test it, he creates a program that graphically displays the location of the detected pressure and technical information about the device's current state. What types of input and output are used by this program?

	Input	Output
(A)	Visual	Tactile
(B)	Visual	Audible
(C)	Tactile	Visual
(D)	Tactile	Audible

35. Which of the following statements correctly describes a procedure?

    I. A procedure can be used in any program as long as the original procedure can be located.
    II. A procedure is able to work in any program without translation, regardless of the language the program is coded in.
    III. A procedure can be reused throughout a program.

    (A) I only
    (B) I and II only
    (C) I and III only
    (D) II and III only

36. Why is it generally considered a better idea to use procedures in a program? **Select two answers.**

    (A) Procedures make a program easier to read because they can collapse complex algorithms into individual lines.
    (B) Procedures make a program easier to share because procedures used in the program will always be in the same file.
    (C) Procedures are easier to read because they keep blocks of code together.
    (D) Procedures make a program easier to modify because editing a repeated algorithm in a procedure only requires editing the procedure.

37. What is the benefit of using a programming library?

    (A) Programming libraries include procedures for common functions, such as exponents, which saves programmers from having to make such procedures themselves.
    (B) Programming libraries make it easy to translate code from one programming language to another.
    (C) Programming libraries allow people to derive code from a compiled program because they correspond between compiled code and high-level code.
    (D) Programming libraries allow users to send procedures from their own programs between each other.

38. The following question uses a robot in a grid. The robot is presented as a triangle, which is initially in the lower-left square of the grid and facing toward the top of the grid.

Starting Grid

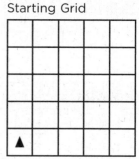

Ending Grid

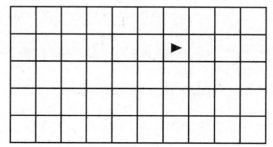

PROCEDURE ziz( )	PROCEDURE zag( )
{	{
MOVE_FORWARD( )	ROTATE_RIGHT( )
MOVE_FORWARD( )	}
MOVE_FORWARD( )	
}	

Which of the following programs will place the robot in the ending grid location?

(A) Line 1: ziz( )
    Line 2: zag( )
    Line 3: ziz( )
    Line 4: ziz( )

(B) Line 1: ziz( )
    Line 2: zag( )
    Line 3: ziz( )

(C) Line 1: zag( )
    Line 2: zag( )

(D) Line 3: zag( )
    Line 1: ziz( )
    Line 2: ziz( )
    Line 3: ziz( )

39. The following question uses a robot in a grid. The robot is presented as a triangle, which is initially in the lower row of the grid facing up. Which of the following calls to moveAndTurn will result in the robot's landing on the star?

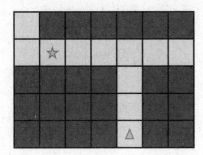

PROCEDURE moveAndTurn ( )
{
  MOVE_FORWARD()
  MOVE_FORWARD()
  MOVE_FORWARD()
  ROTATE_RIGHT()
  ROTATE_RIGHT()
  ROTATE_RIGHT()
}

(A) moveAndTurn( )

(B) moveAndTurn( )
    moveAndTurn( )

(C) moveAndTurn( )
    moveAndTurn( )
    moveAndTurn( )

(D) moveAndTurn( )
    moveAndTurn( )
    moveAndTurn( )
    moveAndTurn( )

40. The following question uses a robot in a grid. The robot is presented as a triangle, which is initially in the lower-left row of the grid and is facing up. Which of the following calls to moveAndTurn will result in the robot's landing on the star?

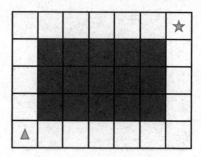

Line 1:   PROCEDURE moveAndSpin (x, y)
Line 2:   {
Line 3:   REPEAT x TIMES
Line 4:   {
Line 5:   MOVE_FORWARD()
Line 6:   }
Line 7:   REPEAT y TIMES
Line 8:   {
Line 9:   ROTATE_RIGHT ()
Line 10:   }

Select two answers.

(A) moveAndSpin(4,1)
    moveAndSpin(6,0)
(B) moveAndSpin(0,1)
    moveAndSpin(6,3)
    moveAndSpin(4,0)
(C) moveAndSpin(7,3)
(D) moveAndSpin(0,7)

ANSWER KEY

1. **C**	11. **D**	21. **A, C**	31. **C**
2. **D**	12. **B**	22. **B**	32. **D**
3. **A**	13. **D**	23. **C**	33. **D**
4. **B**	14. **A**	24. **C**	34. **C**
5. **B**	15. **B**	25. **D**	35. **C**
6. **D**	16. **C**	26. **A**	36. **A, D**
7. **C**	17. **D**	27. **B**	37. **A**
8. **B**	18. **D**	28. **C**	38. **A**
9. **B**	19. **D**	29. **A**	39. **B**
10. **A**	20. **A, B**	30. **C**	40. **A, C**

ANSWERS EXPLAINED

1. **(C)** The data structure called list contains the numbers with the following indexes.

list	11	35	6	0
index	1	2	3	4

The index starts at 1, not 0.

The program then displays the results of calling the procedure Mystery with the parameter list. A procedure is an abstraction.

A For Each loop will iterate through a list starting at index 1 and going to the end of the list.

sum = 0
sum = sum + 11 = 0 + 11 = 11
sum = sum + 35 = 11 + 35 = 46
sum = sum + 6 = 46 + 6 = 52
sum = sum + 0 = 52 + 0 = 52

The LENGTH (list) command is equal to the size of the list. In this case LENGTH (list) = 4.

The final line of the procedure returns sum/LENGTH (list) = 52/4 = 13.

2. **(D)** The data structure called list contains the numbers with the following indexes.

list	11	35	6
index	1	2	3

The program then displays the results of calling the procedure Mystery with the parameter list. A procedure is an abstraction.

When trying to find the maximum or minimum, set the initial number to the first element is the list, not 0.

max = list(1) = 11

A For Each loop will iterate through a list starting at index 1 and going to the end of the list.

If(11 > max) no
If(35 > max) yes max = 35
If(6 > max) no

Return 35

3. **(A)** There are two data structures in this problem.

list1	1	1	35	6	76	4	98
index	1	2	3	4	5	6	7

list2
index

A For Each loop will iterate through the list starting at index 1 and going to the end of the list.

If the item MOD 2 = 0 (even number) the item will be appended to the end of list2.

If(1 MOD 2 = 0) false
If(1 MOD 2 = 0) false
If(35 MOD 2 = 0) false
If(6 MOD 2 = 0) true list2(6)
If(76 MOD 2 = 0) true list2 (6, 76)
If(4 MOD 2 = 0) true list2 (6, 76, 4)
If(98 MOD 2 = 0) true list2 (6, 76, 4, 98)

DISPLAY list2 [6, 76, 4, 98]

4. **(B)** The data structure called list contains the numbers with the following indexes.

list1	11	35	6	2
index	1	2	3	4

Line 2: Will display the call to the procedure Mystery with the parameter list [11, 35, 6, 1].

Line 6: sum = list(1)

sum = 11

Line 7: count = 1

Line 8: The abstraction LENGTH (list) is equal to the size of list, which in this case is 4.

$n = 4$

Line 9: This REPEAT loop will iterate four times.

1st pass	sum = sum + list(1) sum = 11 + 11 = 22	count = count + 1 count = 1 + 1 = 2
2nd pass	sum = sum + list(2) sum = 22 + 35 = 57	count = count + 1 count = 2 + 1 = 3
3rd pass	sum = sum + list(3) sum = 57 + 6 = 63	count = count + 1 count = 3 + 1 = 4
4th pass	sum = sum + list(3) sum = 63 + 2 = 65	count = count + 1 count = 4 + 1 = 5

Return sum/count

Return 65/5 = 13

Note this procedure does not return the average. To return average the sum should have been initialized to 0, not the first element in the list. Also, the sum should have been divided by the size of the list, which was 4, not 5.

5. **(B)** There are two data structures in this problem.

list1	1	1	35	6	76	4	98
index	1	2	3	4	5	6	7

list2
index

A For Each loop will iterate through the list starting at index 1 and going to the end of the list.

If the item MOD 2 = 1 (odd number) the item will be appended to the end of list2.

If(1 MOD 2 = 1) true list2(1)
If(1 MOD 2 = 1) true list2 (1, 1)
If(35 MOD 2 = 1) true list2(1, 1, 35)
If(6 MOD 2 = 0) false
If(76 MOD 2 = 0) false
If(4 MOD 2 = 0) false
If(98 MOD 2 = 0) false

DISPLAY list2 [1, 1, 35]

6. **(D)** There are two data structures in this problem.

list1	1	1	35	6	76	4	98
index	1	2	3	4	5	6	7

list2
index

A For Each loop will iterate through the list starting at index 1 and going to the end of the list.

If the item MOD 2 = 0 (even number) AND item MOD = 1 (odd number) the item will be appended to the end of list2. Since no number can be both an even and odd number at the same time, list2 will be appended.

list2 [ ]

7. **(C)** There are two data structures in this problem.

list1	1	1	35	6	76	4	98
index	1	2	3	4	5	6	7

list2
index

A For Each loop will iterate through the list starting at index 1 and going to the end of the list.

If the item MOD 2 = 0 (even number) OR item MOD = 1 (odd number) the item will be appended to the end of list2. Since number will always be either even or odd at the same time, list2 will be appended by all numbers in list2.

list2 [1, 1, 35, 6, 76, 4, 98]

8. **(B)** There is one data structure in this problem.

list1	1	1	35	6	76	4	98
index	1	2	3	4	5	6	7

max = 1

A For Each loop will iterate through the list starting at index 1 and going to the end of the list.

If(1 > max) ----- false max = 1
If(1 > max) ----- false If(35 > max) ----- true
max = 35 If(6 > max) -----false
If(76 > max) ----- true max = 76
If(4 > max) ----- false
If(98 > max) ----- true max = 98

98

9. **(B)** While the program will display the correct answer, it will not work in every case. The correct format is to set max equal to the first element of the list instead of setting max equal to zero. If the test case was filled with all negative numbers this program would contain a logical error.

Col 1	Col 2
1 > 0 true	max = 1
1 > 1 false	no change
35 > 1 true	max = 35
6 > 35 false	no change
76 > 35 true	max = 76
4 > 76 false	no change
98 > 76 true	max = 98

DISPLAY 98

10. **(A)**

If $p = 0$

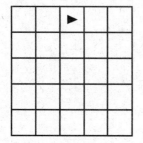

If $p = 1$

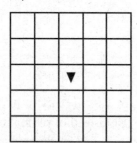

If $p = 3$

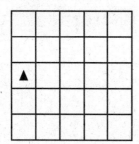

If $p = 4$

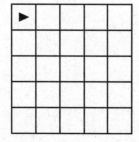

If $p = 5$

If p is greater than 5, then the robot will repeat the above pattern.

11. **(D)** If the robot rotates left then moves forward it will go out of the grid and result in an error.

$p = 1$

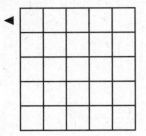

12. **(B)**

When $p = 1$

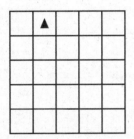

When $p = 2$

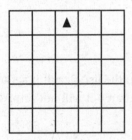

When $p = 3$

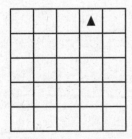

When $p = 4$

13. **(D)** The program is intended to return the largest number but returns the smallest number. To work as intended, the conditional should be item > result. Starting at result = 0 eliminates the numbers being negative.

Result	List	Is Item Less than Result?
0	1	False
−2	−2	True
−2	3	False
−2	0	False
−7	−7	True

14. **(A)** The program is intended to return the smallest number in the list. Result is set correctly to the first item in the list before the loop executes.

Result	List	Is Item Less than Result?
1		
1	1	False
−2	−2	True
−2	3	False
−2	10	False
−7	−7	True

15. **(B)** The program is intended to return the smallest number in the list. Result is set to 0 before the loop executes. Since no number in the list is less than 0 it will not return 1, which is the correct smallest value in the list.

Result	List	Is Item Less than Result?
0		
0	1	False
0	5	False
0	9	False
0	10	False

16. **(C)** The program returns and is intended to return the largest number in the list. Result is set to the first element in the list before the loop executes. If result was set to 0 the program would not work as intended.

Result	List	Is Item Greater than Result?
−3		
−3	−3	False
−3	−5	False
−3	−200	False
−1	−1	True

17. **(D)** Rotate left rotates the robot 90 degrees counterclockwise. After the robot rotates it moves forward one space.

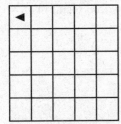

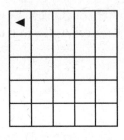

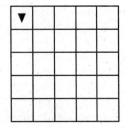

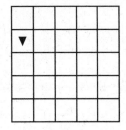

18. **(D)** The robot cannot move off the grid. The first move forward would result in an error.

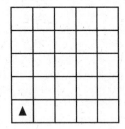

19. **(D)**

First Loop

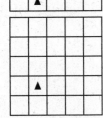

Second Loop

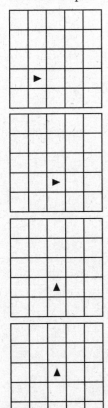

Rotate right

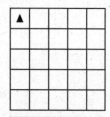

20. **(A), (B)**

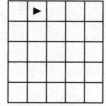

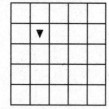

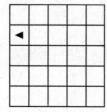

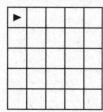

21. **(A), (C)**

$p = 0$

$p = 1$

$p = 2$

22. **(B)** Result keeps on reassigning itself to 0. This is not accumulating the values in the data structure.

Scores	Count	Result
	0	0
10	1	10
		0
10	2	10
		0
15	3	15

Display $15/3 = 5$

23. **(C)** To find the maximum number the condition should be item > max.

24. **(C)** If a number MOD 2 = 1, it signals that the number is odd. If a number MOD 2 = 0, it signals that the number is an even number.

25. **(D)** A number MOD 3 = 0 would be divisible by 3. For a number to be divisible by 5, item MOD 5 = 0. For this program to work as intended, both cases must be true. Since both need to be true, the logical AND needs to be used.

26. **(A)** Test the swap using any nonequal numbers. In this case I used 3 for x and 6 for y to test the swap. If the swap works, $x = 6$ and $y = 6$.

x	y	Temp
3	6	3
6	3	

27. **(B)** For the item to be added to x, the number must be equal to the item.

(D) The program will not have an error.

(A) and (C) are incorrect because of the selection statement.

28. **(C)** The selection statement is if the item MOD number is equal to 0, then the number is divisible by that number.

(A) and (D) are incorrect because the program runs with no errors.

(B) is incorrect because the selection statement is MOD, not =.

29. **(A)** If a number MOD 15 = 0, it indicates that the number is divisible by 15. All other answer choices are incorrect due to the wrong selection statement.

30. **(C)**

x = 10

LENGTH(arr) = 3

10 − 3 = 7

7 MOD 4 = 3

arr[3] = "Puppies"

31. **(C)** There are three data structures in this problem.

list1	1	35	6	76	−4	98
index	1	2	3	4	5	6

list2	5	1	8	96	−4
index	1	2	3	4	5

list3
index

This program will call the abstraction Mystery with list1, list2, and list3 as parameters.

A For Each loop will iterate through every item in list1.

If the item is found in list2 OR the item is less than 0, the item will be appended to the end of list3.

Is 1 found in list2 ----**YES** OR is item < 0 ----**NO**
Is 35 found in list2 ----**NO** OR is item < 0 ----**NO**
Is 6 found in list2 ----**NO** OR is item < 0 ----**NO**
Is 76 found in list2 ----**NO** OR is item < 0 ----**NO**
Is -4 found in list2 ----**YES** OR is item < 0 ----**YES** List3[-4]
Is 98 found in list2 ----**NO** OR is item < 0 ----**NO**

-4

32. **(D)**

x	y	z
~~5~~	~~10~~	~~15~~
~~20~~	-10	-5
-35		

33. **(D)**

x	y	z
5	10	15
-20	-10	-5
-35		

34. **(C)** A touchpad is sensitive to touch, which is a tactile input because it involves a detection of physical contact. The specific output for the program is visual, as it shows the exact location of the touch from a graphical perspective.

(A) and (B) mistake the input as visual, which it is not, as it is not dependent on anything based on light.

(D) mistakes the output for audible, which is untrue because the description mentions no audio.

35. **(C)** I and III are correct and describe the primary benefits of a procedure. II is incorrect as, in most cases, a procedure can only be used with the same programming language that it was written in without translation.

36. **(A), (D)** Procedures make it easier to read a program block by moving complex algorithms outside of the main method (and, if properly named, making the purpose closer to plain English). They also make it easier to modify because one change to the procedure means that all calls will follow the new code.

(B) is incorrect because methods can be imported or inherited from other classes.

(C) is incorrect because the code is transplanted out of the original block, meaning that viewing the entire code requires jumping to different places.

37. **(A)** Libraries contain functions that are useful for most users, but that are not directly supported by the bare language. While a method such as an exponent function might be easy to write, saving the programmer from having to do so makes the programming process more efficient.

(B) is incorrect because libraries are not designed for translating code.

(C) is incorrect because libraries do not support decompiling; that must be handled by other programs.

(D) is incorrect because libraries are created and managed by the language writers, not individual users.

38. **(A)** The below grid calls ziz, zag, ziz, ziz in that order.

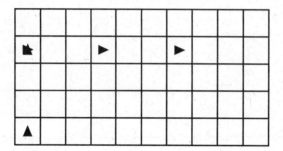

39. **(B)** The moveAndTurn procedure moves three times and then rotates 270 degrees. To land on the star the procedure moveAndTurn must be called twice.

40. **(A), (C)** The first answer choice (A) gets the robot on the square moving clockwise, and then the third (C) gets the robot to the square counterclockwise.

The Internet

7

BIG IDEA 6: THE INTERNET

"*The Internet is just the world passing around notes in a classroom.*"

—Jon Stewart

Chapter Goals

- Autonomous systems of the internet
- How the internet functions
- IP
- Packets
- SSL/TLS
- Domain name system
- Simple mail transfer protocol
- Fault tolerant
- Phishing

- Public key encryption
- Abstractions in the internet
- IPv4/IPv6
- TCP/IP
- Routers
- Internet service provider
- Hypertext transfer protocol
- Redundancy
- Distributed denial of service attack
- Symmetric key encryption

Autonomous Systems of the Internet

The internet connects devices and networks from all over the world. The internet is a physical network of fiber optics, radio transmitters, and cabling. In 1995, there were 16 million internet users. In 2017, there were 4156 million users. Devices and networks that make up the internet are connected and communicate using addresses and protocols. Evolving internet protocols, including those for addresses and names, have allowed for this rapid growth.

A computer network is a group of computers that use common protocols to exchange information and share resources. The internet is a high-level abstraction made up of networks. The internet is redundant, fault tolerant, and hardware and open source driven. Hardware such as wires, cables, ISPs, routers, and servers all work together to make up the internet.

Examples of these common protocols are as follows:

Internet protocol (IP) is responsible for addressing and routing your online requests. For a device to connect to the internet it is first assigned an internet protocol address.

IPv4/IPv6

When the internet was founded in the 1960s, the creators did not predict the need for billions and billions of IP addresses. Currently we are switching between the fourth and fifth versions of the internet protocol. The fourth version (IPv4) uses 32 bits to store IP addresses. 32 bits can hold 2^{32} IP addresses. 2^{32} when multiplied out is 4,294,967,296 unique addresses. The newer version, IPv6, uses 128 bits, which can hold 2^{128} IP addresses. This is equivalent to 3400000000000000000000000000000000000 unique addresses.

Switching from IPv4 to IPv6 is an increase in the capacity by $2^{128} - 2^{32} = 2^{96}$ devices.

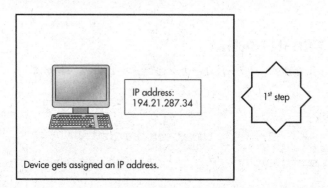

This IP address is not permanently assigned to a user's device and can change at any time.

Transmission control protocol/internet protocol (TCP/IP) is the protocol used to interconnect network devices on the internet.

Data traveling in the internet is broken down into small chunks of data called *packets*. TCP/IP protocols guide the rules on how data is subdivided into packets before transmission.

Trailer End of Packet	Data	Header: Sender's IP Address Receiver's IP Address Packet #

TCP/IP, the transmission control protocol/internet protocol, is the set of rules, or protocols, used to exchange data between hardware devices connected to the internet.

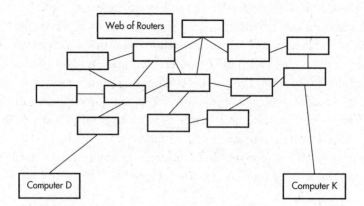

The paths packets travel from computer D to computer K will not be the same. Because packets can travel different paths, they will arrive at the target computer out of order. The paths packets take are guided physically by routers.

If a packet is not received, the TCP/IP protocol will request the sender resend the missing packet. The IP addresses of both the sender and receiver are found in the header of the packet. When all packets are received, the packets will be put together using the packet numbers found in the header to form the original binary message.

The process from computer D to computer K is called *end-to-end architecture*. The breaking down and assembling of the packets is done at each end. What happens to the packets in the middle is hidden from the user in an abstraction.

SSL/TLS

Secure sockets layer (SSL) is the technology for keeping the internet secure and safeguarding the data that is being sent between two systems. Transport layer security (TLS) is a more secure version of SSL. SSL has been replaced by TLS.

Internet Service Provider (ISP)

Most computers are not directly connected to the internet, but instead are connected to an internet service provider (ISP). An ISP connects a local device to the internet.

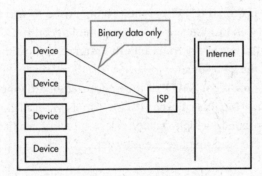

To access a site, you will need the target site's IP address. For example: 31.13.77.36 can be used to access Facebook.

Domain Name System (DNS)

Facebook is located at the IP address 31.13.77.36. It is difficult to remember 31.13.77.36 when you want to access Facebook. The domain name system (DNS) will translate a readable name into the IP address. This allows users to not have to look up the IP address every time they need to access a site. The DNS is designed to make IP addresses more readable and is analogous to a phonebook for looking up a person's phone number. When you type *facebook.com* the DNS server will translate your readable address to an IP address.

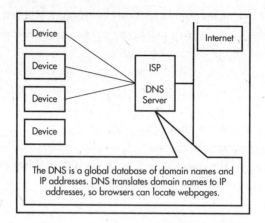

DNS is managed by hierarchies.

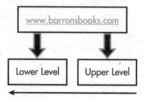

Hypertext transfer protocol (HTTP) is the protocol used to transfer data from remote servers over the web. All web browsers use HTTP protocol to communicate with web servers. The HTTP protocol is also necessary to handle the request sent to the web server, and the response received from the web server.

Simple mail transfer protocol (SMTP) is the internet standard for electronic mail (email).

The Internet Engineering Task Force (IETF): The mission of the IETF is to make the internet work better by producing high-quality, relevant technical documents that influence the way people design, use, and manage the internet.

Functions/Characteristics of the Internet

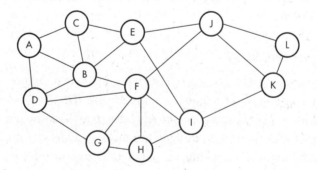

The diagram at the bottom of page 258 is a model of the internet. Notice there are many paths for data to travel. This redundancy in paths creates a fault-tolerant design. For example, there are many paths computer A can take if it wants to communicate with computer F:

    A – B – F

    A – C – E – I – F

    A – D – B – F

    A – D – G – F

The reason for redundant paths is if one path is broken the data will travel a different path. For example, if line A–B is broken then the data will only travel to or from A from C or D.

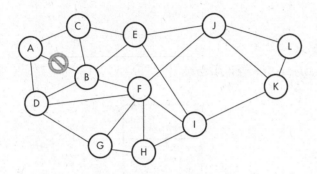

    Having A and B disabled will not stop traffic between A and F. The fault-tolerant nature of the internet will cause the data to be re-routed.

    A – C – E – I – F

    A – D – B – F

    A – D – G – F

How many lines need to be cut to completely isolate A?

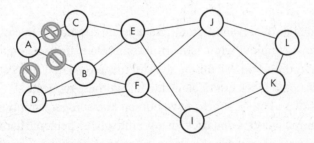

    You would have to cut three lines to completely isolate A.

    Point-to-point connections are where devices are directly connected with no intervening computers. On the other hand, end-to-end communications between computers are not necessarily directly connected. These computers must rely on other machines to relay their messages.

    All data traveling on the internet is in the form of binary data. Light sent through the fibers are most commonly generated by either an LED or a laser. These specialized optical transmitters "flash" the light to represent digital binary data, either on or off.

If information is traveling through fiber optics, a binary 1 would be "light on" and a binary 0 would be "light off." Light pulses sent through fiber optics are commonly generated by lasers or LED. Copper wire would send binary data as pulses of voltage.

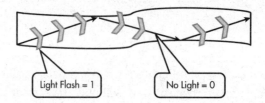

Cybersecurity

Distributed Denial-of-Service Attack

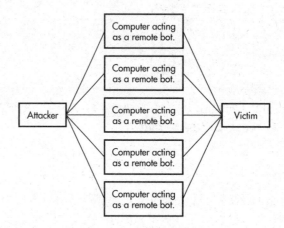

A distributed denial-of-service (DDoS) attack is an attempt to make an online service unavailable by overwhelming it with traffic from multiple sources. Computers can be controlled remotely, and thousands of computers can make repeated requests on the targeted website. This traffic could block out or slow down legitimate requests.

Phishing, viruses, and other attacks have human and software components. Phishing is directing users to unrelated sites that trick the user into giving personal data. Phishing attacks have become sophisticated, and can trick even experienced computer users into giving bank information.

This trust model of the internet has a trade-off between rapid growth and security. Cyberwar and cybercrime have widespread and potentially devastating effects. Antivirus software and firewalls can help avoid viruses but often have hidden viruses contained in them. The same open standards that fueled the growth of the internet have left the users of the internet open to such attacks.

To increase security encryption is used.

Symmetric key encryption uses the same public key for both encryption and decryption. The one key is a shared secret and relies on both sides keeping their key secret. Encryption uses cryptographic algorithms to encrypt data.

Symmetric Key Encryption

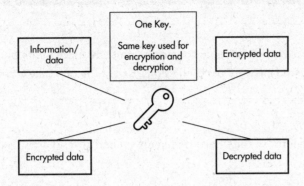

Public Key Encryption

Public key encryption uses two keys—one private and one public. Anyone with the public key can encrypt data, and the public key is a semi-secret. To decrypt, a second key, which is private, is needed.

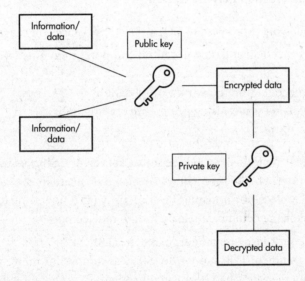

1. What are the benefits of the internet's having an end-to-end architecture? **Select two answers.**

   (A) New devices are more easily connected since they do not need to be registered on a central server.

   (B) Computational processes do not have to worry about a server's being online to work.

   (C) Computers can send unencrypted messages without having to worry about their being intercepted.

   (D) Data can be sent and interpreted faster.

2. Which of the following protocols are NOT utilized by devices on the internet?

   (A) IP—Routers that deliver data to a central computer then direct the data to its designation

   (B) TCP—Delivers data from network to applications

   (C) TLS—Encrypts messages using symmetric cryptography

   (D) None of the above

3. From 1995 to 1999, a protocol called secure sockets layer (SSL) was used to provide security on the internet. The protocol was declared obsolete in 2015; however, it had long since been replaced by transport layer security (TLS) following its release in 1999. Which of the following could be a reason for the replacement?

   (A) Older sites could easily migrate from SSL to TLS.

   (B) Upon the creation of TLS, support for SSL was removed from web browsers.

   (C) SSL's security measures had been circumvented, so evolving internet protocols had to be changed to maintain integrity of data.

   (D) All internet protocols are replaced within five years of their initial release.

4. In IPv6, the address length compared to IPv4 is quadrupled from 2^{32}. How many addresses can be created using IPv6?

   (A) 2^{16}

   (B) 2^{32}

   (C) 2^{64}

   (D) 2^{128}

5. What is the purpose of transitioning from IPv4 to IPv6?

    (A) IPv4 has been found to be too insecure for modern communication.
    (B) The rise of internet-connected devices means that the number of available unique IPv4 addresses is sharply decreasing, and IPv6 will allow for more addresses.
    (C) IPv4 is too slow to be useful in modern communications.
    (D) It is easier to spoof an IPv4 address, as compared to an IPv6 address.

6. Which of the following describes the characteristics of the internet and its systems?

      I. Content filtering
     II. Hierarchical organization
    III. Redundant connections

    (A) II only
    (B) I and III only
    (C) II and III only
    (D) I, II, and III

7. In the following URL, what is the lowest level of the domain's syntax hierarchy?

    `tovuti.net/ukurasa`

    (A) `tovuti.net/ukurasa`
    (B) `net/ukurasa`
    (C) `net`
    (D) `ukurasa`

8. For an IP address similar to 184.89.187.64, which of the following is an example of hierarchy in IP addresses?

    (A) Every four digits correspond to different hierarchical parts of the URL, such as `.com` or `.org`.
    (B) The first few digits of an address identify the network, while the rest specify a device on the network.
    (C) Higher-level networks have addresses that start with numbers in a specific range.
    (D) There is no hierarchy in IP addresses.

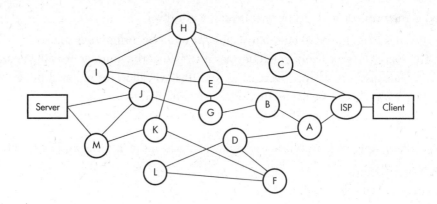

9. Look at the network map above. At least how many connections must be damaged to prevent the client and server from communicating? Assume that the system is fault-tolerant and that the connection between the client and the ISP cannot be damaged.

(A) 1

(B) 2

(C) 3

(D) 4

10. Which of the following illustrates how the internet's hierarchy can improve scalability?

(A) Clients can automatically demand the low-level www domain to save the number of communications.

(B) All requests sharing the same top-level domain, such as .edu, run through the same server.

(C) URLs with https:// ensure that the client is prepared to utilize TLS.

(D) Since the IP address gives the target's network, transmissions can look for the network first instead of immediately searching for the individual target.

11. How does redundancy improve the scaling of the internet?

(A) Redundancy leads to every communication being repeated, which keeps the data from being lost.

(B) Redundancy leads to every communication being repeated, which ensures that the connected devices do not disconnect from each other.

(C) Redundancy makes end-to-end connections more reliable, which means that more devices are able to communicate without interruption.

(D) Redundancy makes end-to-end connections more reliable, which ensures that computers are always on the internet.

12. How does the DNS hierarchy scale the system?

(A) DNS files are distributed to client computers in a hierarchical manner to ensure that new devices can quickly become connected.

(B) Since URLs are arranged in a hierarchical system, it is easier to find websites.

(C) A DNS server only finds data for computer clients in a specific category (e.g., smartphones, PCs, etc.).

(D) Since URLs are arranged in a hierarchical system, it is easier for new websites to be added and organized into the DNS.

13. Why are most websites designed to work within the boundaries of current web protocols, even when it limits a website's capabilities?

(A) Because the protocols are supported by all current web browsers, potential incompatibilities are minimized.

(B) It is illegal to go beyond the boundaries of current protocols.

(C) Current protocols are the limit of web technology, so going further is impossible.

(D) If a protocol is exceeded, an ISP will assume the website to be broken or malicious and block it.

14. The internet is built on open standards. In this context, what does "open" mean?

(A) The standards are made freely available and can be used by anyone.

(B) The standards cannot be utilized in proprietary software of any form.

(C) The standards can be used in any program that is used exclusively to access the web.

(D) The official standards can be made, updated, and edited by anyone.

15. In many old dial-up internet systems, images would typically be "filled in," meaning that the image would only appear up to a certain height, which would slowly increase. Which of the following describes why this occurs?

(A) Data packets travel quickly on dial-up systems, but they were encrypted using complex algorithms and took time to decipher.

(B) Data packets travel slowly on dial-up systems, so each portion of the image was displayed as it was received.

(C) Data packets involving images do not transfer on dial-up, so each packet was transmitted individually on another method.

(D) Data packets containing images could not be transferred on dial-up connections.

16. What is the purpose of the transmission control protocol/internet protocol (TCP/IP) suite?

(A) It controls the way that data is made into packets, addressed, transmitted, and reassembled.

(B) It enables the transmission of text communication in both directions.

(C) It controls the encryption of messages sent over a network using symmetric-key encryption.

(D) It controls the removal of electronic mail messages from a server.

17. What role do the secure sockets layer (SSL) and transport layer security (TLS) protocols play in web communication?

(A) Neither protocol plays any role; they are vestigial features from the early internet.

(B) SSL and TLS manage directory services and their use online.

(C) SSL and TLS encrypt communications to ensure that the data cannot be read if it is intercepted.

(D) SSL and TLS are used to initiate server connections.

18. DNS responses often do not have digital signatures, as that feature must be specifically added by the administrator. Why might this be a problem?

    (A) There is no way to determine if the IP address given was temporarily added or modified by a malicious third party.
    (B) There is no way to determine if the IP address given was permanently added or modified by a malicious third party.
    (C) There is no way to determine if a user is redirected to a malicious DNS.
    (D) There is no way to determine if a URL was improperly entered by the requesting user.

19. Which of the following is an example of cybersecurity being implemented through hardware?

    (A) To protect against phishing links, an email filter warns users that the email was sent from a suspicious address.
    (B) To protect against the Meltdown and Spectre vulnerabilities, Intel redesigned their processors to better separate processes and privilege levels.
    (C) To protect against the Heartbleed vulnerability, the cryptography toolkit OpenSSL was redesigned to ignore data requests that would result in a buffer overflow.
    (D) To protect against malicious programs, all files downloaded to a computer are scanned for viruses by an antivirus program.

20. Which of the following is an example of the effects that cyber attacks can have on the world at large?

    (A) Theft of personal information such as financial information
    (B) Interruption of essential governmental services
    (C) Loss or theft of confidential business work
    (D) All of the above

21. A common way that DDoS attacks are propagated is via *botnets*. These are networks created by infected machines that secretly perform commands for the malicious purpose without informing their users. Why might this method be preferred by cyber criminals for the purpose of DDoS attacks? **Select two answers.**

    (A) A botnet is the only way to ensure that the attack comes from many different IP addresses.
    (B) Botnets do not require the attacker to be revealed, since computers in a botnet do not communicate with a centralized server.
    (C) Since botnets can contain many different computers, DDoS attacks can be made much more powerful.
    (D) It is easier to program attacks with botnets as opposed to without them.

22. Which of the following is NOT an example of a human component within a cyber attack?

    (A) An advertisement tells users to download a certain antivirus program, which is really a virus or piece of spyware.
    (B) A website, which has been hacked, utilizes backdoor protocols in the browser or operating system to secretly download and run a virus.
    (C) A user is sent an email containing a link to an "interesting article," which is a website that utilizes backdoor protocols in the browser or operating system to secretly download and run malware.
    (D) A user is sent an email with an attached "PDF file," which is really an executable that installs and runs malware.

23. How is math utilized in cryptography?

    (A) The length of a string determines whether it should be encrypted.
    (B) Individual bits are given new values that are randomly generated using mathematical principles.
    (C) Bits and group of bits (e.g., characters) are modified by utilizing mathematical and algebraic principles.
    (D) Math is not used; cryptographic algorithms are purely logic-based.

24. How do open standards ensure the security of encrypted data?

    (A) Open standards have their flaws publicly documented, which means there are more people that can repair or mitigate those flaws.
    (B) Open standards are always backed by large corporations that can ensure the security through resources.
    (C) It is illegal to crack open standards, so security is guaranteed.
    (D) It is impossible to crack open standards because the specifications are private.

25. Suppose that a certain encryption program works by taking a number n and replacing every letter in the message with a letter n places after it. Numbers follow a similar pattern, but other characters such as spaces are unaffected. Thus, "ab d7 %" would become "bc e8 %" if $n = 1$. (If the calculated place number is too high, it rolls over to the beginning.) Could this be decrypted using symmetric encryption? If so, what would be the encryption key?

    (A) Yes, the key would be equal to $n * 1.5$.
    (B) Yes, the key would be equal to n.
    (C) Yes, the key would be equal to the numerical value of the first encrypted character.
    (D) No

26. What is the advantage of using public key encryption for encrypted communications?

    (A) A message cannot be decrypted without permission from the receiver.
    (B) Anyone can encrypt and decrypt a message, but he or she needs a key from the receiver.
    (C) A message can only be encrypted by someone who knows the receiver, regardless of whether he or she has a key.
    (D) Anyone can encrypt a message to the receiver without having to know how to decrypt it.

ANSWER KEY

1.	**A, B**	8.	**B**	15.	**B**	22.	**B**
2.	**D**	9.	**B**	16.	**A**	23.	**C**
3.	**C**	10.	**D**	17.	**C**	24.	**A**
4.	**D**	11.	**C**	18.	**C**	25.	**B**
5.	**B**	12.	**D**	19.	**D**	26.	**D**
6.	**C**	13.	**A**	20.	**D**		
7.	**A**	14.	**A**	21.	**B, C**		

ANSWERS EXPLAINED

1. **(A)**, **(B)** End-to-end architecture facilitates connecting new devices and networks on the internet. Operations such as encoding are handled in the communicating end nodes of the network, as opposed to some part of the network itself such as a router. This makes it easier to add new devices, since they do not need to be registered with a server that handles these operations; it also means that processes can be performed without worry that a server's going offline will be an interruption.

   (C) End-to-end architecture does not prohibit interception.

   (D) End-to-end does not affect transmission speed; additionally, interpretation is far slower on a client computer than on a server.

2. **(D)** All three of these are utilized.
   Internet protocol (IP) is responsible for addressing and routing your online requests. TCP is the protocol used to interconnect network devices on the internet. TLS provides security by encrypting messages.

3. **(C)** TLS is stronger and more secure than SSL, and the evolving nature of internet standards meant that the replacement occurred.

   (A) Changing the security protocol would require the site to be turned off (a major inconvenience).

   (B) SSL was retained in most browsers for compatibility reasons.

   (D) If this were correct, TLS would have fallen out of use by 2004, but it is still utilized today.

4. **(D)** The amount of valid addresses is 2^b, where b is the number of bits in the address. In IPv4, there were 32 bits. If IPv6 has quadrupled the number of bits then $4 \times 32 = 128$ bits. Hence, 2^{128} is a really big number.

   For completeness but beyond the scope of the AP test, 2^{128} is equal to 340,282,366,920, 463,463,373,607,431,768,211,456.

   (B) is incorrect; 2^{32} is the value of IPv4.

   (A) and (C) are not any form of IP.

5. **(B)** IPv4 supports 2^{32} (4,294,967,296) addresses. Since one must be assigned to every device, whether client or server, the number of open addresses is slowly decreasing. IPv6 increases the length of IP addresses and, therefore, supports far more addresses overall.

(A) The IP protocol is not related to security.

(C) The IP protocol is not related to speed.

(D) Address spoofing is simply replacing one address with another, regardless of whether it is IPv4 or IPv6.

6. **(C)** The internet is hierarchically organized to ensure that sites are easily found and routed. It has redundant connections to ensure that data can be passed to its destination even when there is a failure in one connection. Content filtering is not a part of the internet; it is performed by other systems such as parental controls.

7. **(A)** URLs are arranged with the lowest level first, which in this case is `tovuti.net/ukurasa`. The upper-level domain is `ukurasa`.

(B) This is a subdomain of the top-level domain `net`. (C) `ukurasa` is the top-level domain. (D) refers to a specific path within the `www` domain, so it is not included in the domain hierarchy.

8. **(B)** A certain portion of the IP address represents the higher-level network, while the rest represents the specific device.

(A) IP addresses are not designed to correspond with URLs, which are merely a more human-readable way to specify IPs (through the DNS).

(C) would have been correct in the early days of the internet, but rapid expansion caused this structure to be abandoned.

(D) is incorrect because of the network/host structure of IP addresses.

9. **(B)** For a fault-tolerant system, such as this, to fail, the sender and receiver must be isolated from each other. The easiest way to do this is to cut all the connections around either. Since the server has fewer connections, 2 is the answer.

(A) would be correct if the ISP/client connection were not deemed unbreakable, but that fact means that the connection count must move up to the ISP.

(C) is the number of connections to the ISP, so it would be correct if the server had more connections.

(D) is incorrect in any sense.

10. **(D)** Searching for the network makes it easier to find a computer by reducing the number of network blocks that need to be checked.

(A) `www` is not used by all websites.

(B) Top-level domains determine the portion of the DNS utilized, not the server.

(C) `https://` is not a part of the hierarchy.

11. **(C)** Redundancy means that computers can stay connected even when a connection is damaged, as there are other connections that pick up the slack. This means that communications are firmer and that it is easier to add new devices since the communications required to set them up can still be performed.

(A) and (B) are incorrect because redundancy does not refer to repeated communications.

(D) Computers can be taken off the internet through means not including connection (such as power loss, corrupted drivers, and turning off the device).

12. **(D)** It is easier to add new websites since they only have to be added to a subset (e.g., all `.com`, all `.edu`, etc.) of all URLs. This also makes it easier to deal with organization, since each subset is invariably smaller and easier to sort than the entire list of websites would be.

(A) DNS files are sent to ISPs, not individual devices.

(B) This is correct, but does not refer to scalability.

(C) DNS servers are not designed in this way.

13. **(A)** Utilizing protocols that aren't current means that most web browsers would be incompatible. This makes no sense for a website, which typically requires as many people as possible to be able to be view it.

(B) There is no legal body that could control this.

(C) Major companies, such as Google, are creating new protocols and web standards using current technology, which can lead to some differences between browsers.

(D) ISPs rarely filter based on the website's behavior; they only block if they are reported or contain banned content.

14. **(A)** Open standards allow anyone to access and utilize them.

(B) would make producing any internet-related proprietary software impossible, as HTTP, TCP/IP, and TLS are essentially required to contact any server.

(C) The same applies here, as these standards are necessary to use online features such as updates and help queries.

(D) Standards must still pass the muster of organizations, such as the World Wide Web Consortium.

15. **(B)** Dial-up is slow by current standards, so packets would rarely be received quickly enough to patch the entire image. This means that browsers would display what they had, which was only a portion of the image, until the last packet was received.

(A) Dial-up is slow and there is little reason to encrypt those files, as it would make the process of displaying images even longer.

(C) Images can be transferred over dial-up (additionally, most computers wouldn't have had a second method of transmission).

(D) would not allow images to be used.

16. **(A)** TCP/IP describes packetization, addressing, transmission, and assembly.

   (B) describes telnet.

   (C) describes transport layer security.

   (D) describes post office protocol.

17. **(C)** SSL and TSL are currently being used to encrypt and keep web communication safe.

   (A) While this could be argued for SSL, TLS is still very much in use, so it is false.

   (B) This describes the lightweight directory access protocol (LDAP).

   (D) misrepresents SSL and TLS's role; the process of initiation is handled by other protocols, with a key-sharing "handshake" being a portion of this.

18. **(C)** A digital signature is a string encrypted with a special private key; a user can decipher it using a public key to verify that the (unencrypted) message came from a legitimate source. This protects against malicious redirects since the malicious server would not know the private key used for verification; the fact that it is NOT present makes this kind of attack harder to notice.

   (A) refers to a cache poisoning attack.

   (B) is a server hack.

   (D) is a misspelling; none of these would be affected by a signature since the signature is merely added to the found IP address, regardless of how the IP address came to be in the DNS server.

19. **(D)** Software components, such as antivirus software and firewalls, can prevent malicious software from being executed (or, at least, alert the user). Hardware components can be designed to prevent the exploitation of hardware quirks (think Meltdown and Spectre). Lastly, human components, such as not running suspicious programs and ignoring phishing links, can keep the average person safe from many attacks.

20. **(D)** Cyber attacks can have a variety of motivations and effects, but all three of these are incredibly commonplace.

   (A) An example of theft of personal information such as financial information is keyloggers and spyware that are propagated through phishing links.

   (B) An example of interruption of essential governmental services is the WannaCry ransomware, which caused services in Great Britain's NHS system to be unavailable for some time.

   (C) An example of loss or theft of confidential business work is Shamoon, which destroyed business-related data at Saudi Arabia's national oil company.

21. **(B), (C)** A botnet both hides the instigator of the attack (since they are at the same level as all other machines in the botnet) and makes it easy to get multiple IP addresses to request data.

   (A) DDoS can also be done utilizing SYN floods, IP spoofing, and amplification attacks.

   (D) Programming a botnet requires attention to be given to communication, roles, and resource consumption.

22. **(B)** Since the virus is downloaded automatically, without the user's knowledge or involvement, there is no human component.

In (A), (C), and (D), the user must be involved, so there is a human component; this is downloading the program, clicking the article link, or opening the disguised executable, respectively.

23. **(C)** Cryptography works on mathematical principles to shift each character in an encrypted message.

(A) A message that requires encryption could be any length.

(B) This would be useless for encryption since random numbers could never be connected to their original values.

(D) This would make cryptographic algorithms nearly impossible, since they are normally made by modifying the numeric value of a piece of data. It is much easier to modify this using math.

24. **(A)** Open standards publish all of their technical specifications publicly, so people are more able to know about and understand flaws. This means that there are more people who can program and suggest fixes.

(B) Open standards can be published by a company or team of any size, so long as the specifications are public.

(C) Open standards are not government-backed (and even that would not ensure security since people break the law).

(D) The specifications of open standards are public by design.

25. **(B)** This is symmetric encryption because the numeric key can be plugged into both an encrypting and a decrypting algorithm. (Note that most encryption algorithms, symmetric or not, are more complicated than this.) The key would be equal to n since that is the exact distance between the original and the new characters.

(A) The resulting key would be floating-point, which may result in an incorrect answer depending on the system and scenario.

(C) That number could not show the relationship between the original message and the encrypted message (as it ONLY relates to the encrypted one).

(D) An algorithm using the original key can be made.

26. **(D)** Since public key encryption uses two keys, the encrypting public key can be shared, allowing anyone to write a message. That message can only be read by the person with the private key, but it can be written and encrypted without knowing that key.

(A) While this is correct in most cases, a stolen key can be used without the receiver's permission.

(B) This would be correct for symmetric encryption, as one key allows for both actions, but that is not true in public key encryption.

(C) This would be impossible to implement since there is no way to definitively prove the knowledge of the receiver.

Global Impact

8

BIG IDEA 7: GLOBAL IMPACT

"Be the change that you wish to see in the world."

—Mahatma Gandhi

Chapter Goals

- Changing the way people interact
- e-commerce
- Creative Commons
- Targeted advertisement
- Legal and ethical concerns
- Moore's law
- Digital Millennium Copyright Act (DMCA)
- Short message service
- Digital divide
- Cloud computing
- GPS
- Video conferencing

Changing the Way People Interact

Computing has changed the way people interact and communicate in daily life. Because of the internet, people can collaborate, share, and maintain relationships around the world. Most people can share large videos or send short messages (SMS) from almost any place at any time.

Video Conferencing

Video conferencing and video chat have made commutations cheaper and more flexible. For example, the grading of the performance task currently is graded by using video conferencing. Employees can work remotely and still have FaceTime with team members. Video chat is used frequently in mobile apps documenting life events for parents, friends, and future employees.

e-commerce

e-commerce refers to the purchase and sale of goods and/or services via electronic channels such as the internet. e-commerce allows customers to overcome geographical barriers and can allow them to purchase products anytime and from anywhere. Not only are they selling products, but they are also selling the metadata collected in the transaction.

e-commerce affects the economy by creating jobs and eliminating them at the same time. Some jobs have not been eliminated but they have been changed. For example, marketers still need ways to get people to visit their site, buy something, and come back to do it again. However, marketers can now use large data sets to target audiences who are likely to buy their product. For example, the author of this text bought himself a puppy online as a reward for writing this book. Not only did the author, Seth, get the advertisement below with the correct breed of purchased dog, but it also used the author's kid's name.

Targeted Advertisement

Email, SMS, video chat, cloud computing, and text-based chat have fostered new ways to communicate and collaborate. Social media has enabled us to communicate with a greater number of people on a global scale. The internet has even changed the way people date and work. Along with the benefits to work, the internet also provides many distractions that hurt productivity.

Social Media

Social media sites changed the way people share information. Social media makes spreading ideas easier and faster than it was in the past. Facebook has become so powerful that they have become catalysts for uprisings in the Middle East and a great influencer of political elections worldwide. News of events is shared in real time as the events are breaking. However, it is just as easy to post incorrect information as it is correct information. News that was previously obtained from established newspapers can now be created by anyone with no accuracy checks on the data being shared. Determining the credibility of a source requires considering and evaluating the reputation and credentials of the authors, publishers, site owners, and/or sponsors. This is difficult as the news sources intend to be credible. Information from a source is considered relevant when it supports an appropriate claim or the purpose of an investigation.

Short Message Service

Short message service (SMS), which is the formal name for text messages, delivers minimal content to a mass amount of people. The majority of people have limitations and do not include everyone.

Digital Divide

This barrier to communication is called the digital divide and is the differing access to computing and the internet based on socioeconomic or geographic characteristics. The global distribution of computing resources raises issues of equity, access, and power. Access to internet, phones, or computers is limited and many people cannot afford access. Some people may have the finances to own these devices but choose not to use them or don't have the knowledge to use them.

Data Generators

As systems are linked together by sensors, including geographic location sensors, we are faced with a new set of ethical and legal questions, such as security, privacy, transparency, data ownership, and sharing of copyrighted material. For example, an iPhone has a proximity sensor, accelerometer/motion sensor, ambient light sensor, moisture sensor, gyroscope, compass, barometer, Touch ID, Face ID, and thermal sensors. What the iPhone does with the data generated by these sensors should be a concern to the user.

The amount of data available is overwhelming. For example, just by knowing the name of the author of this book, you could easily look up his address, the type of car he drives, and even pictures taken by satellite of his backyard. Search engines use complex algorithms to show results when using a search engine. Trends from search engines can be used as predictors of public interest.

Global Positioning System

Global positioning systems (GPS) and related technologies have changed how humans travel, navigate, and find information related to geolocations. GPS was originally created by the U.S. Department of Defense to improve military navigation. Innovations such as Uber not only use GPS to locate destinations, but they also use it to record if a driver is speeding or making short stops. GPS can also predict weather and road hazards, making travel safer and more convenient.

Cloud Computing

Cloud computing fosters new ways to communicate and collaborate. By using cloud applications people from remote locations can work on and make live changes to documents. If your personal equipment breaks, for example, a flash drive or hard drive, your data would be safe if you were also saving your information to a cloud server. The drawback of using a cloud as a server is that the user would need an active internet connection to access data. As with all internet activity, security and privacy are a constant concern for users.

Privacy and Security

Security provides and protects information's confidentiality, integrity, and availability. Security protects that data from cyber attacks and hacking. Privacy assures that personal information is collected, processed, protected, and destroyed legally and fairly. Privacy is the right to control the data generated by one's usage of computing innovations and restrict the flow of that data to third parties.

Privacy and security are concerns with any interaction on the internet. Once a company's security or privacy has been compromised it takes years, if ever, for customers to trust it again. Target, Ashley Madison, AOL, Yahoo, and Facebook are examples of large companies that have had their data compromised, with some of those companies never recovering consumers' trust.

Data Storage

Industries that use the internet rely heavily on digital storage to run their businesses. Storage needs increase every day as users generate significant amounts of valuable data daily. For example, the National Security Agency (NSA) data storage center in Utah is estimated to have between 1 and 5 zettabytes of storage.

Storage needs increase frequently, and companies need to predict storage costs as they increase.

Moore's Law

Moore's law is used to plan future research and development based on anticipated increases in computing power. Moore's law states that microprocessor processing power doubles about every 18 months, especially relative to cost and size. According to Moore's law, new computer models are consistently smaller, lighter, faster, and more powerful than earlier models for the same price. Moore's law is not actually a law but an approximation that companies use to plan for future costs.

The accessibility of high-powered computers and public data has enabled crowdsourced "citizen science" problem solving. For example, the ground-breaking wide study of the behavior of fireflies was done by many scientists over long distances. It could cause setbacks for scientists in regards to collecting data. An important tenet of science is the replication of an experiment. By publishing experimental results publicly, a large number of scientists can perform the experiment and compare the results to determine if the data is incorrect or suggest a problem with the process.

Crowdsourcing

Crowdsourcing enables innovation by providing the ability to access and share information. For example, in your creative performance task coding, hints could be found on websites such as Stack Overflow, which crowdsources questions and answers on coding tips. You could ask the "crowd" for feedback, and anyone with access can provide answers. The accuracy of the answers can vary.

Crowdsourcing can also be used for fundraising. Anyone can raise money for almost any cause; however, with the ease of posting legitimate crowdsourcing causes, it is equally easy to post false causes.

Distributed solutions can scale to solve some problems. A distributed solution is a collection of independent computers that appears to its users as a single coherent system. An example of a distributed solution is the internet itself. The internet has an enormous size but no single authority while sharing hardware such as routers and servers. To the user of the internet it appears to directly connect to websites when in reality it is a combination of many machines working in collaboration.

Creative Commons

Open access and Creative Commons have enabled broad access to digital information. Creative Commons is an American nonprofit organization that is dedicated to expanding the range of creative works available for others to build upon and share legally. The Creative Commons license is a public copyright license that allows for free distribution of copyrighted work. Creative Commons is used to give people the right to use, share, and build upon an author's work. These licenses allow creators to communicate which rights they reserve, and which rights they waive for the benefit of recipients or other creators. Creative Commons licenses can vary from letting others copy, distribute, display, and perform only original copies of their work while not allowing modification without the author's permission to allowing for modification if credit is given to the author. There are six different levels of this license.

Digital Millennium Copyright Act

The Digital Millennium Copyright Act (DMCA) is an extension of copyright laws that prevent the use of devices that allow duplication of copyrighted materials and limit the liability of online service providers. The DMCA has been a benefit and a challenge to making copyrighted digital material widely available. DMCA was signed into law by President Clinton on October 28, 1998. The DMCA's principal innovation in the field of copyright is the exemption from direct and indirect liability of internet service providers and other intermediaries. File, music, and movie sharing on the internet is outlawed by the DMCA.

DIRECTIONS: Each of the questions or incomplete statements below is followed by four suggested answers or completions. Select the one that is best in each case.

1. How have text-based systems (email, SMS, chat, etc.) affected modern communications? **Select two answers.**

   (A) Text-based communication between people can be handled more quickly and reach more people than traditional communications.
   (B) It is harder to communicate emotion, as these systems do not support this in any form.
   (C) People are guaranteed to only connect with people they know or need to work with.
   (D) It is easier to share digital work through attachments, embeds, and hyperlinks.

2. Which of the following are benefits to having information easily accessible?

   I. Information can be easily found by researchers, which can improve experimental and investigative findings.
   II. Information can be easily found by students, who can use it to improve their understanding of a topic.
   III. Information can be easily checked by third parties, which ensures that it is always correct and up-to-date.

   (A) I only
   (B) I and II only
   (C) II and III only
   (D) I, II, and III

3. A government agency publishes data from a recent experiment it conducted. How could making this data public be useful?

   (A) By enabling researchers to access the data, it allows them to replicate the experiment and determine if the results are similar.
   (B) It enables any person to determine if the results are correct through a simple glance.
   (C) It allows the public to decide if the experiment costs too much, given its allocated budget.
   (D) It allows the public to decide whether the experiment should have been done, based on the results.

4. What does it mean to say that social media has "enhanced dissemination"?

   (A) Social media has no effect on the ability to spread and share ideas compared to pre-internet newspapers.
   (B) Social media makes spreading short, simplistic ideas easier than it was in the past.
   (C) Social media makes spreading an idea difficult due to increased disagreement among users.
   (D) Social media makes spreading an idea easier and faster than it was in the past.

5. Which of the following is an example of how global positioning systems (GPS) have affected human navigation? **Select two answers.**

   (A) GPS can be used to calculate the most efficient route to a location.
   (B) GPS can be used to inform people of nearby points-of-interest such as restaurants.
   (C) GPS is used to give people information about points-of-interest such as user reviews.
   (D) GPS is used to communicate with other drivers or commuters.

6. Which of the following is an example of a sensor network leading to enhanced interaction?

   (A) At a theme park, pressure-sensitive pads in the ground cause different aspects of the surrounding area to move when they are walked over.
   (B) At a mall, security cameras are used to monitor the activity of patrons.
   (C) At a hospital, a digital system is used to schedule doctor-patient interactions such as checkups and surgical procedures.
   (D) At a news station, a digital system is used to send locations to reporting teams.

7. What is an example of a way that a "smart grid" could assist with human capabilities?

   (A) The grid could control the temperature of an A/C or heating unit directly.
   (B) The grid could prevent blackouts altogether.
   (C) The grid could distribute power in the most efficient manner possible, ensuring that all users are capable of using power.
   (D) The grid could ensure that all computers on it are properly updated.

8. Which of the following areas has the internet had a major effect on?

   (A) Commerce
   (B) Access to information
   (C) Education
   (D) All of the above

9. Which of the following is a NEGATIVE effect that the web has on productivity?

   (A) It is harder to efficiently communicate with team members since this requires an exceptionally high-end internet connection.
   (B) It is harder to verify the authenticity of productivity-related communications.
   (C) It is easier to access activities that are unrelated to work, creating potential distractions.
   (D) It is easier to damage the infrastructure (i.e., network) of a workplace or similar environment.

10. Which of the following would be an example of "citizen science" that utilizes technology?

(A) People take pictures of wildlife using an app that sends information about species and location to researchers.

(B) A specially fitted camera records the hair and eye color of people that are in a certain public square.

(C) An advertising firm tests several potential commercials among members of a focus group and determines how demographics such as gender and race affect reactions.

(D) An app sends basic diagnostic information about errors and crashes to its developer.

11. Which of the following is an example of using many contributions to benefit society?

(A) A jigsaw simulation game determines the picture by randomly selecting images that are found on the internet with specific dimensions.

(B) An encyclopedia is made freely available with contributions made by college professors.

(C) News aggregators take articles from many different sources, which ensures that people have access to news from many different viewpoints.

(D) A tech company has a small percentage of its users try out the beta version of their products to get feedback on the features and functionality.

12. Which of the following are new models of collaboration that have been created through crowdsourcing? **Select two answers.**

(A) Small teams and businesses can collaborate with the general public to receive financing for projects.

(B) A moderately sized development team can have members of the general public edit and improve a beta's source code.

(C) A development team can invite a small amount of potential users to give comments on a current beta build.

(D) A project that had been abandoned can be remade and finished by another group made up of members of the general public.

13. How has the rise of mobile computing led to new applications?

(A) Since mobile devices are typically always on and internet-connected throughout the day, applications can assume that a user is capable of using it at any time.

(B) Mobile devices make audio-based communication much easier.

(C) Since mobile devices are much smaller, they are easier to modify from a hardware perspective.

(D) By design, it is easier to modify a mobile device's firmware.

14. Which of the following describes an impact that machine learning has had on its given field?

(A) Medicine—machine learning can be used to determine the conditions that indicate a disease, leading to better diagnosis.

(B) Business—algorithms can be produced through machine learning that ensure the efficient use of resources such as money allocated to advertising.

(C) Science—machine learning can be used to organize data and determine noteworthy values collected in scientific research.

(D) All of the above

15. How does the ability to share information lead to additional innovation?

   (A) Sharing information allows people with identical perspectives to assess and create innovations based on the information.
   (B) Sharing information allows people with different perspectives to assess and create different innovations based on the same information.
   (C) Sharing information enables different people to develop the same innovation, which proves how strong the underlying idea is.
   (D) Sharing information enables people to better understand other innovations.

16. The website Napster was originally created as a hub for peer-to-peer communications that were used to transfer music. The website was shut down after a lawsuit and was later reformatted into a music store. Why might this lawsuit have occurred?

   (A) Napster was unable to regulate the transfers to ensure that they did not allow for music piracy.
   (B) Napster's communications are peer-to-peer, which are inherently illegal.
   (C) Napster's communications were not run through a government server that ensured a lack of malicious activity.
   (D) Napster was created before music streaming was considered legal.

17. Which of the following is an ethical concern of software and content licensing?

   (A) A license might unfairly damage a buyer's ability to exercise their rights regarding ownership.
   (B) A license typically forbids copying the software or content for non-personal use.
   (C) A license might forbid the use of the software for illegal purposes such as the creation of malware.
   (D) None of the above

18. Suppose that a web browser on a mobile device collects information about login information and geolocation. Is this a security concern?

   (A) Yes, because both of these could be used for malicious purposes such as identity theft.
   (B) Only the login information, as geolocation is meaningless on the internet.
   (C) Only the geolocation, as login information is unrelated to personal information.
   (D) No, because neither is particularly tied to a person's identity.

19. The web browser Puffin advertises complete anonymity on the internet by having all website requests run through Puffin's servers. How does this enable anonymity?

   (A) The servers compress the data leaving the server, which ensures that it will not be decrypted.
   (B) The server does not store any information about the client.
   (C) The servers act as a proxy, which means that all interactions within a website are done through Puffin's servers rather than the user's devices.
   (D) The servers are designed to scan data running through them for viruses, which prevents spyware from reaching the client computer.

20. How does technology enable the collection and use of information about individuals and groups?

(A) Algorithms translate human thought into information.
(B) Algorithms are utilized to translate machine code into English and to collect and store the information.
(C) Computers collect data about the actions performed by groups and individuals, which can be processed into usable information using algorithms.
(D) Computers collect data about text that is typed by groups and individuals, which can be processed into usable information using algorithms.

21. Which of the following is an example of targeted advertising being misused at an aggregate level?

(A) Allowing housing and employment advertisements to not be shown to certain minorities, which violates two civil rights laws
(B) Sending ads designed to scare viewers to frighten them
(C) Allowing advertisements that deliberately lie to be viewed on the platform
(D) Determining advertisements for a specific person based on information that was obtained through a privacy policy violation

22. Which of the following is a question about intellectual property (IP) that is raised specifically by modern informational systems?

(A) How can an IP holder prevent his or her content from being copied?
(B) How can an IP holder prevent his or her content from being distributed?
(C) How can an IP holder determine whether other work does not utilize his or hers outside of the bounds of fair use?
(D) How can an IP holder deal with violating content that is on a server located outside of his or her country?

23. Which of the following is an example of a business impact of open source programs and libraries?

(A) Many open source programs and libraries are copyleft, which forbids their reuse.
(B) Many open source programs and libraries are copyleft, which forbids them from being used in any program with a more restrictive license.
(C) Many open source programs and libraries are in the public domain, which means that they cannot be used in a commercial setting.
(D) Many open source programs and libraries forbid businesses from accessing their source code.

24. Which of the following is NOT a consequence of the disparity in online access?

(A) Rural areas are less likely to receive internet access because of the high cost of laying a connection.
(B) Companies that are not listed online may have a harder time gaining a consumer base.
(C) People that live in poorer regions are less able to communicate because they do not have access to some methods of communication.
(D) Political supporters that are too poor to access the internet are less able to communicate with each other and their representatives.

25. How has the rise of mobile and wireless networking impacted innovation?

    (A) Devices can be controlled remotely.
    (B) Finished innovations can be distributed to any customer instantaneously.
    (C) An innovation that normally requires the use of a wire can be redesigned to be wireless with little effort.
    (D) Communication used for innovation can be performed by more devices in more locations.

26. Which of the following is NOT an issue raised by the global distribution of computing resources?

    (A) How would a developing computer market be affected if it had less powerful computers than the rest of the world?
    (B) What impact does the lack of internet in some areas have on their well-being?
    (C) If a country suddenly gains a large amount of computing-related resources, how will that affect the balance of world power?
    (D) If a new type of hardware can be created with any computing resources, how will that affect the price of the hardware?

27. Which of the following is an effect that the "digital divide" has on the given group?

    (A) Teachers without computers are unable to grade work at all.
    (B) Students without computers have a harder time accessing resources and programs for schoolwork.
    (C) Mathematicians without computers cannot evaluate calculus expressions such as integrals.
    (D) Taxi and carpool drivers without computers cannot find efficient routes.

28. Which of the following is a method of search refinement that is based on Boolean logic?

    (A) Excluding results of a genre
    (B) Filtering results by decade published
    (C) Only including results with specific data values
    (D) All of the above require Boolean logic

29. Which of the following are ways that technology has affected plagiarism? **Select two answers.**

    (A) Copying information verbatim is much easier since it can be done using cut-and-paste commands.
    (B) It is easier to plagiarize out of sloth since computers cannot expedite the process of citation.
    (C) It is easier to detect plagiarism through the use of services that automatically check text against the web.
    (D) Copying information verbatim is much harder due to the use of web scripts that prevent the copying of website material.

ANSWER KEY

1.	**A, D**	9.	**C**	17.	**A**	25.	**D**
2.	**B**	10.	**A**	18.	**A**	26.	**D**
3.	**A**	11.	**C**	19.	**C**	27.	**B**
4.	**D**	12.	**A, B**	20.	**C**	28.	**D**
5.	**A, B**	13.	**A**	21.	**A**	29.	**A, C**
6.	**A**	14.	**D**	22.	**D**		
7.	**C**	15.	**B**	23.	**B**		
8.	**D**	16.	**A**	24.	**A**		

ANSWERS EXPLAINED

1. **(A), (D)** Text-based communication is now the speed of a connection (rather than the mail service), and digital work can be shared either through URL links or dedicated methods within the system.

   (B) Emotion can be indicated through wording and symbolism (emoticons/emojis).

   (C) Most systems cannot filter messages in this manner (see junk mail).

2. **(B)** I and II describe uses for information, and making that information easier to access improves both of these effects. III is incorrect because information is not always checked; and checks made do not necessarily lead to changes to articles.

3. **(A)** An important tenet of science is the replication of an experiment. By publishing the results publicly, a large number of scientists can perform the experiment and compare the results to the government's to determine if the data is incorrect or suggest a problem with the methodology.

   (B) mistakes this for a simple examination of the results, which is not enough.

   (C) discusses finances, which is not something that the experiment's results could demonstrate. (This information might still be available online; it just won't be in the published results.)

   (D) The connection between results and necessity is fallacious; a necessary test might still have expected results. By this logic, there would be no repetition since already known facts would be considered solid, when they are not.

4. **(D)** Dissemination means "the act or process of dispersion or spreading something," so "enhanced dissemination" means that it improves this process.

   (A) and (C) do not correctly describe the enhancement, while (B) is too narrow in its scope.

5. **(A), (B)** GPS is used to determine location. With (A), this determines the position of the start and end for the path, allowing the computer to map a path from there. (B) determines the position of the user and the nearby POIs so they can be found and mapped, allowing the user to navigate to them more easily.

   (C) describes data about the POIs that does NOT include location.

   (D) is possible (by placing messages at specific geographic locations) but does not have a major effect on navigation.

6. **(A)** The pressure sensors in the pads are used to interact with certain aspects of the environment such as moving parts or sound effects.

   (B) The interaction (e.g., sending a security guard to a store being robbed) is not triggered by a sensor.

   (C) and (D) The system is only used for organization and nonbinding communication, not a stimulus for interaction.

7. **(C)** Efficient power distribution ensures that all users on the system are able to utilize power without one system taking too much.

   (A) and (D) An electrical grid cannot directly affect a machine's software since power is separate from communication features.

   (B) Some blackouts (e.g., severe weather damage to power cables) cannot be avoided on a software level.

8. **(D)** It has affected commerce by making it easier to find and remotely order items. It has affected access to information through the free and searchable nature of much of the internet (think Wikipedia). It has affected education by enabling the publishing of educational guides and enabling better interaction between students and teachers (if used properly).

9. **(C)** Even with administrator-set filters, it is possible to access non-work-related websites such as video platforms and games, which distracts the worker and leads to lost productivity.

   (A) disregards both the relatively low-speed requirements of most communication tools and other methods such as the telephone and face-to-face interaction, which can still be used.

   (B) can be subverted through the use of cryptographic protocols such as digital signatures.

   (D) is untrue as long as the system administrator has placed security protocols such as a firewall and tiered restrictions in place.

10. **(A)** This is citizen science because it allows members of the general public to provide information in this research (presumably to determine wildlife areas and migration patterns).

    In (B), (C), and (D), nonresearchers are not actively involved in the process of collecting and submitting data, so it is not citizen science.

11. **(C)** News aggregators take contributions from many different sources and reporters to keep users informed from multiple ends of the political spectrum.

(A) Jigsaws have little impact on society (and may be detrimental if those images are not used with permission).

(B) This limits the contributions to college professors, so there are not many contributions.

(D) This is incorrect for the same reasons as (B), since the percentage of users that beta test is small.

12. **(A), (B)** Crowdsourcing refers to aspects of the project coming from the public, and in both of these cases some aspect is from the public (financing in (A) and the source code in (B)).

(C) The testers were specifically picked; therefore, this is not crowdsourcing.

(D) This is not crowdsourcing, because the original project was not specifically put up for the purposes of editing.

13. **(A)** Mobile phones are very close to always-on, so apps can be designed to be used at any time, extending their reach.

(B) Smartphones tend to be no easier to use than much simpler cellular phones.

(C) Smaller pieces of hardware are harder to replace and limit the amount of extensions that can be made at any given time.

(D) Most mobile devices, through both design and limited inputs, are harder to edit from a firmware perspective.

14. **(D)** All three of these are legitimate uses. AI is built to examine factors such as genome sequences to better determine the presence of diseases. Machine algorithms are used to determine the ads that a person is most likely to react to, which ensures that money is not being wasted on advertising to the uninterested; machine learning is used to determine these factors. Additionally, having a computer search and organize data makes it easier to find statistical outliers and other useful information in less time; machine learning is used to determine what information could be considered useful.

15. **(B)** Different people can develop different innovations in different ways, so communication enables more people to access the innovation leading to it.

(A) No two people have fully identical perspectives.

(C) This is possible but unlikely, as the different perspectives would lead to different approaches in most cases.

(D) This is a true statement, but does not explicitly connect to additional innovation.

16. **(A)** Transferring peer-to-peer meant that the music files did not go through a central server to be examined. Unfortunately, this meant that there was no way to ensure that the music was not copyrighted, so Napster was unable to operate amid the liabilities of infringement.

(B) Peer-to-peer communications are the foundation of local networks and the internet itself.

(C) Such a server does not (and should never) exist.

(D) Napster was used for transfers, not streaming (and streaming music has never been illegal, per se).

17. **(A)** Licenses are written to determine what a person cannot do with software and content (e.g., illegally copying and selling a CD is forbidden by most licenses), and this can overlap with ownership rights if it is poorly or maliciously written (e.g., forbidding the resale of a purchased CD without DRM implemented). Removing rights in this manner is unethical, though not necessarily illegal if the license is properly worded. The other choices are not ethical concerns since nonpersonal copying and cyber crimes are violations of the law.

18. **(A)** The login information could be used to access personal information such as the information stored on a bank or college application website. The geolocation could be used to piece together a person's address or daily routine, which also would have a use for identity thieves. As a result, the web browser must be able to keep this information secure and dispose of it as soon as possible.

    (B), (C), and (D) misunderstand the potential concern of one of these.

19. **(C)** Puffin's browser uses proxy servers. If a Puffin user googles the phrase "test," the Google server views the Puffin servers as the requester. This means that the exact requester is hidden from the web server, making it harder to track the user.

    (A) and (D) deal with security, not anonymity.

    (B) would make it impossible to send the information back to the user.

20. **(C)** Computers collect data and metadata for the sake of organization and the developer's intention. Algorithms process this into information. For example, Google collects data about searches; if a person searches regularly for articles about animals, then Google's algorithm can use this data to produce information relating to their interest in animals.

    (A) misses the in-between of the computational device.

    (B) incorrectly suggests that this information is stored in English, which is false, as digital information is always stored in binary.

    (D) limits the data to text that is typed, which is too narrow for many information-gathering algorithms.

21. **(A)** Preventing certain minorities from viewing a housing listing violates the Fair Housing Act of 1968, and preventing certain minorities from viewing a job listing violates the Civil Rights Act of 1964. Targeted advertising easily allows both, despite this. Allowing such a crime this easily for any listing is an aggregate flaw (as it applies to the entire system).

    (B) is wholly unethical, but it is only a misuse at an individual level since it only targets one person.

    (C) is criminal activity (deliberately false advertising is very much a crime) but is more a problem with the platform holder than the targeting itself.

    (D) is criminal since the data was obtained outside of a legal agreement, but it also only targets one person.

22. **(D)** Since intellectual property laws are different depending on the country holding the data, it can be difficult for IP holders to assert copyright claims and take down violating websites if the other government does not pursue that. Since things cannot be easily blocked on the internet, many things may remain up despite this.

(A), (B), and (C) discuss concepts that would exist even without modern informational systems (though the concerns might not be as widespread, they're still there).

23. **(B)** Many open source programs are placed under a copyleft license such as GPL or CC SA. This means that any derivative works may not be placed under a more restrictive license, which is required for most commercial products. This, effectively, forbids the commercial use of these technologies.

(A) does not correctly describe copyleft restrictions.

(C) Open source does not necessarily mean that the described software is in the public domain; additionally, software in the public domain specifically would allow it to be used in any instance.

(D) Open source licenses only forbid the commercial reuse of code, as opposed to any commercial interaction.

24. **(A)** While the statement about cable-laying cost is true, it is a cause of the disparity rather than a consequence.

(B) demonstrates a business consequence.

(C) demonstrates a social consequence.

(D) demonstrates a political consequence.

25. **(D)** Wireless networking allows internet-based communication, such as email, to be used by any device that supports wireless communication in any location where they could access the internet. Without this, only hard-wired devices in a networked location, such as an office, could be used. This enables better communication among innovators.

(A) Wireless technologies such as RF, which did not communicate over a network, existed before wireless networking.

(B) Physical innovations cannot be transferred instantaneously.

(C) A redesign can be difficult, depending on the technology being altered.

26. **(D)** The fact that it can use any resources means that the distribution of exact resources (e.g., minerals and processing factories) does not affect the issue of cost, at least not directly.

(A) describes a question of resource equity.

(B) describes a question of resource access.

(C) describes a question of how resource differences affect power.

27. **(B)** Students without computers still need to access the internet and utilize programs such as PowerPoint for certain assignments. Even when there are public access points such as a library, this can be a huge handicap.

(A) Most grade calculations are either too subjective for a computer (e.g., writing assignments) or are simple math calculations (e.g., percentage of correct answers on a multiple-choice test). A computer can make these easier but is by no means required.

(C) Most calculus problems can be performed by hand. While some require a computer/calculator and others are sped up using the same, the answer's reach is too broad.

(D) Reasonably efficient routes can be found using a map and knowledge of a city's typical traffic conditions. Like (A) and (C), a computer speeds up this process but is not required.

28. **(D)** All three of these methods utilize Boolean logic. They find the given value of an item, compare it to the target using Boolean logic, and use that result in another Boolean logic comparison to determine whether it should be added to the result list.

29. **(A), (C)** Both of these statements describe effects on plagiarism. Plagiarism is easier to perform because it is easier to mindlessly CTRL+C and CTRL+V than put in the effort of writing the entire original out by hand. At the same time, automation makes it easier to detect plagiarism since services can automatically check text against previous papers and other websites.

(B) Citations can be made more quickly through the use of websites such as EasyBib and built-in features such as Microsoft Word's References tab.

(D) While these scripts do exist, they are not widely used since they must be deliberately placed by the site owner and limit legitimate citations.

Practice
Tests

1. Ⓐ Ⓑ Ⓒ Ⓓ	25. Ⓐ Ⓑ Ⓒ Ⓓ	49. Ⓐ Ⓑ Ⓒ Ⓓ
2. Ⓐ Ⓑ Ⓒ Ⓓ	26. Ⓐ Ⓑ Ⓒ Ⓓ	50. Ⓐ Ⓑ Ⓒ Ⓓ
3. Ⓐ Ⓑ Ⓒ Ⓓ	27. Ⓐ Ⓑ Ⓒ Ⓓ	51. Ⓐ Ⓑ Ⓒ Ⓓ
4. Ⓐ Ⓑ Ⓒ Ⓓ	28. Ⓐ Ⓑ Ⓒ Ⓓ	52. Ⓐ Ⓑ Ⓒ Ⓓ
5. Ⓐ Ⓑ Ⓒ Ⓓ	29. Ⓐ Ⓑ Ⓒ Ⓓ	53. Ⓐ Ⓑ Ⓒ Ⓓ
6. Ⓐ Ⓑ Ⓒ Ⓓ	30. Ⓐ Ⓑ Ⓒ Ⓓ	54. Ⓐ Ⓑ Ⓒ Ⓓ
7. Ⓐ Ⓑ Ⓒ Ⓓ	31. Ⓐ Ⓑ Ⓒ Ⓓ	55. Ⓐ Ⓑ Ⓒ Ⓓ
8. Ⓐ Ⓑ Ⓒ Ⓓ	32. Ⓐ Ⓑ Ⓒ Ⓓ	56. Ⓐ Ⓑ Ⓒ Ⓓ
9. Ⓐ Ⓑ Ⓒ Ⓓ	33. Ⓐ Ⓑ Ⓒ Ⓓ	57. Ⓐ Ⓑ Ⓒ Ⓓ
10. Ⓐ Ⓑ Ⓒ Ⓓ	34. Ⓐ Ⓑ Ⓒ Ⓓ	58. Ⓐ Ⓑ Ⓒ Ⓓ
11. Ⓐ Ⓑ Ⓒ Ⓓ	35. Ⓐ Ⓑ Ⓒ Ⓓ	59. Ⓐ Ⓑ Ⓒ Ⓓ
12. Ⓐ Ⓑ Ⓒ Ⓓ	36. Ⓐ Ⓑ Ⓒ Ⓓ	60. Ⓐ Ⓑ Ⓒ Ⓓ
13. Ⓐ Ⓑ Ⓒ Ⓓ	37. Ⓐ Ⓑ Ⓒ Ⓓ	61. Ⓐ Ⓑ Ⓒ Ⓓ
14. Ⓐ Ⓑ Ⓒ Ⓓ	38. Ⓐ Ⓑ Ⓒ Ⓓ	62. Ⓐ Ⓑ Ⓒ Ⓓ
15. Ⓐ Ⓑ Ⓒ Ⓓ	39. Ⓐ Ⓑ Ⓒ Ⓓ	63. Ⓐ Ⓑ Ⓒ Ⓓ
16. Ⓐ Ⓑ Ⓒ Ⓓ	40. Ⓐ Ⓑ Ⓒ Ⓓ	64. Ⓐ Ⓑ Ⓒ Ⓓ
17. Ⓐ Ⓑ Ⓒ Ⓓ	41. Ⓐ Ⓑ Ⓒ Ⓓ	65. Ⓐ Ⓑ Ⓒ Ⓓ
18. Ⓐ Ⓑ Ⓒ Ⓓ	42. Ⓐ Ⓑ Ⓒ Ⓓ	66. Ⓐ Ⓑ Ⓒ Ⓓ
19. Ⓐ Ⓑ Ⓒ Ⓓ	43. Ⓐ Ⓑ Ⓒ Ⓓ	67. Ⓐ Ⓑ Ⓒ Ⓓ
20. Ⓐ Ⓑ Ⓒ Ⓓ	44. Ⓐ Ⓑ Ⓒ Ⓓ	68. Ⓐ Ⓑ Ⓒ Ⓓ
21. Ⓐ Ⓑ Ⓒ Ⓓ	45. Ⓐ Ⓑ Ⓒ Ⓓ	69. Ⓐ Ⓑ Ⓒ Ⓓ
22. Ⓐ Ⓑ Ⓒ Ⓓ	46. Ⓐ Ⓑ Ⓒ Ⓓ	70. Ⓐ Ⓑ Ⓒ Ⓓ
23. Ⓐ Ⓑ Ⓒ Ⓓ	47. Ⓐ Ⓑ Ⓒ Ⓓ	71. Ⓐ Ⓑ Ⓒ Ⓓ
24. Ⓐ Ⓑ Ⓒ Ⓓ	48. Ⓐ Ⓑ Ⓒ Ⓓ	72. Ⓐ Ⓑ Ⓒ Ⓓ

Practice Test 1

Time: 120 minutes
72 questions

DIRECTIONS: Each of the questions or incomplete statements below is followed by four suggested answers or completions. Select the one that is best in each case and then fill in the appropriate letter in the corresponding space on the answer sheet.

Consider the following code.

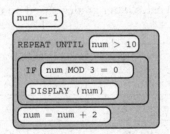

```
num ← 1

REPEAT UNTIL (num > 10)
    IF (num MOD 3 = 0)
        DISPLAY (num)
    num = num + 2
```

1. What is displayed as a result of executing the code segment?

(A) 1 3 5 7 9

(B) 1 5 7

(C) 3 9

(D) 3

Consider the following code segment.

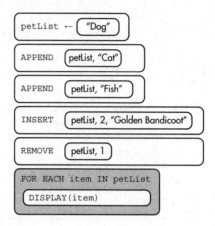

2. What is displayed as a result of executing the code segment?

(A) Dog Cat Fish Golden Bandicoot

(B) Dog Cat Fish

(C) Dog Golden Bandicoot Cat Fish

(D) Golden Bandicoot Cat Fish

Students at a high school receive letter grades based on the following scale:

Score	Letter Grade
90 or above	A
Between 80 and 89 inclusive	B
Between 70 and 79 inclusive	C
Below 70	D

3. Which of the following code segments will display the correct letter grade for a given score?

I.
```
IF ( score ≥ 90)
{
     DISPLAY ( "A")
}
IF ( score ≥ 80 AND score ≤ 89)
{
     DISPLAY ( "B")
}
IF ( score ≥ 70 AND score ≤ 79)
{
     DISPLAY ( "C")
}
```

```
        IF ( score < 70)
        {
            DISPLAY ( "D")
        }
II.  IF ( score ≥ 90)
        {
            DISPLAY ( "A")
        }
        ELSE
        {
          IF ( score ≥ 80 AND score ≤ 89)
          {
              DISPLAY ( "B")
          }
          ELSE
          {
            IF ( score ≥ 70 AND score ≤ 79)
            {
                DISPLAY ( "C")
            }
            ELSE
            {
                DISPLAY ( "D")
            }
          }
        }
III. IF ( score ≥ 90)
        {
            DISPLAY ( "A")
        }
        IF ( score ≥ 80 AND ≤ 89)
        {
            DISPLAY ( "B")
        }
        IF ( score ≥ 70 AND ≤ 79)
        {
            DISPLAY ( "C")
        }
        IF ( score < 70)
        {
            DISPLAY ( "D")
        }
```

(A) I only

(B) III only

(C) I and II only

(D) I, II, and III

4. Colors can be represented by decimal values from 0 to 255. If each pixel in a photo is a combination of three color values, what is the minimum number of bits needed to store a pixel?

   (A) 512
   (B) 256
   (C) 24
   (D) 8

5. Which of the following is a true statement about data transmitted over the internet?

   (A) All data traveling over the internet is binary.
   (B) Packets are received in the same order that they are sent.
   (C) Redundancy in the design of the internet is overseen by the Internet Engineering Task Force (IETF).
   (D) The domain name system (DNS) has been challenged by the Digital Millennium Copyright Act (DMCA).

6. Which of the following is **NOT** a reasonable amount of time when executing a program?

   (A) $100\,x$
   (B) $x^2 + 4x$
   (C) $x^3 + x^4$
   (D) 3^x

7. What should replace <condition missing> so that the program below displays TRUE 60% of the time?

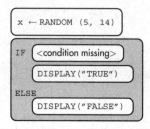

   (A) $x < 6$
   (B) $x \geq 6$
   (C) $x > 10$
   (D) $x \leq 10$

8. What percentage of the time will the program display an even number?

```
Line 1: num ← RANDOM(1,10)
Line 2: IF ( num < 5 AND num MOD 2 = 0)
Line 3: {
Line4:     DISPLAY(num)
Line 5: }
```

(A) 10%

(B) 20%

(C) 40%

(D) 50%

9. What will the following program display?

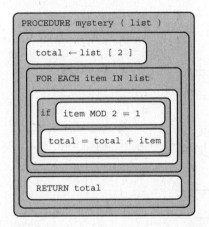

(A) 35

(B) 41

(C) 81

(D) 95

A flowchart is a way to visually represent an algorithm. The flowchart below uses the following building blocks.

Block		Explanation
Oval	(oval)	The start or end of the algorithm
Rectangle	(rectangle)	One or more processing steps, such as a statement that assigns a value to a variable
Diamond	(diamond)	A conditional or decision step, where execution proceeds to the side labeled true if the condition is true and to the side labeled false otherwise
Parallelogram	(parallelogram)	Display a message

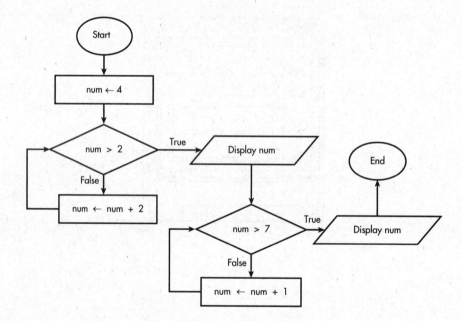

10. What will the program above display?

(A) 2 8

(B) 4 8

(C) 2 7

(D) 3 7

300   AP COMPUTER SCIENCE PRINCIPLES

11. Why is programming code written in a high-level language ran through a compiler before it can be run?

 (A) The compiler ensures that the program will have no bugs.
 (B) The computer cannot directly understand upper-level programming code. The compiler must translate code into machine code.
 (C) The compiler installs the new or updated program onto the computer.
 (D) The computer interfaces with the compiler to determine how to run the program.

12. Which of the following does **NOT** need to be considered when determining the credibility of a source?

 (A) Author's reputation and credentials
 (B) Use of persuasive techniques within the source
 (C) Publisher's reputation and credentials
 (D) Sponsorship of the article or publisher

13. The code segment below is intended to swap the variables *a* and *b* using a temporary variable, *temp*. What can replace <Missing Code> so the algorithm works as intended?

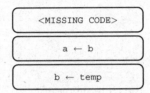

(A)
```
temp ← a
```

(B)
```
b ← a
```

(C)
```
temp ← b
```

(D)
```
b ← temp
```

14. In 2018, the company Cambridge Analytica was found to have collected data regarding millions of Facebook users. This was done by utilizing a loophole in Facebook's data-collection policy, where apps connected to Facebook could collect information on a person's friends without the friends' permission. Which of the following concepts does this demonstrate?

(A) If security-related protections are ignored, the curation of data by commercial groups can be exploited.

(B) If privacy-related protections are ignored, the curation of data by commercial groups can be exploited.

(C) If security-related protections are ignored, the curation of data by governmental programs can be exploited.

(D) If privacy-related protections are ignored, the curation of data by governmental programs can be exploited.

15. Consider the following code segment, which uses the variables a, b, and c.

$a \leftarrow 2$
$b \leftarrow a + a$
$c \leftarrow b + a$
$a \leftarrow c + a$
DISPLAY(a)
DISPLAY(b)
DISPLAY(c)

What is displayed by running the code segment?

(A) 3 3 6
(B) 8 4 6
(C) 11 3 8
(D) 3 11 3

16. Which best describes the role of hypertext transfer protocol/internet protocol (HTTP/IP)?

(A) The foundation of data communication for the World Wide Web
(B) The set of rules for the path packets taken on the route-tolerant internet
(C) It regulates the amount of people allowed on the internet at what time
(D) A core protocol of the domain name system

17. What is the minimum number of lines needing to be cut to completely isolate F?

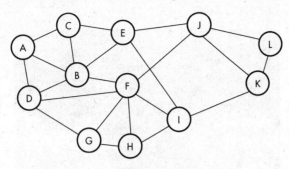

(A) 0

(B) 4

(C) 6

(D) 8

18. By switching from IPv4, which can store 2^{32} IP addresses, to IPv6, which can store 2^{128} IP addresses, how many more IP addresses will become available?

(A) Twice as many IP addresses

(B) 2^2 as many IP addresses

(C) 96 as many IP addresses

(D) 2^{96} as many addresses

19. What should replace <condition missing> so that the following program segment displays true if the number parameter is a multiple of 3 or 5 and otherwise false?

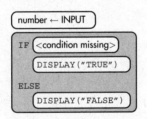

(A) `number MOD 3 = 0 OR number MOD 5 = 0`

(B) `number MOD 3 = 0 AND number MOD 5 = 0`

(C) `number/3 = 0 OR number/5 = 0`

(D) `number/3 = 0 AND number/5 = 0`

20. Which of the following is NOT metadata for the following picture of my dog Novack the 3rd taken in front of PETCO field?

(A) The picture of the dog

(B) The location of where the picture was taken

(C) The time the picture was taken

(D) The memory space taken up by the picture

21. Which of the following would be the highest-level domain for the website *www.example.com* according to the guidelines of the domain name system (DNS)?

(A) https

(B) example

(C) www

(D) com

Instruction	Explanation
Robot	
If the robot attempts to move to a square that is not open or is beyond the edge of the grid, the robot will stay in its current location and the program will terminate.	
Text: MOVE_FORWARD () **Block:** MOVE_FORWARD	The robot moves one square forward in the direction it is facing.
Text: ROTATE_LEFT () **Block:** ROTATE_LEFT	The robot rotates in place 90 degrees counterclockwise (i.e., makes an in-place left turn).
Text: ROTATE_RIGHT () **Block:** ROTATE_RIGHT	The robot rotates in place 90 degrees clockwise (i.e., makes an in-place right turn).
Text: CAN_MOVE (direction) **Block:** CAN_MOVE direction	Evaluates to true if there is an open square one square in the direction relative to where the robot is facing; otherwise evaluates to false. The value of direction can be left, right, forward, or backward.

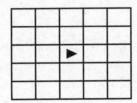

```
REPEAT (RANDOM( 0,1) )
{
    ROTATE_RIGHT ( )
}
REPEAT (RANDOM( 0,2) )
{
    MOVE_FORWARD ( )
}
```

22. What are the possible landing spaces for the robot?

(A)
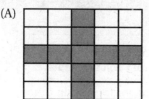

(B)
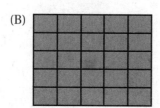

(C)
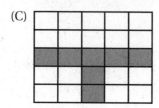

(D)
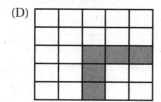

23. **Algorithm A**

Step 1: Set sum equal to 0.

sum ← 0

Step 2: Set count = 1.

count ← 1

Step 3: Add list[count] to sum.

sum ← sum + list[count]

Step 4: Add 1 to count.

Step 5: Repeat steps 3 and 4 until count is equal to LENGTH (list).

Step 6: Set ave to sum divided by count.

ave ←sum / count

Step 7: Return step 6.

Algorithm B

Step 1: Set sum equal to 0.

sum ← 0

Step 2: Set count = 1.

count ← 1

Step 3: Add list[count] to sum.

sum ← sum + list[count]

Step 4: Add 1 to count.

Step 5: Set ave to sum divided by count.

ave ←sum / count

Step 6: Repeat steps 3, 4, and 5 until count is equal to LENGTH (list).

Step 7: Return the last value calculated in step 5.

(A) Algorithm A calculates average in all cases, while Algorithm B does not.

(B) Algorithm B calculates average in all cases, while Algorithm A does not.

(C) Neither Algorithm A nor Algorithm B calculates average correctly.

(D) Both Algorithm A and Algorithm B calculate average correctly, but Algorithm A is more efficient.

24. Which of the following is true of a binary number ending in 1?

(A) The number MOD 2 = 0.

(B) The number is even.

(C) The number MOD 2 = 1.

(D) The number would be negative.

25. The procedure findSum is intended to return the sum of the numbers in the list called numbers. The procedure does not work as intended.

```
PROCEDURE findSum (numbers)
{
    sum ← numbers[1]
    FOR EACH number IN numbers
    {
       sum = sum + numbers[number]
    }
    RETURN (sum )
}
```

Which of the following test case values of numbers will return the correct value?

(A) numbers [1, 1, 35, 6]

(B) numbers [0, 1, 35, 6]

(C) numbers [11, 35, 6]

(D) numbers [3, 5, 11, 6]

26. Which of the following is NOT an example of using citizen science as a possible solution?

(A) The behavior of fireflies during the summer months

(B) The behavior of the mysterious and wonderful jellyfish on the beach or water

(C) Collecting recordings using ultrasonic microphones and sonograms of bats

(D) Calculating PSAT scores for a school district

27. Which of the following best characterizes a low-level language?

(A) A language that is easier for humans to program

(B) A language that is easier for humans to debug

(C) A language that is easier for a computer to interpret but difficult for humans to interpret

(D) A language that is built for beginner programmers

28. Why is it typically far easier to read code written in a high-level language when compared to a lower-level language?

(A) High-level languages tend to be written so computers can process the code quickly.

(B) High-level languages tend to be closer to machine code, which makes it easier to understand.

(C) High-level languages tend to be written for more experienced programmers to use, which implicitly makes them easier to read.

(D) High-level languages tend to be closer to natural language, by utilizing simplified abstractions with descriptive names.

29. In the computing language JAVA, the programmer can add a support class using the `import` command, which is followed by the full path to the support class. The path is ordered from the most abstract class to the least and does not skip any level.

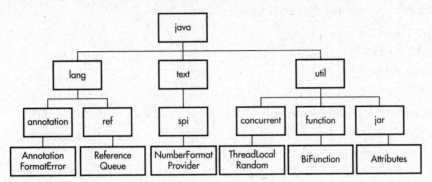

Suppose that the programmer wants to access the class `ThreadLocalRandom`. Using the partial hierarchy above, determine which of the following commands would properly import `ThreadLocalRandom`.

(A) `import java.util.concurrent.ThreadLocalRandom`
(B) `import ThreadLocalRandom.concurrent.util.java`
(C) `import java.ThreadLocalRandom`
(D) `import java.util.function.ThreadLocalRandom`

30. Convert DA_{HEX} to a binary number.

(A) 10101100_{BIN}
(B) 11001010_{BIN}
(C) 11110000_{BIN}
(D) 1101010_{BIN}

31. Assume a particular system stores text by connecting eight-bit sequences. Each character in a string is one sequence, with the number used corresponding to its place in the alphabet (thus, a would be `00000001`, b would be `000000010`, c would be `000000011`, and so on). In this system, what would be the binary representation of the word dog?

(A) `00000010000001111100000111`
(B) `00000111000011110000000100`
(C) `00000100000011110000000111`
(D) `00000100000001001000000111`

PRACTICE TEST 1

32. The abstraction Draw(magnitude, direction) is used to draw line segments at a given magnitude and direction (north, south, east, or west) starting at the tip of the first vector to the tail of the second vector. Consider the following program, where the vector starts in the upper-left corner of a grid of dots.

Draw(3, east)
Draw(2, east)
Draw(3, south)
Draw(1, west)

Which of the following represents the figure that is drawn by the program?

(A)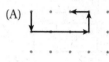

(B)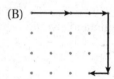

(C)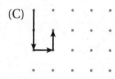

(D)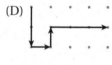

33. Select the highest-level hardware abstraction.

    (A) Transistor
    (B) Motherboard
    (C) Computer
    (D) Memory

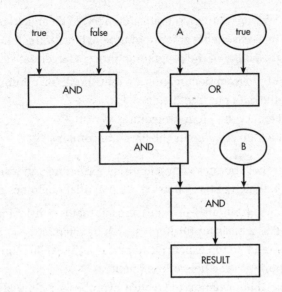

34. What is the value of RESULT?

   (A) True when both A and B are true
   (B) True when either A or B are true
   (C) Always true
   (D) Always false

35. An economist wants to understand how changes in supply and demand affect the inflation rate of a country. What is a benefit of using a simulation?

   (A) A simulation would be more cost-effective and easier to create than an experiment done to an entire country.
   (B) A simulation would be able to account for every variable that would affect supply and demand.
   (C) Simulations can only be run once, so they are guaranteed to be close to real life, where an experiment like this could only happen once.
   (D) Simulations have as much of an effect on the real world as an actual experiment of this scale would.

36. Which of the following is true about data compression?

   (A) Data compression can be used for pictures and video only.
   (B) Lossless data compression is the best compression under all conditions.
   (C) Data compression can be used to reduce the size of a file for storage or transmission.
   (D) Lossy compression cannot be used when sending pictures.

37. A programmer is writing a program that is intended to be able to process large amounts of data in a reasonable amount of time. Which of the following considerations is likely to affect the ability of the program to process larger data sets?

(A) The amount of program documentation that should be minimized
(B) The order of the data put into the data set
(C) How much memory the program requires to run
(D) How many program statements the program contains

38. A certain company collaborates with scientists by creating and testing simulations for scientific research. Which of the following are potential outcomes of this?

(A) If a simulation continuously provides a result that is considered abnormal, this could be used as a basis for further research by scientists.
(B) If a concept would be too expensive to perform in real life, the company could create a simulation with the help of the scientists.
(C) If scientists need information to create a hypothesis, a simulation can be used to provide the information necessary.
(D) All of the above

39. To show the impact of gerrymandering, the website FiveThirtyEight created an interactive web page that allows the user to switch between several different maps of congressional districts that are based around different goals (e.g., favor one of the major parties, make elections competitive, make elections compact). Which of the following would NOT be a useful metric with which to analyze this data?

(A) Overall results—the likely makeup of Congress based on the likely winner of each district. (Some seats are listed as "competitive.")
(B) County splits—the number of times that a county is divided into multiple districts.
(C) Racial makeup—the number of districts that are a majority of a certain race (or have no majority).
(D) Third-party wins—the number of districts that would likely be won by an independent candidate or third party.

40. Why does updating a file require more memory than reading a file?

(A) A read file only needs certain parts loaded to memory, but an updating file requires the entire file to be in memory.
(B) A read file requires no memory, so the updating file would always require more.
(C) A read file requires the entire file loaded, but an updating file requires both the original version and the updated version in memory.
(D) A read file only uses the hard disk, while an updating file requires both the hard disk and the RAM.

41. Why do computing innovations tend to lead to legal concerns?

(A) Lawyers are unfamiliar with the laws governing computing innovations because they involve multiple states.
(B) There are no laws on the internet concerning copyrights.
(C) Laws involved in these concerns were often created before the advent of computers, meaning that they may not cover certain aspects of new technology.
(D) There is no way to hide your IP address on the internet, so laws are easily enforced.

42. How has the Digital Millennium Copyright Act benefited efforts to make copyrighted material available?

    (A) By preventing the circumvention of copy protection, material can be placed on any website but can only be viewable or usable by paying customers.

    (B) By preventing the circumvention of copy protection, there are many sites that can hold the material with no digital-rights management software involved.

    (C) By enabling the takedown of illegal material holders, paid outlets such as Netflix and Hulu are able to compete and provide the material legally.

    (D) By enabling the takedown of illegal material holders, there are more sites remaining that hold the content legally.

43. What is a major disadvantage of the internet's model of trust?

    (A) A trusted website can have a large amount of power over a computer, so improper trusts can be very damaging if the website is malicious.

    (B) A trusted website has power over the computer's ROM, which could be very damaging if the website is malicious.

    (C) A trusted website cannot have encrypted communications, which means any data sent can be read by an interceptor.

    (D) A trusted website can still download malicious code even if it is blocked by a firewall.

44. The program below will return TRUE if the last digit of a is equal to the last digit of b. Example:

    ```
    if a = 34 and b = 94 the program will return true.
    if a = 11 and b = 35 the program will return false.
    if a = 6 and b = 86 the program will return true.
    ```

    Which code below can replace <Missing Code> so the procedure would return TRUE?

    ```
    Line 1: PROCEDURE lastDigit (a, b)
    Line 2: {
    Line 3: <Missing Code>
    Line 4: RETURN (true)
    Line 5: ELSE
    Line 6: RETURN (false)
    Line 7: }
    ```

    (A) IF (a = b)
    (B) IF (a /10 = b /10)
    (C) IF (a != b)
    (D) IF (a MOD 10 = b MOD 10)

45. The Caesar cipher is an encryption technique that is a substitution cipher replacing a letter with a different letter a fixed number of positions down the alphabet. For example, of a shift of 3 the message "cat" would translate to "fdw." The Caesar cipher is an example of what type of encryption?

    (A) Asymmetric encryption
    (B) Public key encryption
    (C) Home key encryption
    (D) No key encryption

46. What is the purpose of a digital certificate in secured communications?

    (A) Certificates ensure that the communication system has been examined by a third party.

    (B) Certificates ensure that the server's own security features have been examined by a third party and is using public key encryption and ensuring that the transactions are being kept confidential.

    (C) Certificates ensure that the server contacted in the secure connection is the actual server and not a copycat.

    (D) Certificates ensure that the website's code has been created by a professional programmer.

47. Which of the following illustrate ways that the internet facilitates collaboration?

    I. People can communicate more quickly, enabling teams to work together regardless of distance.

    II. Online technologies such as messaging and file transfers make it easier to send visuals that can be pertinent for projects.

    III. File-sharing protocols enable documents to be saved in the cloud and edited by all team members.

    (A) I only

    (B) I and III only

    (C) II and III only

    (D) I, II, and III

48. A web browser contacts a domain name system (DNS) server using IPv4 and pages a request for a website's address. Which of the following could NOT be a potential response?

    (A) 92.11.198.113

    (B) 174.260.45.144

    (C) 128.198.232.65

    (D) 54.116.188.246

49. The International Engineering Task Force develops internet protocols such as SMTP and HTTP. Are all websites required to use IETF protocols?

    (A) Yes, as the use of IETF protocols is legally enforced.

    (B) Yes, as IETF protocols are required by all web browsers.

    (C) No, as the use of standards is not enforced by any government body.

    (D) No, as IETF protocols are merely frameworks for proprietary protocols.

50. Which of the following types of components is necessary to cyber security?

    I. Software

    II. Hardware

    III. Human

    (A) I only

    (B) III only

    (C) I and II only

    (D) I, II, and III

51. What is the maximum number of searches required if using a linear search on a list containing 2000 numbers?

(A) 2000

(B) 1000

(C) 11

(D) 1

52. What will the following program display?

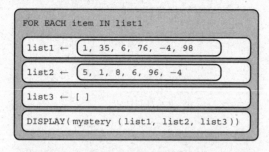

(A) [ ]

(B) [1, 6, −4]

(C) [4, 6, −4]

(D) [1, 35, 6, 76, 4, 98, 5, 1, 8, 96, −4]

53. What is the value of sum displayed after this algorithm is run?

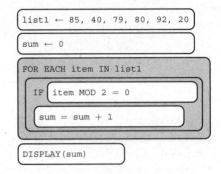

(A) 0

(B) 4

(C) 6

(D) Error?

54. What will the following program display?

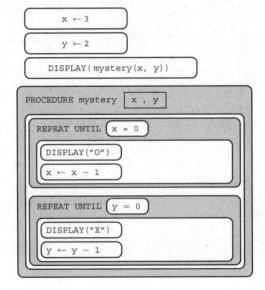

(A) OXXOXXOXX

(B) OXXOO

(C) OOOOXXX

(D) The program is an infinite loop.

55. What will the result of the displayed program be?

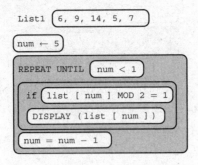

(A) 9, 5, 7

(B) 6, 14

(C) 14, 6

(D) 7, 5, 9

56. What will the output of the following program be?

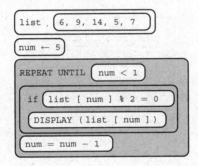

(A) 9 5 7

(B) 14 6

(C) 14

(D) 7 5 9

Consider the following code segment.

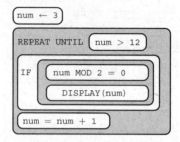

57. What will the executed code display?

(A) All odd numbers between 3 and 12

(B) All even numbers between 1 and 12

(C) All even numbers between 3 and 12

(D) All odd numbers between 1 and 12

58. What should replace <condition missing> so the program below displays TRUE 60% of the time?

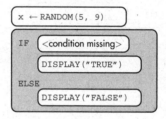

(A) x MOD 2 = 0

(B) x MOD 5 = 0

(C) x MOD 2 = 1

(D) x MOD 5 = 5

59. What percentage of the time will the program display a number?

```
num ← RANDOM(1,20)
IF ( num > 5 AND num < 13 AND num MOD 2 = 0)
{
    DISPLAY(num)
}
```

(A) 20%

(B) 10%

(C) 25%

(D) 75%

60. What is the following program displaying?

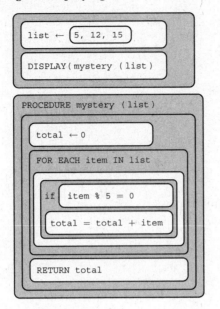

(A) 37

(B) 27

(C) 25

(D) 20

61. What is the code below displaying?

```
Line 1: x ← 2
Line 2: y ← 0
Line 3: WHILE ( y < 15 AND y MOD 3 = 1 )
Line 4: {
Line 5: DISPLAY (y)
Line 6: y ← y + 1
Line 7: }
```

(A) 0

(B) 2, 4, 6, 8, 10, 12, 14

(C) 3, 6, 9, 12

(D) 3, 6, 9, 12, 15

62. What is the code segment displaying?

```
c ← 17
x ← 4
x ← 14 MOD 2
c ← c * x
DISPLAY (c)
```

(A) 68

(B) 0

(C) 17

(D) 34

63. What does the algorithm display?

```
a ← (4 MOD 3) + (7 MOD 2) * 3
DISPLAY (a)
```

(A) 3

(B) 7

(C) 4

(D) 5

64. What will the following algorithm display?

```
x ← (64 MOD 8)*(54 MOD 8)*(127 MOD 64)*(8 MOD 3)*(53 MOD 4)
DISPLAY (x)
```

(A) 0

(B) 1,512

(C) 756

(D) 48

65. What will y display?

```
x ← 7
y ← 8
temp ← x + y
x ← y
y ← x
temp ← x + y
y ← temp + 4
DISPLAY (y)
```

(A) 15

(B) 0

(C) 16

(D) 20

66. What is the value of *x*?

$$w \leftarrow 34 \text{ MOD } 15$$
$$y \leftarrow 21 \text{ MOD } 6$$
$$x \leftarrow (y + 15) * w$$

   (A) 23

   (B) 101

   (C) 72

   (D) 15

67. Why is it more effective to put abstractions in a program than to repeat code?
Select two answers.

   (A) Abstractions make it harder to edit because every extraction is saved on a distinct file.

   (B) Abstractions simplify editing by requiring only one edit to the abstraction rather than every instance of the code.

   (C) Using abstractions takes up less space than repeating code, which makes the program easier to read.

   (D) Abstractions are guaranteed to work in every instance they are used if they work once.

68. The following question uses a robot in a grid of squares. The robot is represented by a triangle, which is initially facing right. Which code can replace <Missing Code> to have the robot end up in the safe place?
Select two answers.

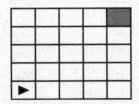

Where *x* = 5

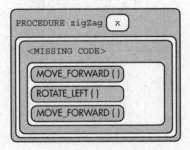

   (A) Repeat Until *x* = 5

   (B) Repeat *x* TIMES

   (C) FOR EACH *x* IN LIST

   (D) IF *x* equals GOAL_REACHED

69. The findings from a project are typically presented using a graph as opposed to a table or raw data. Why might this be?

   Select two answers.

   (A) Graphs can be easily placed into a slideshow or document, while tables cannot.

   (B) Graphs can show trends that might not be easily seen with raw data.

   (C) Graphs are able to show all of the detail necessary to understand data.

   (D) Graphs are easier to read and interpret at a glance.

The question below uses a robot in a grid of squares. The robot is represented by the triangle, which is initially in the top-left square of the grid and facing toward the top of the grid.

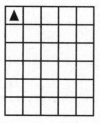

Code for the procedure Mystery is shown below. Assume that the parameter *p* has been assigned a positive integer value (e.g., 1, 2, 3, …).

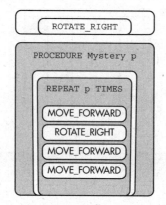

70. Which of the following shows the result of calling the procedure for any value of *p*?
    Select two answers.

    (A)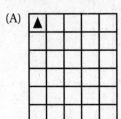

    (B)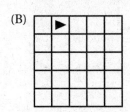

    (C)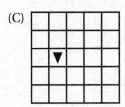

    (D) Error. The robot leaves the grid.

71. A theme park wants to create a simulation to determine how long it should expect the wait time to be at its most popular ride. Which of the following characteristics for the virtual patrons would be most useful?
    Select two answers.

    (A) Ride preference—denotes whether a patron prefers roller coasters, other thrill rides, gentle rides, or no rides
    (B) Walking preference—denotes how far a patron is willing to walk in between rides
    (C) Food preference—denotes the type of food that a patron prefers to eat (e.g., chicken, burgers, salads)
    (D) Ticket type—denotes whether the patron has a single-day pass, a multi-day pass, or an annual pass

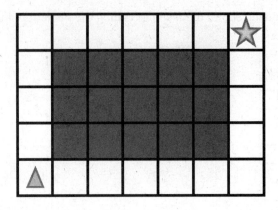

```
Line 1: PROCEDURE moveAndSpin (x, y)
Line 2: {
Line 3: REPEAT x TIMES
Line 4: {
Line 5: MOVE_FORWARD()
Line 6: }
Line 7: REPEAT y TIMES
Line 8: {
Line 9: ROTATE_RIGHT ()
Line 10:}
```

72. What procedure below will result in the robot landing on the star?

   (A) moveAndSpin(4,1)
       moveAndSpin(6,0)

   (B) moveAndSpin(0,1)
       moveAndSpin(6,3)
       moveAndSpin(4,0)

   (C) moveAndSpin(7,3)

   (D) moveAndSpin(0,7)

ANSWER KEY

1. **C**	19. **A**	37. **C**	55. **D**
2. **D**	20. **A**	38. **D**	56. **B**
3. **C**	21. **D**	39. **C**	57. **C**
4. **C**	22. **D**	40. **C**	58. **C**
5. **A**	23. **D**	41. **B**	59. **A**
6. **D**	24. **C**	42. **C**	60. **D**
7. **D**	25. **B**	43. **D**	61. **A**
8. **B**	26. **C**	44. **D**	62. **B**
9. **C**	27. **C**	45. **C**	63. **C**
10. **B**	28. **D**	46. **B**	64. **A**
11. **B**	29. **A**	47. **D**	65. **D**
12. **B**	30. **D**	48. **B**	66. **C**
13. **A**	31. **C**	49. **C**	67. **B, C**
14. **B**	32. **B**	50. **D**	68. **A, B**
15. **B**	33. **C**	51. **A**	69. **B, D**
16. **A**	34. **D**	52. **C**	70. **A, B**
17. **C**	35. **A**	53. **B**	71. **A, B**
18. **D**	36. **C**	54. **C**	72. **A, B**

ANSWERS EXPLAINED

1. **(C)**

Step 1: num = 1

Step 2: Enter the repeat until:

num	Is num > 10	Is num MOD 3 = 0	Display	num = num + 2
1	False			3
3	False	Yes	3	5
5	False			7
7	False			9
9	False	Yes	9	11
11	True			

num	num > 10	num MOD 3	num MOD 3 = 0	Display
1	False	1	False	
3	False	0	True	3
5	False	2	False	
7	False	1	False	
9	False	0	True	9
11	True			

The program will display the values 3 9.

(A) While num has all the values 1 3 5 7 9 11 it will only display if num MOD equals 0. Only 3 and 9 MOD 3 will equal 0.

(B) Here, 1 MOD 3 equals 1, which would make the "If" statement false so 1 will not display; 5 MOD 3 equals 2, which would make the "If" statement false so 5 will not display; and 7 MOD 3 equals 1, which would make the "If" statement false so 7 will not display.

(C) Correct.

(D) Here, 9 MOD 3 is also equal to 0 and will display.

2. **(D)**

*petList is initialized containing the value Dog

petList [Dog]

- The value Cat is added to the end of petList
- petList [Dog Cat]
- The value Fish is added to the end of petList
- petList [Dog Cat Fish)]

The value Golden Bandicoot is added at position 2 of petList and shifts all values after position 2 to the right.

- petList [Dog Golden Bandicoot Cat Fish]
- The value in position 1 of petList is removed, and all values to the right of position 1 are shifted to the left: petList [Golden Bandicoot Cat Fish]

Each item in petList is displayed, resulting in [Golden Bandicoot Cat Fish].

3. (C)

I.

Test case score		Predicted grade if	Boolean	Displayed grade	Correct?
92	A	score >= 90	true	A	yes
80	B	score >= 80 and score <= 89	true	B	yes
75	C	score >= 70 and score <= 79	true	C	yes
40	D	score < 70	true	D	yes

II.

Test case score		Predicted grade if	Boolean	Displayed grade	Correct?
92	A	score >= 90	true	A	yes
80	B	score >= 80 and score <= 89	true	B	yes
75	C	score >= 70 and score <= 79	true	C	yes
40	D	score < 70	true	D	yes

III. Logically I, II, and III should all work. However, IF (score $\geq$ 80 AND $\leq$ 89) is incorrect syntax and results in an error. Correct syntax would be IF (score $\geq$ 80 AND score $\leq$ 89).

Both I and II are true only.

4. (C)

256	128	64	32	16	8	4	2	1
	1	1	1	1	1	1	1	0

Determine the minimum number of bits to hold the number 254:

254	126	62	30	14	6	2
−128	−64	−32	−16	−8	−4	−2
126	62	30	14	6	2	0

It takes 8 bits to hold the number 255.

Three colors would require 8 bits $\times$ 3 = 24 bits.

(A) $512 = 83$.
(B) The amount of numbers between 0 and 255 is 256.
(C) Correct.
(D) Eight bits can only hold one color.

5. **(A)** The internet uses fiber optic cables that transmit data as "on" or "off," which is represented in binary as 0 or 1.

(B) Due to the fault-tolerant nature of the internet, packets will travel in different directions through the internet. Since packets travel in different directions, they will arrive at their destination in a different order than that in which they were sent.

(C) There is no central governing body that controls the design of the internet.

(D) The Digital Millennium Copyright Act does not relate to the internet naming convention.

6. **(D)** Correct. Exponential growth $= 3^x$. (A) Only exponential growth is not reasonable. Polynomial growth is acceptable. (B) Only exponential growth is not reasonable. Polynomial growth is acceptable. (C) Only exponential growth is not reasonable. Polynomial growth is acceptable.

7. **(D)** There are 10 numbers between 5 and 14 inclusive.

5 6 7 8 9 10 11 12 13 14

For the condition to evaluate to true 60% of the time, six of the ten numbers must be included.

5, 6, 7, 8, 9, 10

(A) $x < 6$ would only include one number and would result in being true 10% of the time.
(B) $x \geq 6$ would include nine numbers and would result in being true 90% of the time.
(C) $x > 10$ would include four numbers and would result in being true 40% of the time.
(D) Correct. $x \leq 10$ would include six numbers and would result in being true 60% of the time.

8. **(B)** num can be 1, 2, 3, 4, 5, 6, 7, 8, 9, or 10.

Of the above numbers 1, 2, 3, and 4 are less than five.

Of those above numbers 2 and 4 are also even.

Two out of 10 numbers would make line 2 true, which is 20%.

(A) Ten percent (10%) would be one out of 10 numbers.
(B) Correct.
(C) Forty percent (40%) would be four out of 10 numbers.
(D) Fifty percent (50%) would be five out of 10 numbers.

9. **(C)**

list	11	35	6
index	1	2	3

Total = 35

Total	11 MOD 2 = 1 true	35 MOD 2 = 0
35	Total = total = 35 + 11 = 46	Total = 46 + 35
		Final total = 81

Returns 81

10. **(B)**

Step 1: Start the program.

Step 2: Set num = 4.

Step 3: Is 4 > 2 evaluates to true.

Step 4: Display 4.

Step 5: Is 4 > 7 evaluates to false.

Step 6: Set num = 5.

Step 7: Is 5 > 7 evaluates to false.

Step 8: Set num = 6.

Step 9: Is 6 > 7 evaluates to false.

Step 10: Set num = 7.

Step 11: Is 7 > 7 evaluates to false.

Step 12: Set num = 8.

Step 13: Is 48 > 7 evaluates to true.

Step 14: Display 8.

Step 15: End the program.

11. **(B)** Most modern programming languages have abstractions that must be converted to machine code. A compiler translates upper-level code into readable low-level code.

(A) Bugs exist in programs that are compiled.

(C) Installation indicates the creation of support files and registry keys, neither of which the compiler itself makes.

(D) The compiled program is typically run as an executable or by the programming environment; this is dependent on the language and environment involved, not the compiler.

12. **(B)** It is extremely difficult to determine the credibility of a source. The author, publisher, or sponsorship reputation is a factor, but at the time of writing this book all of these can be easily faked. So, while the correct answer is (B), it is still a gray area.

13. **(A)** When solving a swap, for organization set up sample numbers in for the variables.

In this case I picked the numbers 5 and 13, but the numbers could have been of any value.

a	b
5	13

If the swap is successful, the values will be swapped.

a	b
13	5

(A) Correct. Taking sample values of $a = 5$ and $b = 13$ results in:

temp	a	b
5	5	13
	13	5

(B) Taking sample values of $a = 5$ and $b = 13$ results in:

temp	a	b
	5	5
	5	0

(C) Taking sample values of $a = 5$ and $b = 13$ results in:

temp	a	b
5	5	13
	5	5

(D) Taking sample values of $a = 5$ and $b = 13$ results in:

temp	a	b
	5	13
0	0	0

14. **(B)** Correct. Cambridge Analytica was able to get its data utilizing Facebook's own policy, which, intentionally or not, represented a blasé attitude toward protecting user privacy that will hopefully be replaced.

(A) The data was retrieved using Facebook's own tools, which means that there was no security protection being exploited.

(B) Correct.

(C) Facebook is not a governmental program.

(D) Again, Facebook is not a governmental program.

15. **(B)**

a	b	c	DISPLAY
2̶	4	6	
8			

8 4 6

16. **(A)**

(A) HTTP/IP is the set of rules for transferring files through the internet.

(B) The path taken by packets on the internet varies frequently depending on current speed and cost of traveling a particular path.

(C) This is the definition of a packet, not HTTP.

(D) This is the definition of transmission control protocol, not HTTP.

17. **(C)** The internet is built to be redundant. If one line is cut, the internet is designed to take a different path.

To isolate F:

F–B needs to be cut.

F–J needs to be cut.

F–I needs to be cut.

F–H needs to be cut.

F–G needs to be cut.

F–D needs to be cut.

(A) F can still communicate, leaving six paths.

(B) F can still communicate, leaving two paths.

(C) Correct.

(D) There are only six paths out of computer F.

18. **(D)** Every time the exponent is increased by one, it means that there will be $2x$ as many IP addresses available. In this scenario, the exponent increases by 96, meaning that the amount of IP addresses would double 96 times. This can be mathematically represented as 2^{96}.

(A) Doubling the amount of IP addresses would change from 2^{32} to 2^{33}.

(B) This would result in four times as many IP addresses.

(C) Although the exponent increased by 96, this means that IPv6 would double the current amount of IPs 96 times, not multiply the current amount by 96.

(D) Correct.

19. **(A)** MOD is an operation commonly used to test for multiples. It returns the remainder after dividing the input by a specified number. If the remainder is 0, then the input is a multiple of the specified number. In this case, we want the function to return true for inputs that are multiples of either 3 or 5, so (A) would correctly replace the missing condition.

    (A) Correct.
    (B) Although it uses modulus, it only returns true for multiples of both 3 and 5, excluding all numbers that are multiples of one but not the other.
    (C) Division cannot be used to find multiples. The only number that would return true is 0.
    (D) Division cannot be used to find multiples. The only number that would return true is 0.

20. **(A)** Metadata is data describing things stored on a computer. While metadata for images or videos can include image sizes, location, date and time, run time, memory space, and resolution, it does not include the pictures and videos themselves.

21. **(D)** The guidelines of the domain name system state that the highest-level domain starts with the organizational name, in this case, *www.example.com*. Anything following the organizational name is a lower level of the website domain.

22. **(D)** The robot starts in the center facing to the right. The entire code segment shown is only run once, so finding the answer can be accomplished by going through all the possibilities separately.

    Assuming that the first random number is 0, do not rotate right at all. The robot can either move forward 0, 1, or 2 times, so all the spaces directly in front of the robot's original position are potential landing spaces.

    If the first random number is 1, rotate right once. The robot can either move forward 0, 1, or 2 times, so all the spaces to the right of the robot's original position are potential landing spaces.

    (A) This answer misinterprets the rotation command as if the robot could rotate right up to three times. It can only rotate right once.
    (B) This answer interprets the code as if it repeats on a loop. The entire segment is only run once.
    (C) This answer misinterprets the rotation command as if the robot could rotate right up to two times. It can only rotate right once.
    (D) Correct.

23. **(D)** For Algorithm A, the algorithm has a variable "sum" initialized to zero and a variable "count" initialized to 1. The algorithm uses count to identify each value in the list and adds them to the sum. At the end, "sum" is the sum of all the values in the list and "count" is the total number of values in the list. Taking sum and dividing by count gives us the correct average.

For Algorithm B, the algorithm has a variable "sum" initialized to zero and a variable "count" initialized to 1. The algorithm uses count to identify each value in the list and adds them to the sum. Each time a number is added to sum and increases the count, the algorithm calculates the average of all the numbers added to sum so far. Although calculating the average at each step takes more time and is, therefore, less efficient, it does the math correctly and results in the correct final values for sum, count, and average.

(A) Algorithm A does calculate the average, but Algorithm B does as well.
(B) Algorithm B does calculate the average, but Algorithm A does as well.
(C) Both Algorithm A and B calculate the average correctly.
(D) Correct.

24. **(C)** If a binary number (base 2) ends in a 1 it will be an odd number.
An odd number MOD 2 would equal 1.
If a number MOD 2 = 0, that would represent an even number.

25. **(B)** When finding the total in a data structure the variable needs to be set to 0. In this example, sum is set to the first element in the data structure. The error is this algorithm is counting the first number in the data structure twice. The reason why numbers [0, 1, 35, 6] did not have an error is because the first number in the data structure is 0. If 0 is counted twice it will not result in an error. For all other sets here, the first number in the data structure is counted twice.

26. **(C)** Citizen science is a practice where data is collected either completely or in part by everyday people. This would not work for collecting recordings of bats using ultrasonic microphones and sonograms because everyday people do not know much about using ultrasonic microphones or sonograms.

(A) This would be an example of citizen science because people can report their observations of fireflies during summer months.
(B) This would be an example of citizen science because people can report their observations of jellyfish.
(C) Correct.
(D) This would be an example of citizen science because people can report their PSAT scores and they can be compared to other scores in the given county.

27. **(C)** A great example of a lower-level language to answer this question is binary. All information is presented as a jumble of 1's and 0's. The computer can read binary easily as transistors are either 0 (off) or 1 (on); however, information in binary cannot be read by people on the spot.

    (A) It is hard to program in a low-level language because you have to think about what you want to do, then translate it into the language piece by piece.
    (B) It is hard to debug a program in a low-level language because you have to translate each part of your code into a language you can easily read to identify errors.
    (C) Correct.
    (D) Beginner programmers need a language that is easy to read and has commands as close to normal language as possible.

28. **(D)** High-level languages use commands and abstractions that have names similar to their functions. When you code in a high-level language, these names make it easier to remember what each part of the code does.

    (A) High-level languages typically take more time for the computer to process. High-level languages are typically used for the ease of the programmer.
    (B) Machine code is typically written in binary, which is a lower-level language.
    (C) High-level languages are for experienced and beginning programmers alike.
    (D) Correct.

29. **(A)** The problem states that the command starts with the most abstract class and goes to the least abstract without skipping. The most abstract class in the given chart is JAVA, so the command should start there. To reach ThreadLocalRandom, there is only one possible path.

    (A) Correct.
    (B) The correct classes are listed, but they are in the incorrect order.
    (C) This lists the first and last class but skips the classes in between.
    (D) This lists the right number of steps but follows the incorrect path.

30. **(D)** When converting hexadecimal to binary, each digit in hexadecimal can be represented by four digits in binary. (D) is the value 13, so converting to binary = 1101. (A) is the value 10, so converting to binary = 1010. Combine the two digits' binary conversions to reach 11011010.

8	4	2	1
1	1	0	1
8	4	2	1
1	0	1	0

11011010

31. **(C)** For the numerical positions of each letter in the word *dog*, *d* is in position 4, *o* is in position 15, and *g* is in position 7 (of the alphabet). In eight-digit binary, *d* is represented by 4 in binary, 00000100; *o* would be 00001111; and *g* would be 00000111.

32. **(B)** This chart correctly displays the output of the given code segment. The other charts all begin by going south instead of going 3 west.

33. **(C)** Hardware abstractions are the larger-level components that people interact with. Although most people do not know much about small pieces such as circuits and transistors, they do know how to use a computer and a mouse. Using these computer parts from lowest to highest would be transistor, memory, motherboard, and, at the highest level, computer.

    (A) Transistors are a lower-level abstraction than the computer because they are a component of the computer.
    (B) Motherboards are a lower-level abstraction because they are part of the computer.
    (C) Correct.
    (D) Memory is a part of the computer and, therefore, a lower-level abstraction.

34. **(D)** Regardless of the values of A and B, the first logic gate says true and false and will always return false. Every statement that false feeds into is an "And" statement. When one part of the "And" statement is false, it will return false regardless of the outcome of the other statement. Therefore, the value of result will always be false.

    (A) The values of A and B do not matter due to the outcome of the first statement.
    (B) The values of A and B do not matter due to the outcome of the first statement.
    (C) The outcome of the first statement makes every statement including result return as false.
    (D) Correct.

35. **(A)** Simulations are often used as opposed to real-world experiments because they are cheaper and easier.

    (A) Correct.
    (B) Simulations cannot account for every variable due to a lack of exact circumstances and the possibility of human error.
    (C) Simulations can be altered and run multiple times.
    (D) Simulations can predict the real world, but leave room for error and would not affect people the same way.

36. **(C)** Data compression is used to reduce the size of files for storage or transmission quite frequently. It can be either lossless or lossy, depending on the circumstances.

    (A) Data compression can be used on multiple types of files.
    (B) Lossless data compression is not ideal when you need to fit certain storage requirements.
    (C) Correct.
    (D) Lossy compression is used to send pictures.

37. **(C)** If a program requires a large amount of memory to run, it may not be able to process larger data sets.

   (A) Programming documentation does not affect a program's ability to process data and run.
   (B) The order of the data in the set is most likely irrelevant.
   (C) Correct.
   (D) The number of program statements will have a slight effect on run time, but it will not be a major issue when processing larger data sets.

38. **(D)** Computer simulations can provide heuristic solutions to experiments that cannot be performed in real life. They can also predict outcomes of given situations in reference to scientific research. All three statements are true here, making (D) the best answer choice.

39. **(C)** The website contains information about political parties and elections; it has nothing to do with race.

   (A) It has information on parties and popular opinions in each district that could be used to predict outcomes.
   (B) It can be used to analyze the splits in each county by dividing it into popular opinion of each district.
   (C) Correct.
   (D) The website contains information on favor of parties in each district.

40. **(C)** Reading a file and writing a file require different memory requirements. Writing to files requires the original file plus an updated version of the file that is being worked on. This becomes obvious when working on large Word files such as this book.

   (A) The entire file is needed in both cases.
   (B) Read files require memory.
   (C) Correct.
   (D) Both files use the same memory.

41. **(B)**

   (A) Lawyers must know the laws to pass the bar. Multiple state companies are not new.
   (B) There are enforceable laws on the internet.
   (C) Correct. The internet has changed the way we live our lives so quickly that new rules need to be adaptive.
   (D) Proxy servers can hide your IP address.

42. **(C)** The Digital Media Copyright Act is a federal copyright law that was meant to curb internet piracy of digital media. The DMCA updated copyright protection in relation to use on computers and other electronic devices.

43. **(D)** For the internet to be successful, humanity must be able to trust the security, safety, and privacy of a trusted site. However, with so many parts working together a user can never be 100% sure a site is truly trustworthy. If a site is labeled trusted it does not guarantee that the site does not contain malicious code.

44. **(D)** Any number modulus 10 will always return the rightmost digit of that number; for example, 96 MOD 10 = 6, 104 MOD 10 = 4. Testing to see if the number MOD 10 results of each number are equal will test to see if the last digits are the same numbers.

(A) 34 = 94 is false while the last numbers are equal

If they're equal, check the entire number, not just the last digit.

(B) 34/10 = 3 and 94/10 = 8

These two numbers have the same last digit, so they should return true.

A number/10 does not isolate the last digit.

(C) 34 is not equal to 94

Not equal does not check the last digit of the number.

(D) Correct.

34 MOD 10 = 4 and 94 MOD 10 = 4

A number MOD 10 will give the ones place of the number in all cases.

45. **(C)** A Caesar cipher is an example of asymmetric encryption. The person encoding the message uses his or her private key, sends the encoded message, and then tells that person the private key so that he or she can decode the message.

46. **(B)** A digital certificate is an electronic "password" that allows organizations to exchange data securely over the internet using the public key infrastructure. The information within the message or transaction is kept confidential. It may only be read and understood by the intended sender and receiver.

(A) Having systems examined by a third party does not ensure security.

(B) Correct.

(C) It does ensure it is the actual server, but it also needs to encrypt the data.

(D) What makes someone a professional?

47. **(D)** The internet facilitates collaboration in many ways. It does allow for many people to work together quickly and easier.

I	A team can work together quickly regardless of distance.
II	Online technologies make sending messages and files easier.
III	Cloud technology creates shared editing tools.

48. **(B)** IPv4 is a type of internet networking protocol that functions as an address for devices connected to a network. IPv4 addresses are commonly found in the format of xxx.xxx.xxx.xxx, the largest number being 255.

49. **(C)** The nature of the internet is freedom from being controlled by a government body. No single computer or group of computers controls the internet. The internet is not centrally managed but is a collection of local area networks.

(A) Protocols are not legally enforced.

(B) Nothing is required, but that is not saying that everything will work.

(C) It does ensure it is the actual server, but it also needs to encrypt the data.

(D) The internet protocols are not frameworks but are needed so that all computers can "talk" to other computers regardless of brands or price.

50. **(D)** To successfully protect a company from cyber attacks it must contain software, hardware, and a human element to protect itself. The company needs educated users to not trust seemingly innocent links, as well as hardware, such as firewalls and software, to protect against malware.

51. **(A)** If a sorted or an unsorted list contains 2000 numbers, the best-case scenario is finding the number on the first guess. The worst-case scenario is searching 2000 times. A linear search is the only choice for finding a number in an unsorted list. If the list is sorted a binary search is generally faster.

52. **(C)**

List1	1	35	6	76	−4	98
List2	5	1	8	6	96	−4
List3						

DISPLAY(mystery (list1, list2, list3))

53. **(B)**

List1	1	35	6	76	−4	98
List2	5	4	8	6	96	−4
List3	1	6	−4			

If an element from list1 is in list2 append the number to list3.

List1	85	40	79	80	92	20

Sum = 0

If item MOD 2 = 0	Sum = 0
85 MOD 2 = 1	Sum = 0
40 MOD 0 = 0	Sum = 1
79 MOD 0 = 1	Sum = 1
80 MOD 2 = 0	Sum = 2
92 MOD 2 = 0	Sum = 3
20 MOD 2 = 0	Sum = 4

Sum = 4

54. **(C)**

X	Y
3	2

DISPLAY(mystery(3,2))

X	Output
3	O
2	O
1	O
0	O

Y	Output
2	X
1	X
0	X

OOOOXXX

55. **(D)**

List1	6 9 14 5 7

Num = 5

Num 5	7 MOD 1 = 1	Display 7
4	5 MOD 2 = 1	Display 5
3	14 MOD 2 = 0	
2	9 MOD 2 = 1	Display 9
1	6 MOD 2 = 0	

7 5 9

56. **(B)**

List1	6	9	14	5	7

Num = 5

Num 5	7 % 2 = 1	
Num 4	5 % 2 = 1	
Num 3	14 % 2 = 0	Display 14
Num 2	9 % 2 = 1	
Num 1	6 % 2 = 0	Display 6

6 14

57. **(C)**

Num	Is Num > 12	Num MOD 2 = 0	Output
3	No	No	
4	No	Yes	4
5	No	No	
6	No	Yes	6
7	No	No	
8	No	Yes	8
9	No	No	
10	No	Yes	10
11	No	No	
12	No	Yes	12
13			

4 6 8 10 12

58. **(C)** Possible random numbers 5, 7, and 9 are returned by the method Random(5, 9).

To represent true, 3 of the 10 numbers should have the possibility of being chosen.

5 6 7 8 9	
x MOD 2 = 0 would hit the two numbers 6 and 8	
x MOD 5 = 0 would hit the one number 5	
x MOD 2 = 1 would hit the required three numbers 5, 7, and 9	5 7 9
x MOD 5 = 5 would hit 0	

The only choice that selects 3 out of the 5 numbers is x MOD 2 = 1.

59. **(A)**

Random 1 2 3 4 5 6 7 8 9 10 11 12 13 14 15 16 17 18 19 20

Num > 5 is 3/4

And

Num < 13 and even is 6 out of 20

2/10 * 100 = 20%

60. **(D)**

List 1	5	12	15

Total = 0
5 MOD 5 = 0   total = 0 + 5 = 5
12 MOD 5 = 2
15 MOD 5 = 0   total = 5 + 15 = 20
Answer = 20

61. **(A)** While 1 is less than 15 and 1 MOD 3 = 1, not 0, the loop only executes one time.

x	y	Output	
2	0	0	
	1		

62. **(B)**

c	x
~~17~~	~~4~~
0	0

63. **(C)** The order of operations is to do what's inside the parentheses first:

$a \leftarrow 1 + 1 * 3$

Then multiply:

$a \leftarrow 1 + 3$

Then add.

$a \leftarrow 4$

64. **(A)** Solve using the correct order of operations:

$x \leftarrow (0) *$ anything in the world is 0

$x \leftarrow 0$

65. **(D)**

x	y	Temp
~~7~~	~~8~~	~~15~~
8	8	
		16
	20	

66. **(C)**

$w = 34 \text{ MOD } 15 = 4$

$y = 21 \text{ MOD } 6 = 3$

$x = 18 * 4 = 72$

w	y	x
4	3	72

67. **(B), (C)** Abstractions reduce the level of complexity of a program by allowing the programmer to code the abstraction once but class the abstraction as many times as needed. The abstraction also can compartmentalize the code, so if there is an error the programmer knows where the error is.

68. **(A), (B)** The first two choices result in the robot being in a safe place. The call to the MOVE_FORWARD method moves the robot one space. The call to the ROTATE_LEFT method rotates the robot 90 degrees counterclockwise. FOR EACH *x* IN LIST is incorrect because the For Each loop is used with a data structure that does not exist in this problem. IF *x* equals GOAL_REACHED just does not work.

69. **(B), (D)** Graphs can illustrate trends in a manner that is easier to digest than the numbers that make up raw data. Tables can be added to an office suite's applications just as easily as graphs can be, and different types of graphs can only show specific aspects of data (e.g., a line graph only shows trends, while a pie chart only shows proportions).

70. **(A), (B)** If the robot rotates left, then moves forward, it will go out of the grid and result in an error.

$p = 1$

When $p = 0$ the robot will not move and will remain in the current location. For any value of p other than 0 it will result in an error due to the robot going outside the grid.

71. **(A), (B)** A person's ride preferences and willingness to walk have the most effect on what they ride first (willingness to walk via distance to the ride from the gate), which has the most effect on lines. While the variables in the last two choices may have some effect (people may go to rides near the places they eat, and annual passholders may be more likely to try for less popular rides), they have a small enough effect that they can be ignored if necessary.

72. **(A), (B)**

Choice (A) runs the robot along the top of the grid to the star.
Choice (B) runs the robot along the bottom of the grid to the star.
Choice (C) places the robot off the grid.
Choice (D) just spins the robot 7 times but does not change the location of the robot.

ANSWER SHEET
Practice Test 2

1. Ⓐ Ⓑ Ⓒ Ⓓ
2. Ⓐ Ⓑ Ⓒ Ⓓ
3. Ⓐ Ⓑ Ⓒ Ⓓ
4. Ⓐ Ⓑ Ⓒ Ⓓ
5. Ⓐ Ⓑ Ⓒ Ⓓ
6. Ⓐ Ⓑ Ⓒ Ⓓ
7. Ⓐ Ⓑ Ⓒ Ⓓ
8. Ⓐ Ⓑ Ⓒ Ⓓ
9. Ⓐ Ⓑ Ⓒ Ⓓ
10. Ⓐ Ⓑ Ⓒ Ⓓ
11. Ⓐ Ⓑ Ⓒ Ⓓ
12. Ⓐ Ⓑ Ⓒ Ⓓ
13. Ⓐ Ⓑ Ⓒ Ⓓ
14. Ⓐ Ⓑ Ⓒ Ⓓ
15. Ⓐ Ⓑ Ⓒ Ⓓ
16. Ⓐ Ⓑ Ⓒ Ⓓ
17. Ⓐ Ⓑ Ⓒ Ⓓ
18. Ⓐ Ⓑ Ⓒ Ⓓ
19. Ⓐ Ⓑ Ⓒ Ⓓ
20. Ⓐ Ⓑ Ⓒ Ⓓ
21. Ⓐ Ⓑ Ⓒ Ⓓ
22. Ⓐ Ⓑ Ⓒ Ⓓ
23. Ⓐ Ⓑ Ⓒ Ⓓ
24. Ⓐ Ⓑ Ⓒ Ⓓ
25. Ⓐ Ⓑ Ⓒ Ⓓ

26. Ⓐ Ⓑ Ⓒ Ⓓ
27. Ⓐ Ⓑ Ⓒ Ⓓ
28. Ⓐ Ⓑ Ⓒ Ⓓ
29. Ⓐ Ⓑ Ⓒ Ⓓ
30. Ⓐ Ⓑ Ⓒ Ⓓ
31. Ⓐ Ⓑ Ⓒ Ⓓ
32. Ⓐ Ⓑ Ⓒ Ⓓ
33. Ⓐ Ⓑ Ⓒ Ⓓ
34. Ⓐ Ⓑ Ⓒ Ⓓ
35. Ⓐ Ⓑ Ⓒ Ⓓ
36. Ⓐ Ⓑ Ⓒ Ⓓ
37. Ⓐ Ⓑ Ⓒ Ⓓ
38. Ⓐ Ⓑ Ⓒ Ⓓ
39. Ⓐ Ⓑ Ⓒ Ⓓ
40. Ⓐ Ⓑ Ⓒ Ⓓ
41. Ⓐ Ⓑ Ⓒ Ⓓ
42. Ⓐ Ⓑ Ⓒ Ⓓ
43. Ⓐ Ⓑ Ⓒ Ⓓ
44. Ⓐ Ⓑ Ⓒ Ⓓ
45. Ⓐ Ⓑ Ⓒ Ⓓ
46. Ⓐ Ⓑ Ⓒ Ⓓ
47. Ⓐ Ⓑ Ⓒ Ⓓ
48. Ⓐ Ⓑ Ⓒ Ⓓ
49. Ⓐ Ⓑ Ⓒ Ⓓ
50. Ⓐ Ⓑ Ⓒ Ⓓ

51. Ⓐ Ⓑ Ⓒ Ⓓ
52. Ⓐ Ⓑ Ⓒ Ⓓ
53. Ⓐ Ⓑ Ⓒ Ⓓ
54. Ⓐ Ⓑ Ⓒ Ⓓ
55. Ⓐ Ⓑ Ⓒ Ⓓ
56. Ⓐ Ⓑ Ⓒ Ⓓ
57. Ⓐ Ⓑ Ⓒ Ⓓ
58. Ⓐ Ⓑ Ⓒ Ⓓ
59. Ⓐ Ⓑ Ⓒ Ⓓ
60. Ⓐ Ⓑ Ⓒ Ⓓ
61. Ⓐ Ⓑ Ⓒ Ⓓ
62. Ⓐ Ⓑ Ⓒ Ⓓ
63. Ⓐ Ⓑ Ⓒ Ⓓ
64. Ⓐ Ⓑ Ⓒ Ⓓ
65. Ⓐ Ⓑ Ⓒ Ⓓ
66. Ⓐ Ⓑ Ⓒ Ⓓ
67. Ⓐ Ⓑ Ⓒ Ⓓ
68. Ⓐ Ⓑ Ⓒ Ⓓ
69. Ⓐ Ⓑ Ⓒ Ⓓ
70. Ⓐ Ⓑ Ⓒ Ⓓ
71. Ⓐ Ⓑ Ⓒ Ⓓ
72. Ⓐ Ⓑ Ⓒ Ⓓ
73. Ⓐ Ⓑ Ⓒ Ⓓ
74. Ⓐ Ⓑ Ⓒ Ⓓ

Practice Test 2

> **DIRECTIONS:** Each of the questions or incomplete statements below is followed by four suggested answers or completions. Select the one that is best in each case and then fill in the appropriate letter in the corresponding space on the answer sheet.

1. What should replace <condition missing> so that the program below displays TRUE 10% of the time?

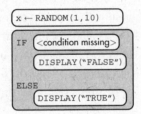

(A) x < 1
(B) x < = 1
(C) x < 9
(D) x <= 9

2. Consider the following code segment, which uses variables *x*, *y*, and *z*.

What would the following program display?

```
Line 1: x ← 6
Line 2: y ← 12
Line 3: z ← 24
Line 4: if ( y MOD x = 0 )
Line 5: {
Line 6: x ← y
Line 7: }
Line 8: if ( z MOD x = 0 )
Line 9: {
Line 10: z ← x
Line 11: }
Line 12: DISPLAY (x, y, z)
```

(A) 6 12 24
(B) 12 12 12
(C) 24 24 24
(D) 12 24 24

3. Which of the following is NOT an example of a DDoS attack?

(A) A botnet of 20,000 computers located across the world training its resources to simultaneously flood a website with requests to log in
(B) An anonymous group creating 10,000 bots that are programmed to order on a pizza application that prevents real users' access to the pizza-ordering site
(C) A group of friends creating a thread of tweets on their Twitter accounts
(D) A flood of login requests to a testing site preventing real students from taking the test

4. Tickets prices to Fun Land are given below.

Ticket Type	Price in Rubies
Child	90
Adult	100
Senior	80

If it is your birthday the ticket has a discount of $5.

A programmer is creating an algorithm to set the ticket price to Fun Land. Which of the following code segments correctly sets the value of ticketPrice?

(A)
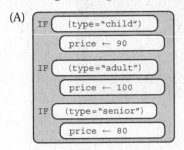

```
IF (type="child")
    price ← 90
IF (type="adult")
    price ← 100
IF (type="senior")
    price ← 80
```

(B)
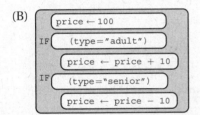

```
price ← 100
IF (type="adult")
    price ← price + 10
IF (type="senior")
    price ← price - 10
```

(C)
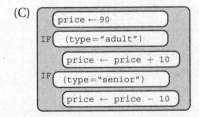

```
price ← 90
IF (type="adult")
    price ← price + 10
IF (type="senior")
    price ← price - 10
```

(D)
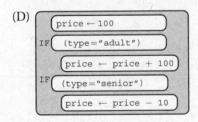

```
price ← 100
IF (type="adult")
    price ← price + 100
IF (type="senior")
    price ← price - 10
```

The following picture was taken by a smartphone.

5. Which of the following is NOT metadata?

    (A) The average value of the green pixels in the picture
    (B) The geographic location where the picture was taken
    (C) The date the photo was taken
    (D) The filename

6. What will the following algorithm display after running the code below?

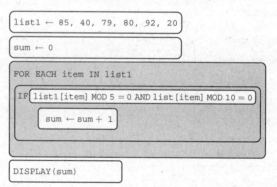

```
list1 ← 85, 40, 79, 80, 92, 20

sum ← 0

FOR EACH item IN list1
    IF list1[item] MOD 5 = 0 AND list[item] MOD 10 = 0
        sum ← sum + 1

DISPLAY(sum)
```

    (A) 1
    (B) 2
    (C) 3
    (D) 4

A flowchart is a way to visually represent an algorithm. The flowchart below uses the following building blocks.

Block	Explanation
Oval	The start or end of the algorithm
Rectangle	One or more processing steps, such as a statement that assigns a value to a variable
Diamond	A conditional or decision step, where execution proceeds to the side labeled `true` if the condition is true and to the side labeled `false` otherwise
Parallelogram	Display a message

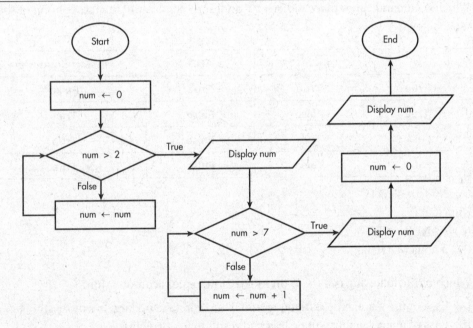

7. What will the above program display?

(A) 2 8 14

(B) 4 8 8

(C) 2 7 0

(D) Nothing due to an infinite loop

8. Two computers calculate the same equation

   $a \leftarrow 1/3$

   A second computer calculates

   $b \leftarrow 1/3$

   If a does not equal b, what error has occurred?

   (A) Roundoff error

   (B) Overflow error

   (C) Hexadecimal conversion error

   (D) a will equal b on all computers

9. Which of the following data structures is NOT a candidate for a binary search?

   (A) A list of students in size order

   (B) A list of numbers from smallest to largest

   (C) A list of words from a poem about sunshine in the order they appear in the poem

   (D) A list of words in a dictionary

10. Which command can replace <Missing Condition> to result in the last column of the table below?

a	b	a AND b	<Missing Condition>
True	True	True	False
True	False	False	True
False	True	False	True
False	False	False	True

   (A) NOT (a AND b)

   (B) a OR b

   (C) a AND (a AND b)

   (D) b AND (a AND b)

11. Which of the following is a trade-off inherent in lossless compression?

   (A) Ease of use—it can be difficult to email and can take up large memory storage.

   (B) Loss of image quality will be less and result in a blurry image.

   (C) Some of the data will be lost and cannot be recovered.

   (D) Loss of number and size of pixels

The following question uses a robot in a grid of squares. The robot is represented by a triangle, which is initially facing right.

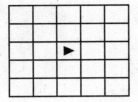

12. What are the possible landing spots for the robot after executing the following program?

y ← RANDOM(0, 2)

```
Line 1: x ← RANDOM (0,2)
Line 2: REPEAT x TIMES
Line 3: {
Line 4: ROTATE_LEFT( )
Line 5: }
Line 6: REPEAT x TIMES
Line 7: {
Line 8: MOVE_FORWARD( )
Line 9: }
```

(A)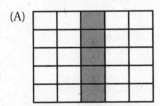

(B)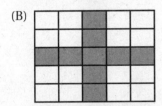

(C)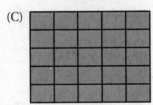

(D)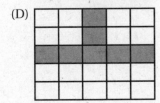

13. Which of the code below will correctly swap the frog with the bear?

animal

(A) ```
    temp = animal[1]
    animal[1] = animal[3]
    animal[3] = temp
    ```
(B) ```
    temp = animal[1]
    animal[1] = animal[2]
    animal[2] = temp
    ```
(C) ```
    animal[1] = animal[2]
    animal[2] = animal[1]
    ```
(D) ```
    animal[3] = animal[1]
    animal[1] = animal[3]
    ```

14. What is the value displayed after the algorithm is run?

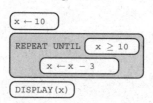

(A) 0
(B) 1
(C) 10
(D) 12

15. An algorithm has n number of steps. Which of the following would be considered a reasonable number of steps?

(A) n^n
(B) $4^n + 8n^2$
(C) $100n^4$
(D) 3^n

ASCII	Hex	ASCII	Hex	ASCII	Hex
0	30	L	4C	g	67
1	31	M	4D	h	68
2	32	N	4E	i	69
3	33	O	4F	j	6A
4	34	P	50	k	6B
5	35	Q	51	l	6C
6	36	R	52	m	6D
7	37	S	53	n	6E
8	38	T	54	o	6F
9	39	U	55	p	70
A	41	V	56	q	71
B	42	W	57	r	72
C	43	X	58	s	73
D	44	Y	59	t	74
E	45	Z	60	u	75
F	46	a	61	v	76
G	47	b	62	w	77
H	48	c	63	x	78
I	49	d	64	y	79
J	4A	e	65	z	7A
K	4B	f	66		

ASCII is a character-encoding scheme that uses 7 bits to represent each character. The hexadecimal (base 16) values 30 through 7A represent the letters and numbers shown in the table above.

16. What ASCII character is represented by the binary (base 2) number 01101101?

(A) m

(B) p

(C) H

(D) f

17. What would be a good use of constants when initializing variables at the beginning of a program?

 I. To represent the maximum capacity of people allowed in a restaurant for fire safety

 II. To represent the mathematical value of Newton's constant

 III. To represent how much time is left in a game

(A) I and II only

(B) I and III only

(C) I, II, and III

(D) II and III only

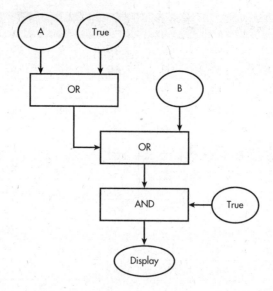

18. What does the above algorithm display?

    (A) True always
    (B) False always
    (C) When A is false, the algorithm is false.
    (D) When B is false, the algorithm is false.

19. What is displayed after running the algorithm below?

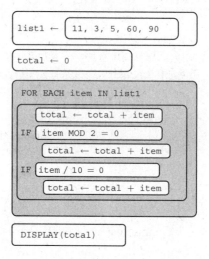

```
list1 ←   11, 3, 5, 60, 90

total ← 0

FOR EACH item IN list1
    total ← total + item
IF  item MOD 2 = 0
        total ← total + item
IF  item / 10 = 0
        total ← total + item

DISPLAY(total)
```

    (A) 0
    (B) 240
    (C) 169
    (D) 150

20. Which of the following can be represented by a single binary digit?

(A) Time

(B) Date

(C) Geographic location

(D) Light on/light off

21. What is displayed as a result of executing the following code segment?

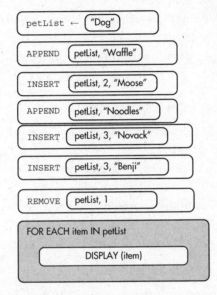

```
petList ← "Dog"

APPEND    petList, "Waffle"

INSERT    petList, 2, "Moose"

APPEND    petList, "Noodles"

INSERT    petList, 3, "Novack"

INSERT    petList, 3, "Benji"

REMOVE    petList, 1

FOR EACH item IN petList
    DISPLAY (item)
```

(A) Moose Benji Novack Waffle Noodle

(B) Dog Cat Fish

(C) Dog Golden Bandicoot Cat Fish

(D) Golden Bandicoot Cat Fish

22. Lisa took high-definition pictures of her new dog, Waffles. She emailed the pictures to her grandmother in Miami. When her grandmother opened the pictures she noticed that the images were not crisp and the pictures appeared blurry. Which of the following could be a possible explanation for the blurry pictures?

(A) When emailing the pictures the file was broken down into packets that were not assembled in the correct order.

(B) The picture files were compressed using lossy compression so the file could be small enough to be emailed.

(C) The picture files were compressed using lossless compression so the file could be small enough to be emailed.

(D) Every time you email a picture some of the picture data will be lost in transmission.

23. Why is cryptography essential to cyber security?

(A) Cryptography secures internet communications by ensuring that they cannot be read if they are intercepted.

(B) Cryptography is used to prevent publicly accessible files on a server from being edited.

(C) Cryptography secures internet communications by preventing a third party from hijacking a connection.

(D) Cryptography does not allow data on a server to be edited by anyone, ensuring the data's integrity.

24. A 10-megapixel camera takes pictures made up of 10 million pixels. A pixel contains red, green, and blue values between 0 and 255. A photo-editing software adds a value of 40 to every red pixel. If the red value is greater than 255 it saves the red value as 255. What type of transformation is the photo-editing software using?

(A) Lossless transformation
(B) Lossy transformation
(C) Addition transformation
(D) Frequency transformation

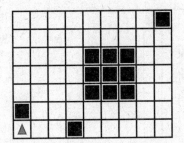

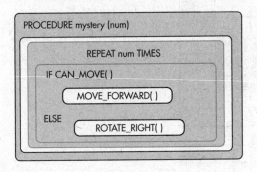

25. Where would the robot end up after running the following code?

```
Line 1: mystery ( 4 )
Line 2: ROTATE_LEFT( )
Line 3: ROTATE_LEFT( )
Line 4: mystery( 5 )
```

(A)

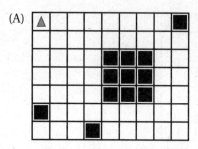

(B)

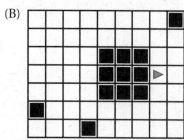

(C)

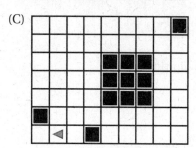

(D)

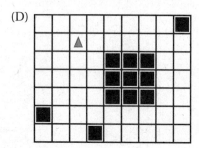

26. Order the numbers from lowest to highest.

    I. AC_{HEX}

    II. 82_{DEC}

    III. 110111_{BIN}

  (A) I, II, and III

  (B) III, II, and I

  (C) II, III, and I

  (D) I, III, and II

27. Find the error in the following low-level programming code.

```
10111001 11010010 0000011 100001001 00001110 00000000 00000000
10111001 11100001 00010000 10001001 00001110 00000010 00000000
10100001 00000000 00000000 1001011 00011110 00000010 00000000
00000011 11000011 10111111 00000100 00000000 100001001 00001110
00000000 00000000 10111001 11100001 00010000 10001001 00001110
00000010 00000000 10100001 00000000 00000000 1001011 00011110
00000010 00000000 00000011 11000011 10100011
```

(A) The 17th 1 needs to be changed to a 0.
(B) This is too difficult. To determine errors, it would be considerably easier to use an upper-level language.
(C) The 34th 0 should be a 1.
(D) The 84th digit should be a 1.

28.

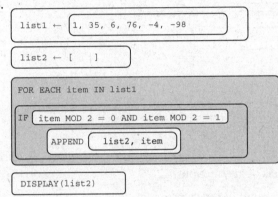

```
list1 ← 1, 35, 6, 76, -4, -98

list2 ← [    ]

FOR EACH item IN list1

IF  item MOD 2 = 0 AND item MOD 2 = 1

        APPEND  list2, item


DISPLAY(list2)
```

(A) [ ]
(B) [−4 , −98]
(C) [1, 35, 6, 76, −4, −98]
(D) [6, 4, 98]

29. What is displayed after running the below algorithm?

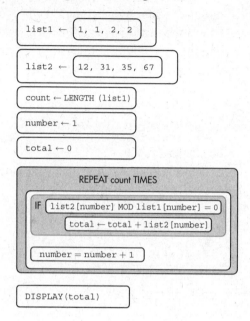

```
list1 ← 1, 1, 2, 2

list2 ← 12, 31, 35, 67

count ← LENGTH (list1)

number ← 1

total ← 0

REPEAT count TIMES

IF  list2[number] MOD list1[number] = 0
        total ← total + list2[number]

    number = number + 1

DISPLAY(total)
```

(A) 145

(B) 12

(C) 133

(D) 43

30. Hardware is built using multiple levels of abstractions.

Which of the following hardware are listed in order from high to low?

(A) Computer, transistor, motherboard

(B) Logic gate, transistor, computer

(C) Computer, motherboard, transistor

(D) Logic gate, motherboard, transistor

31. Credit card companies use a combination of technology and humanity to fight fraud. Fraud detection uses algorithms across massive amounts of data collected from millions of customers and hundreds of millions of cards. What type of algorithm would be best used for fraud detection?

   (A) Brute force algorithm
   (B) Heuristic algorithm
   (C) Searching algorithm
   (D) Optimization algorithm

32. An algorithm compares the user-inputted number **number** to the randomly selected number **randomNumber** and calls the method **checkForInEquality()** if the two values are different. What should replace <Missing Code> in the following algorithm?

```
<Missing Code>
{
checkForInEquality()
}
```

   (A) IF(number = randomNumber)
   (B) IF(number = true AND randomNumber = drawing)
   (C) IF(number ≠ randomNumber)
   (D) IF(number = true OR randomNumber = true)

33. A common type of heuristic algorithm for chess is alpha-beta pruning. This algorithm evaluates moves but automatically stops if the current move is proven to be worse than the current "best solution." In addition, if a certain early step is found to be bad, any moves involving that step are also ignored, regardless of whether they have already been tested. Why is this used?

   (A) This method will always procure the best solution because all moves with early flaws are ignored.
   (B) Finding the best solution could take a long time, so ignoring certain branches that appear to be useless means that fewer solutions need to be checked.
   (C) This method never works, but it requires far fewer resources than other algorithms.
   (D) Finding the best solution requires far more computer power with this method, which makes it more likely to be accurate.

34. The algorithm below should display the total value contained in list1, not counting the value 13. So, if list1 contained [2, 13, 4], the algorithm should display 6. What line of code can replace <Missing Code> so the algorithm will work as intended?

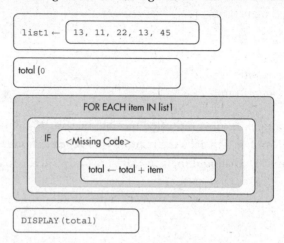

(A) `list1 = 13`

(B) `item = 13`

(C) `list1 ≠ 13`

(D) `item ≠ 13`

35. For the following data structure, which search algorithm would work as intended to find the value 35?

numbers[1,43,23,65,76,34,33,12,94,576,55,35,3456,3,25854,2357,1,4,0,43]

(A) Linear search

(B) Binary search

(C) Bubble sort

(D) Insertion sort

36. How many lines need to be cut to completely isolate computer E from computer C?

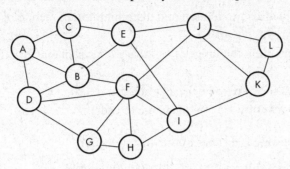

(A) 0

(B) 3

(C) 6

(D) 8

37. Data traveling in the internet is broken down into small chunks of data called packets. What protocol guides the rules on how data is subdivided into packets before transmission?

(A) TCP/IP

(B) DNS

(C) FTP

(D) HTTP

38. Convert $2A_{HEX}$ to a binary number.

(A) 00101010_{BIN}

(B) 11001010_{BIN}

(C) 11110000_{BIN}

(D) 11111111_{BIN}

39. Which of the following is NOT indicative of a phishing attack?

(A) A professional origination that the user is a member of asks in an email to click on a link to rectify a discrepancy with an account. The email resembles previous legitimate official correspondence.

(B) An email with the user's personal information, including the name, position, company, and work phone number, directs the user to click a link to input her social security number to verify that the user is accurate.

(C) An email asks the user to call the phone number on the back of his or her credit card to verify purchases made in the past 24 hours.

(D) A virus pops up on the computer asking the user to call a phone number to protect his IP address from hackers.

40. What is the role of the Digital Millennium Copyright Act (DMCA)?

(A) DMCA criminalizes production and dissemination of technology, devices, or services of copyrighted works.

(B) DMCA is expanding the range of creative works available for others to build upon legally and to share.

(C) DMCA allows software to be used at no cost.

(D) DMCA provides software free of charge to users.

41. Which of the following is a cause of the digital divide?

(A) Lack of access to the technology due to affordability

(B) Lack of knowledge on how to use technology

(C) Lack of access to technology due to location

(D) All of the above

42. A fast food company selling burgers wants to increase speed at the drive thru. They create a simulation that shows a decrease in wait time by 20% if they implement a touchscreen ordering system instead of using employees to take orders. When the restaurant implemented the simulation in a real-world situation the wait time did decrease; however, the overall sales also decreased 40%. What could have been the reason for the failure?

(A) The simulation had considered all variables.

(B) The simulation might not have considered human preference for ordering food from people instead of using a touchscreen.

(C) The simulation had worked as intended.

(D) Wait time and sales are directly proportional, and, therefore, the simulation worked as intended.

43. An API (application program interface) provides the following methods:

getStudentScores(studentName): returns the total value of all test scores added together from the named student.

getNumberOfTests(studentName): returns the number of tests taken by the named student.

Which of the following code segments will display the named student's average using only the above API and common math functions?

(A) `DISPLAY ( getStudentScores("Lisa Reichelson") / getNumberOfTests("Lisa Reichelson"))`

(B) `DISPLAY ( getStudentScores( ) / getNumberOfTests( ))`

(C) `DISPLAY ( getNumberOfTests( ) / getStudentScores( ))`

(D) `DISPLAY (getAverage("Lisa Reichelson"))`

44. A user attempts to enter the site "Facebook.com," but is instead directed to a fake Facebook site designed to collect information from the user. Which system is being infected for this misdirection?

(A) The IP address of the user is infected.

(B) The domain name server (DNS) is infected.

(C) The fault-tolerant nature of the internet disabled the connection to Facebook.

(D) Facebook's IP address could have switched from IPv4 to IPv6.

45. What is the minimum number of searchers for a binary search using an ordered list of 100 numbers?

(A) 0

(B) 1

(C) 8

(D) 100

46. What is the minimum number of binary digits needed to store the number 56?

(A) 1

(B) 3

(C) 5

(D) 6

47. Which of the following are benefits to having information be easily accessible and changeable?

I. Information can be easily found by researchers and citizens, which can improve experimental and investigative findings.

II. Information can be easily found by students, who can use it to improve their understanding of a topic.

III. Information can be easily checked by third parties, which ensures that it is always correct and up-to-date.

(A) I only

(B) I and II only

(C) II and III only

(D) I, II, and III

48. In what order will the numbers appear after running the algorithm below?

```
a ← 4
  DISPLAY(1 + a)
a ← a + 2
DISPLAY(a)
IF(a < 0)
{
      DISPLAY(−3 + a)
      DISPLAY(a / 2)
}
ELSE
{
      DISPLAY(1 − (a))
      DISPLAY(a)

}
```

(A) 5, 7, −6, 7

(B) 5, 6, −5, 6

(C) 5, 6, 3, 3

(D) 5, 7, 4, 3.5

49. In the following URL, what is the highest level of the domain's syntax hierarchy?
https://www.tovuti.net/ukurasa

(A) www

(B) tovuti

(C) net

(D) ukurasa

50. What is the value displayed after the algorithm is run?

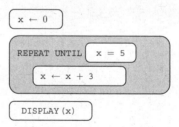

(A) 0

(B) 1

(C) 10

(D) This algorithm will not display any number due to an infinite loop.

The question below uses a robot and a grid of squares. The robot is represented as a triangle, which is initially in the bottom-left square facing toward the top of the grid.

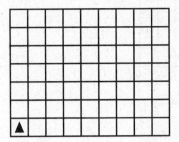

The following algorithm is run on the robot above.

```
Line 1: move ← RANDOM(0 , 4)

Line 2: count < RANDOM(0, 8)

Line 3: REPEAT move TIMES

Line 4: REPEAT count TIMES

Line 5: {

Line 6: MOVE_FORWARD()

Line 7: }

Line 8: ROTATE_RIGHT()
```

51. Which of the following are possible landing spots for the robot?

(A)

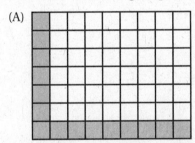

(B)

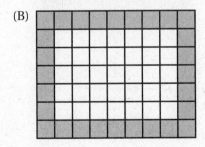

(C)

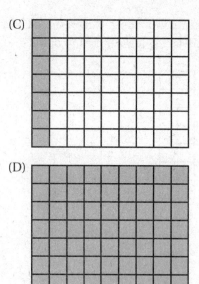

(D)

52. What role does a compiler have in processing a high-level language?

(A) The compiler ensures that the program will have no runtime errors.

(B) The computer cannot directly understand high-level languages, so an intermediate program, such as a compiler, is needed to translate the code into machine code so that the computer can understand.

(C) The compiler checks for updates and installs programs onto the computer.

(D) The compiler speeds up runtime of a program.

53. What is displayed after the following algorithm is run?

```
Line 1: temp ← 132
Line 2: DISPLAY (convertApproxTemp( temp ))
Line 3:
Line 4: PROCEDURE(temp)
Line 5: {
Line 6:   RETURN( (5 x (temp - 32)) / 10)
Line 7: }
```

(A) 132

(B) 50

(C) 100

(D) 32

54. A 10mp camera will take pictures with 10 million pixels. Each pixel will contain a red, green, and blue value. If the red, green, and blue values are represented by the three hexadecimal numbers (00, A3, 16), what are the equivalent decimal numbers?

(A) 0, 163, 22
(B) 0, 103, 16
(C) 0, 22, 15
(D) 0, 19, 16

55. What could a single binary value represent?

(A) Volume on a radio
(B) Temperature in Celsius
(C) Is a light on or off
(D) Time

a	*b*	*a* AND *b*	<Missing condition>
T	T	T	F
T	F	F	T
F	T	F	T
F	F	F	T

56. What could replace the missing condition to get the results in the fourth column?

(A) *a* OR *b*
(B) NOT(*a* OR *a*)
(C) NOT(*a* AND *b*)
(D) NOT *b*

57. Which of the following will evaluate to "TRUE"?

  I. (TRUE AND FALSE)
 II. (NOT (FALSE OR FALSE))
III. (TRUE AND FALSE) OR (TRUE OR FALSE)

(A) I only
(B) I and III only
(C) I, II, and III
(D) II and III

PRACTICE TEST 2   369

58. Which of the following is an example of a DDoS attack?

(A) Receiving an email with a false link designed to trick users into entering social security numbers

(B) Using a key to decrypt encrypted asymmetrical encrypted data

(C) Using thousands of infected computers to constantly request to log into a website so actual users cannot log on

(D) Infecting a DNS server to direct traffic to the incorrect IP address

59. When sending a picture from your phone to your friend's phone using a mobile application, what is true about the packets of information sent?

(A) Packets are sent by the quickest path possible in the correct order.

(B) Packets are sent in multiple paths and can be received out of order.

(C) Packets are received in the order that they are sent.

(D) All of the above

60. Which of the following algorithms can be used to determine if a number is even or odd?

(A)
```
LINE 1: Number ← INPUT( )
LINE 2: If( NUM MOD 2 = 0)
LINE 3: {
LINE 4: DISPLAY ("even")
Line 5: }
```

(B)
```
LINE 1: Number ← INPUT( )
LINE 2: If( NUM = even)
LINE 3: {
LINE 4: DISPLAY ("even")
Line 5: }
```

(C)
```
LINE 1: Number ← INPUT( )
LINE 2: If( NUM MOD 2 = 0)
LINE 3: {
LINE 4: DISPLAY ("EVEN")
Line 5: }
Line 6: ELSE
Line 7:{
Line 8: DISPLAY("ODD")
Line 9: }
```

(D)
```
LINE 1: Number ← INPUT( )
LINE 2: If( NUM MOD 3 = 0)
LINE 3: {
LINE 4: DISPLAY ("EVEN")
Line 5: }
Line 6: ELSE
Line 7:{
Line 8: DISPLAY("ODD")
Line 9: }
```

61. What should replace <Missing Code> in order to make the following program return true when the first element of the array is equal to the last element of the array?

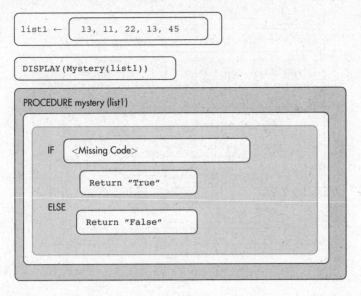

(A) if (list1 = list1)
        return "true"
(B) if (list1[0] = list1[1])
        return "true"
(C) if (list1[1] = list[LENGTH(list1)])
        return "true"
(D) if (list1[0] = list1[LENGTH(list1)-1])
        return "true"

62. Which of the following test cases will not find the maximum number in the list?

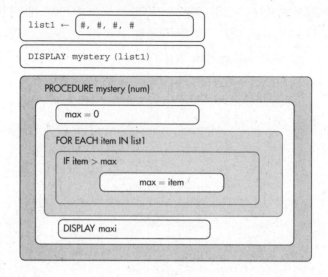

(A) list1[23, 67, 3]

(B) list1[0, 0, 0, 0]

(C) list1[−23, −67, −3, −7]

(D) list1[4]

63. What will the above initialization result in?

$a \leftarrow 34$

$b \leftarrow a \times 10$

$c \leftarrow a - 65 \times -1$

$d \leftarrow a + b$

$e \leftarrow a$ MOD b

$f \leftarrow c$ MOD d

$g \leftarrow e$ MOD f

DISPLAY (g)

(A) 99

(B) 34

(C) 3

(D) 99

64. Is a binary search always the fastest search when searching for a number in a sorted list?

(A) A binary search is always faster with a sorted list.

(B) No, the first pass of a linear search has a chance of finding the correct number.

(C) For a large list, binary searches are always faster.

(D) For a large list, linear searches are always faster.

65. Which of the following concepts pose a problem that cannot be solved with an algorithm?

    (A) Asymmetric cryptography
    (B) Pointer variable
    (C) One-way function
    (D) Reinforcing feedback loop

66. Which of the following would NOT make a problem unsolvable?

    (A) An algorithm can only answer the problem with "yes" or "no."
    (B) An algorithm could take too long to find the solution.
    (C) An algorithm tends to produce an incorrect answer with certain input values.
    (D) An algorithm provides an output in floating-point decimal form.

67. Why do sorting algorithms have varying levels of efficiency?

    (A) Each method of sorting requires a different number of comparisons.
    (B) Try to use something other than "get lucky" maybe—particle sorts and other algorithms rely partly on luck.
    (C) Each sorting method is designed to work with specific arrangements of lists.
    (D) Older methods are naturally less efficient.

68. Why is it important to find an efficient solution to a problem?

    (A) An efficient solution makes it harder to copy an algorithm.
    (B) An efficient solution makes it easier to analyze larger data sets.
    (C) An efficient solution uses more computer resources, which ensures that the results are correct.
    (D) An efficient solution can be solved in a reasonable amount of time.

69. Which of the following can be represented by a single binary number?
    Select two answers.

    (A) The position of an object in a grid of squares representing the position of a 2-d array
    (B) Do you have a puppy?
    (C) Is your puppy named "Waffles"?
    (D) The speed of a puppy chasing a squirrel

70. Most algorithms are designed to both run quickly and use as little RAM as possible. Why?
    Select two answers.

    (A) If an algorithm uses more memory than is available in the computer, it can cause a segmentation fault and a subsequent crash.
    (B) Modern computer programs cannot use more memory than is available as a result of Moore's law.
    (C) If an algorithm uses more memory than there is in the computer, the program will be forced to use virtual memory, which slows down the process.
    (D) If an algorithm uses more memory than the computer has, the program's results will be corrupted.

71. Why are internet protocols used?
    Select two answers.

    (A) Internet protocols make the internet scalable and encourage growth.
    (B) Internet protocols are needed to slow the growth of the internet.
    (C) Internet protocols are a set of rules to ensure the internet can work and transmit information across different equipment used within the internet.
    (D) Internet protocols are specific to the hardware attached to the internet.

72. Which of the following algorithms will display "3" if the number entered by the user contains a "3" in the ones place? (Both 3 and 503 contain a 3 as the first digit. 734 and 4 do not contain a 3 in the first digit.)
    Select two answers.

    ```
    novack <-- input ( )
    ```

    (A) If(novack = 3)
    ```
            DISPLAY (3)
    ```
    (B) If(num / 3 = 0)
    ```
            DISPLAY (3)
    ```
    (C) if(num / 10 = 3)
    ```
            DISPLAY (3)
    ```
    (D) if(num MOD 10 = 3)
    ```
            DISPLAY(num MOD 3)
    ```

73. When should a heuristic algorithm be used?

    (A) When determining which files could have been exposed to a virus before actually checking all files contained on the computer
    (B) Calculating the average score for the national SAT test
    (C) Finding the quickest way to drive from Orlando, Florida, to Cold Foot, Alaska
    (D) Finding the lifetime batting average for Mookie Wilson

74. A simulation for a color choicer should result in 25% BLUE. Which of the following could replace the missing condition?

Select two answers.

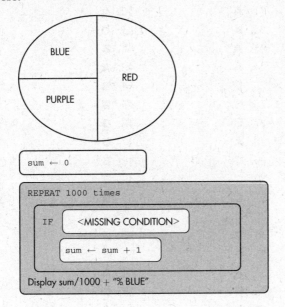

Display sum/1000 + "% BLUE"

(A) `RANDOM(1,4) < 2`

(B) `RANDOM(250,1000) < 251`

(C) `RANDOM(1,2) > 1`

(D) `RANDOM(5,8) > 7`

ANSWER KEY

1. **D**		20. **D**		39. **C**		58. **C**
2. **B**		21. **A**		40. **A**		59. **B**
3. **C**		22. **B**		41. **D**		60. **A**
4. **B**		23. **A**		42. **B**		61. **C**
5. **A**		24. **A**		43. **A**		62. **C**
6. **C**		25. **D**		44. **B**		63. **B**
7. **D**		26. **B**		45. **B**		64. **B**
8. **A**		27. **B**		46. **D**		65. **A**
9. **C**		28. **A**		47. **D**		66. **A**
10. **A**		29. **C**		48. **B**		67. **C**
11. **A**		30. **C**		49. **B**		68. **B**
12. **D**		31. **C**		50. **D**		69. **B, C**
13. **B**		32. **C**		51. **B**		70. **A, C**
14. **C**		33. **B**		52. **B**		71. **A, C**
15. **C**		34. **D**		53. **B**		72. **A, D**
16. **A**		35. **A**		54. **A**		73. **C**
17. **A**		36. **B**		55. **C**		74. **A, D**
18. **A**		37. **A**		56. **C**		
19. **B**		38. **A**		57. **D**		

ANSWERS EXPLAINED

1. **(D)** The program picks a random number from 1 to 10. If it displays false when x is less than or equal to 9, it will display false 90% of the time. Therefore, it will display true the remaining 10% of the time.

   (A) The program picks a random number from 1 to 10. If it only displays false when x is less than one, it would never display false. (Displays true 100% of the time)

   (B) The program picks a random number from 1 to 10. If it displays false when x is less than or equal to 1, it will display false 10% of the time. (Displays true 90% of the time)

   (C) The program picks a random number from 1 to 10. If it displays false when x is less than 9, it will display false 80% of the time. (Displays true 20% of the time)

   (D) Correct.

2. **(B)** To solve this problem, use the following trace:

$x = 6, y = 12, z = 24$ [The three variables are initialized at these values.]

If(12 MOD 6 = 0) [true, MOD is the remainder after dividing the first number by the second]

This statement is true, so set x to the value of y.

$x = 12, y = 12, z = 24$

If(24 MOD 12 = 0) [true]

This statement is true, so z is set to the current value of x.

That leaves a final answer: $x = 12, y = 12, z = 12$.

3. **(C)** A DDoS attack is when computers are used to overload a particular system or website with requests in an attempt to prevent actual users from accessing the system. It would take an incredibly high level of requests to execute a DDoS attack, so a group of friends posting on Twitter would not cause any harm. The other three choices are all DDoS attacks.

4. **(B)** The price is initialized as 90 rubies. If the visitor is an adult, 10 rubies are added to the price, resulting in an adult ticket price of 100 rubies. If the visitor is a senior, 10 rubies are subtracted from the price, resulting in a senior ticket price of 80 rubies. In any case, the final "If" statement checks to see if Birthday is true. If it is true, 5 rubies are discounted from the price.

(A) The price based on type of visitor is correctly assigned, but it fails to discount 5 rubies when it is the visitor's birthday.
(B) Correct.
(C) The price based on type of visitor is not correctly assigned. It initializes price as 100, resulting in an adult price of 110 and a senior price of 90.
(D) The price based on type of visitor is correctly assigned, but it fails to include an "If" statement to discount for the visitor's birthday.

5. **(A)** Metadata is data collected on other data, such as pictures, videos, and other files. Examples of metadata include location, date and time, runtime, color data, and filename. The average value of a pixel is the actual data, not metadata.

6. **(C)** This program contains a list of numbers, list1, and a variable "sum," which is initialized to zero. It goes through each item contained in list1 and checks it against an "If" statement, if(item MOD 5 = 0 and item MOD 10 = 0). [If item MOD num = 0, it means that item is divisible by num.] If the number is divisible by both 5 and 10, the program adds one to the sum. The numbers in list1, 40, 80, and 20, are all divisible by both 5 and 10, so the program returns 3.

7. **(D)** Solve the problem with the following trace:

Num = 0 [the variable num is initialized to 0]

If(num > 2) [num is 0, so this statement is false]

The above statement returns false, so set num equal to num.

Now, num = 0.

If(num > 2) [num is still 0, so this statement is false]

The above statement returns false, so set num equal to num.

You can go through the above statements as many times as you like, but you'll start to notice that you repeat the same steps over and over. Num starts out as zero, the statement always returns false, and num does not change. Therefore, the program gets stuck in an infinite loop and returns nothing.

8. **(A)** Depending on the computer and the language you are coding in, division may result in either whole number results or answers with a certain number of decimal places. The number of decimal places may not be consistent across computers due to differences in rounding. (One computer may round to three places; another may truncate to five places.) This is called a roundoff error.

(A) Correct.
(B) An overflow error occurs when the computer receives a number that is too large or has too many decimal places for the computer to handle.
(C) This problem works with simple fractions and has nothing to do with hexadecimal values.
(D) Depending on the program and the data type a and b are stored as, the values could be rounded differently.

9. **(C)** A binary search works by taking an ordered list and repeatedly dividing it in half. If the halfway point is greater than the number we are searching for, we only look at the first half, and divide the list repeatedly in this manner until we locate the value we are looking for. This works for alphabetized lists as well.

A binary search requires the given list to be organized in a specific order. Numbers should be ordered by size, and words should be ordered alphabetically.

(A) The students are listed in size order (with numbers), which means that a binary search would work.
(B) The numbers are in size order, so a binary search would work.
(C) Correct.
(D) The words are in alphabetical order, so a binary search would work.

10. **(A)** The statement "NOT (*a* and *b*)" would return the exact opposite of every Boolean shown in the column "(*a* and *b*)." This parameter matches the Booleans listed in the missing-condition column.

(A) Correct.
(B) *a* and *b* would return true if either *a* or *b* were true. However, on the first line you find that both *a* and *b* are true, but the missing condition is false.
(C) This statement would return true only if both *a* and (*a* and *b*) returned true. However, on the third line, see that the missing condition returns true when both *a* and (*a* and *b*) return false.
(D) This statement would return true only when *b* and (*a* and *b*) return true. However, on the fourth line, see that the missing condition returns true when both *b* and (*a* and *b*) return false.

11. **(A)** Lossless compression does not lose any image quality, but it can result in large files that are difficult to transfer and store.

(A) Correct.
(B) There is not image quality lost in lossless compression.
(C) There is no data lost in lossless compression.
(D) Number and size of pixels qualifies as data, and there is not data lost in lossless compression.

12. **(D)** The Random(*a*, *b*) procedure returns a random number from *a* to *b*. In this example, *x* is set to a random number from 0 to 2. All possible values for *x* are 0, 1, or 2. The ROTATE_LEFT is contained in a loop that will iterate the value of *x*. The robot will rotate counterclockwise either 0, 90, OR 180 degrees. The MOVE_FORWARD method is contained in a loop that will iterate either 0, 1, or 2 spaces.

13. **(B)** This question assumes that the images shown are stored in an array named "animal." Animal[1] is the frog, animal[2] is the bear, and so on. The goal is to switch the frog with the bear. Do so by using an initialized variable called "temp." See the trace below:

Temp	Animal[1]	Animal[2]	Explanation
Null	Frog	Bear	This is how the variables should be initialized
Frog	Frog	Bear	Temp stores the original info from animal[1] so it isn't lost
Frog	Bear	Bear	Animal[1] is then set to the value of animal[2]
Frog	Bear	Frog	Animal[2] is set to the value of temp, thus switching the original values of animal[1] and animal[2]

(A) Although this utilizes temp correctly to switch variables, it incorrectly switches animal[1] with animal[3], meaning that the frog will be switched with the sheep.
(B) Correct.
(C) Without using temp, the two variables can't be switched. When you replace animal[1] with animal[2], the computer deletes the frog originally held in animal[1], and you end up with two bears.
(D) This attempts to switch the frog and the sheep. Additionally, it fails to utilize temp, the computer replaces the sheep with the frog, and the image of the sheep is lost.

14. **(C)** Variable x has an initial value of 10. After that, there's a repeat statement: repeat until x is greater than or equal to 10. On the first run, notice that 10 is equal to 10, so there's no need to execute the command under the repeat statement. Simply return the current x value, 10, and then end the program segment.

15. **(C)** Both number of steps and runtime for a given algorithm can be modeled with either numbers or expressions. Any algorithm that can be executed in a "reasonable amount of time" is modeled by a polynomial, not an exponential expression. This means that there cannot be any variables, such as the variable n as an exponent of a number. The other answer choices all have a variable exponent.

16. **(A)** To convert binary to hexadecimal, break the binary into sets of four. Recall that if the number is greater than 9, it must be switched into letters. A is 10, B is 11, and so on.

First, convert the first four numbers, 0110. See the chart below.

Next, convert the second four numbers, 1101. See the chart below.

0	1	1	0
8	4	2	1

This results in:

1	1	0	1
8	4	2	1

Now, there's D.

That leaves the value 6D in hexadecimal, and, using the chart, that corresponds with the letter M.

17. **(A)** When you initialize constant variables at the beginning of the program, you should only represent things that are not subject to change. While a mathematical constant and max capacity of a restaurant clearly fall within these parameters, time left in a game does not. Since timers constantly count backward to zero, option 3 would not be a good choice for a constant variable.

(A) Correct.
(B) I is a good option, but III is not.
(C) I and II are good options, but III is not.
(D) II is a good option, but III is not.

18. **(A)** Examine the logic gates in order, one at a time. The first one is an "Or" statement that takes in "A" and true. Since it's an "Or" statement, only one parameter must be true, so this gate will always return true. For the next gate, there's another "Or" statement that takes in "B" and the outcome of the first gate, which is true. This also only requires a true and therefore will always return true. The final logic gate is an "And" statement that takes in a true and the outcome of the second gate, which will be true. Since both statements are true, the final outcome will always be true.

19. **(B)** It is important to understand the loop and the "If" statements. The loop runs once for each item in the list. The loop adds the given item to total. It adds the given value again if 2 MOD of the given value = 0 (meaning that it is an even number). It adds the given value again if the value/10 = 0 (meaning it is divisible by 10).

To solve the problem, use the following trace:

Total:

0 [the total was initialized as zero]

11 [the loop adds the first item to total, MOD of this value is not zero and it is not divisible by 10, so it is added only one time]

3 [the loop adds the second item to total, 2 MOD 3 is not zero and it is not divisible by 10, so it is only added one time]

5 [the loop adds the third item to total, 5 MOD 2 is not zero and it is not divisible by 10, so it is only added one time]

60 [60 MOD 2 is zero but is not divisible by 10, so this value is added to total 2 times]

90 [90 MOD 2 is zero and it is not divisible by 10, so this value is added to total 2 times]

Therefore, 240 is the final value of total, and it is displayed at the end of the program.

20. **(D)** One binary digit can only display two numbers, either 0 or 1. This means that it can only represent situations with two options (think "yes" or "no" situations). Therefore, light on or light off can be represented with one binary digit.

(A) There are 24 hours in a day, thus time cannot be represented by a single binary digit.

(B) There are 12 months in a year and 28 days in a month, thus the current date cannot be represented by a single binary digit.

(C) Geographic location is represented by latitude/longitude coordinates, which cannot be represented by a single binary digit.

(D) Correct.

21. **(A)** We will solve the problem using a trace of petlist:

Petlist:

Dog [petlist is initialized with one item, Dog]

Dog, Waffle [add a second item, Waffle, to petlist when the code says "append"]

Dog, Moose, Waffle [add another item at index 2 when the code says insert with given number 2]

Dog, Moose, Waffle, Noodle [add another item, Noodle, to petlist when the code says "append"]

Dog, Moose, Novack, Waffle, Noodle [add another item at index 3 when the code says insert with given number 3]

Dog, Moose, Benji, Novack, Waffle, Noodle [add another item at index 3 when the code says insert with given number 3]

Moose, Benji, Novack, Waffle, Noodle [remove the item at index 1]

The final display of all the items in the list: Moose, Benji, Novack, Waffle, Noodle.

22. **(B)** Odds are when emailing a picture, you'll have to compress it so that the file is small enough to fit in the email. Most of the time, this is done using lossy compression, which loses data and often makes the picture look blurry or pixelated.

   (A) If the packets were not assembled in the correct order, there would not be a visible picture.
   (B) Correct.
   (C) If the image was compressed using lossless compression, there would be no reduction in image quality.
   (D) It depends on the situation and the original size of the image.

23. **(A)** People use cryptography to secure internet connections, so that they cannot be read by a third party when intercepted.

   (A) Correct.
   (B) Cryptography cannot stop publicly accessible files from being edited. It simply obscures the information to prevent it from being read by an unwanted third party.
   (C) Although it keeps the third party from viewing the information, it cannot stop them from hijacking connections altogether.
   (D) Cryptography has nothing to do with editing data stored on servers.

24. **(A)** This is an example of a lossless transformation. Because the exact parameters for transforming the original are known, the given steps can be reversed to revert the edited photo back to the original.

   (A) Correct.
   (B) Because the steps are known, they can easily be reversed and, therefore, no data is lost.
   (C) Addition transformation is not a type of data transformation.
   (D) Frequency transformation is not a type of data transformation.

25. **(D)** The easiest method to solve a robot problem is to run through the steps of the code as if you are the computer. The method, Mystery, takes in an integer "num," which is how many times to repeat the steps given in Mystery. Mystery is called twice in the given program lines, and you can see each step the robot goes through in the grid below (final location is circled):

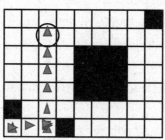

26. **(B)** The best strategy to solve this problem is to convert all numbers into base 10. See the charts below, the first for hexadecimal and the second for binary.

A(10)	C(12)
16	1

$160 + 12 = 172$

1	1	0	1	1	1
32	16	8	4	2	1

$32 + 16 + 4 + 2 + 1 = 55$

$AC_{HEX} = 172$, 82_{DEC}, and $110111_{BIN} = 55$. From lowest to highest, the order is 110111, 82, AC.

27. **(B)** Coding in binary is far too difficult. Finding the error in this code, even if you could interpret it, would not be possible because you do not know the intended purpose. Coding is done in higher-level language because binary, a low-level language, is too hard for most people to read.

28. **(A)** In this problem there are two lists, list1 and list2. List1 has numbers in it; list2 is empty. There's a loop that goes through each item found in list1 and appends the item to list2. If 2 MOD of a number equals 1, the number is odd. If 2 MOD of the number equals zero, then the number is even. You'll notice very quickly that a number can never be both even and odd, so the code never adds any numbers to list2, and it returns as empty.

29. **(C)** In this problem there are two lists, list1 and list2. There's a variable count, set to the value of the length of list1. The given program iterates through each item in list1 by repeating "count" times. There is an "If" statement that checks if each item at a given index of list1 is divisible by an item at the given index of list2. If the "If" statement is true, the item at the given index in list2 is added to the variable total. For Each iteration, "number" (the index in each list) is increased by 1.

Code:	Total:
IF(12MOD1 = 0)	12
IF(31MOD1 = 0)	43
IF(35MOD2 = 0)	43
IF(67MOD2 = 0)	43

The code then displays total.

30. **(C)** Computers are the highest-level hardware component. The motherboard of the computer is one of the larger computer parts, so that is the second-highest-level hardware component. Transistors are far smaller components that make up the motherboard and other electrical components, so they are the lowest-level hardware component.

31. **(C)** Searching algorithms are ideal in this context. A credit card company would want to search through the given data for potentially fraudulent purchases, so they would simply code the computer to search for characteristics of fraudulent activity.

    (A) Brute force algorithms would not be efficient for a system that contains "hundreds of millions" of data.
    (B) When it comes to something serious, such as detecting credit card fraud, a heuristic solution runs the risk of missing potentially fraudulent activity.
    (C) Correct.
    (D) An optimization algorithm does not make sense in this context. Optimization algorithms run several possible solutions and test each for efficiency.

32. **(C)** The given code is meant to call the method checkForInEquality if the variables "number" and "randomNumber" are different values. Looking at the answer choices, it's clear that the missing code will be an "If" statement. The goal is to call the method if the "If" statement returns true, and given the information in the problem, it should return true if number and random number are not equal. Therefore, the statement IF(number $\neq$ randomNumber) will be the correct answer.

    (A) This would return true if the two numbers were equal, but our goal is to return true when the two numbers are not equal.
    (B) "Number" is just an integer, and integer values cannot equal true. This answer choice does not make sense.
    (C) Correct.
    (D) "Number" is just an integer, and integer values cannot equal true. This answer choice does not make sense.

33. **(B)** For problems that would take a long time to solve, computer programmers often use "heuristic" solutions, or solutions that are approximate and not exact. Ignoring certain branches that appear to be useless makes sense because heuristics are most commonly used to solve a problem in a shorter amount of time.

    (A) Heuristic methods do not always produce the best solution, because they use approximations to create a solution in a reasonable amount of time.
    (B) Correct.
    (C) If the method never works, it would not be used to find a solution.
    (D) Although this method is practical, it is only practical because it uses a smaller amount of computer power than most methods; that way, the solution is produced in a reasonable amount of time.

34. **(D)** For this program, our goal is to add each item to total if the item does not equal 13.

   (A) This incorrectly checks if list1 = 13, but you cannot check to see if an array equals a single numerical value.
   (B) This would add the item to total only if the item were equal to 13. Our goal is to add every number that is not 13.
   (C) This incorrectly checks if list1 ≠ 13, but you cannot compare an array to a single numerical value.
   (D) Correct.

35. **(A)** A linear search iterates through each value in a given list and checks each in its given order. It does not require them to be sorted.

   (A) Correct.
   (B) This would not work in this scenario. A binary search requires lists to be sorted.
   (C) Bubble sorts do not find a given value; they are simply used to sort a list.
   (D) Insertion sorts do not find a given value; they are simply used to sort a list.

36. **(B)** Looking at the diagram, computers E and C are directly next to each other in the network diagram. C has three connections, and E has four connections, so cutting off all the connections for C would completely isolate it and prevent transmission between computers E and C.

37. **(A)** Transmission control protocol/internet protocol guides the rules on how packets should be formed for transmission.

   (A) Correct.
   (B) DNS is the naming system for IP addresses.
   (C) FTP is the file transfer protocol, but it does not break the data into packets; it only transfers the data from place to place.
   (D) HTTP is the hypertext transfer protocol; it controls how internet commands are processed and how messages are transmitted.

38. **(A)** Convert hexadecimal to binary using the following conversion:

2	A(10)
16	1

Multiply down the column and add the totals, which gives us $32 + 10 = 42$ in decimal.

Now, convert to binary.

128	64	32	16	8	4	2	1
0	0	1	0	1	0	1	0

$42 - 32 - 8 - 2 = 0$.

The final binary conversion is 00101010_{BIN}.

39. **(C)** If an email asks you to call a number that is given in the email, it is most definitely a scam. However, if it asks you to call the number on your official credit card, that number is safe because it is directly linked to your personal bank.

(A) Visual similarities of correspondence between current and past emails from someone claiming to be a professional are common. Scammers go well out of their way to create realistic scam emails. Do not trust something simply because it looks professional.

(B) Never give anyone your social security number online if they ask for it in that manner. Anyone can find information on you online, so the fact that they know your name and place of work is not motivation for trust.

(C) Correct.

(D) Never trust any pop-ups on your computer. They are a sign of a virus, so get your computer scanned immediately and do not click on or give information to the pop-up browser.

40. **(A)** The Digital Millennium Copyright Act is meant to prevent copyright infringement on the internet.

(A) Correct.

(B) You cannot legally build upon or borrow the creative works of others without following the laws surrounded by copyright infringement.

(C) There are no laws/protocols that allow for all software to be used at no cost.

(D) There are no laws/protocols that allow for all software to be used at no cost.

41. **(D)** The digital divide exists due to the lack of access to technology whether the cause be geographic location, lack of education, or cost. The best answer choice is all of the above, (D).

42. **(B)** A good simulation takes into account all the variables for a given situation. If the simulation showed an increase when the real-world results showed a decrease, that is a sign that at least one variable has not been taken into account.

(A) The simulation clearly did not take all variables into consideration, because the actual results were so far from the simulation.

(B) Correct.

(C) Incorrect. A simulation that has a highly incorrect prediction is most likely not working correctly.

(D) Incorrect. Wait time and sales are not directly proportional.

43. **(A)** This requires an understanding of both programming and simple math functions. The question uses the given API. When you call a program's API, you must put information in for each required parameter, thus the random name used when each function was called. This particular line is meant to find the average value. To find the average of any given set of numbers, you need to divide the sum of all the numbers by the quantity of numbers. In this case, divide the sum of the scores by the number of scores.

(A) Correct.

(B) This fails to put in a name for the parameter of each function.

(C) This fails to put in a name for the parameter of each function and incorrectly calculates the average.

(D) This does not use the functions given in the API.

44. **(B)** Any issues with a website name entered into the browser can be attributed to DNS, or domain name server. This is the system involved with the commonplace names of webpages.

   (A) The IP address of the user would not redirect them from a given site they typed into their browser.
   (B) Correct.
   (C) The fault-tolerant nature of the internet is meant to keep it working, not to cause issues when visiting websites.
   (D) This would not be attributed to a virus.

45. **(B)** A binary search is looking for a particular number in a set of numbers. It splits the ordered list down the middle. If the number in the middle is not the number the computer is searching for, it uses greater or less than to determine which half it should search through next. This process is repeated until the correct number is found. Assuming this is done as quickly as possible, the computer could get lucky and find the number on the first try.

46. **(D)** In binary, it would take a minimum of six digits to represent the decimal number 56. See the table below.

32	16	8	4	2	1
1	1	0	0	0	0

   (A) The highest number that can be stored with 1 binary digit is 1.
   (B) The highest number that can be stored with 3 binary digits is 7.
   (C) The highest number that can be stored with 5 binary digits is 31.
   (D) Correct.

47. **(D)** Having information that is easy to access and change is good because both citizens and students can learn, and those who already know the information can verify that it is correct.
   (A) I is true, but there are other true options as well.
   (B) I and II are true, but there are other true options as well.
   (C) II and III are true, but there are other true options as well.
   (D) Correct.

48. **(B)** Solve using the following trace:

A	Current Display	Explanation
4		A is initialized to this value
4	5	Displays current A value +1
6	5	A increases by 2
6	5,6	Displays current A value
6	5,6	A is not negative, if statement false
6	5,6,−5,6	Executes else statement

49. **(B)** The highest level within a given name is the actual site name, such as "Facebook" or "Google."

   (A) "www" is common across multiple domains, but doesn't count as the highest part of a given domain.
   (B) Correct.
   (C) "net" is common across multiple domains, but doesn't count as the highest part of a given domain.
   (D) "ukurasa" is the lowest part of the given domain.

50. **(D)** To solve this problem, use a trace.

x	Explanation
0	x initialized at 0
3	Repeat until $x = 5$, and it didn't equal 5, so add 3
6	Repeat until $x = 5$, and it didn't equal 5, so add 3
9	Repeat until $x = 5$, and it didn't equal 5, so add 3

   After a while of tracing you'll notice that it continues to increase and always will, never reaching a point where $x = 5$; therefore, you are left with an endless loop, and the program never reaches its final statement to return the value of x.

51. **(B)** The best strategy for solving a robot question is to run through the code as if you are the robot. The variable "move" stores a random number between 0 and 4. Lines 4 through 7 will be repeated "move" times. Within that outer loop is an inner loop that is repeated "count" times. The variable "count" stores a random number between 0 and 8. The inner loop will repeat Line 6 "count" times. For example, if the outer loop is set to 3 and the inner loop is set to 2, line 6 would be repeated 6 times. After finishing the outer loop line 8 will rotate the robot right.

   (A) This only shows half of the possible landing spaces.
   (B) Correct.
   (C) This only shows the possible landing spaces if move was a random number between 0 and 1.
   (D) This includes incorrect possible landing spaces; see explanation above.

52. **(B)** A compiler's purpose is to take a high-level language written by a programmer and translate it into low-level machine code.

   (A) A compiler often has error checking after you compile, but these errors are syntax errors, not runtime errors.
   (B) Correct.
   (C) Compilers don't update and install programs on the computer.
   (D) The compiler cannot speed up runtime; runtime depends on number of statements and code size.

53. **(B)** The given code starts by initializing temp at 132. It contains a procedure that takes in temp, subtracts 32, multiplies that value by 5, and then divides that value by 10. The procedure is called in the display function on line 2. When doing the math, ((5x (temp − 32)) / 10, displays the value 50.

54. **(A)** Solve this problem by converting the three hexadecimal numbers into decimal with the conversions below:

0	0
16	1

A	3
16	1

1	6
16	1

Multiply down the columns and then add, which leaves 0, 163, and 22.

(A) Correct.
(B) Incorrect. See conversions above.
(C) Incorrect. See conversions above.
(D) Incorrect. See conversions above.

55. **(C)** A single binary digit can only represent two numbers, 0 and 1. When applied to a real-life situation, it leaves two options, so it must model a situation with only two options (think yes or no situations)—in this case, whether a light is on or off.

(A) Volume of a radio has more than two settings, so this can't be represented by a single binary digit.
(B) Temperature has more than two possible values.
(C) Correct.
(D) Time has more than two possible values.

56. **(C)** In the a AND b column, the Boolean outcome is always opposite of the missing condition column, so you know that "NOT(a AND b)" suits the missing condition.

(A) In the first column, both a and b are true. However, the missing condition returns false, so the missing condition cannot be "a OR b."
(B) In the first column, a is true and not a is false. The missing condition returns false, so the missing condition cannot be "NOT a OR a."
(C) Correct.
(D) In the third row, b returns true. The missing condition also returns true, so the missing condition cannot be "NOT b."

57. **(D)** II will evaluate as true because the inside statement "false or false" would return false but is reversed to true due to the "Not" statement on the outside.

III will evaluate as true because the right statement "true or false" will return true, and is part of the larger statement, (true and false) or "true", and since one term is true the final statement will return true.

(A) The statement "true and false" will return false because one of the statements is false.

(B) Statement I will return false.

(C) Statement I will return false.

(D) Correct.

58. **(C)** A DDoS attack is when thousands of computer bots are used to flood a website with requests, thus preventing actual users from accessing the site.

(A) An attack involving an email would qualify as a phishing attack.

(B) This is encryption, not a DDoS attack.

(C) Correct.

(D) This is not a DDoS attack.

59. **(B)** Packets can travel through multiple paths and be received out of order but are reassembled correctly upon receipt.

(A) Packets are sent quickly but aren't necessarily sent in the correct order.

(B) Correct.

(C) Packets can be sent out of order.

(D) Some of the above statements were incorrect.

60. **(A)** When determining whether a number is even, modulus that number by 2. If the outcome is zero, the number is even. If the outcome is one, the number is odd.

(A) This correctly displays when a number is even, but does nothing when a given number is odd.

(B) The computer does not have a meaning for the phrase "even," and we cannot check the status of numbers in that manner.

(C) Correct.

(D) This takes the MOD of the given number by 3 when it should be by 2, and tells us nothing about the status of the number.

61. **(C)** The goal is to return true when the first element in list1 is equal to the last element in list1. To do so, check the first element in the list by calling list1[1], then compare it to the last statement, list1[Length(list1)] using an "If" statement.

(A) You cannot compare the entirety of list1; you must call list1 at a certain index to reach the numbers within it.

(B) This test assumes the array starts at an index of 1, so the list doesn't have an index of 0.

(C) Correct.

(D) This checks the first number against the second to last number.

62. **(C)**

    (A) There will be no problem because the max value is greater than 0.

    (B) There will be no problem because all the values in the given array are 0.

    (C) Correct. This will work for any case so long as the numbers in the list are not negative. It cannot find the max in a given list if every number is negative and the original max is set to 0, because the computer will determine that none of the given numbers are greater than 0, and 0 will be returned in place of the max.

    (D) There will be no problem because all the values in the array are greater than 0.

63. **(B)** Solve the following problem with a trace:

A	B	C	D	E	F	G
34	340	99	374	34	99	34

Follow the code line by line as if you are the computer and fill in the values of each number. It starts off as simple arithmetic. When you get to the MOD lines, do recall that (smaller number) MOD (bigger number) will always return the smaller number. The final value for g is of 34.

64. **(B)**

    (A) It depends on the situation; you could get lucky on the first try with either method.

    (B) Correct. The fastest method always depends on the situation. Technically speaking, you could get lucky on the first try whether it be a binary search or a linear search, so binary is not guaranteed to be the best method.

    (C) Size is irrelevant because you could get lucky on your first try with either method. Since a binary search halves the number of objects needed to search after every pass, the larger the list the more likely a binary search is faster. However, a binary search only works on sorted lists.

    (D) Size is irrelevant because you could get lucky on your first try with either method.

65. **(A)** Asymmetric cryptography requires two keys, and you wouldn't be able to both encrypt and decrypt within one algorithm.

Exponential growth is not considered reasonable growth. This is not considered a reasonable amount of time for an algorithm to solve a problem.

66. **(A)**

    (A) Correct. Undecidable problems cannot be solved correctly and consistently with an algorithm. A yes or no problem can be solved by returning a Boolean, so the problem would not be undecidable.

    (B) An inability to answer problems with certain input values makes it undecidable. An algorithm must be able to find a solution in a reasonable amount of time. Exponential growth is not a reasonable amount of time.

    (C) Producing incorrect answers given certain input values makes it undecidable.

    (D) Answering with floating point may result in the wrong number of decimal places, making the problem undecidable.

67. **(C)**

   (A) The number of comparisons depends on pure luck for how many iterations it takes to find the correct answer.
   (B) Length is irrelevant. In an unsorted list using a linear search, the first object selected could be the correct object. In using a binary sort, the object in the middle of the data structure could be the object being searched for.
   (C) Correct. There are several different types of searching, such as binary searches and linear searches. Depending on whether it is sorted and pure luck of your searching technique, one method may prove to be more efficient than another.
   (D) This is not true. If things were consistently less efficient, we would stop using them.

68. **(B)**

   (A) Efficient solutions and readability have no relation.
   (B) Correct. Efficient solutions can solve problems regardless of the data size. You want to avoid inefficient solutions that decrease in efficiency as data size increases.
   (C) The goal of an efficient solution is to solve the problem while using the smallest possible amount of computer resources.
   (D) Solutions need to be solved in a reasonable amount of time. On this AP test exponential growth is not considered a reasonable amount of time.

69. **(B), (C)** A single binary digit can only hold two answers. In this case, both answers are yes or no.

   (A) This would require x and y variables. Multiple numbers cannot be stored in a single binary number.

   (D) Speed would require multiple numbers, which is beyond the scope of a single binary number.

70. **(A), (C)** The upper limit on software is the allowable memory. Care should be taken to not exceed this limit. If the upper limit is reached virtual memory will be used, which would slow down the runtime of the algorithm. The worse case would be the computer will crash due to lack of memory. Moore's law is a rule of thumb that the number of transistors on a chip doubles every two years while the costs are halved. While computers have large memory, multiple tabs open can easily use up all your memory and start using virtual memory, which slows down the computer.

71. **(A), (C)** Internet protocols give the internet the capacity to be changed in size or scale. The purpose of internet protocols is to ensure that different brands and types of equipment can all be used to transmit information uniformly throughout the internet.

   (A) Correct. The internet protocols are not enforced by law.
   (B) Internet protocols are made to ensure efficiency of internet usage and communication, not to slow the growth of the internet.
   (C) Correct.
   (D) Internet protocols are uniform across all types of hardware.

72. **(A), (D)** If the number inputted was 3 there is no work to be done. If a number ends in 3, taking the number and MOD by 3 will strip the last number out and display the number 3.

(B) is incorrect because any number divisible by 3 does not necessary end in the number 3 (for example, 9).

(C) will only work if the number is 30. However, 30 does not end in the number 3, so it is incorrect.

73. **(C)** Heuristics should be used when you have a lot of data to sort through to find a solution, and your solution does not have to be precise. Finding the quickest driving distance would be an example of a heuristic solution because you can find an approximate shortest distance.

(A) Heuristics can save time in only checking files likely exposed to viruses.
(B) The average for a national test would require an exact solution.
(C) Correct.
(D) A player's lifetime batting average should be an exact value.

74. **(A), (D)**

(B) returns true 25% of the time because it returns true when a random number from 1 to 4 is less than 2.

(C) returns true 25% of the time because it returns true when a random number from 1 to 1000 is less than 251.

Appendix

Appendix

Appendix A

PERFORMANCE TASK: EXPLORE IMPACT OF COMPUTING INNOVATIONS

Overview

Computing innovations impact our lives in ways that require considerable study and reflection for us to fully understand them. In this performance task, you will explore a computing innovation of your choice. A computing innovation is an innovation that includes a computer or program code as an integral part of its functionality. Your close examination of this computing innovation will deepen your understanding of computer science principles.

Please note that once this performance task has been assigned as an assessment (rather than as practice), you are expected to complete the task with minimal assistance from anyone. For more clarification, see the "Guidelines for Completing the Through-Course Performance Tasks" section.

You will be provided with a minimum of 8 hours of class time to develop, complete, and submit the following:

- **A computational artifact**
- **Written responses**

General Requirements

For this performance task, you are required to select and investigate a computational innovation to:

- Analyze a computing innovation's impact on society, economy, or culture and explain how this impact could be beneficial and/or harmful;
- Explain how a computing innovation consumes, produces, or transforms data; and
- Describe how data-storage, data-privacy, or data-security concerns are raised based on the capabilities of the computing innovation.

You are also required to:

- Investigate your computing innovation using a variety of sources (e.g., print, online, expert interviews);
- Provide in-text citations of at least three different sources that helped you create your computational artifact and/or formulate your written responses;

  o At least two of the sources must be available online or in print; your third source may be either online, in print, or a personal interview with an expert on the computing innovation.

o At least two of the sources must have been created after the end of the previous academic year.

■ Produce a computational artifact that illustrates, represents, or explains the computing innovation's intended purpose, its function, or its effect; and

■ Provide written responses to all the prompts in the performance task about your computational artifact and computing innovation.

Submission Requirements

1. Computational Artifact

Your computational artifact must provide an illustration, representation, or explanation of the computing innovation's intended purpose, its function, or its effect. The computational artifact must not simply repeat the information supplied in the written responses and should be primarily nontextual.

Submit a video, audio, or PDF file. Use computing tools and techniques to create one original computational artifact (a visualization, a graphic, a video, a program, or an audio recording). **Acceptable multimedia file types include: .mp3, .mp4, .wmv, .awi, .mov, .wav, .aif, or .pdf format. PDF files must not exceed three pages. Video or audio files must not exceed 1 minute in length and must not exceed 30 MB in size.**

2. Written Responses

Submit one PDF file in which you respond directly to each of the following prompts. Clearly label your responses 2a–2e in order. Your responses must provide evidence of the extensive knowledge you have developed about your chosen computing innovation and its impact(s). Write your responses so they would be understandable to someone who is not familiar with the computing innovation. Include citations, as applicable, within your written responses. Your responses to prompts 2a–2d combined must not exceed 700 words. The references required in 2e are not included in the final word count.

Computational Artifact

2a. Provide information on your computing innovation and computational artifact. (Must not exceed 100 words.)

■ Name the computing innovation that is represented by your computational artifact.

■ Describe the computing innovation's intended purpose and function.

■ Describe how your computational artifact illustrates, represents, or explains the computing innovation's intended purpose, its function, or its effect.

2b. Describe your development process, explicitly identifying the computing tools and techniques you used to create your artifact. Your description must be detailed enough so that a person unfamiliar with those tools and techniques will understand your process. (Must not exceed 100 words.)

Computing Innovation

2c. Explain at least one beneficial effect and at least one harmful effect the computing innovation has had, or has the potential to have, on society, economy, or culture. (Must not exceed 250 words.)

2d. Using specific details, describe:

- the data your innovation uses;
- how the innovation consumes (as input), produces (as output), and/or transforms data; and
- at least one data-storage concern, data-privacy concern, or data-security concern directly related to the computing innovation.

(Must not exceed 250 words.)

2e. Provide a list of at least three online or print sources used to create your computational artifact and/or support your responses through in-text citation to the prompts provided in this performance task.

- At least two of the sources must have been created after the end of the previous academic year.
- For each online source, include the complete and permanent URL. Identify the author, title, source, the date you retrieved the source, and, if possible, the date the reference was written or posted.
- For each print source, include the author, title of excerpt/article and magazine or book, page number(s), publisher, and date of publication.
- Include in-text citations for the sources you used.
- Each source must be relevant, credible, and easily accessed.

Appendix B

CHECKLIST FOR EXPLORE WRITTEN REPORT

Picking Your Computing Innovation

Is your computing innovation an innovation that includes a computer or program code as an integral part of its functionality?	yes/no
Does your innovation have a beneficial effect on society, economy, or culture?	yes/no
Does your innovation have a harmful effect on society, economy, or culture?	yes/no
Does your innovation have at least two sources that have been created after the end of the previous academic year?	yes/no

Computational Artifact

A computational artifact is something created by a human using a computer and can be, but is not limited to, a program, an image, an audio, a video, a presentation, or a webpage file. The computational artifact could solve a problem, show creative expression, or provide a viewer with new insight or knowledge.

Computing innovations may be physical computing innovations such as Google glasses or self-driving cars, nonphysical computer software such as a cell phone app, or computing concepts such as e-commerce or social networking, which rely on physical transactions conducted on the internet.

Identifies the computing innovation.	yes/no
Provides an illustration, representation, or explanation of the computing innovation's intended purpose, function, or effect.	yes/no
Was your artifact created using a computational tool?	yes/no

Purpose means the intended goal or objective of the innovation.

Function means how the innovation works (e.g., consumes and produces data).

The artifact will **NOT** be awarded a point if:

There is no artifact.	No point
The artifact is not a computational artifact.	No point
The innovation identified in the artifact does not match the innovation described in the written response.	No point
The artifact does not identify the innovation clearly.	No point
The artifact does not illustrate, represent, or explain the innovation's intended purpose, function, or effect.	No point
The artifact illustrates a feature of the innovation instead of the purpose, function, or effect.	No point
The computational artifact doesn't clearly illustrate, represent, or explain as required in the scoring criteria AND the written response describes the innovation's intended purpose and function without explaining how the computational artifact illustrates, represents, or explains the intended purpose, function, or effect.	No point

Response 2a

Did you name the computing innovation that is represented by your computational artifact?	yes/no
Did you describe the computing innovation's intended purpose and function?	yes/no
Did you describe how your computational artifact illustrates, represents, or explains the computing innovation's intended purpose, its function, or its effect?	yes/no
Is your response under 100 words?	yes/no

The artifact will **NOT** be awarded a point if:

The identified innovation is not a computing innovation.	No point
The written statement gives an effect.	No point

Response 2b

Was your computational artifact created by a computational tool?	yes/no
Did you explain the multistep process of how you created your computational artifact?	yes/no

Response 2c

Did you identify a beneficial effect of the identified or described computing innovation and how it relates to society, economy, or culture?	yes/no
Did you identify a harmful effect of the identified or described computing innovation and how it relates to society, economy, or culture?	yes/no

An effect may be an impact, a result, an outcome, and so on.

Beneficial and/or harmful effects are contextual and interpretive; identification includes both the classification of the effect as beneficial or harmful and justification for that classification.

The following will **NOT** be awarded a point if:

The described innovation is not a computing innovation.	No point
The response is missing the adjectives *harmful* or *beneficial* (or synonyms thereof).	No point
The response is missing a plausible beneficial effect.	No point
The response is missing a plausible harmful effect.	No point
The identified effect is actually a purpose for using the computing innovation (e.g., allows me to make videos to share with my family).	No point
The identified effect is actually a function or use of the computing innovation (e.g., self-driving cars can drive me to work).	No point
The identified effect is not a result of the use of the innovation as intended (e.g., a self-driving car is not intended to crash; therefore, its exposure to hacking is not an effect of its intended use).	No point
The explanation does not connect one of the effects to society, economy, or culture.	No point

Response 2d

Identifies the data that the identified or described computing innovation uses	yes/no
Explains how that data is consumed, produced, or transformed	yes/no
Identifies one data-storage, data-privacy, or data-security concern related to the identified or described computing innovation	yes/no

Data types include integers, numbers, Booleans, text, image, video, audio, and signals. Data that infer these types, like fingerprints, temperature, music, length, pictures, etc., are allowed.

Data-collection devices (e.g., sensors, cameras) are not data.

The following will **NOT** be awarded a point if:

The described innovation is not a computing innovation.	No point
The response does not state the specific name of the data or simply says "data."	No point
The response confuses or conflates the innovation with the data; the response fails to explain what happens to the data.	No point
The response confuses the source of the data with the data.	No point
The response identifies or describes a concern that is not related to data.	No point

Response 2e

References, through in-text citation, at least three different sources	yes/no

In-text citations may be provided in any way that acknowledges the source:

- "According to…" or "As written in *The New York Times*…"
- Parenthetical
- Footnotes
- Numerical superscripts with corresponding footnote
- Number system with a corresponding reference

The following will **NOT** be awarded a point if:

The response contains a list of sources only, no in-text citations.	No point
The response contains less than three in-text citations.	No point
There are not three in-text citations with corresponding references.	No point

Appendix C

PERFORMANCE TASK: CREATE APPLICATIONS FROM IDEAS
Overview

Programming is a collaborative and creative process that brings ideas to life through the development of software. Programs can help solve problems, enable innovations, or express personal interests. In this performance task, you will be developing a program of your choice. Your development process should include iterative designing, implementing, and testing of your program. You are strongly encouraged to work with another student in your class.

Please note that once this performance task has been assigned as an assessment (rather than as practice), you are expected to complete the task with minimal assistance from anyone other than your collaborative peer(s). For more clarification see the "Guidelines for Completing the Through-Course Performance Tasks" section.

You will be provided with a minimum of 12 hours of class time to complete and submit the following:

- **A video of your program running**
- **Individual written responses about your program and development process**
- **Program code**

Scoring guidelines and instructions for submitting your performance tasks are available on the AP Computer Science Principles course home page.

Note: Students in nontraditional classroom environments should consult a school-based AP coordinator for instructions.

General Requirements

This performance task requires you to develop a program on a topic that interests you or that solves a problem. During the completion of this performance task, you will iteratively design, implement, and test your program. You will provide written responses to prompts about your program and specific program code that are significant to the functionality of your program. It is strongly recommended that a portion of the program involve some form of collaboration with another student in your class; for example, in the planning, designing, or testing (debugging) part of the development process. Your program development must also involve a significant amount of independent work writing your program code, in particular, algorithm(s) and abstraction(s) that you select to use as part of your written response to describe how the program code segments help your program run.

You are required to:

- Independently develop an algorithm that integrates two or more algorithms and that is fundamental for your program to achieve its intended purpose;
- Develop an abstraction that manages the complexity of your program;
- Create a video that displays the running of your program and demonstrates its functionality;
- Write responses to all the prompts in the performance task; and
- Submit your entire program code.

Program Requirements

Your program must demonstrate a variety of capabilities and implement several different language features that, when combined, produce a result that cannot be easily accomplished without computing tools and techniques. Your program should draw upon mathematical and logical concepts, such as use of numbers, variables, mathematical expressions with arithmetic operators, logical and Boolean operators and expressions, decision statements, iteration, and/or collections.

Your program must demonstrate:

- Use of several effectively integrated mathematical and logical concepts from the language you are using;
- Implementation of an algorithm that integrates two or more algorithms and integrates mathematical and/or logical concepts; and
- Development and use of abstractions to manage the complexity of your program (e.g., procedures, abstractions provided by the programming language, APIs).

Submission Requirements

1. Video

Submit one video in .mp4, .wmv, .avi, or .mov format that demonstrates the running of at least one significant feature of your program. **Your video must not exceed 1 minute in length and must not exceed 30 MB in size.**

2. Written Responses

Submit one PDF file in which you respond directly to each prompt. **Clearly label your responses 2a–2d in order. Your response to all prompts combined must not exceed 750 words, exclusive of the program code.**

Program Purpose and Development

2a. Provide a written response or audio narration in your video that

- identifies the programming language;
- identifies the purpose of your program; and
- explains what the video illustrates.

(Must not exceed 150 words.)

2b. Describe the incremental and iterative development process of your program, focusing on two distinct points in that process. Describe the difficulties and/or opportunities you encountered and how they were resolved or incorporated. In your description clearly indicate whether the development described was collaborative or independent. At least one of these points must refer to independent program development. *(Must not exceed 200 words.)*

2c. Capture and paste a program code segment that implements an algorithm (marked with an **oval** in **section 3** below) and that is fundamental for your program to achieve its intended purpose. This code segment must be an algorithm you developed individually on your own, must include two or more algorithms, and must integrate mathematical and/or logical concepts. Describe how each algorithm within your selected algorithm functions independently, as well as in combination with others, to form a new algorithm that helps to achieve the intended purpose of the program. *(Must not exceed 200 words.)*

2d. Capture and paste a program code segment that contains an abstraction you developed individually on your own (marked with a **rectangle** in **section 3** below). This abstraction must integrate mathematical and logical concepts. Explain how your abstraction helped manage the complexity of your program. *(Must not exceed 200 words.)*

3. Program Code

Capture and paste your entire program code in this section.

- Mark with an **oval** the segment of program code that implements the algorithm you created for your program that integrates other algorithms and integrates mathematical and/or logical concepts.

- Mark with a **rectangle** the segment of program code that represents an abstraction you developed.

- Include comments or acknowledgments for program code that has been written by someone else.

Appendix D

GRAPHICAL ORGANIZER FOR WRITTEN REPORT OF THE CREATE PERFORMANCE TASK

Response 2a

Identify your programming language used.	yes/no
Identify the purpose of your program (what the program is attempting to do).	yes/no
Explain what your video illustrates.	yes/no
Is your response under 150 words?	yes/no

Purpose is the intended goal or objective of the program. Function means how the program works.

Response 2b

Identify two program development difficulties or opportunities that occurred in developing your program.	yes/no
Describe how the two identified difficulties or opportunities are resolved or incorporated into your program.	yes/no
Describe or outline steps used in the incremental and iterative development process to create the entire program.	yes/no
Is your response under 200 words?	yes/no

Development processes are iterative and cyclical in nature and require students to reflect *and* improve on what they have created. Examples of iterative development could include reflection, revision, testing and refining, and improvements based on feedback.

The incremental and iterative development process does not need to be a formal method such as waterfall, top-down, bottom-up, agile, and so on.

Response earns the point if it identifies two opportunities, or two difficulties, or one opportunity and one difficulty *and* describes how each is resolved or incorporated.

The following will **NOT** be awarded a point if:

The process for determining the program idea does not address the development process used to create the entire program.	No point
The response does not indicate iterative development.	No point
Refinement and revision are not connected to feedback, testing, or reflection.	No point
The response only describes the development at two specific points in time.	No point
The response does not describe how the difficulties or opportunities were resolved or incorporated.	No point

Response 2c

Selected code segment implements an algorithm that includes at least two or more algorithms.	yes/no
At least one of the included algorithms uses mathematical or logical concepts.	yes/no
Explains how one of the included algorithms functions independently.	yes/no
Describes what the selected algorithm does in relation to the overall purpose of the program.	yes/no
Is your response under 200 words?	yes/no

The algorithm being described can utilize existing language functionality or library calls.

Response earns the point even if the algorithm was not newly developed (i.e., a student's re-implementation of the algorithm to find the minimum value).

Mathematical and logical concepts can be a part of the selected algorithm or part of either of the included algorithms.

Mathematical concepts include mathematical expressions using arithmetic operators and mathematical functions.

Logical concepts include Boolean algebra and compound expressions.

The following will **NOT** be awarded a point if:

The selected algorithm consists of a single instruction.	No point
The selected algorithm consists solely of library calls to existing language functionality.	No point
The selected algorithm does not include mathematical or logical concepts.	No point
The response only describes what the selected algorithm does without explaining how it does it.	No point
The response does not explicitly address the program's purpose.	No point
The code segment consisting of the selected algorithm is not included in the written responses section or is not explicitly identified in the program code section.	No point
The algorithm is not explicitly identified (i.e., the entire program is selected as an algorithm, without explicitly identifying the code segment containing the algorithm).	No point

Response 2d

Explains how the student-developed abstraction manages the complexity of the program.	yes/no
Is your response under 200 words?	yes/no

Responses that use existing abstractions to create a new abstraction, such as creating a list to represent a collection (e.g., a classroom, an inventory), would earn this point.

The following will **NOT** be awarded a point if:

The explanation does not apply to the selected abstraction.	No point
The abstraction is not explicitly identified (i.e., the entire program is selected as an abstraction, without explicitly identifying the code segment containing the abstraction).	No point

Appendix E

AP COMPUTER SCIENCE PRINCIPLES EXAM REFERENCE SHEET

As AP Computer Science Principles does not designate any particular programming language, this reference sheet provides instructions and explanations to help students understand the format and meaning of the questions they will see on the exam. The reference sheet includes two programming formats: text based and block based.

Programming instructions use four data types: numbers, strings, lists, and Booleans. Instructions from any of the following categories may appear on the exam:

- Assignment, Display, and Input
- Arithmetic Operators and Numeric Procedures
- Relational and Boolean Operators
- Selection
- Iteration
- List Operations
- Procedures
- Robot

Instruction	Explanation
Assignment, Display, and Input	
Text: a ← expression **Block:** ` a ← expression `	Evaluates expression and assigns the result to the variable a.
Text: DISPLAY (expression) **Block:** ` DISPLAY expression `	Displays the value of expression, followed by a space.
Text: INPUT () **Block:** INPUT	Accepts a value from the user and returns it.

Instruction	Explanation
Arithmetic Operators and Numeric Procedures	

Text and Block:
`a + b`
`a - b`
`a * b`
`a / b`
	The arithmetic operators +, -, *, and / are used to perform arithmetic on `a` and `b`.
	For example, `3 / 2` evaluates to `1.5`.

Text and Block: `a MOD b`	Evaluates to the remainder when `a` is divided by `b`. Assume that `a` and `b` are positive integers. For example, `17 MOD 5` evaluates to `2`.

Text:
`RANDOM (a, b)`
Block:
`RANDOM a, b`
	Evaluates to a random integer from `a` to `b`, including `a` and `b`.
	For example, `RANDOM (1, 3)` could evaluate to 1, 2, or 3.

Relational and Boolean Operators	

Text and Block:
`a = b`
`a ≠ b`
`a > b`
`a < b`
`a ≥ b`
`a ≤ b`
	The relational operators =, ≠, >, <, ≥, and ≤ are used to test the relationship between two variables, expressions, or values.
	For example, `a = b` evaluates to `true` if `a` and `b` are equal; otherwise, it evaluates to `false`.

Text:
`NOT condition`
Block:
`NOT (condition)`
	Evaluates to `true` if condition is `false`; otherwise evaluates to `false`.

Text:
`condition1 AND condition2`
Block:
`(condition1) AND (condition2)`
	Evaluates to `true` if both `condition1` and `condition2` are `true`; otherwise, evaluates to `false`.

Text:
`condition1 OR condition2`
Block:
`(condition1) OR (condition2)`
	Evaluates to `true` if `condition1` is `true` or if `condition2` is `true` or if both `condition1` and `condition2` are `true`; otherwise, evaluates to `false`.

Instruction	Explanation
Selection	

Text:
`IF (condition)`
`{`
    `<block of statements>`
`}`
Block:
 	
IF `condition`
`block of statements`
	The code in `block of statements` **is executed if the Boolean expression** `condition` **evaluates to** `true`; **no action is taken if** `condition` **evaluates to** `false`.

Text:
`IF (condition)`
`{`
    `<first block of statements>`
`}`
`ELSE`
`{`
    `<second block of statements>`
`}`
Block:
 	
IF `condition`
`first block of statements`
ELSE
`second block of statements`
	The code in `first block of statements` **is executed if the Boolean expression** `condition` **evaluates to** `true`; **otherwise, the code in** `second block of statements` **is executed.**

Iteration	

Text:
`REPEAT n TIMES`
`{`
    `<block of statements>`
`}`
Block:
 	
REPEAT n TIMES
`block of statements`
	The code in `block of statements` **is executed** n **times.**

Instruction	Explanation

Text:
REPEAT UNTIL (condition)
{
    <block of statements>
}
Block:
 	
REPEAT UNTIL condition
  block of statements
	The code in block of statements is repeated until the Boolean expression condition **evaluates to** true.

List Operations

For all list operations, if a list index is less than 1 or greater than the length of the list, an error message is produced and the program terminates.

Instruction	Explanation
Text: list[i] **Block:** list [i]	Refers to the element of list at index i. The first element of list is at index 1.
Text: list[i] ← list[j] **Block:** list [i] ← list [j]	Assigns the value of list[j] to list[i].
Text: list ← [value1, value2, value3] **Block:** list ← [value1, value2, value3]	Assigns value1, value2, and value3 to list[1], list[2], and list[3], respectively.

Text:
FOR EACH item IN list
{
    <block of statements>
}
Block:
 	
FOR EACH item IN list
  block of statements
	The variable item is assigned the value of each element of list sequentially, in order from the first element to the last element. The code in block of statements is executed once for each assignment of item.

Text: INSERT (list, i, value) **Block:** INSERT [list, i, value]	Any values in list at indices greater than or equal to i are shifted to the right. The length of list is increased by 1, and value is placed at index i in list.

Instruction	Explanation

Text:
`APPEND (list, value)`
Block:
`APPEND [list, value]`
	The length of `list` is increased by 1, and `value` is placed at the end of `list`.

Text:
`REMOVE (list, i)`
Block:
`REMOVE [list, i]`
	Removes the item at index `i` in `list` and shifts to the left any values at indices greater than `i`. The length of `list` is decreased by 1.

Text:
`LENGTH (list)`
Block:
`LENGTH [list]`
	Evaluates to the number of elements in `list`.

Procedures	

Text:
`PROCEDURE name (parameter1,`
`parameter2, ...)`
`{`
`    <instructions>`
`}`
Block:
`PROCEDURE name [parameter1, parameter2,...]`
`instructions`
	A procedure, `name`, takes zero or more parameters. The procedure contains programming instructions.

Text:
`PROCEDURE name (parameter1,`
`parameter2, ...)`
`{`
`    <instructions>`
`RETURN (expression)`
`}`
Block:
`PROCEDURE name [parameter1, parameter2,...]`
`instructions`
`RETURN (expression)`
	A procedure, `name`, takes zero or more parameters. The procedure contains programming instructions and returns the value of `expression`. The `RETURN` statement may appear at any point inside the procedure and causes an immediate return from the procedure back to the calling program.

Instruction	Explanation
Robot	
If the robot attempts to move to a square that is not open or is beyond the edge of the grid, the robot will stay in its current location and the program will terminate.	
Text: MOVE_FORWARD () Block: MOVE_FOREWARD	The robot moves one square forward in the direction it is facing.
Text: ROTATE_LEFT () Block: ROTATE_LEFT	The robot rotates in place 90 degrees counterclockwise (i.e., makes an in-place left turn).
Text: ROTATE_RIGHT () Block: ROTATE_RIGHT	The robot rotates in place 90 degrees clockwise (i.e., makes an in-place right turn).
Text: CAN_MOVE (direction) Block: CAN_MOVE direction	Evaluates to true if there is an open square one square in the direction relative to where the robot is facing; otherwise evaluates to false. The value of direction can be left, right, forward, or backward.

Index